Microsoft® Office Access 2003
A Beginner's Guide

Robert Sheldon

McGraw-Hill/Osborne

New York   Chicago   San Francisco
Lisbon   London   Madrid   Mexico City
Milan   New Delhi   San Juan
Seoul   Singapore   Sydney   Toronto

The McGraw·Hill Companies

McGraw-Hill/Osborne
2100 Powell Street, 10th Floor
Emeryville, California 94608
U.S.A.

To arrange bulk purchase discounts for sales promotions, premiums, or fund-raisers,
please contact **McGraw-Hill**/Osborne at the above address. For information on translations
or book distributors outside the U.S.A., please see the International Contact Information page
immediately following the index of this book.

Microsoft® Office Access 2003: A Beginner's Guide

1234567890 FGR FGR 019876543

ISBN 0-07-223142-4

Publisher   Brandon A. Nordin
Vice President & Associate Publisher   Scott Rogers
Acquisitions Editor   Lisa McClain
Project Editor   Laura Sackerman
Acquisitions Coordinator   Athena Honore
Technical Editor   Greg Guntle
Copy Editor   Kathy Krause
Proofreader   Laura Sackerman
Indexer   Julie Kawabata
Composition   Carie Abrew, Jean Butterfield
Illustrators   Kathleen Fay Edwards, Melinda Moore Lytle, Michael Mueller
Series Design   Jean Butterfield
Series Cover Design   Sarah F. Hinks

This book was composed with Corel VENTURA™ Publisher.

About the Author

Robert Sheldon has worked as a technical consultant and writer for more than 10 years. As a consultant, he has managed the development and maintenance of web-based and client-server applications and the databases that support those applications. In addition, he has designed and implemented various Access and SQL Server databases and has used SQL to build databases, create and modify database objects, query and modify data, and troubleshoot system- and data-related problems. Robert has also written or co-written eight books on various computer-related technologies, one of which received a Certificate of Merit from the Puget Sound Chapter of the Society for Technical Communication. In addition, two of the books that Robert has written focus exclusively on SQL Server design and implementation, and one focuses on programming in SQL. Robert has also written and edited a variety of other documentation related to SQL databases and other computer technologies. In addition, his writing includes material outside the computer industry—everything from news articles to ad copy to legal documentation—and he has received two awards from the Colorado Press Association.

Contents at a Glance

PART I
The Access Database

1 Working with Access Databases 3

2 Creating a Data Model 23

3 Managing Access Tables 47

4 Managing Table Properties 71

5 Managing Table Relationships 101

6 Managing Database Security 117

PART II
Data Access and Modification

7 Modifying Data in an Access Database 141

8 Finding, Sorting, and Filtering Data 161

9 Importing, Exporting, and Linking Data 183

10 Querying an Access Database 211

11 Adding Expressions to Your Queries 239

PART III
Access Data Objects

12 Creating and Configuring Forms 267

13 Creating and Configuring Reports 299

14 Creating and Configuring Data Access Pages 327

15 Creating Macros and Modules 363

PART IV
Appendixes

A Answers to Mastery Checks 389

B Keyboard Shortcuts 421

Index 427

Contents

ACKNOWLEDGMENTS xv
INTRODUCTION xvii

PART I
The Access Database

1 Working with Access Databases 3
Critical Skill 1.1 Use the Access 2003 Interface 4
    Opening Access 4
    Reviewing the Access Interface 6
Critical Skill 1.2 Open an Access 2003 Database File 9
    Reviewing the Database Window 11
    Project 1-1 Opening the Northwind Database 15
Critical Skill 1.3 Create an Access 2003 Database File 15
    Creating a Blank Database 17
    Creating a Database File from an Existing File 17
    Creating a Database File from a Template 18
    Configuring the Database Properties 19
    Project 1-2 Creating Access 2003 Database Files 20
Module 1 Mastery Check 21

2 Creating a Data Model 23
  Critical Skill 2.1 Understand Relational Databases 24
    Structured Data 24
    Normalized Data 26
    Associated Data 28
  Critical Skill 2.2 Learn about SQL 31
    SQL as a Database Language 32
  Critical Skill 2.3 Create a Data Model 33
    Identifying Entities 34
    Normalizing Data 35
    Identifying Relationships 36
    Refining the Design 37
    Project 2-1 Creating a Data Model 38
  Module 2 Mastery Check 44

3 Managing Access Tables 47
  Critical Skill 3.1 View Tables in a Database 48
    Opening a Table in Datasheet View 48
    Opening a Table in Design View 51
  Critical Skill 3.2 Create Tables in a Database 53
    Creating a Table in Design View 55
    Creating a Table in Datasheet View 59
    Creating a Table by Using the Table Wizard 60
    Project 3-1 Adding Tables to the Consumer Advocacy Database .. 63
  Critical Skill 3.3 Modify Table Settings 65
    Changing the Field Name or Description 66
    Changing the Data Type 66
    Changing the Primary Key 66
    Adding and Deleting Fields 67
    Changing the Field Order 68
    Project 3-2 Modifying Table Settings 68
  Module 3 Mastery Check 69

4 Managing Table Properties 71
  Critical Skill 4.1 Configure General Field Properties 72
    Setting the Field Size 75
    Formatting the Field Data 75
    Providing an Input Mask 77
    Creating a Caption 78
    Providing a Default Value 80
    Requiring Values and Allowing Blank Fields 81
    Using Unicode Compression 82

Configuring the IME Settings 83
Applying Smart Tags 83
Configuring Numerical Data 84
Determining New Values 85
Critical Skill 4.2 Define Validation Rules 85
Critical Skill 4.3 Create Field Indexes 88
Viewing Field Indexes 89
Critical Skill 4.4 Configure Lookup Field Properties 89
Setting Lookup Properties 90
Critical Skill 4.5 Configure Table Properties 92
Configuring Table Object Properties 92
Configuring Table Design Properties 93
Project 4-1 Configuring Table Properties 94
Module 4 Mastery Check 98

5   Managing Table Relationships 101
Critical Skill 5.1 Work with Relationships in an Access Database 102
Understanding Access Relationships 102
Navigating the Relationships Window 104
Critical Skill 5.2 Create Relationships Between Tables 106
Defining a Table Relationship 106
Enforcing Referential Integrity 107
Configuring the Join Properties 109
Saving the Relationships Layout 110
Critical Skill 5.3 Modify Existing Relationships 111
Editing Relationships 111
Deleting Relationships 112
Project 5-1 Creating Table Relationships 112
Module 5 Mastery Check 115

6   Managing Database Security 117
Critical Skill 6.1 Password-Protect Your Database File 118
Critical Skill 6.2 Apply User-Level Security 119
Managing Access Workgroups 120
Managing Security Accounts 123
Assigning Permissions to Security Accounts 128
Critical Skill 6.3 Encode and Decode Your Database File 132
Encoding the Database File 132
Decoding the Database File 133
Project 6-1 Configuring User-Level Security 134
Module 6 Mastery Check 137

PART II
Data Access and Modification

7 Modifying Data in an Access Database 141

   Critical Skill 7.1 Insert Data into a Table 142

      Creating a New Record 142

      Inserting Data into a Field 143

      Working with Property Restrictions 147

      Copying and Moving Data 149

   Critical Skill 7.2 Update Data in a Table 152

      Editing Field Data 152

      Setting Keyboard Options 154

   Critical Skill 7.3 Delete Data from a Table 156

     Project 7-1 Manipulating Data in the Consumer Advocacy Database 156

   Module 7 Mastery Check 159

8 Finding, Sorting, and Filtering Data 161

   Critical Skill 8.1 Find Data in a Table 162

      Finding Values in a Table 162

      Finding and Replacing Values in a Table 165

   Critical Skill 8.2 Sort Data in a Table 167

      Sorting Values in a Single Field 168

      Sorting Values in Multiple Fields 169

   Critical Skill 8.3 Filter Data in a Table 170

      Filtering by Selection 171

      Filtering by Excluded Selection 172

      Filtering by Form 174

      Creating Advanced Filters 175

     Project 8-1 Finding, Sorting, and Filtering Data 178

   Module 8 Mastery Check 181

9 Importing, Exporting, and Linking Data 183

   Critical Skill 9.1 Import Data into Your Database 184

      Importing Data from an Access Database 184

      Importing Data from a dBase Database 187

      Importing Data from an Excel Spreadsheet 187

      Importing Data from a Text File 192

      Importing Data from an XML File 194

   Critical Skill 9.2 Link Data to an External Data Source 195

      Linking to an Access Database 196

      Linking to a dBase Database 197

      Linking to an Excel Spreadsheet 198

      Linking to a Text File 199

     Project 9-1 Importing and Linking Data to the Consumer Advocacy Database 199

Critical Skill 9.3 Export Data out of Your Database 202
    Exporting Data to an Access Database 202
    Exporting Data to a dBase Database 203
    Exporting Data to an Excel Spreadsheet 204
    Exporting Data to a Text File 205
    Exporting Data to an XML File 207
    Project 9-2 Exporting Data out of the Consumer Advocacy Database 207
  Module 9 Mastery Check 209

10 Querying an Access Database 211
  Critical Skill 10.1 Create a Select Query 212
    Creating a Single-Table Select Query 212
    Creating a Multiple-Table Query 217
    Project 10-1 Adding a Select Query to the Consumer Advocacy Database 219
  Critical Skill 10.2 Create a Crosstab Query 221
  Critical Skill 10.3 Create an Action Query 226
    Creating a Make-Table Query 227
    Creating an Update Query 229
    Creating an Append Query 231
    Creating a Delete Query 233
    Project 10-2 Creating Action Queries 234
  Module 10 Mastery Check 237

11 Adding Expressions to Your Queries 239
  Critical Skill 11.1 Work with Expressions 240
    Using Operators in an Expression 241
    Using Functions in an Expression 244
    Using Identifiers in an Expression 246
    Using Literals in an Expression 247
  Critical Skill 11.2 Add Expressions to Your Queries 248
    Creating Criteria Expressions 248
    Creating Calculated Field Expressions 253
    Creating Queries with Aggregate Functions 255
  Critical Skill 11.3 Use Expression Builder to Create Expressions 258
    Project 11-1 Creating Expressions in a Query 260
  Module 11 Mastery Check 263

PART III
Access Data Objects

12 Creating and Configuring Forms 267
  Critical Skill 12.1 Navigate the Design View Interface 268
    Opening a New Form in Design View 268
    Working with the Design View Windows 270

Critical Skill 12.2 Add Controls to a Form 275
   Adding a Control to a Form 275
   Creating an Option Group 279
   Formatting a Control 280
   Applying Conditional Formatting 281
Critical Skill 12.3 Configure Control Properties 283
   Configuring Format Properties 284
   Configuring Data Properties 284
   Configuring Event Properties 286
   Configuring Other Properties 286
Critical Skill 12.4 Create Special Forms 288
   Creating Forms with Multiple Tabs 288
   Creating Subforms 289
   Creating Switchboards 292
   Project 12-1 Creating a Form in the Consumer Advocacy Database 294
   Module 12 Mastery Check 297

13 Creating and Configuring Reports 299
Critical Skill 13.1 Create Reports in Design View 300
   Opening a New Report 300
   Navigating the Design View Interface 302
   Adding Controls to a Report 303
   Using Multiple Columns in a Report 305
Critical Skill 13.2 Configure Headers and Footers 307
Critical Skill 13.3 Sort and Group Data 310
   Configuring Group Headers and Footers 312
   Summarizing Grouped Data 314
Critical Skill 13.4 Use Parameter Queries in a Report 317
   Adding Parameter Values to a Report 318
   Project 13-1 Creating a Report in the Consumer Advocacy Database 319
   Module 13 Mastery Check 324

14 Creating and Configuring Data Access Pages 327
Critical Skill 14.1 Learn about Data Access Pages 328
   Working with Data Access Pages 328
   Viewing Data Access Pages 330
Critical Skill 14.2 Create a Data Access Page 332
   Opening a New Data Access Page in Design View 332
   Navigating the Design View Interface 334
   Adding Controls to a Data Access Page 337
   Adding HTML Paragraphs to a Data Access Page 338
   Adding a Theme to a Data Access Page 340

Critical Skill 14.3 Group Data in a Data Access Page   342
    Working with Group Sections in the Design Grid   342
    Summarizing Data   345
Critical Skill 14.4 Add Special Controls to a Data Access Page   349
    Adding a Spreadsheet to a Data Access Page   349
    Adding a Chart to a Data Access Page   352
    Adding a PivotTable to a Data Access Page   354
    Project 14-1 Creating a Data Access Page in the Consumer Advocacy Database . .   356
Module 14 Mastery Check   360

15 Creating Macros and Modules   363
Critical Skill 15.1 Create Macros for Events   364
    Using the Macro Window   364
    Creating a Basic Macro   366
    Adding Conditions to a Macro   368
Critical Skill 15.2 Assign Macros to Events   371
    Adding a New Macro   372
    Project 15-1 Create a Macro for an Event   373
Critical Skill 15.3 Create Modules for Events   375
    Understanding VBA   375
    Using the Microsoft Visual Basic Window   379
    Creating a Class Object Module   381
    Project 15-2 Create a Module for an Event   381
Module 15 Mastery Check   384

PART IV
Appendixes

A Answers to Mastery Checks   389
    Module 1: Working with Access Databases   390
    Module 2: Creating a Data Model   392
    Module 3: Managing Access Tables   394
    Module 4: Managing Table Properties   396
    Module 5: Managing Table Relationships   399
    Module 6: Managing Database Security   401
    Module 7: Modifying Data in an Access Database   403
    Module 8: Finding, Sorting, and Filtering Data   405
    Module 9: Importing, Exporting, and Linking Data   407
    Module 10: Querying an Access Database   409
    Module 11: Adding Expressions to Your Queries   411
    Module 12: Creating and Configuring Forms   413

Module 13: Creating and Configuring Reports 415

Module 14: Creating and Configuring Data Access Pages 417

Module 15: Creating Macros and Modules 419

B Keyboard Shortcuts 421

Editing Data in Datasheet View and Form View 422

Navigating Fields and Records in Datasheet View 423

Navigating Fields and Records in Form View 425

Index 427

Acknowledgements

*M*icrosoft Office Access 2003: A Beginner's Guide could never have come together if not for the editors and staff at McGraw-Hill/Osborne. I particularly want to acknowledge and thank Greg Guntle, the technical editor, for his grasp of the material and his tireless efforts at keeping me on track; and Kathy Krause, the copy editor, whose attention to detail and insightful feedback proved invaluable time and again. I also want to thank Lisa McClain, the acquisitions editor; Athena Honore, the acquisitions coordinator; and Laura Sackerman, the project editor; for pulling this project together and keeping it moving forward in a smooth and professional manner—and for their continued and invaluable help along the way. In addition, I want to acknowledge all the other editors, proofreaders, indexers, designers, illustrators, and other participants whose efforts made this book possible. Finally, I want to thank my agent, Danielle Jatlow at Waterside Productions, Inc., for her help in moving forward on this project and for tending to the details.

Introduction

In these times of home computers, global networks, and the Internet, the term "database" has become a household word, and most computer users are no doubt aware of how extensively databases are used to store data and provide information to a variety of people in a variety of circumstances. Database systems can range from simple desktop applications to mainframe solutions that support multiple layers of application and business logic and that are accessed by users around the world. However, for many people and businesses, the simpler the better, and a desktop application is more than they need to store and manage data.

Microsoft Office Access has been at the forefront of database desktop applications since its introduction. With the release of Access 2003, Microsoft provides an even more powerful desktop application that supports the database needs of a wide range of users—from the home user who wants to store information about a CD collection to the business owner who wants to track customer orders. Access makes it easy to create databases and add data that can be accessed and manipulated at any time. In addition to providing a flexible database environment, Access 2003 allows you to develop data-driven applications that can be used to access and manipulate data and keep it current. With Microsoft Office Access 2003, you can create different types of interface objects that allow you to work with the data in the database in a manner that is both simple and efficient.

Regardless of how you plan to use Access, *Microsoft Office Access 2003: A Beginner's Guide* will provide you with the information you need to create and manage an Access database and data-driven application. Because it uses a task-oriented structure, this book allows you to work through the steps necessary to create an Access database, manage objects within the database, query and manipulate data stored in database tables, and manage the forms, reports, data access pages, macros, and modules that provide front-end access to that data. The goal of this book is to provide you with a valuable resource that is clear, concise, relevant, and manageable.

Who Should Read This Book

Because Access is such a robust, flexible, and easy-to-implement application, it can be used both at home and at the office. If your goal is to learn to work efficiently with Access, *Microsoft Office Access 2003: A Beginner's Guide* can help. You'll find this book useful if you are

- A home user who wants to create a simple database for an information store such as an address book, a CD collection, or recipes

- A home-based business owner who wants to create a database application for such tasks as managing customers and contacts, tracking inventories, or recording orders

- A manager or owner of a small business who needs a database solution that is both easy and inexpensive to implement

- A developer or other employee working within an organization who is tasked with the development of an Access solution

- A group manager within a larger company who needs a database solution that meets immediate needs within the group

- A director, staff member, or volunteer at a nonprofit organization that requires a database solution that is simple and inexpensive to implement

- Any other individual who wants to learn how to create and manage an Access data-driven application

Nearly anyone who is new to Microsoft Office Access will be able to benefit from *Microsoft Office Access 2003: A Beginner's Guide.* In addition, users who have had experience with earlier versions of Access will be able to use the book to refresh their skills and update them to Access 2003.

What the Book Covers

Microsoft Office Access 2003: A Beginner's Guide is divided into three parts. Each part contains a set of modules that help explain how to create an Access database and data-driven application. In addition to the three parts, *Microsoft Office Access 2003: A Beginner's Guide* contains two appendixes that include information that supplements the material presented in the three parts.

Description of the Book's Content

The following outline describes the content of the book and shows how the book is broken down into task-focused modules.

Part I: The Access Database

Part I provides you with a foundation for creating an Access database and the tables that store the data within the database. You'll learn how to create a data model, create tables, and manage table properties. You'll also learn how to set up relationships between tables and manage database security.

Module 1: Working with Access Databases   This module introduces you to the Access interface and to Access database files. You'll learn how to open a database file and navigate the database window. You'll also learn various methods for copying and creating database files.

Module 2: Creating a Data Model   This module introduces you to structured query language (SQL) and relational databases. The module then explains how to create a data model that defines the table structure within your database. The model defines the tables, the fields (columns) within the tables, and the relationships between the tables.

Module 3: Managing Access Tables   In this module, you'll learn how to add tables to your database. The module explains how to create the tables and how to add fields to them. The module also introduces you to data types and explains how to configure each field with a data type. You'll also learn how to add a primary key to a table.

Module 4: Managing Table Properties   This module explains how to configure table and field properties. You'll learn how properties vary depending on a field's data type. You'll also learn how to configure default values, input masks, and validation rules for different types of fields, and you'll learn how to create lookup tables that provide values to fields.

Module 5: Managing Table Relationships   In this module, you'll learn about the different types of relationships that can exist between tables in a database. The module also explains how relationships can be used to enforce data integrity. In addition, the module explains how to create relationships between tables and how to view the relationships that exist in a database.

Module 6: Managing Database Security   In this module, you'll be introduced to how security is implemented in Access and within the objects in an Access database. You'll learn how to password-protect your database file, how to apply user-level security, and how to encode and decode your database file.

Part II: Data Access and Modification

Part II explains how to access and modify data in an Access database. You'll also learn how to find, sort, and filter data as well as import, export, and link data. In addition, you'll learn how to query a database and how to add expressions to your queries.

Module 7: Modifying Data in an Access Database   This module describes the various ways in which you can modify the data in your database. You'll learn how to insert and edit data in fields with different data types and with different property restrictions. You'll also learn how to copy and move data, from individual fields to entire records. Finally, you'll learn how to delete data from a table.

Module 8: Finding, Sorting, and Filtering Data   In this module, you'll learn how to find values in a table as well as find and then replace data. The module also explains how to sort values in a single field and values in multiple fields. In addition, the module describes how to create filters that allow you to display a subset of records in a table. You'll learn how to create different types of filters that vary in complexity, depending on the type of data you want to display.

Module 9: Importing, Exporting, and Linking Data   This module explains how to import data from different types of data sources into your Access database. You'll also learn how to export data to different types of files and formats. In addition, you'll learn how to link data from within your database to an external data source.

Module 10: Querying an Access Database   In this module, you'll learn how to add queries to your database. The module explains how to create queries that can select data from one or more tables and present that data in one view. You'll also learn how to create queries that filter the data so that your query results contain only a subset of the data as it is stored in the underlying tables. In addition, you'll learn how to create action queries that allow you to modify data in the tables.

Module 11: Adding Expressions to Your Queries
This module defines what an expression is and describes the parts that make up an expression. The module also explains how to create expressions and how to use them in your queries so that they display only the information that you want to include in the query results.

Part III: Access Data Objects

Part III explains how to create the data objects that support a data-driven application. You'll learn how to create and configure forms, reports, and data access pages. You'll also learn how to create macros and modules that can be used to enhance the functionality of your forms and reports.

Module 12: Creating and Configuring Forms
In this module, you'll learn how to add forms to your database. The module describes how to add controls to the forms to allow users to retrieve and present data in a meaningful way. The module also describes how to format the forms and controls to improve data presentation.

Module 13: Creating and Configuring Reports
This module describes how to add reports to your database. You'll learn how to create a basic report and configure headers and footers in that report. You'll also learn how to create a report that contains grouped data. In addition, you'll learn how to use parameter queries in a report.

Module 14: Creating and Configuring Data Access Pages
This module introduces you to data access pages and explains how to create them. You'll learn how to add and format controls, as well as add and format Hypertext Markup Language (HTML) text. You'll also learn how to group data on the page and add spreadsheets and charts.

Module 15: Creating Macros and Modules
In this module, you'll learn how to create macros that perform the actions triggered by events on forms and reports. You'll also learn how to associate a macro with an event property. In addition, you'll be introduced to Visual Basic for Applications (VBA) and you'll learn how to create a basic module that can respond to an event.

Appendix A: Answers to Mastery Checks
This appendix provides the answers to the Mastery Check questions listed at the end of each module.

Appendix B: Keyboard Shortcuts   This appendix describes the keyboard shortcuts that help users navigate through and manipulate data in different data views.

Module Content

As you can see in the outline, *Microsoft Office Access 2003: A Beginner's Guide* is organized into modules. Each module focuses on a set of related tasks. The module contains the background information you need to understand the various concepts related to those tasks, explains the steps necessary to perform the tasks, and provides examples that demonstrate various concepts. In addition, each module contains other elements to help you better understand the information covered in that module:

- **Progress Check**   Each module contains one or two sets of questions interspersed within the content of the module. The questions help you understand the key points presented in a particular section. The answers to these questions are provided at the bottom of the page on which the questions appear.

- **Ask the Expert**   Each module contains one or two Ask the Expert sections that provide information on real-world questions that you might have about the information presented in the module.

- **Mastery Check**   Each module ends with a Mastery Check that lets you test yourself on the information and skills you learned in that module. The answers to the Mastery Check questions are in Appendix A.

Microsoft Office Access 2003: A Beginner's Guide is organized into a logical structure that corresponds to the process of creating an Access data-driven application. Each module builds on previous modules so that you're continually applying the skills that you learned earlier to the information you're being taught in the current module. By the end of the book, you'll have created a database and tables within that database, configured relationships between the tables, queried and modified data within the database, and created data objects that allow you to view and modify the data.

Because of the book's organization, it is recommended that you work through the modules in the order that they're presented. If you already have experience with Access databases, you might want to use the book more as a reference and simply skip to the module that provides the information that you're looking for. However, most readers should start at the beginning and work their way through each module.

Module Projects

In addition to the module elements already mentioned (Progress Check, Ask the Expert, and Mastery Check), each module includes one or two projects that allow you to apply the information that you learned in the module to an actual database. Each project is broken down into steps that walk you through the process of completing a particular task. One of the projects in Module 9 uses related files that you can download from McGraw-Hill/Osborne's web site at http://www.osborne.com.

The projects are based on a database that you'll create for a consumer advocacy organization. You'll create the database file, the tables, and other objects in the database; you'll add data to those tables; and then you'll manipulate that data. You'll also create the objects that turn the database into an application. Because the projects build on one another, it is best that you complete them in the order that they're presented in the book. Once you've completed all the projects, you'll have a data-driven application that you can copy, build upon, or simply use as a reference. And, better still, you'll have the skills that you need to start creating data-driven applications on your own.

Part I

The Access Database

Module 1

Working with Access Databases

CRITICAL SKILLS

1.1   Use the Access 2003 Interface

1.2   Open an Access 2003 Database File

1.3   Create an Access 2003 Database File

Microsoft Office Access 2003 is a relational database management system (RDBMS) that stores data safely and efficiently, allowing easy access to that data for viewing and modification. An RDBMS is a system made up of one or more programs that store, manage, manipulate, and return data. However, Access is more than just an RDBMS. Access allows you to develop complete data-driven applications that provide users with the ability to view and manipulate data in a user-friendly environment that supports up-to-date reports and Web-based access. In this module, I introduce you to the Access interface and database files. You'll learn how to maneuver through the interface and database as well as how to open and create database files. From the skills you develop in this module, you'll be able to go on to create the data objects necessary to build a robust data-driven application that meets your specific needs.

CRITICAL SKILL
1.1 Use the Access 2003 Interface

As is the case with any program in the Microsoft Office System, the Access 2003 interface is made up of a main window that contains the elements necessary to take advantage of the various features and functions that the application has to offer. Specifically, the main Access application window allows you to create and open database files and manipulate the structure and properties of the database within those files, as well as manage the data contained in the database. To perform these functions, you should first have an understanding of the Access interface and how features and functions are accessed through that interface.

Opening Access

Of course, before you can begin to do anything in the Access interface, you must first open the application. As with any application, the steps necessary to open Access will vary depending on your operating system, how that system is configured, and what shortcuts you might have created. If you're uncertain about how to open an application in a specific operating system, be sure to check the product documentation for that system.

Now let's take a look at Figure 1-1, which shows you how to launch Access through the Start menu in Windows XP. The steps necessary to launch Access are fairly straightforward: Click the Start menu, point to All Programs, point to Microsoft Office, and click Microsoft Office Access 2003.

NOTE

In Windows XP, you can also pin an application to the Start menu, add a shortcut to the taskbar, or add a shortcut to the desktop. In addition, you can double-click an Access database file in Windows Explorer to launch Access and open that file. Again, be sure to check the product documentation for your operating system if you have any questions about opening an application.

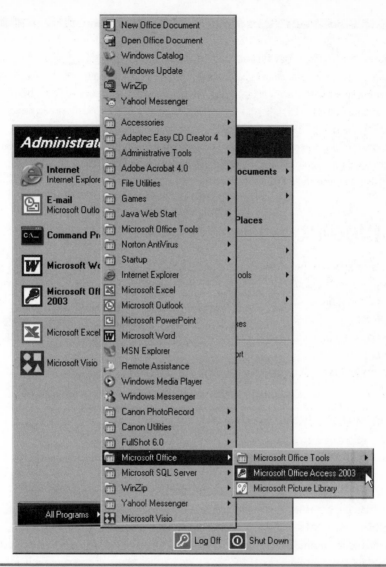

Figure 1-1 Launching the Access 2003 application from the Start menu in Windows XP

When Access is launched, the main window appears with the Getting Started task pane open. Except for the menus and toolbar, the rest of the window is blank, as shown in Figure 1-2.

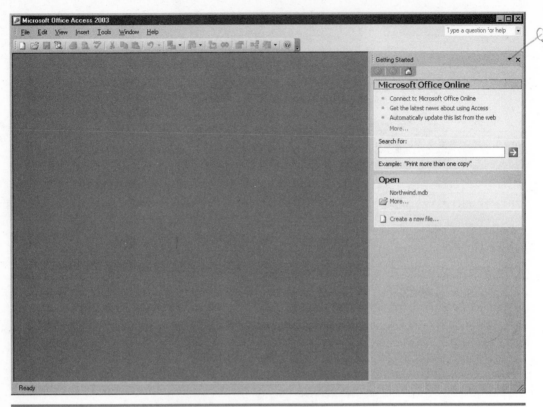

Figure 1-2 The main application window in Access 2003

Reviewing the Access Interface

Typical of Microsoft Office applications, a menu bar sits at the top of the main window. Which menus are displayed and which options are available in each menu depends on whether a database file is open and what object is selected within that file. Table 1-1 provides an overview of each menu. As you move through the book, you'll delve into many of these options in more detail; the table is meant only to provide you with a basic understanding of the options.

If you've already used Office applications, many of the menu items will be familiar to you. Take the time now to open each menu so that you can get a sense of some of the tasks that can be performed.

Beneath the set of menu items in the main window is the Database toolbar, which allows you to perform single-click actions, rather than having to access the menu options. As with menu options, the buttons' availability on the toolbar depends on whether a database file is open and which object is selected. Again, you will be provided with more details about many

Menu	Allows you to
File	Open and close files, import and export data, back up databases, create new files, print data, and view database properties
Edit	Cut, copy, and paste data; delete and rename objects; and manage groups
View	View database objects and their properties, specify which object properties are displayed, arrange icons, and display toolbars
Insert	Create new database objects
Tools	Check spelling, view relationships, analyze database components, configure security, set up replication, manage databases, use database-related tools, link to other Office products, set options, register ActiveX controls, and customize the interface
Window	Set display options
Help	Open Access help, link to resources, and activate the Access application

Table 1-1 Options on the Access 2003 Menu Bar

of the toolbar buttons as you progress through the book. However, if you're already familiar with Office applications, you should be comfortable with most of the buttons, which allow you to take such actions as opening or saving a file; cutting, copying, or pasting text; or printing documents. If you want to know what function a button performs, simply point to the button with your mouse, and a ScreenTip will appear, describing the option.

The Database toolbar is displayed by default. However, you can also display the Web toolbar, which provides browser-like functionality similar to what you would find in Internet Explorer. For example, you can link to a web site that is listed in your Favorites folder. When you click one of the links, your browser opens and displays the web page. Any action that you take on the Web toolbar is displayed in a separate browser window. To display the Web toolbar, right-click the menu area at the top of the interface and select Web.

NOTE

Right-clicking the menu area allows you to display or to close the Database toolbar, the Web toolbar, and the Task Pane window. You can also use this method to access the Customize dialog box, which allows you to customize the menu options and toolbars.

Using the Access Task Panes

As you can see in Figure 1-2, the Getting Started task pane is opened when Access is launched. Getting Started is one of a number of task panes available to you. To access a task pane different from the current one, click the drop-down arrow at the top of the task pane and select the name of the task pane that you want to display. You can display only one task pane at a time. However, you can use the Back and Forward buttons to return to previously opened task panes. In addition, you can click the Home button to return to the Getting Started task pane.

If the task pane window is not displayed, you can right-click the menu area of the main application window and click Task Pane. This process will open the Getting Started task pane.

Now let's take a closer look at the various task panes. Table 1-2 provides an overview of each of the task panes available when you open Access. Be sure to review each task pane so that you understand the features that each one has to offer and what functions can be performed.

Task pane	Allows you to
Getting Started	Follow links to relevant information and web sites, use the search functionality, follow links to recently opened Access files, open other files, and create a new file. If you enter a search, the Search Results task pane is opened, and the search results are displayed in that window. If you click More, the Open dialog box appears, and you can browse your local computer and network for additional files. If you click the Create A New File link, the New File task pane is opened.
Help	Search the Access Help files and display a Help-related table of contents. When you implement a search, the Search Results task pane is opened, and the search results are displayed in that window. You can also connect to web sites relevant to Access and Office.
Search Results	Display the results of your searches. You can specify a search directly on the Search Results pane.
File Search	Search for files that contain a specified phrase. You can also specify a search location and a file type. If you specify Advanced File Search, you can specify whether to search file text or properties, and you can specify a search condition.
Clipboard	Display content saved to the clipboard. This applies only to content stored in an Access database file, not in other applications. You can then paste the contents to a table in the database. In addition, you can set options that determine when the Clipboard task pane will appear.
New File	Create a blank database, blank data access page, or project. You can also create a database or project from an existing file. In addition, you can create a database or project based on a predefined template.

Table 1-2 Task Panes in Access 2003

Ask the Expert

Q: Two of the links on the New File task pane refer to creating projects. You can create a project, which is different from creating a database, by using existing data or by using new data. What is an Access project?

A: To understand what an Access project is, you should first look at the types of database engines supported by Access: Jet and SQL Server. Jet is the traditional database engine used by Access. A typical Access database file, which uses the .mdb extension, is a self-contained file that holds the database, the data contained within that database, and the application objects used to access and manipulate data. The application objects can include such items as forms, reports, macros, and modules, all of which are covered later in this book. In other words, an .mdb file—or Jet database file—contains the entire data-driven application. Typically, when a reference is made to an Access database, it is referring to a Jet database file that has an .mdb extension.

A project, on the other hand, uses the SQL Server database engine and takes an .adp extension. The .adp extension is taken from the acronym ADP, which stands for Access data project. An .adp file contains only the application objects. The database itself, as well as the data stored in the database, is contained in SQL Server. As a result, an Access project file represents the front-end portion of a data-driven application that uses SQL Server as the back end. Because this book is written for the beginning Access user, it focuses on Jet-based .mdb files, often referring to them simply as Access database files or Access databases. However, as you become more comfortable with Access, you might want to experiment with Access projects and SQL Server databases. Keep in mind, however, that for basic, single-user, data-driven applications, a Jet database is more than adequate for most of your needs.

CRITICAL SKILL

1.2 Open an Access 2003 Database File

Once you've opened the Access application, you're ready to open an Access database (.mdb) file. The database file is a complete package. Unlike a database created in a more complex RDBMS, such as SQL Server, a Jet database includes all its primary components in the .mdb file. This includes the objects that make up the database as well as the data itself. In addition, an .mdb file can contain forms. A *form* is a customized interface window that provides a front end to the data in the database, allowing users to access that data without having to maneuver through the tables that hold the data. (Forms are covered in detail in Module 12.) Together these components make up a complete data-driven application, allowing each .mdb file to stand on its own, as is the case with any other Office file.

You can open an .mdb file from one of two task panes: Getting Started or File Search. Getting Started provides two methods for opening a file, both of which are located in the Open section of the task pane:

● Click the name of one of the database files that was most recently opened. By default, up to four files are displayed. When you first install and open Access, the Northwind.mdb file is displayed.

● Click the More link to launch the Open dialog box. From there, maneuver to the appropriate folder and open the file as you normally would, usually by double-clicking the filename.

You can change the number of recently opened files displayed by clicking Options in the Tools menu. When the Options dialog box appears, select the General tab and then set the appropriate number of files in the Recently Used Files List drop-down list. Note that the Options command on the Tools menu is grayed out unless a database file is open.

NOTE

If the Northwind.mdb file was not installed when you installed Access, you can install it at any time by using the Add Or Remove Programs utility in the Control Panel. When you update Access, be sure to select the Choose Advanced Customization Of Application check box, and then add the Northwind sample database. For more information on updating an installed application, check the product documentation for your operating system.

You can also use the File Search task pane to find and then open an Access database file. Simply provide the necessary search parameters and click Go. For example, to perform a basic search for the Northwind.mdb file, type **Northwind.mdb** in the text box named Search Text, select a location from the Search In drop-down list, and click Go. In the search result, click the filename to open the Northwind database. From the search results, you can also create a new file from the existing file, copy the file link to the clipboard, or view the properties for that database file.

NOTE

You can also open an Access database file through one of the methods supported by your version of the Windows operating system. For example, in Windows XP, you can open a file through Windows Explorer or the Start menu simply by clicking or double-clicking the filename. If Access is not open when you open the file, this process will also launch the application.

Reviewing the Database Window

When you open an Access database file, several events occur:

- The database window appears and displays information about the database objects. By default, the Tables object type is selected.

- A switchboard appears if Access is configured to display one. A *switchboard* is a form that provides links to other forms that allow you to manipulate data in the database.

- The task pane window closes.

For now, let's focus on the database window. I cover forms and switchboards in detail in Module 12. Because forms are objects separate from the database, they don't affect the database window or the underlying data structure (though they do represent one type of data object).

If you take a look at Figure 1-3, you'll see the database window for the Northwind database. (The switchboard for this application was closed right after the database file was opened, so you won't see it in the figure.) Notice that, in the left pane, there is a list of object types and groups. The right pane contains a list of objects for the selected object type. For

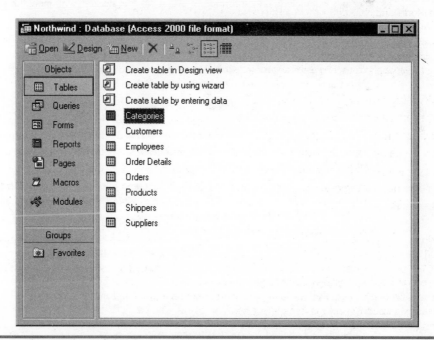

Figure 1-3 The Northwind database window in Access 2003

Working with Access Databases

example, the Tables object type is selected by default when you open a database file. As a result, the right pane displays a list of tables in the database, along with links to tools that allow you to create additional tables. If you were to select the Queries object type, a list of predefined queries would be displayed in the right pane.

Table 1-3 describes each of the object types that appears in the database window. Note that I've provided only an overview of the types. I go into each object type in greater detail in later modules.

Object type	Description
Tables	The basic structures that hold the data within the database. A table is organized into a set of rows and columns that contain related data. You can view the contents of a table as you would an Excel spreadsheet. For example, the Northwind database contains the Employees table, which contains related information about the company's employees. (See Modules 3 through 5.)
Queries	Objects that contain predefined requests for data. Each query asks a formalized question, and the response from the database is returned as a set of data. For example, a query might ask the database for a list of customers who live within a specified region and who have bought products within the last year. The query results will include only information about those customers who meet the search criteria. (See Modules 10 and 11.)
Forms	Interface windows that provide a user-friendly mechanism for interacting with data or for accessing other forms. For example, you can create a form that allows a user to display customer information one record at a time. The user can then view and edit that information as necessary. (See Module 12.)
Reports	Objects that contain predefined report definitions. The reports that are generated from these definitions can calculate and summarize data and display that data in a format that provides current information on an as-needed basis. For example, you can create a report that allows managers to view the total revenues generated by specific sales staff during specific times. (See Module 13.)
Pages	Refers to data access pages, which are Hypertext Markup Language (HTML) documents that allow users to view data on the Web. For example, you can create a data access page to allow your sales staff to view product inventories through their web browsers. (See Module 14.)
Macros	Objects that contain predefined actions that are taken in response to specified events. When the events occur, the macros run automatically and the tasks are completed according to the defined actions. For example, you can create a macro that displays a message box if the users enter certain information into a form's text box. (See Module 15.)
Modules	Objects that contain procedures written in Visual Basic. Modules can perform most actions that macros can perform; however, modules are generally more powerful and versatile than macros. For example, you can create a module that distinguishes between different types of errors. (See Module 15.)

Table 1-3 Object Types in the Access Database Window

Working with Groups

In addition to the main object types listed in the database window, you'll notice that a Favorites group is listed in the Groups section. A *group* in Access 2003 is a collection of shortcuts to various objects stored in the database file. For example, you can group together a set of forms and reports along with the underlying tables that support them. Because a group is nothing more than a collection of shortcuts to the specific objects, the objects themselves are not affected by the groups. As a result, you can change group names, delete groups, add object shortcuts to groups, or delete shortcuts—and the objects will be unaffected.

By default, the Groups section includes only the Favorites group, which contains no initial shortcuts. You can add an object shortcut to the Favorites group or to any other group by taking the following steps:

1. Right-click the object name in the database window to open the shortcut menu.

2. Point to Add To Group. A list of groups appears.

3. Click the group name.

In addition, you can create groups to meet your specific needs. This can be useful if you want to group objects according to tasks or to user types. To create a new group, take the following steps:

1. Click the Edit menu, point to Groups, and then click New Group.

2. When the New Group dialog box appears, enter the name of the group in the New Group Name text box.

3. Click OK. The new group should now be listed in the Groups section of the database window. You can now add object shortcuts to the group.

TIP

You can create a new group when adding an object to a group by right-clicking the object, pointing to Add To Group in the shortcut menu, and then clicking New Group (rather than clicking a group name). When the New Group dialog box appears, enter the new group name and click OK.

Working with the Toolbar

Returning again to Figure 1-3, you'll notice that the database window also includes a toolbar that allows you to perform various actions on database objects. For example, you can open a table so that you can display the contents in a row/column format. Table 1-4 describes the buttons on the toolbar. Not all buttons are the same for each object type, although most buttons are shared by the different types.

Toolbar button	Description
Open	Opens the selected object. For example, if you select the Categories table (in the Northwind database) and then click Open, the data within the table will be displayed. This button is available only for tables, queries, forms, and data access pages.
Design	Opens the selected object in Design view, which allows you to view object definitions and layouts. For example, you can edit query definitions or modify form layouts.
New	Creates a new object for the selected object type.
Delete	Deletes a selected object.
Display buttons	Changes how information is displayed in the database window. You can display large or small icons or list objects with or without object descriptions.
Preview	Previews the selected reports. This button is available only for reports.
Run	Executes the selected macro. This button is available only for macros.

Table 1-4 Toolbar Buttons in the Access Database Window

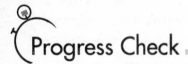

Progress Check

1. Which task pane appears when you open Access?

2. What file extension does an Access database file take?

3. Which database engine does an Access project use?

4. How do you open a database file from the Getting Started task pane?

1. Getting Started

2. .mdb

3. SQL Server

4. Click the name of one of the database files that was most recently opened, or click the More link to launch the Open dialog box.

Project 1-1 Opening the Northwind Database

In this project, you'll open the Northwind database file. If you didn't install the file when you installed Access, you'll need to do that now. (Use the Add Or Remove Programs utility in the Control Panel to install the database file.) You will not be taking any actions with the objects or data at this time—only familiarizing yourself with the process and reviewing the interface.

Step by Step

1. Open Access 2003. The main Access window should appear and display the Getting Started task pane.

2. In the Getting Started task pane, click the Northwind.mdb link. If the Northwind.mdb file is not displayed, click the More link, navigate to the correct folder, and double-click the file. (By default, the file is in the Program Files\Microsoft Office\Office 11\Samples folder.) The Getting Started task pane will close, and the Northwind database file will open, displaying a welcome screen. The welcome screen was developed specifically for the Northwind database.

3. Read the welcome screen, and then select the Don't Show This Screen Again check box.

4. Click OK.

5. Close the Main Switchboard window by clicking the X in the upper-right corner of the window. You do not need to be concerned with the switchboard at this time.

6. In the database window, click each of the object types and review the objects. For each object type, highlight an object, and then review the menu and toolbar options to determine which ones are available for that particular object. Do not make any changes to the database, the objects, or the data.

Project Summary

The process of opening any Access database (.mdb) file is similar to the steps you took in this practice. You could have also opened the file (and launched Access) through Windows Explorer or through other methods supported by your operating system. The advantage to the .mdb file is that it is essentially a self-contained unit, allowing you to open the file as you would any other Office document.

CRITICAL SKILL
1.3 Create an Access 2003 Database File

Now that you've been introduced to the Access interface and to database files, you're ready to create your own .mdb files. Access supports three types of new database files: files that contain blank databases, database files based on existing files, and database files based on templates. If you take a look at Figure 1-4, you'll see that all three types of files can be created from the New File task pane.

Figure 1-4 The New File task pane in the Access interface

NOTE

You can open the New File task pane by clicking the Create A New File link on the Getting Started task pane, by selecting New File from the drop-down list at the top of the task pane window, or by clicking the New button on the Database toolbar. Also note that the Recently Used Templates section appears only if a template has been used.

Although we'll be reviewing all three methods for creating an .mdb file, the file creation process that we'll be most concerned with throughout the book is the one that allows you to create a blank database. In fact, most of the projects will be geared toward creating a data-driven application based on the blank database file that you'll create later in this module. By developing an application from scratch, you'll gain a better understanding of how to create and modify the data objects and manipulate data within the database. With this knowledge, you'll find it easier to work with files that were created from other files or that were based on templates.

Creating a Blank Database

A blank database file, as the name implies, is simply a blank database. The database itself contains no tables, and no other data objects—such as queries or forms—are associated with the database. The process for creating a blank database file is very simple. (In fact, Access makes creating any new database file very easy.)

To create a blank database, take the following steps:

1. In the New File task pane, click the Blank Database link.

2. In the File Name text box of the File New Database dialog box, type the name of the new database file.

3. Click Create.

When you click Create, a database window for the new file appears, and the New File task pane closes. From the new window you can define data objects, configure database properties, and add and manipulate data.

Creating a Database File from an Existing File

You might find that you want to create an .mdb file that is based on a file that already exists. For example, you can create a file based on the Northwind database. That way you'll have a complete application that you can modify without having to worry about unintentionally changing the original Northwind file. You might also find that you want to create a new application that is similar to Northwind, in which case all you'll need to do is modify the copied application according to your own specifications.

Whatever reason you have for creating a new file from an existing file, the steps for doing so are as follows:

1. In the New File task pane, click the From Existing File link.

2. Browse to the file that you want to copy.

3. Select the file and click Create New.

NOTE

Access automatically assigns a name to the new file, based on the name of the original file. To rename the file, click the More link on the Getting Started task pane. When the Open dialog box appears, right-click the new file, click Rename, and type in the new name. Then click Open to launch the file or click Cancel to close the Open dialog box without opening the file.

Once the new file is created, you can manipulate the data objects and the data to suit your specific needs. The original file will be unaffected.

Creating a Database File from a Template

One of the most useful aspects of Access is the ability to create a complete data-driven application, and indeed, by the end of this book, you'll be able to do just that. However, to make this task easier, Access includes templates that represent complete applications. In some cases, a template application might meet your needs closely enough that you'll be able to set up an entire application in a matter of minutes, and all you'll need to do is tweak the package that has been provided.

Access allows you to choose a template from a set of templates installed on your computer or from templates available online. To help you take advantage of the templates, Access includes the Database wizard, which steps you through the process of creating a data-driven application based on the specified template. The number of steps that the wizard walks you though varies according to which template you use. For some templates, you must make decisions about the type of data that will be stored in the database and the layout of the forms used.

To create a database file based on a template on your computer, take the following steps:

1. In the New File task pane, click the On My Computer link in the Templates section. The Templates dialog box appears.

2. Select the Databases tab, and then select a template.

3. Click OK. The File New Database dialog box appears.

4. In the File Name text box, type the name of the file.

5. Click Create. The Database wizard appears.

6. Follow the steps in the wizard. When you've reached the last screen, click Finish. The new database and application are created, and a switchboard appears.

Once you've created the new file, you can modify the data objects as necessary. You can also add data to the database and manipulate the data.

Configuring the Database Properties

The database contained in an .mdb file is itself a data object, just as tables and forms are data objects. Like these objects, the database object is associated with a set of properties, which you can access by selecting Database Properties from the File menu. Figure 1-5 shows the Summary tab of the Northwind.mdb Properties dialog box. The Summary tab is selected by default when you open the dialog box.

For the most part, the database properties are self-explanatory, and many of them you can modify as necessary. Table 1-5 describes each of the tabs in a database's Properties dialog box.

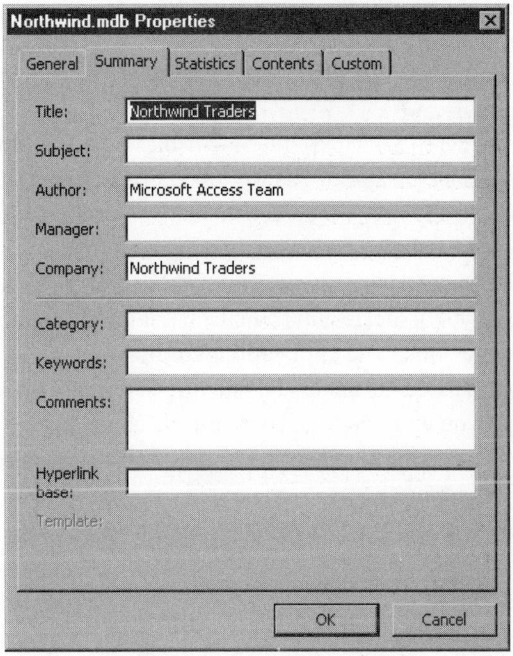

Northwind.mdb Properties ☒

General | Summary | Statistics | Contents | Custom

Title:	Northwind Traders
Subject:	
Author:	Microsoft Access Team
Manager:	
Company:	Northwind Traders
Category:	
Keywords:	
Comments:	
Hyperlink base:	
Template:	

OK   Cancel

Figure 1-5 The Summary tab of the Northwind.mdb Properties dialog box

Tab	Description
General	Provides details about the database file, such as size, location, and dates created, modified, and accessed.
Summary	Provides descriptive details about the database file, such as a title for the application, the author, the company, keywords, and general comments.
Statistics	Provides the dates that the file was created, modified, and accessed, as well as information about the last revision.
Contents	Provides a list of data objects contained in the data file, including tables, queries, forms, reports, data access pages, macros, and modules.
Custom	Provides information that can be used to help locate the database file without having to use a filename.

Table 1-5 Tabs in a Database Properties Dialog Box

Project 1-2 Creating Access 2003 Database Files

In this project, you'll create two database files—one that is based on the Northwind database and one that contains a blank database. The Northwind-based file will be used in subsequent projects to extract data. In addition, I recommend that you use this file when you want to view features in the Northwind database, work with data objects, or manipulate data, thus preserving the original file should you need to re-create the working copy.

The second file that you'll create will form the basis for the application that you'll develop as you work through the book. The application will be based on a consumer advocacy organization that must track membership and that offers a limited amount of merchandise for sale to its members. As you work through later projects in this book, you'll get a better sense of the organization and its application needs. For this project, you need only create the .mdb file that will be used in later projects.

Step by Step

1. If it is not already open, open Access 2003.

2. Click the Create A New File link. The New File task pane appears.

3. Click the From Existing File link. The New From Existing File dialog box appears.

4. Browse to the Northwind.mdb file. It should be located in the Program Files\Microsoft Office\Office11\Samples folder.

5. Select the Northwind.mdb file and click Create New. The Northwind1.mdb file is created. The Northwind welcome screen appears, and the New File task pane closes.

6. Select the Don't Show This Screen Again check box.

7. Click OK. The Main Switchboard window appears.

8. Close the Main Switchboard window by clicking the X in the upper-right corner of the window.

9. Close the database window by clicking the X in the upper-right corner of the window.

10. On the Database toolbar, click the New button. The New File task pane appears.

11. Click the Blank database link. The File New Database dialog box appears.

12. Type **ConsumerAdvocacy** in the File Name text box.

13. Click Create. The database window for the new file appears, and the New File task pane closes.

Project Summary

You should now have two new Access database files stored on your system. The first—Northwind1.mdb—is a duplication of the original Northwind database file. The second— ConsumerAdvocacy.mdb—contains only a blank database and no data objects or data. You'll be adding objects and data in later projects. At this point, you should browse your hard disk to verify that both files have been created. Be sure to back up the files as you would any other document.

✓ Module 1 Mastery Check

1. Which toolbar is displayed by default at the top of the main Access window?

   A. Database

   B. Web

   C. Task Pane

   D. Query Design

2. From which task panes can you open a file?

   A. Search Results

   B. File Search

C. New File

D. Getting Started

3. Which database engine does a typical Access data file use?

4. What object types are listed in the database window?

5. What do you use the Design button for in the toolbar on the database window?

6. Which group is included in a database file by default?

7. Which type of object contains predefined requests for data?

A. Forms

B. Reports

C. Queries

D. Pages

8. Which type of object contains procedures written in Visual Basic?

A. Modules

B. Reports

C. Macros

D. Pages

9. How do you add an object shortcut to a group?

10. Which toolbar button on the database window should you use to execute a macro?

A. New

B. Run

C. Preview

D. Open

11. What are the three types of new database files supported by Access?   *mab*
    adp

12. What methods can you use to open the New File task pane?

13. What steps do you take to create a blank database?

14. From which sources can you choose a template to create a database file?

15. How do you access the properties of a database object?

Module 2

Creating a Data Model

CRITICAL SKILLS

2.1 Understand Relational Databases

2.2 Learn about SQL

2.3 Create a Data Model

In Module 1, I explained how to create an Access database (.mdb) file. As you'll recall, one type of .mdb file that you can create contains only a blank database, and from there you must add tables in order to be able to store data in the database. You can also add other data objects, such as forms and reports, to create a data-driven application. However, before you do any of that, you should have some sort of plan of how you want to structure the database. In other words, you should determine what tables to create and what information they will contain. One way to do that is to develop a data model that adheres to the principles of relational theory (which form the basis of a relational database design), that takes into account clearly defined business requirements, and that incorporates the functionality supported by the relational database management system (RDBMS), which, in this case, is Access. In this module, I introduce you to relational databases and structured query language (SQL), the database programming language used to define databases and the data they contain. I then describe the steps necessary to develop a data model that can be used to create the tables in your Access database.

CRITICAL SKILL
2.1
Understand Relational Databases

In 1970, Dr. E. F. Codd published his historic work, "A Relational Model of Data for Large Shared Data Banks" in the journal *Communication of the ACM,* Volume 13, Number 6 (June 1970). In that work, Codd describes the components of a relational data structure that both protects data and allows that data to be viewed and manipulated while minimizing the risks to the data itself. It is Codd's relational model that forms the basis on which today's RDBMSs are built.

The relational model is based on the mathematical principles of set theory and predicate logic, which define a database structure that maintains data consistency and accuracy. Fortunately, you do not have to be a mathematician to incorporate the principles of the relational model in your database design. You should, however, be familiar with the basic characteristics that help to define that model. An understanding of these characteristics—structured data, normalized data, and associated data (relationships)—will provide you with the foundation you need to create an effective data model that you can use to create the necessary tables in your Access database file.

Structured Data

According to the relational model, all data is organized into structures known as relations. A *relation* is a set of related data collected into columns and rows to form a table-like structure. Each relation is made up of one or more *attributes,* which are subsets of similar data that form the columns within the relation. Figure 2-1 shows an example of a relation that collects information about authors into its structure. Notice that in this relation there are three attributes: FirstName, LastName, and YearBorn.

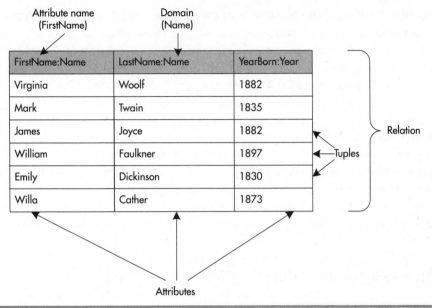

Figure 2-1 A relation made up of three attributes

Data is collected in a relation in tuples. A *tuple* is another subset of data that forms a row within the relation. A tuple provides a record of a related set of data. For example, the James Joyce row in Figure 2-1 represents one of the author tuples in the authors relation.

In addition to relations, attributes, and tuples, the relational model also defines domains. A *domain* specifies the type of data that can be stored in an attribute. For example, in Figure 2-1, the Name domain has been applied to the FirstName and LastName attributes. Any data added to those attributes must conform to the restrictions defined by the Name domain.

Most RDBMSs, including Access, define components that are counterparts to the objects defined in the relational model. In most cases, the terms *table, column,* and *row* are used to refer to relation, attribute, and tuple, respectively. In some cases, such as with Access, the term *field* is used to refer to an attribute, and the term *record* is used to refer to a row.

Although the meanings of the terms used in the relational model are not exactly the same as the terms used by RDBMSs—the relational model is based on mathematical principles, and RDBMSs are concerned with the physical implementation of that model—the meanings are close enough for the purposes of this book. However, the term "domain" is not quite as straightforward as the other terms, although even that term has what can be considered a counterpart ("data type") in the RDBMS.

Access uses data types to restrict the type of data that can be inserted into fields. A *data type* is a constraint that is placed on a field when you create the table that contains that field.

The data type defines the format of the data that can be entered into the field. A domain, on the other hand, can provide a far more comprehensive set of restrictions, such as defining the format *and* restricting the values that can be entered. As you work through the book, you'll use data types and other types of constraints to restrict the data that you can enter into a field. (Data types are discussed in Module 3.)

Normalized Data

In addition to defining how data should be structured, the relational model addresses how data should be organized within that structure. The process of organizing the data to conform to the relational model is referred to as *normalization*. When you normalize data, you're trying to minimize redundant data while preserving the integrity of that data. The goal is to prevent data inconsistency and the loss of data. To achieve this goal, the relational model identifies a number of rules, referred to as *normal forms*.

When Codd first presented the relational model, he defined three normal forms. Since then, more normal forms have been added; however, the first three still cover most situations you'll run into when designing an Access database. For this reason, we'll cover only the first three normal forms in this section. However, many books cover the relational model in more detail, so be sure to check one out if you want more information about normalizing data.

First Normal Form

The first normal form acts as a foundation for the entire normalization process. For data to be in conformance with the first normal form, it must meet the following requirements:

- Each field within a record must contain only one value.

- Each record in a table must contain the same number of values.

- Each record in a table must be different.

Let's take a look at Figure 2-2, which shows part of the Employees table as it appears in the Northwind database in Datasheet view. The figure illustrates a table that is in conformance with the first normal form.

TIP

You can open the Employees table in Datasheet view by opening the Northwind database, selecting the Tables object type in the database window, and double-clicking the Employees table.

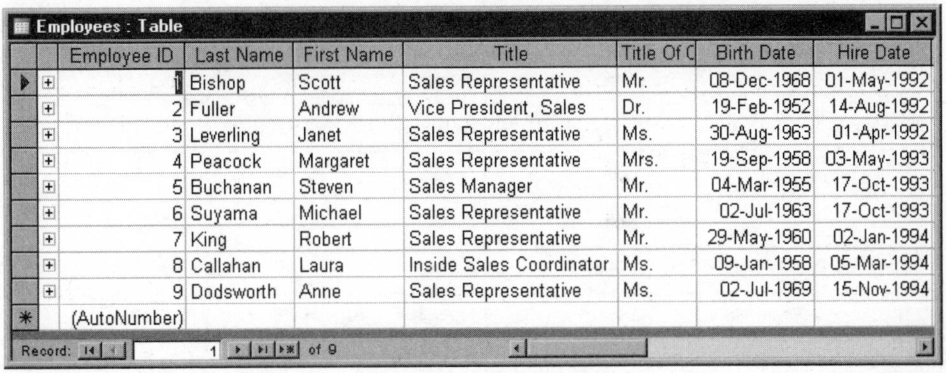

Employees : Table

	Employee ID	Last Name	First Name	Title	Title Of C	Birth Date	Hire Date
+	1	Bishop	Scott	Sales Representative	Mr.	08-Dec-1968	01-May-1992
+	2	Fuller	Andrew	Vice President, Sales	Dr.	19-Feb-1952	14-Aug-1992
+	3	Leverling	Janet	Sales Representative	Ms.	30-Aug-1963	01-Apr-1992
+	4	Peacock	Margaret	Sales Representative	Mrs.	19-Sep-1958	03-May-1993
+	5	Buchanan	Steven	Sales Manager	Mr.	04-Mar-1955	17-Oct-1993
+	6	Suyama	Michael	Sales Representative	Mr.	02-Jul-1963	17-Oct-1993
+	7	King	Robert	Sales Representative	Mr.	29-May-1960	02-Jan-1994
+	8	Callahan	Laura	Inside Sales Coordinator	Ms.	09-Jan-1958	05-Mar-1994
+	9	Dodsworth	Anne	Sales Representative	Ms.	02-Jul-1969	15-Nov-1994
*	(AutoNumber)						

Record: 1 of 9

Figure 2-2 The Employees table in the Northwind database

Notice that each field within a record contains only one value. For example, the first record (row) contains a value of 1 in the Employee ID field and a value of Bishop in the Last Name field. Even values that contain two words, such as those in the Title field, represent a single value. Now notice that each record contains the same number of values. For example, the first record and the fifth record each contain six values. (Assume for now that the view of the Employees table shown in Figure 2-2 represents the entire table.)

Finally, you can see that every record in the Employees table is different. Even if two employees share the same name, the Employee ID field uniquely identifies each record, so each record will be unique. This does not mean that values cannot be repeated within a field. For example, more than one record shares the Sales Representative value in the Title field, but each record, taken as a whole, is unique.

Second Normal Form

For data to be in the second normal form, it must first conform to the rules of the first normal form. In addition, all fields in the table must be dependent on the entire primary key. A *primary key* is one or more fields that uniquely identify the records in a table. No values in a primary key can be repeated. If a primary key is made up of more than one field, the combination of values in those fields cannot be repeated, although you might be able to repeat values within the individual field, depending on how that field is configured. (For more information on primary keys, see Module 3.)

To get a better idea of how the second normal form is applied, let's take a look at Figure 2-3. Because different books and different authors can share the same name, the primary key for this table is made up of three fields: BookTitle, AuthorFName, and AuthorLName. As a result, the remaining fields must be dependent on all three of the primary key fields. However, this is clearly not the case. For example, the Publisher field is dependent on the BookTitle field but

BookTitle	AuthorFName	AuthorLName	Publisher	PublisherContact
The Bone People	Keri	Hulme	197	SHE3456
Painted Bird	Jerzy	Kosinski	192	CAD1345
White Noise	Don	DeLillo	479	NAT3588
Geek Love	Katherine	Dunn	334	RAN3009
Ordinary People	Judith	Guest	276	CAM2876
The Milagro Beanfield War	John	Nichols	198	HOR9754

Figure 2-3 This table violates the second and third normal forms.

is not dependent on the AuthorFName and AuthorLName fields. Consequently, this table violates the conditions of the second normal form. To bring the data stored in this table into conformance with the second normal form, you need to store nondependent data in separate tables or separate the book information from the author information.

Third Normal Form

The third normal form is essentially an extension of the second normal form. For data to be in conformance with the third normal form, it must be in conformance with the second normal form and non-primary-key fields must be independent of each other (while still being dependent on all fields in the primary key). For example, if you refer again to Figure 2-3, you'll see that the PublisherContact field violates the third normal form. This field is dependent on the Publisher field, not on the fields in the primary key. Without the Publisher field, the PublisherContact field would have no meaning. The PublisherContact information should be stored in a table specific to publishers.

Associated Data

One other aspect of the relational model that you should take into consideration when creating a data model is the definition of the relationships between tables. A *relationship* is an association between tables that links the data in those tables in a meaningful way. This process helps to ensure the integrity of the data so that actions taken in one table do not adversely affect the data in other tables.

When you begin to identify the tables in your data model, you'll also need to identify the relationships between those tables. This will help you determine whether additional tables are

Ask the Expert

Q: Are there ever times when you would intentionally violate the rules of normalization?

A: Although most database designers strive to normalize a database as much as possible, there are times when issues of performance override the need for a purely normalized structure. The process of violating the rules of normalization, which is referred to as *denormalization,* is sometimes necessary, particularly with regard to the second and third normal forms. A fully normalized database is often more complicated to query (to request information from the tables) because the queries must span multiple tables, thereby affecting performance. As a result, denormalizing the structure to some degree might represent a significant enough improvement in performance to warrant the design modification. Even so, the ultimate goal of a normalized structure is to ensure data integrity, so denormalizing the database must be done with a great deal of caution.

needed and whether the data is being organized in a logical manner. When creating your data model, you'll identify three types of relationships:

- **One-to-one**   A record in the first table is related to only one record in the second table, and a record in the second table is related to only one record in the first table.

- **One-to-many**   A record in the first table is related to one or more records in the second table, but a record in the second table is related to only one record in the first table.

- **Many-to-many**   A record in the first table is related to one or more records in the second table, and a record in the second table is related to one or more records in the first table.

Let's take a look at an example that helps explain the various types of relationships. Figure 2-4 shows four tables that contain information about books and authors. The tables are associated with one another through the three types of relationships.

The first relationship that we'll look at is the many-to-many, which exists between the Authors table and the Titles table. For each author, there can be one or more books, and for each book, there can be one or more authors. Whenever a many-to-many relationship exists between two tables, you should create a third table, which is referred to as a *junction table*, that establishes two one-to-many relationships. The junction table in this case is the AuthorTitles table.

In the figure, relationships are represented by lines drawn between the related tables. The "many" side of the relationship is represented by the three-pronged end (sometimes referred to

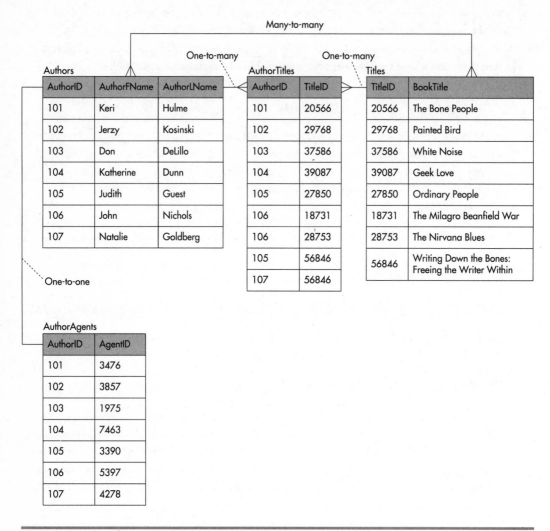

Figure 2-4 Identifying relationships between tables

as a crow's foot). Because a many-to-many relationship exists between Authors and Titles, both sides of the line use the "many" notation.

A one-to-many relationship exists between the Authors table and the AuthorTitles table. For every author, there can be one or more records in the AuthorTitles table, but for each AuthorTitles record, there can be only one author. The same type of relationship exists between the Titles and AuthorTitles tables. For every title, there can be one or more records in the AuthorTitles table, but for every AuthorTitles record, there can be only one title. However, by creating these two one-to-many relationships, you're preserving the many-to-many relationship between the Authors table and the Titles table while maintaining a normalized structure.

The last relationship that we'll look at is the one-to-one relationship, which exists between the Authors table and the AuthorAgents table. For every author, there can be only one AuthorAgents record, and for every AuthorAgents record, there can be only one author.

Progress Check

1. What are a relation, an attribute, and a tuple in the relational model?

2. What rules must data adhere to in order to meet the requirements of the first normal form?

3. Which normal form states that all fields in the table must be dependent on the entire primary key?

4. What three types of relationships should you identify when you are developing a data model?

CRITICAL SKILL
2.2 Learn about SQL

Now that you have a basic understanding of the relational model, you're just about ready to begin developing a data model for an Access database. However, before you begin the process of creating a model, I want to introduce you to SQL, the language used by RDBMSs to implement the relational model. Although SQL does not implement the model exactly, it has nonetheless has become the standard used by most relational databases. You should note, however, that you do not need to know SQL in order to create your data model, although a basic understanding of the language will provide you with a better understanding of Access.

In 1986, the American National Standards Institute (ANSI) published the first standard for SQL, although prior to that products were already being released that were based on the SQL

---

1. A relation is a set of related data collected into columns and rows to form a table-like structure. Each relation is made up of one or more attributes, which are subsets of similar data that form the columns within the relation. A tuple is another subset of data that forms a row within the relation. A tuple provides a record of a related set of data.

2. Each field within a record must contain only one value, each record in a table must contain the same number of values, and each record in a table must be different.

3. The second normal form

4. One-to-one, one-to-many, and many-to-many

model. Since 1986, ANSI and the International Standards Organization (ISO) have released two major revisions: SQL-92 and SQL:1999.

Despite the attempts to standardize SQL, not all products are in conformance with the standard, although most achieve at least some level of compliance. However, each product, including Access, supports some language elements that extend the base SQL standard or that deviate from that standard. The result is that SQL statements can vary from one product to the next, although you'll fine a great number of similarities among products. Even so, when you use SQL within the environment of a specific RDBMS, you need to know how the language is implemented in that product.

NOTE

As a beginning Access application developer, you do not need to be too concerned about the intricacies of SQL at this time. Access, for the most part, builds the SQL statements you'll need to interact with data in the database. You do not need to learn SQL in order to build an application. However, as you become more comfortable with Access and want to build more complex queries, you'll find that you'll want to spend some time learning more about the language as it is implemented in Access.

SQL as a Database Language

SQL was developed to support the creation of relational databases, the management of objects within those databases, and the manipulation of data stored in those objects. Despite its universal application, SQL is very different from other languages such as C and Java. Those languages are procedural in nature; they define how operations are performed and the order in which they're performed. SQL, on the other hand, is nonprocedural in nature. Its focus is on the results of an operation; the underlying system determines how operations are processed.

With the release of the SQL:1999 standard, SQL has become more procedural in nature, and many RDBMSs have implemented procedural-like capabilities within their products. However, SQL continues to lack many of the basic programming functions that most other computer languages possess. At the same time, most of those programming languages cannot manipulate data as effectively as SQL can. As a result, SQL is often used in conjunction with a procedural language to build applications that can effectively access data. For this reason, SQL is often considered a *sublanguage* in that it is used within a programming language as a means to access data.

Despite the fact that SQL is often considered a sublanguage and that it is nonprocedural in nature, it is a complete language in terms of relational databases. With SQL—or a product-specific implementation of SQL—you can create database objects, maintain and secure those objects, and add to and manipulate data in the database.

For the purposes of giving you a better understanding of the scope of SQL, this book separates the language's statements into three broad categories:

- **Data Definition Language (DDL)**   SQL statements that create and manage database objects such as tables

- **Data Control Language (DCL)**   SQL statements that control access to specific objects within the database

- **Data Manipulation Language (DML)**   SQL statements used to view, add, modify, and delete data

For the most part, SQL statements in Access work behind the scenes. You do not have to create them or execute them. Instead, you use the Access interface to perform nearly all SQL-related functions. The only exception to this is when you're querying the database. Although a query is a data object that you can create by using the interface, Access also allows you to view and modify the SQL statements that form a query. However, as a beginning Access user, you normally will not need to be concerned about the actual SQL code being used in your queries. The queries that you create through the interface will generally be sufficient for retrieving data from the database.

Progress Check

1. What is the difference between SQL and other computer languages such as C and Java?

2. What are the three main categories of SQL statements?

CRITICAL SKILL
2.3 Create a Data Model

In the first critical skill in this module, I introduced you to the fundamental principles of the relational model. As you'll recall, data should be organized into a specific structure (tables, fields, and records), conform to the rules of normalization (the normal forms), and be associated in

---

1. Languages such as C and Java are procedural in nature; they define how operations are performed and the order in which they're performed. SQL is nonprocedural in nature. Its focus is on the results of an operation; the underlying system determines how operations are processed.

2. Data Definition Language, Data Control Language, and Data Manipulation Language

a meaningful way (through relationships). You can use this information to create a data model that will form the basis of your Access database. The data model acts as a visual representation of the tables and their fields as they will be implemented in your Access database. The model also defines the relationships between the tables, allowing you to see how data is related within the database.

There are many types of data models that you can create, varying in detail and complexity. For example, some data models define the primary key for each table and provide information about interactions between tables, beyond simply representing the three types of relationships. In addition, database designers often create two types of models: the logical data model and the physical data model. The logical model tends to conform more closely to the relational model, whereas the physical model takes into account the environment in which the database will be implemented. For the purpose of designing an Access database, I take a simpler approach, creating one model that provides the basic information you need to create the tables in your database.

NOTE

The notation used for data modeling varies from system to system. There are a number of formalized methods and a wide range of options, with no one system being the "correct" one. Your choice of data modeling system depends on your personal preference and the environment in which you work.

The process of creating a data model for your Access database is fairly straightforward. You must first identify the initial tables and fields, then apply the rules of normalization, and finally identify relationships between tables. With each step, you're refining the model as it evolves into the final blueprint that you'll use to create your tables and their relationships.

Identifying Entities

As you'll recall from the discussion of the data structure in the relational model, data is organized into tables (relations) and fields (attributes). The first step in creating any data model—once you've defined your business requirements—is to identify those initial tables that will form the basis of your database.

At this point in the data modeling process, the initial tables are often referred to as *entities,* which are sets of related data grouped together to form the preliminary tables and fields. So your first steps are to identify the entities and group together the related information.

Let's take a look at an example to give you a better idea of what this process entails. Suppose you're creating an Access database for a bookstore. The owners of the store tell you that they want to be able to store information about authors and their books that are in stock. The author information should include the first name, last name, year of birth, and year of death (if applicable). The book information should include the title, copyright date, publisher, publisher address, and ISBN.

From this information, you can identify the two most obvious entities: authors and books. In addition, you can identify information related to each of these entities. Figure 2-5 shows you how your initial diagram might look. Notice how information has been grouped together to provide you with initial tables and fields. From this information, you can start creating your data model.

Normalizing Data

Once you've identified your entities, you can start applying the rules of normalization and begin to model actual tables. Remember, at this point you're working with the three normal forms. You need to look at each entity and determine whether the attributes listed for that entity need to be further normalized.

Let's return to our example in Figure 2-5. The first entity is Authors. For each author, you must include a first name, last name, year of birth, and year of death. Each of these attributes represents a single value, so you would be able to create fields based on them. However, keep in mind that for a table to be in first normal form each record must be different. In all likelihood, you will not have two authors that share the same first name, last name, data of birth, and date of death, so each row will probably be unique. However, that would mean creating a primary key made up of three or four fields, which makes table relationships more complicated and creates more redundant data. (Table relationships will be explained in more depth in Module 5.) Keep in mind that one of the goals of the relational model is to reduce redundant data. As a result, you should add some sort of author identifier to the table that will serve as a way to reference author records. If you take a look at Figure 2-6, you'll see that the Authors table now includes an AuthorID field.

NOTE

Notice in Figure 2-6 that the names of the fields in the tables have been changed from simple references, such as "Year of birth," to actual field names, as in "YearOfBirth." The naming conventions used for objects in an Access database file are, to some degree, at the discretion of the developer, although Access does limit the length and the type of characters that can be used. My preference is to use mixed case for object names and to make each name one word, which is the convention I'll be following in this book.

Authors	Books
First name	ISBN
Last name	Title
Year of birth	Copyright
Year of death	Publisher
	Publisher address

Figure 2-5 Identifying the Authors entity and the Books entity

Figure 2-6   Normalizing the table structure in your data model

Now let's return to Figure 2-5 and take a look at the Books entity. Notice that one of the attributes is the ISBN, which uniquely identifies each publication. As a result, you do not need to create a unique identifier for the Books table. However, you might have noticed that the publisher's address information violates the third normal form, which states that non-primary key fields must not be dependant on each other: the Publisher address field is dependent on the Publisher field.

The way to work around this is to create another table that contains publisher information, as shown in Figure 2-6. Notice that the Books table now contains only a reference to the publisher (PublisherID) and that the Publishers table contains all the address information. Now you have three tables, each of which should conform to the rules of normalization.

NOTE

Some database architects might choose to normalize address information even more, separating out not only the street address, but also separating out the city, state, postal code, and country, depending on the size of the database and the potential for redundancy. However, for the purposes of this book, the database designs that we'll be looking at provide an adequate level of detail to demonstrate the principles of normalization.

Identifying Relationships

Now that you've established the fundamental structure of your tables, you can begin to identify the relationships between the tables. As you'll recall, the relational model supports three types of relationships: one-to-one, one-to-many, and many-to-many.

Returning again to Figure 2-6, you can see that a relationship exists between the Authors table and the Books table. In this case, one or more authors can write one or more books.

Consequently, a many-to-many relationship exists between these two tables, as shown in Figure 2-7.

A relationship also exists between the Books table and the Publishers table. A book has one publisher, but a publisher can publish many books. As a result, a one-to-many relationship exists between the two tables. Again, a line is drawn between them (as shown in Figure 2-7); this time only one end of the line is drawn with the "many" notation.

The only other table pairing left in the data model is that between the Authors table and the Publishers table. However, as you can see, there is no way that the tables can directly relate to each other, so your current database design includes only two relationships.

Refining the Design

As you'll recall from our discussion on relationships, a many-to-many relationship is physically implemented by adding a junction table between the two related tables. For the many-to-many relationship shown in Figure 2-7, you must add a table that allows you to create two one-to-many relationships. That way, multiple authors can be associated with one book, multiple books can be associated with one author, and multiple authors can be associated with multiple books.

If you take a look at Figure 2-8, you'll see how an additional junction table—AuthorBooks—can be used to establish two one-to-many relationships. A one-to-many relationship now exists between the Authors and AuthorBooks tables, and a one-to-many relationship exists between the Books and AuthorBooks tables. As a result, a direct relationship no longer exists between Authors and Books, although the many-to-many relationship is still implied.

Your data model for the authors and books is basically complete. You should note, however, that many data models also identify the primary keys and foreign keys. A *primary key,* as you'll recall, is one or more fields that uniquely identify the records in a table. A *foreign key* works with a primary key to enforce a relationship between two tables. Foreign keys, as well as primary keys, are discussed in Module 3.

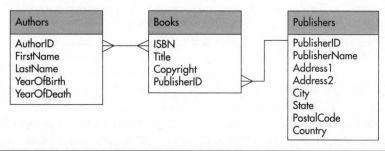

Figure 2-7 Identifying the relationships between tables

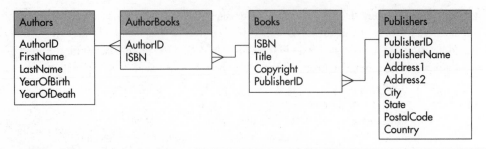

Figure 2-8 Adding the AuthorBooks table to the data model

Project 2-1 Creating a Data Model

In this module, you learned how to apply the principles of the relational model to the process of creating a data model. You will now create a data model for the database that is part of the Access database file you created in Module 1. You created this file (ConsumerAdvocacy.mdb) with a blank database, which means that you must create the tables necessary to hold the data. However, before creating the tables, you should develop a data model that provides a clear blueprint for your table structure.

To complete the steps in this project, you'll first need to read the information below about the consumer advocacy project. You'll also need paper and a pen or pencil—or you can use a drawing program such as Visio—to sketch out the data model.

As you'll recall from Project 1-2 in Module 1, you'll be developing an application for a fictitious consumer advocacy organization. The application must track the organization's membership base and the employees and volunteers who work for the organization. In addition, the organization offers a limited amount of merchandise for sale to its members.

The data model that you will be developing will be based on the following business rules:

- The database must store information about the organization's members. The information must include first name, last name, and middle initial, as well as each member's address, phone numbers, e-mail address, and the date that he or she became a member.

- The database must track the members' orders for merchandise. The information for each order must include the member who placed the order, amount paid, form of payment, order date, status of order, shipped date, products sold, and the quantity of each product.

- The database must track information about the products available for sale to the members. The information must include the name of the product, the quantity in stock and on order, the wholesale price, and the retail price.

- The database must store information about the staff who work for the organization. The information must include the first names, last names, and middle initials, as well as the staff members' addresses, phone numbers, and start dates. The information must also include their positions within the organization as well as who each one's supervisor is.

Although these business rules don't come close to providing all the information that you need to create a complete application, they do provide a starting point for creating a data model. When you need more details to complete the model and develop other components of the application, they will be provided.

Step by Step

1. Identify the main entities that will form the initial foundation for your data model. Remember to review the business rules and pick out the main categories of information.

2. On a piece of paper, draw a rectangle for each entity. Be sure to leave enough room beneath the entity name to record the attributes associated with that entity.

3. For each entity, write down the attributes associated with that entity. At this time, do not worry about normalizing the data or identifying relationships. Your goal is simply to record all the information that should be contained in the database.

Your initial data model should be similar to the following illustration:

Orders	Products	Members	Staff
Member	Product title	First name	First name
Amount	Number in stock	Last Name	Last Name
Form of payment	Number on order	Middle initial	Middle initial
Order status	Wholesale price	Address	Address
Order date	Retail price	Phone numbers	Phone numbers
Shipped date		E-mail address	Position
Products		Begin date	Start date
Quantity			Supervisor

Notice that four preliminary entities have been identified: Orders, Products, Members, and Staff. From this diagram, you can begin to develop a working data model.

4. Your next step is to begin to normalize the data. Let's start with the Orders entity. As you track orders, you must be able to uniquely identify each order. As a result, you should add an identifying field to your table, such as OrderID.

The Orders entity must also reflect the form of payment. Members can pay for an order by check, money order, or one of several different types of credit cards. To minimize redundancy, it would be better to put the form of payment types in a different table.

(continued)

You might have noticed from the business rules that an order can be for more than one product. However, if each record in the Orders table represents an order, then the inclusion of more than one product would violate the first normal form. For the purposes of this exercise, though, we're going to ignore that and simply reference the product in the table. When we begin to identify the relationships between tables, we will address this issue.

5. Next, let's take a look at the Products entity. Again, your database must be able to uniquely identify each product, so you should add an identifying field to your table, such as ProductID.

6. The Members entity will also need a unique identifier. In addition, you will need more specific business requirements for the addresses and telephone numbers. Each address requires two street addresses, city, state, and postal code. In addition, the database must be able to store whatever phone numbers are available for the members, including home, business, cell, and fax.

   The phone numbers present a particular problem because each member will have a different set of phone numbers, in terms of the type of numbers that they have available. For example, some members might have only one phone number, while others may have several. As a result, the best solution is to put the phone numbers in a separate table. That way, you can assign as many phone numbers to a member as necessary without having to store a lot of redundant data or leave a lot of empty values in the Members table.

7. The Staff entity is very similar to the Members entity. The address requirements are the same for both, and you need a unique identifier. However, you need only a home phone number for the staff members. The Staff table must also include information about the staff positions. To minimize redundant data, you should create a separate table for the position types and then reference it from the Staff table.

   Your data model should now be similar to the following illustration:

Orders

OrderID
MemberID
Amount
PaymentID
OrderStatus
OrderDate
ShippedDate
ProductID
Quantity

Products

ProductID
ProductTitle
InStock
OnOrder
WholesalePrice
RetailPrice

FormOfPayment

PaymentID
PaymentType

Positions

PositionID
PositionType

Members

MemberID
NameFirst
NameMI
NameLast
Address1
Address2
City
State
PostalCode
Email
BeginDate

NumberTypes

TypeID
TypeDescrip

PhoneNumbers

NumberID
TypeID
Number
MemberID

Staff

StaffID
NameFirst
NameMI
NameLast
HomePhone
Address1
Address2
City
State
PostalCode
PositionID
StartDate
Supervisor

Notice that there are now eight tables. You still have the original tables, plus additional ones for the form of payment types, the phone number types, the phone numbers, and the staff positions. As you move closer to the final data model, you should incorporate a naming convention into the table and field names.

8. Your next step is to identify the relationships between the different tables. The following table pairs indicate where relationships exist: Orders-Products, Orders-FormOfPayment, Orders-Members, Members-PhoneNumbers, PhoneNumbers-NumberTypes, and Staff-Positions. In addition, a relationship exists within the Staff table—from the Supervisor field to the StaffID field.

(continued)

Your data model should now be similar to the following illustration:

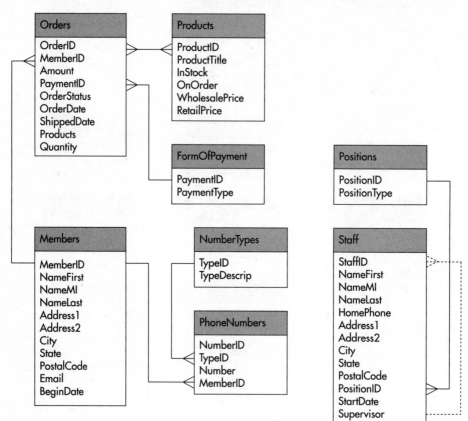

Notice that all the relationships are one-to-many except the one between the Orders table and the Products table, which is many-to-many. Also notice that a dotted line is used to represent the self-referencing relationship within the Staff table.

9. You should now refine your data model to address the many-to-many relationship. To do so, you should add a table between Orders and Products. This allows an order to contain more than one product and a product to be used in multiple orders. The new table should also contain the quantity for each product.

Your data model should now look similar to the following illustration:

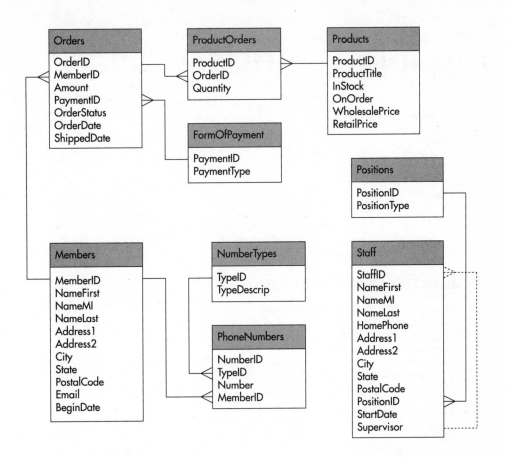

Notice the new ProductOrders table. Now the Orders table does not need any references to quantity or product.

Project Summary

In this project, you created a data model for a consumer advocacy organization. The data model contains the tables necessary to support membership tracking, staff records, products sold, and orders taken for products. The data model will serve as a blueprint for creating tables in your database. You should hang onto the model as you work through the book. It will provide a handy overview of the database as you create other elements of your application.

Module 2 Mastery Check

1. Which structure within the relational model is made up of similar data that form columns within a table-like structure?

   A. Tuple

   B. Attribute

   C. Relation

   D. Domain

2. The _____ is based on the mathematical principles of set theory and predicate logic, which define a database structure that maintains data consistency and accuracy.

3. What is a relation in the relational model?

4. What is a domain in the relational model?

5. What is the common name used in an RDBMS to refer to a relation?

   A. Column

   B. Attribute

   C. Field

   D. Table

6. How does a data type differ from a domain?

7. Which normal form states that each record in a table must be different?

   A. First

   B. Second

   C. Third

   D. Fourth

8. Which normal form is violated if non-primary-key fields are dependent on each other?

   A. First

   B. Second

   C. Third

   D. Fourth

9. You have two tables in your database, one that lists the names of actors and one that lists the names of movies. An actor can appear in one or more movies. A movie can star one or more actors. What type of relationship exists between the two tables?

 A. One-to-one

 B. One-to-many

 C. Many-to-one

 D. Many-to-many

10. You're developing a data model for your Access database. A many-to-many relationship exists between two tables. What should you do?

11. What is SQL?

12. You're working with an Access database and you want to modify the data in one of the tables. Which type of SQL statement will be used to modify the data?

 A. Data Definition Language

 B. Data Control Language

 C. Data Manipulation Language

13. What is a data model?

14. What is the first step that you should take when creating a data model?

 A. Group together related information.

 B. Define the possible relationships that might exist between data.

 C. Identify the initial entities.

 D. Normalize the data structure.

15. You're creating a data model and you've normalized the data structure. What is the next step that you should take?

 A. Define the relationships between tables.

 B. Group together related information.

 C. Denormalize the appropriate structures.

 D. Identify possible entities.

Module 3

Managing Access Tables

CRITICAL SKILLS

3.1 View Tables in a Database

3.2 Create Tables in a Database

3.3 Modify Table Settings

In Module 1 you learned how to create an Access database file, and in Module 2 you learned how to create a data model that could be used to add tables to your database file. As you'll recall, a table is a type of object that is concerned specifically with the storage of data. Before data can be added to a database or manipulated, the tables must have already been created. In this module, you'll learn about the various ways you can create tables, and you'll learn how to modify those tables once they've been created. In addition, this module explains how to open a table and view the data it contains or view the settings that define how the table is configured.

CRITICAL SKILL

3.1 View Tables in a Database

The table is the basic unit of organization within a database. It is made up of a set of fields, each of which defines the type of data that can be inserted into it. For example, a table might be made up of three fields: one that contains text, one that contains numbers, and one that contains dates. Data is stored in the table in the form of records. Each record within a table contains the same number of fields, giving a table the look of an Excel spreadsheet.

A table, like any other object in a database file, is made up of a set of properties that define its characteristics. Many of those characteristics are specific to the fields within the table. For example, a field that contains text data will contain a property setting that defines how many characters each value in that field can contain.

When you view a table, you can choose to display either the data that is stored in that table or the field definitions and properties for that table. You view the data by using Datasheet view, and you view the configuration settings by using Design view.

Opening a Table in Datasheet View

Datasheet view displays a table's records in a column/row structure that includes all the data stored in the table. Access provides several methods for opening a table in Datasheet view. In each case, you must first select the Tables object type in the database window. Then take one of the following steps:

- Double-click the table name.

- Select the table name and then click the Open button at the top of the database window.

- Right-click the table name and then click Open in the shortcut menu.

When the Datasheet view window appears, you can view the contents of the table, navigate to specific records and fields, sort the contents, or take other actions.

CAUTION

You can also modify data when in Datasheet view. Use caution when navigating through the table, and verify any modification that you make. For more information on modifying data, see Module 7.

Navigating the Datasheet View Window

The Datasheet view window provides a number of features that allow you to determine how data from a table is displayed within the column/row structure and which data is displayed. If you'll take a look at Figure 3-1, you can see how the Customers table from the Northwind database is displayed in Datasheet view. As you can see, you can scroll up and down and left to right, which allows you to view all the records in the table. Of course, the need to scroll through the content depends on the number of fields and records in the table. In some cases, all the table's content is displayed at the same time.

When you open a table in Datasheet view, the Database toolbar is replaced by the Table Datasheet toolbar. As you would expect, the toolbar contains a number of options specific to Datasheet view. The toolbar allows you to sort and filter data, find records, or add and delete records. (Modules 7 and 8 describe how to perform these actions.) As is the case with the Database toolbar, each button on the Table Datasheet toolbar has an equivalent option on the menu. For example, to sort records in ascending order (based on the selected field), you can click the Sort Ascending button or click the Records menu, point to Sort, and then click Sort Ascending.

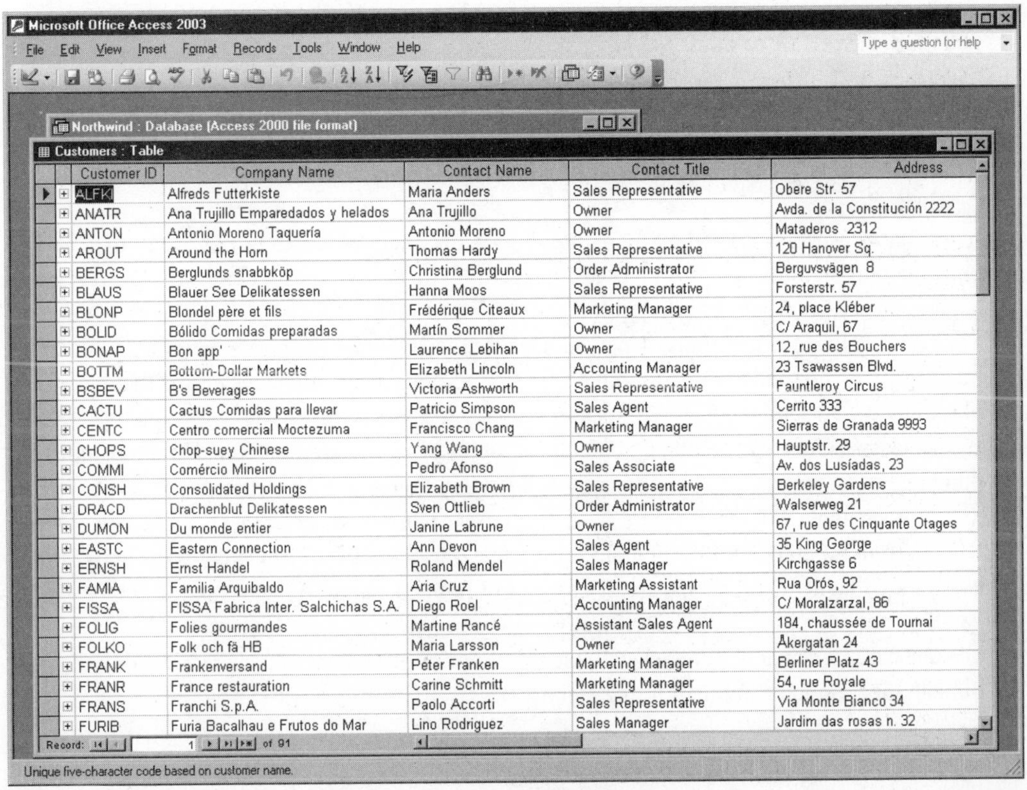

Customer ID	Company Name	Contact Name	Contact Title	Address
ALFKI	Alfreds Futterkiste	Maria Anders	Sales Representative	Obere Str. 57
ANATR	Ana Trujillo Emparedados y helados	Ana Trujillo	Owner	Avda. de la Constitución 2222
ANTON	Antonio Moreno Taquería	Antonio Moreno	Owner	Mataderos 2312
AROUT	Around the Horn	Thomas Hardy	Sales Representative	120 Hanover Sq.
BERGS	Berglunds snabbköp	Christina Berglund	Order Administrator	Berguvsvägen 8
BLAUS	Blauer See Delikatessen	Hanna Moos	Sales Representative	Forsterstr. 57
BLONP	Blondel père et fils	Frédérique Citeaux	Marketing Manager	24, place Kléber
BOLID	Bólido Comidas preparadas	Martín Sommer	Owner	C/ Araquil, 67
BONAP	Bon app'	Laurence Lebihan	Owner	12, rue des Bouchers
BOTTM	Bottom-Dollar Markets	Elizabeth Lincoln	Accounting Manager	23 Tsawassen Blvd.
BSBEV	B's Beverages	Victoria Ashworth	Sales Representative	Fauntleroy Circus
CACTU	Cactus Comidas para llevar	Patricio Simpson	Sales Agent	Cerrito 333
CENTC	Centro comercial Moctezuma	Francisco Chang	Marketing Manager	Sierras de Granada 9993
CHOPS	Chop-suey Chinese	Yang Wang	Owner	Hauptstr. 29
COMMI	Comércio Mineiro	Pedro Afonso	Sales Associate	Av. dos Lusíadas, 23
CONSH	Consolidated Holdings	Elizabeth Brown	Sales Representative	Berkeley Gardens
DRACD	Drachenblut Delikatessen	Sven Ottlieb	Order Administrator	Walserweg 21
DUMON	Du monde entier	Janine Labrune	Owner	67, rue des Cinquante Otages
EASTC	Eastern Connection	Ann Devon	Sales Agent	35 King George
ERNSH	Ernst Handel	Roland Mendel	Sales Manager	Kirchgasse 6
FAMIA	Familia Arquibaldo	Aria Cruz	Marketing Assistant	Rua Orós, 92
FISSA	FISSA Fabrica Inter. Salchichas S.A.	Diego Roel	Accounting Manager	C/ Moralzarzal, 86
FOLIG	Folies gourmandes	Martine Rancé	Assistant Sales Agent	184, chaussée de Tournai
FOLKO	Folk och fä HB	Maria Larsson	Owner	Åkergatan 24
FRANK	Frankenversand	Peter Franken	Marketing Manager	Berliner Platz 43
FRANR	France restauration	Carine Schmitt	Marketing Manager	54, rue Royale
FRANS	Franchi S.p.A.	Paolo Accorti	Sales Representative	Via Monte Bianco 34
FURIB	Furia Bacalhau e Frutos do Mar	Lino Rodriguez	Sales Manager	Jardim das rosas n. 32

Figure 3-1 Displaying the Customers table in Datasheet view

TIP

When you open a table in Datasheet view, the Formatting (Datasheet) toolbar is available but not displayed. To display the toolbar, right-click anywhere in the menu area and then click Formatting (Datasheet). The toolbar allows you to format the individual cells within the table.

Datasheet view also contains navigation buttons at the bottom of the window. The buttons allow you to go to specific records or move to the beginning or end of the records. The active record is indicated by an arrow at the very left of the row that contains the record. If you look again at Figure 3-1, you'll see that the arrow is to the left of the ALFKI value in the Customer ID field. The row that contains this value is the active record.

One other item to note is at the bottom-left corner of the Access application window. In Figure 3-1, notice the words "Unique five-character code based on customer name." This is a description of the selected field. In the case of the Customers table in the figure, the selected field is Customer ID, so the description applies to that field. If no description has been defined for a field, the words "Datasheet view" are displayed.

Viewing the Subdatasheet Window

Returning again to Figure 3-1, you'll notice that each row is preceded by a plus (+) sign. If a plus sign is displayed before a record, that record is related to information in another table. If you click the plus sign, a subdatasheet window appears and displays the related information. At the same time, the plus sign changes to a minus (–) sign, which you would click to close the subdatasheet.

A subdatasheet is related to the record that immediately precedes it. For example, if you click the plus sign for the fourth record (the record with a Customer ID value of AROUT), a subdatasheet displays order information about the customer Around the Horn, as shown in Figure 3-2. This information is displayed because the customer is associated with the records that appear in the subdatasheet. In other words, the subdatasheet displays orders that have been placed by the Around the Horn company.

Subdatasheets are available by default for tables that have an established relationship with other tables. In the case of the subdatasheet shown in Figure 3-2, the Customers table is related to the Orders table. For every record (customer) in the Customers table, there can be one or more records (orders) in the Orders table. In this case, a one-to-many relationship exists between the two tables. (Table relationships are discussed in Modules 2 and 5.)

You can open as many subdatasheet windows in a table as you want. You can also expand all subdatasheet windows, collapse all windows, or remove subdatasheets by selecting the Subdatasheet option from the Format menu.

Customers : Table					
Customer ID	Company Name	Contact Name	Contact Title	Address	
ALFKI	Alfreds Futterkiste	Maria Anders	Sales Representative	Obere Str. 57	
ANATR	Ana Trujillo Emparedados y helados	Ana Trujillo	Owner	Avda. de la Constitución 2222	
ANTON	Antonio Moreno Taquería	Antonio Moreno	Owner	Mataderos 2312	
AROUT	Around the Horn	Thomas Hardy	Sales Representative	120 Hanover Sq.	

	Order ID	Employee	Order Date	Required Date	Shipped Date	Ship Via	Freight	Ship Name
	10355	Suyama, Michael	15-Nov-1996	13-Dec-1996	20-Nov-1996	Speedy Express	$41.95	Around the Horn
	10383	Callahan, Laura	16-Dec-1996	13-Jan-1997	18-Dec-1996	Federal Shipping	$34.24	Around the Horn
	10453	Davolio, Nancy	21-Feb-1997	21-Mar-1997	26-Feb-1997	United Package	$25.36	Around the Horn
	10558	Davolio, Nancy	04-Jun-1997	02-Jul-1997	10-Jun-1997	United Package	$72.97	Around the Horn
	10707	Peacock, Margaret	16-Oct-1997	30-Oct-1997	23-Oct-1997	Federal Shipping	$21.74	Around the Horn
	10741	Peacock, Margaret	14-Nov-1997	28-Nov-1997	18-Nov-1997	Federal Shipping	$10.96	Around the Horn
	10743	Davolio, Nancy	17-Nov-1997	15-Dec-1997	21-Nov-1997	United Package	$23.72	Around the Horn
	10768	Leverling, Janet	08-Dec-1997	05-Jan-1998	15-Dec-1997	United Package	$146.32	Around the Horn
	10793	Leverling, Janet	24-Dec-1997	21-Jan-1998	08-Jan-1998	Federal Shipping	$4.52	Around the Horn
	10864	Peacock, Margaret	02-Feb-1998	02-Mar-1998	09-Feb-1998	United Package	$3.04	Around the Horn
	10920	Peacock, Margaret	03-Mar-1998	31-Mar-1998	09-Mar-1998	United Package	$29.61	Around the Horn
	10953	Dodsworth, Anne	16-Mar-1998	30-Mar-1998	25-Mar-1998	United Package	$23.72	Around the Horn
	11016	Dodsworth, Anne	10-Apr-1998	08-May-1998	13-Apr-1998	United Package	$33.80	Around the Horn
*	:oNumber)						$0.00	

BERGS	Berglunds snabbköp	Christina Berglund	Order Administrator	Berguvsvägen 8	
BLAUS	Blauer See Delikatessen	Hanna Moos	Sales Representative	Forsterstr. 57	
BLONP	Blondel père et fils	Frédérique Citeaux	Marketing Manager	24, place Kléber	
BOLID	Bólido Comidas preparadas	Martín Sommer	Owner	C/ Araquil, 67	
BONAP	Bon app'	Laurence Lebihan	Owner	12, rue des Bouchers	
BOTTM	Bottom-Dollar Markets	Elizabeth Lincoln	Accounting Manager	23 Tsawassen Blvd.	
BSBEV	B's Beverages	Victoria Ashworth	Sales Representative	Fauntleroy Circus	
CACTU	Cactus Comidas para llevar	Patricio Simpson	Sales Agent	Cerrito 333	
CENTC	Centro comercial Moctezuma	Francisco Chang	Marketing Manager	Sierras de Granada 9993	

Record: 1 of 91

Figure 3-2 The subdatasheet window for the Around the Horn customer record

Opening a Table in Design View

As you saw when you opened a table in Datasheet view, you can display the data that is stored in a table. However, there might be times when you want to view the actual *table definition,* the configuration settings that define the structure of the table and determine the type of data that can be stored in that table. You can view a table definition by opening the table in Design view.

The Design view window provides a graphical interface to the table definition. To open a table in Design view, select the Tables object type in the database window and then take one of the following steps:

- Select the table name and then click the Design button at the top of the database window.
- Right-click the table name and then click Design View in the shortcut menu.

When the Design view window appears, you can view details about the fields that make up the table and the individual properties defined for each field.

CAUTION

You can also modify the field definitions and their properties. Use caution when navigating through the Design view window to be certain that you do not make any unintentional modifications to the table. Modifying table settings is discussed in the "Modify Table Settings" section later in this module.

Navigating the Design View Window

The Design view window is very different from what you saw for the Datasheet view window. Figure 3-3 shows the Customers table in the Northwind database, as it appears in Design view. Notice that the window is divided into three distinct sections. The top half, which is organized into a table structure, lists the fields that have been defined for the table. The bottom half provides information specific to the selected field. The left side provides the properties of the selected field, and the right side provides information about the active area of the window.

Each field listed in Design view includes the field name, the data type, and an optional description of the field. For example, the Region field shows the Text data type and a description that reads "State or province." The field list also identifies the primary key, which is indicated by a key icon to the left of the field name. For the Customers table, the primary key is the CustomerID field. If more than one field makes up the primary key, a key icon appears next to each field.

NOTE

You may have noticed that, in Datasheet view, the CustomerID field appears as the Customer ID field (two words). This is because you can configure a display name for the field in the field's properties.

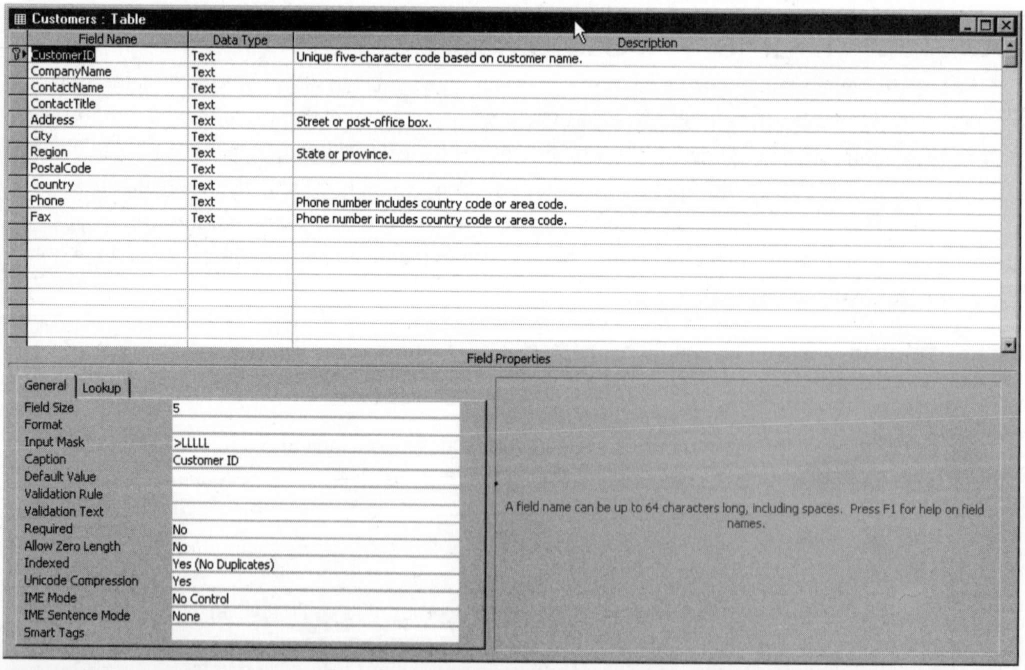

Field Name	Data Type	Description
CustomerID	Text	Unique five-character code based on customer name.
CompanyName	Text	
ContactName	Text	
ContactTitle	Text	
Address	Text	Street or post-office box.
City	Text	
Region	Text	State or province.
PostalCode	Text	
Country	Text	
Phone	Text	Phone number includes country code or area code.
Fax	Text	Phone number includes country code or area code.

Field Properties

General | Lookup

Field Size	5
Format	
Input Mask	>LLLLL
Caption	Customer ID
Default Value	
Validation Rule	
Validation Text	
Required	No
Allow Zero Length	No
Indexed	Yes (No Duplicates)
Unicode Compression	Yes
IME Mode	No Control
IME Sentence Mode	None
Smart Tags	

A field name can be up to 64 characters long, including spaces. Press F1 for help on field names.

Figure 3-3 Displaying the Customers table in Design view

If you again refer to Figure 3-3, you'll notice that the left part of the field properties area includes two tabs: General and Lookup. The General tab is selected by default and includes properties for the selected field. The properties allow you to configure such settings as the field size, validation rules, and whether the field requires a value. The Lookup tab contains a set of properties that provide values—from another table or from a list—for the specified field. The lookup values provide a reference for adding values to the field. (Configuring table properties is discussed in Module 4.)

One other aspect of the Design view window that I want to point out has to do with the toolbar and menu. When you open a table in Design view, the Database toolbar is replaced by the Table Design toolbar and the menu options change. As you've come to expect, the toolbar and new menu options are specific to the Design view window. You can use these options to perform such tasks as creating primary keys, setting up indexes, or viewing table properties.

Progress Check

1. Which view should you use to view the data stored in a table?

2. What is a subdatasheet?

3. What information is displayed in Design view?

CRITICAL SKILL
3.2 Create Tables in a Database

Now that you have an understanding of how to view data in a table and view the table definition, you're ready to create a table. Access provides a number of methods for creating tables:

- Creating a table in Design view

- Creating a table in Datasheet view, which is also referred to as creating a table by entering data

- Creating a table by using the Table wizard

- Creating a table by importing data from another data source

- Creating a table by linking to data in another table

1. Datasheet view

2. A subdatasheet is a window that displays information related to a record displayed in a datasheet view window.

3. Design view displays the configuration settings that define the structure of the table and determine the type of data that can be stored in that table.

Of these options, we will be most concerned with creating a table in Design view. Creating a table in this manner is as close as you can get in Access to creating a table "from scratch." By creating a table in Design view, you'll gain a comprehensive understanding of how tables are defined. As a result, other methods of table creation will be easier because you'll have a better comprehension of the components that make up the table.

NOTE

This section does not cover the last two options—creating a table by importing data and creating a table by linking data. I discuss importing and linking data in Module 9.

Access provides a number of methods that you can use to begin the process of creating a table. These methods can be separated into two broad categories: those that can be accessed through the New Table dialog box and those that can be accessed from the list of tables. In both cases, the database window must be open.

The New Table dialog box allows you to access any of the five methods (listed previously) for creating tables. You can access the dialog box by taking one of the following steps:

- Select the Tables object type in the database window and click the New button.

- Click Table in the Insert menu.

- Click the down arrow in the New Object button on the Database toolbar and then click Table.

When the New Table dialog box appears, you can select the appropriate table creation option, as shown in Figure 3-4. Once you select the option, click OK to begin the table creation process. You can also begin the table creation process by double-clicking the appropriate option.

The database window also allows you to create a table directly from one of the links included in the list of tables (when the Tables object type is selected). By double-clicking

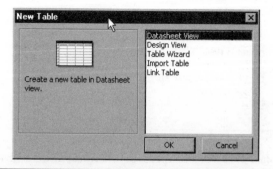

Figure 3-4 The five table creation options in the New Table dialog box

one of the links, you can bypass the need to launch the New Table dialog box. Instead, the links begin the table creation process directly. Figure 3-5 shows the links that are displayed in the database window, as it appears in the Northwind database. Note that the link Create Table By Entering Data allows you to create a table in Datasheet view.

Creating a Table in Design View

Earlier in this module, I described how to view a table in Design view, which provides a graphical interface to the table definition. We'll now look at how to create a table in Design view, only now the Design view window acts as a blank slate on which you must configure the necessary settings that define the structure of the new table.

When you launch the Design view table creation process—either through the New Table dialog box or by clicking the link in the database window—the Design view window appears and is ready for you to start configuring the table, as shown in Figure 3-6. As you can see, no fields exist and, as a result, no field properties are listed. Because a field's properties are dependent on a field's data type, you cannot view or edit those properties until a data type has been assigned to the field.

The first place to start, then, is to add the necessary fields to your table. For each field, you should add a field name, select a data type, and provide a description if applicable. You should also define the table's primary key. You can configure a field's properties after you create that field or after you create all fields. Because I don't discuss configuring table properties until Module 4, assume for now that the properties will be configured after the fields have been defined.

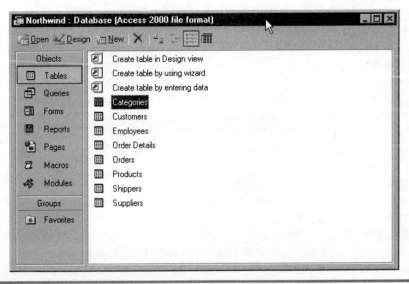

Figure 3-5 The table creation links in the database window

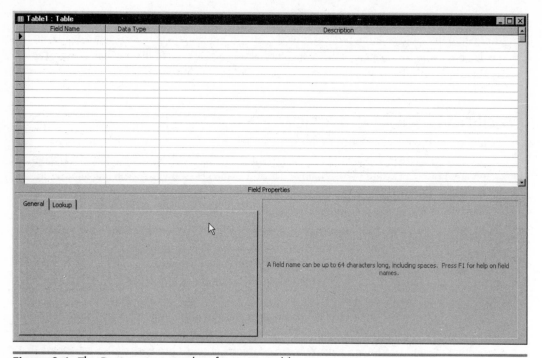

Figure 3-6 The Design view window for a new table

Assigning a Field Name

The first step in adding a field to a table is to type a field name into the Field Name column of the Design view window. Field names can be made up of letters, numbers, and spaces, although a space should not be the first character in a field name. You can also use a mix of uppercase and lowercase letters; however, you cannot exceed 64 characters, including spaces.

When assigning names to fields, be sure to use names that are intuitive. For example, if you're creating a field that lists customers' identification numbers, you might want to name the field something like CustomerID. You should also try to be consistent in the naming conventions you use across fields. For instance, don't use mixed case for one field name (such as CustomerID) and all uppercase for another field name (such as FIRST NAME). You should adopt a naming convention that is used for all objects throughout the database.

Selecting a Data Type

Once you've provided a name for the field, you must select a data type from the drop-down list provided in the Data Type column. As you'll recall, a data type is a constraint that defines the format of the data that can be entered into the field. You can assign only one data type per field. Table 3-1 describes the data types that are supported by Access.

Let's take a look at an example of assigning a data type to a field. Suppose you create a field named BookTitles. The data that will be entered into that field will be mostly characters,

Data Type	Description
Text	A field can contain up to 255 characters that can include letters or numbers. The Text data type can be used for such things as names, job titles, or addresses. Keep in mind that, even if the field contains only numbers, they cannot be calculated, as they can be for the Number and Currency data types. The Text data type is the most common one used, and it is the default.
Memo	A field can contain up to 65,535 characters that can include letters or numbers. The Memo data type can be used for data that requires more than 255 characters (the limitation placed on the Text data type).
Number	A field can contain numerical data that can be mathematically calculated. The Number data type can be used for such data as inventory amounts or employee hours, amounts that can be added together or calculated in some other way.
Date/Time	A field can contain date and time values (for the years 999 through 9999).
Currency	A field can contain currency or other numerical data that can be mathematically calculated. The Currency data type is accurate to 15 digits to the left of the decimal point and 4 digits to the right, making calculations more precise than the Number data type.
AutoNumber	A unique numerical value is automatically assigned to the field for each new record. The AutoNumber data type guarantees that each record is unique. As a result, the field configured with this data type usually serves as the table's primary key. You can configure Access to increment that value by 1 for each record or to assign random numbers.
Yes/No	A field can contain only one of two values. By default, the values are Yes and No, but you can set them to be True/False or On/Off. The field will always support only two options.
OLE Object	A field can contain an embedded object or link to an object such as an Excel spreadsheet or a Word document. (OLE refers to object linking and embedding.)
Hyperlink	A field can contain a hyperlink address. The field can contain up to four parts: display text, a file or web page path, a location within the target file, and a screen tip. Only the file or web page path is required.
Lookup Wizard	A field can contain only values that are included in the referenced table or list. Selecting this option launches the Lookup wizard, which allows you to create a lookup field. Once the source table or list has been defined, Access assigns a data type based on the lookup values.

Table 3-1 Data Types for Fields in a Table

although some titles might include numbers. As a result, you decide to assign the Text data type to the field. For each field, you must determine what type of data will be stored in that field and then select the appropriate data type.

Providing a Description

For any field that you add to a table, you can provide an optional description. Simply type the description in the Description column for that field. The description is important if the field name is not self-explanatory or if special rules restrict the type of data that can be added to a field and you want to list those restrictions. For some fields, however, a description is not necessary. For example, if you have an address-related field named City, a description would probably not be necessary, unless there are specific restrictions on the city that can be entered into the field.

Assigning a Primary Key

As you'll recall from Module 2, the relational model states that every record within a table must be unique. To ensure this uniqueness, one or more fields are configured as the primary key. The primary key ensures that no values (for single-field primary keys) or no sets of values (for multiple-field primary keys) are duplicated. For example, if you configure a single-field primary key that is made up of incremental numbers, each of those numbers must be unique (such as 1001, 1002, 1003, and so on). However, if you configure a multiple-field primary key, the individual fields can contain duplicate values, but the fields taken together cannot contain duplicates. Suppose, for example, that the primary key is made up of the first name and last name. First names can be duplicated and so can last names, but no full names can be duplicated (which is why a primary key using names is usually not a good idea).

To configure a primary key, you must select the field and then take one of the following steps:

● Click the Primary Key button on the Table Design toolbar.

● On the Edit menu, click Primary Key.

● Right-click the field (or one of the fields if multiple fields are selected) and click Primary Key in the shortcut menu.

NOTE

To select more than one field, hold down the CTRL key while clicking each field.

Progress Check

1. What information should you provide when creating a field?

2. What is the greatest number of characters that can be contained in a field name?

3. Which data type should you use for a field that contains numerical values that must be calculated?

4. How many fields in a table can you configure as the primary key?

---

1. For each field, you should add a field name, select a data type, and provide a description if applicable. If the field should be configured as a primary key, specify that as well.

2. 64

3. Number or Currency

4. One or more

Ask the Expert

Q: You state that a primary key can include one or more fields. In what circumstances should you configure a primary key with more than one field?

A: In most cases, you should be able to configure a primary key with only one field. If a field that would qualify as a primary key does not exist within your table, you should consider adding a field that uniquely identifies each record. This approach is usually the safest and most efficient approach to ensuring that your records are unique. In addition, because Access supports the AutoNumber data type, this approach is often the easiest.

However, there are circumstance in which configuring multiple fields as a primary key is a good solution. The best example of this is the junction table. As you'll recall from Module 2, a junction table is one that is added between two tables in which a many-to-many relationship exists. The junction table allows you to create two one-to-many relationships. The junction table usually includes two columns that represent the primary key from each of the original tables. Those two columns, when combined, must contain unique value sets. As a result, those columns make good candidates for the primary key. (See Module 2 for more information on relationships and junction tables.)

Creating a Table in Datasheet View

Earlier in this module, I described how you can use the Datasheet view window to view data in a table. Access also allows you to create a table by using Datasheet view to enter data. A table is then created based on the values you entered into the fields, and the default property settings are assigned to those fields. You can then modify those settings as needed.

To create a table in Datasheet view, you must open the Datasheet view window by double-clicking the Create Table By Entering Data link in the database window or by using one of the other methods for starting the Datasheet view table creation process. When the Datasheet view window appears, all columns and rows are blank, as shown in Figure 3-7.

Once the Datasheet view window is open, you can enter data into the table. You must be certain that the data is accurate and that you've entered it into the appropriate fields. Access assigns data types to the fields based on the data, so incorrect data could result in an incorrect data type, which would mean that inappropriate constraints would be placed on the data.

After you've entered all the data, you simply close the window. You'll be prompted to save the table and give it a name. Once you've done that, you'll be prompted to set the primary key. If you allow Access to create a primary key, it will add a field that is configured with the AutoNumber data type, and it will assign a unique identifier for each row, starting with 1.

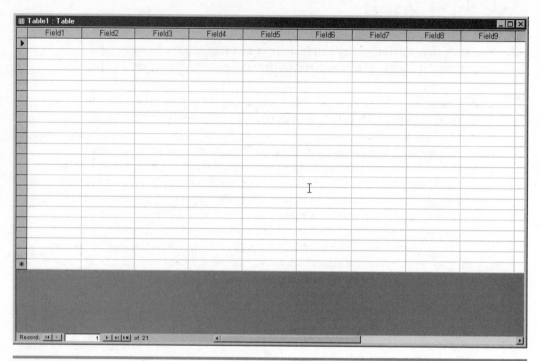

Figure 3-7 Using Datasheet view to create a table

NOTE

In general, I do not recommend using the Datasheet view method to create a table unless it is a very simple table that contains only a small amount of data. For the most part, data should not be added to a table until the table has been properly configured, appropriate constraints have been applied, and relationships have been established. When you use Datasheet view to create a table, the data types assigned by Access and the properties configured are based on the data, when instead the data entered should be limited by the constraints already in place.

Creating a Table by Using the Table Wizard

The Table wizard provides a fast and convenient method for creating a table that uses the default configuration settings assigned to a new table. The wizard provides sample tables that you can use to identify the fields for your new table. The wizard also allows you to name the table, assign a primary key or generate one automatically, and establish relationships with other tables.

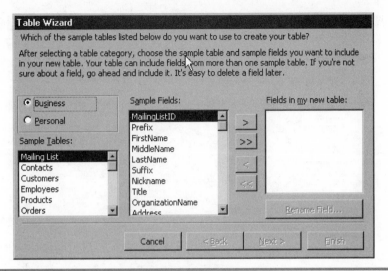

Figure 3-8 The opening screen of the Table wizard

The Table wizard walks you through the steps necessary to create a table. To launch the wizard, double-click the Create Table By Using Wizard link in the database window or use one of the other methods to launch the wizard. The first screen to appear, shown in Figure 3-8, allows you to select from a list of sample tables that each provide fields that you can use in your table.

To add a field to your table, select the field from the Sample Fields list box and then click the right arrow. You can then rename the field by selecting the field name in the Fields In My New Table list box, clicking Rename Field, and entering the new field name.

TIP

You do not need to use fields from the same table. Once you've chosen fields from one table, select another table and then choose fields from that one.

Once you've added the necessary fields to your table, click Next to move to the next screen, shown in Figure 3-9. On this screen, you can name the table and select a primary key option. You can have Access create the primary key for you, or you can configure the primary key manually.

Your next step in creating the table is to determine whether the new table is related to any other tables in the database. Figure 3-10 shows the screen that prompts you for relationship

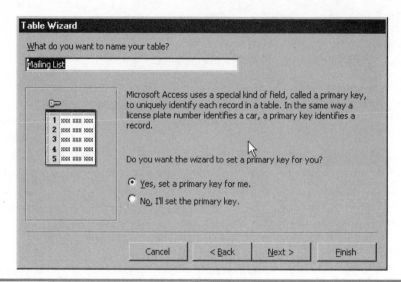

Figure 3-9 Setting the primary key

information. To set a relationship, select the applicable table and click Relationships. You're then prompted to select the type of relationship.

Once you've defined the table relationship, you can then choose to modify the table definition, enter data into the table, or create a form for entering data.

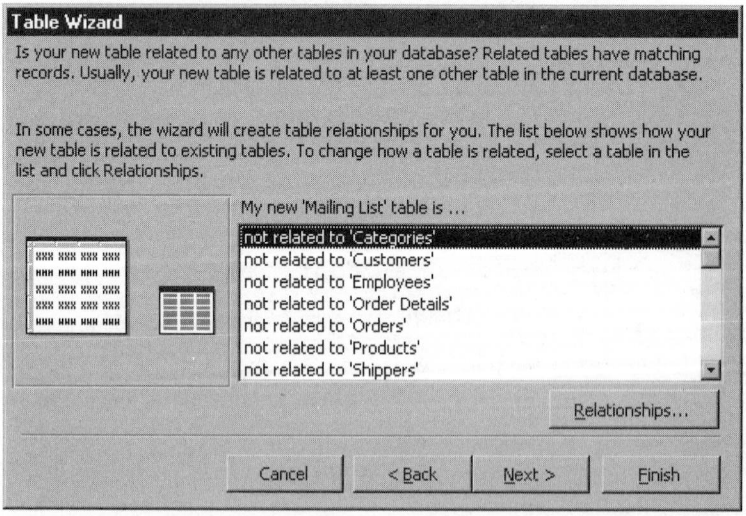

Figure 3-10 Configuring table relationships

| Project 3-1 | # Adding Tables to the Consumer Advocacy Database |

Now that you have an understanding of how to create tables in an Access database, you can create the tables for the application you're developing for the consumer advocacy organization. You will be adding tables to the database file (ConsumerAdvocacy.mdb) that you created in Module 1. The tables will be based on the data model that you created in Module 2. However, as you might recall from that module, data models often reflect the primary keys and the domains. For a data model for an Access database, you might want to show data types rather than domains. As a result, I've revised the data model created in Project 2-1 to include the primary key for each table and the data type for each field. Figure 3-11 shows the revised data model. The primary key fields are shown in bold, and the data types are in parentheses.

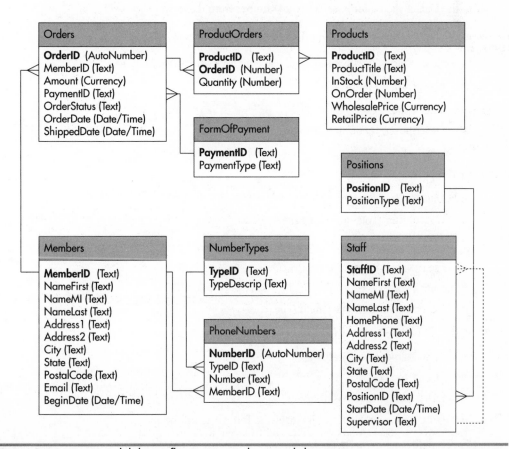

Figure 3-11 Data model that reflects primary keys and data types

(continued)

As you can see, each table includes a primary key made up of one column. The only exception to this is the ProductOrders table, which serves as a junction table between the Orders table and the Products table. From this data model, you can create the tables for your database.

Step by Step

1. If they're not already open, open Access and then open the ConsumerAdvocacy.mdb file.

2. If it is not selected, select the Tables object type, and then double-click the Create Table In Design View link to open the Design view window.

3. The first table that you'll be creating is the Orders table, which includes seven fields. In the first row, type **OrderID** in the Field Name column.

4. In the Data Type column, select AutoNumber from the drop-down list.

5. In the Description column, type **Unique identifier for each order**.

6. In the second row, create a field that uses the following information:

   - Field Name: MemberID
   - Data Type: Text
   - Description: ID of member who placed the order.

7. In the next row, create a field that uses the following information:

   - Field Name: Amount
   - Data Type: Currency
   - Description: Total amount paid for order.

8. In the next row, create a field that uses the following information:

   - Field Name: PaymentID
   - Data Type: Text
   - Description: ID for payment type.

9. In the next row, create a field that uses the following information:

   - Field Name: OrderStatus
   - Data Type: Text
   - Description: Status of order.

10. In the next row, create a field that uses the following information:

    - Field Name: OrderDate
    - Data Type: Date/Time
    - Description: Date order was placed.

11. In the next row, create a field that uses the following information:
    - Field Name: ShippedDate
    - Data Type: Date/Time
    - Description: Date order was shipped.

12. Select the first row, which contains the OrderID field, and then click the Primary Key button on the Table Design toolbar. The OrderID field has now been set up as the primary key. Because the AutoNumber data type was used for this field, unique values will automatically be assigned to the records.

13. In the File menu, click Save. The Save As dialog box appears.

14. In the Table Name text box, type **Orders**, and then click OK.

15. Close the Design View window. Notice that the table has been added to the database window.

16. For each of the remaining tables in the data model, create a table that uses the appropriate field names and data types. Add descriptions as necessary, and be sure to set the primary key for each table. Keep in mind that the primary key for the ProductOrders table is made up of two fields. To select more than one field at a time, press CTRL and then click the participating fields.

Project Summary

In this project, you created the nine tables that are represented in your data model. To create those tables, you used Design view, which allowed you to configure the individual settings for each field. Part of the table creation process is to configure the table and field properties, and normally you would do that when you created the fields. However, because I do not discuss the table and field properties until Module 4, this project had you simply identify the fields, data types, descriptions, and primary keys. You will configure the properties in the next module. Even so, your database now has the necessary tables, which provide you with the basic foundation for your application.

CRITICAL SKILL
3.3 Modify Table Settings

It is not unusual to find that, after you've created your tables, you must modify the field settings. Access allows you to change the field names or descriptions, change data types, change primary keys, add and delete fields, or change the field order. To change a table's settings, open that table in Design view, make the necessary changes, and save your changes.

NOTE

You can also change the field and table properties, which will be discussed in Module 4.

Changing the Field Name or Description

Changing field names and descriptions is a very straightforward process. You simply type in the new information and save the table. Neither change affects the underlying data. However, changing a field name can affect other data objects in your database. For example, you may have queries that specifically reference the field name that you've changed.

Fortunately, Access includes a feature called Name AutoCorrect that updates references in data objects if you change a name in a table. When you open the data object, Access checks whether any names have changed since the last time that the object was saved. Access then corrects the references in the object to be consistent with the new name.

Changing the Data Type

Changing the data type is as easy as changing a field name if no data is stored in the table. However, if the table does contain data, changing a data type can be more complicated. Remember, a data type applies constraints on the data that can be entered into a field. If you change the data type, some data might be lost.

NOTE

If you try to change a data type that could affect data, Access displays a message that tells you how many rows will be affected.

For example, you can change a Number data type to a Text data type because Text fields can include numbers. However, converting a Text field to a Number field can cause problems because the Number data type does not support letters, only numbers. All non-number characters will be deleted.

To change a data type, click the Data Type column for the specific field, select the new data type from the drop-down list, and save the table.

Changing the Primary Key

You might find it necessary to alter the primary key in your table. Perhaps you want to add a column to the existing primary key or designate a different column as the primary key. Access makes changing a primary key as easy as creating one:

- To designate a different field for the primary key, select the new field and click the Primary Key button on the Table Design toolbar. The old primary key is deleted and the new primary key created.

- To add a field to an existing primary key, select the original primary key field and the new field, and then click the Primary Key button. The primary key is updated to include both fields.

- To delete a primary key, select the primary key field and then click the Primary Key button.

Adding and Deleting Fields

You might discover that you want to add fields to or delete fields from your table. You can add a new field to the bottom of the list of fields or insert a field in between other fields. You can also delete any of the existing fields.

CAUTION

When you delete a field, you're also deleting the data contained in that field. If you try to delete a field that contains data, Access warns you about the loss of data.

To add a field at the end of a table, select the Field Name column in the first empty row, enter the field information, and save the table.

To insert a field in between tables, click the field directly below where you want the new field to appear and take one of the following actions:

- Click Rows in the Insert menu.

- Click the Insert Rows button on the Table Design toolbar.

- Right-click the selected row and click Insert Rows in the shortcut menu.

Once you've inserted the new row, enter the field information and save the table.

To delete a field from the table, click the field and then take one of the following actions:

- Press the DELETE key.

- Click Delete Rows in the Edit menu.

- Click the Delete Rows button on the Table Design toolbar.

- Right-click the selected field and click Delete Rows in the shortcut menu.

NOTE

The entire row that contains the field must be selected if you use the DELETE key to remove a field from the table.

Managing Access Tables

3

Once you've deleted the field, save the table. Note that Access will not let you delete a field if a relationship exists between that field and another table.

CAUTION

Before you delete a field, you should ensure that no data objects contain references to that field.

Changing the Field Order

Access allows you to change the order in which fields are listed in your table. Select the row that contains the field that you want to move by clicking the row selector arrow at the left end of the row, and then drag the row to the new location. You can move several rows at the same time by selecting all the rows that you want to move and then dragging them to their new location.

Project 3-2 Modifying Table Settings

As you have seen, once you've created a table, you can modify the table settings. In this project, you'll create a copy of the Members table that you created in Project 3-1 for the consumer advocacy database. In the new table, you'll modify the field settings and change the field order, and then you'll delete the table, returning the database to the state it was in at the end of Project 3-1.

Step by Step

1. If they're not already open, open Access and then open the ConsumerAdvocacy.mdb file.

2. Verify that the Tables object type is selected, and then select the Members table.

3. On the Database toolbar, click the Copy button, and then click the Paste button. The Paste Table As dialog box appears.

4. In the Table Name text box, type **Test**, and then click OK. The Test table is added to the list of tables in the database window.

5. Select the Test table if not already selected, and then click the Design button at the top of the database window. The table opens in Design view.

6. Right-click the Email field, and then click Delete Rows in the shortcut menu. The field is deleted from the table.

7. Right-click the City field, and then click Insert Rows in the shortcut menu. A row is added above the City field.

8. In the Field Name column of the new row, type **Address3**, and then move the cursor to another row. The Text data type is automatically configured for the new field.

9. Select the entire row that contains the BeginDate field, and drag the field to immediately above the Address1 field.

10. In the Field Name column for the PostalCode field, double-click the field name, and then type **ZipCode**.

11. In the Data Type column for the ZipCode field, select the Number data type.

12. Select the NameLast field and then click the Primary Key button on the Table Design toolbar. The original primary key is deleted and a new one is created.

13. Close the table, but do not save the changes.

14. In the database window, right-click the Test table, click Delete in the shortcut menu, and then click Yes to confirm the deletion.

Project Summary

In this project, you modified a number of fields in the Test table. You deleted and added fields, changed the field order, changed a field name and data type, and reconfigured the table's primary key. You could have also modified the field properties when you were making changes. As you can see, Access allows you to make numerous modifications after a table has been created. However, when you modify table settings, you must use caution if data is stored in the table. An inappropriate modification can result in the loss of data.

Module 3 Mastery Check

1. You want to view the table definition for the Employees table. Which view should you use?

2. Which toolbar is displayed when you are viewing the data contained in a table?

   A. Database

   B. Table Design

   C. Table Datasheet

   D. Formatting (Datasheet)

3. How do you display the subdatasheet associated with a record that you're viewing in Datasheet view?

   A. Click the plus sign associated with the record.

   B. Click the minus sign associated with the record.

C. Click the Database Window button on the Table Datasheet toolbar.

D. Click the row selector arrow for that record.

4. How is a table's primary key indicated in Design view?

5. What five methods does Access provide for creating tables?

6. What types of characters can you use in a field name?

7. You're creating a field that will uniquely identify each record in your table. The field values will be a mix of letters and numbers. Which data type should you use?

   A. AutoNumber

   B. Text

   C. Memo

   D. Number

8. How does the Text data type differ from the Number data type?

9. You're creating a new table in the database. You want to create only the basic table at this time, but will refine the table settings at a later time. What settings must you configure when creating the table?

   A. Field names

   B. Data types

   C. Descriptions

   D. Primary key

10. How do you create a table by simply entering data?

11. Which table creation method should you use if you want to select fields from sample tables?

   A. Creating a table in Design view

   B. Creating a table in Datasheet view

   C. Creating a table by using the Table wizard

   D. Creating a table by linking data

12. What feature does Access include that updates field references in a data object if that field name changes?

13. What can happen to data in a table if you change a data type?

14. What happens to data in a field when you delete that field?

15. You want to add a new field to a table after the existing fields. How do you add a field to the end of the listed fields?

Module 4

Managing Table Properties

CRITICAL SKILLS

4.1 Configure General Field Properties

4.2 Define Validation Rules

4.3 Create Field Indexes

4.4 Configure Lookup Field Properties

4.5 Configure Table Properties

A s you learned in Module 3, the process of creating a table involves not only defining the fields for that table, but also configuring the table and field properties. In fact, you would normally configure a field's settings when you define that field. For example, if you're adding a Text field to your table, you can set the field's maximum size and provide a caption for the field, both of which are part of the field's properties. In addition, you can configure the table's properties—those properties not specific to any field—at any point in the table creation process. You can also wait to configure both field and table properties until after you've created all the necessary fields, which is the approach I take in this book in order to demonstrate each component of the table creation process. In this module, you'll learn how to configure table and field properties. Keep in mind, however, that setting the properties is only part of the entire table creation process. You should refer back to Module 3 as necessary for more information about the process.

CRITICAL SKILL
4.1 Configure General Field Properties

For each field in an Access database table, you can configure a set of properties specific to the field. The properties available for a field depend on the data type configured for that field. For example, you can specify the number of decimal places for Numeric and Currency fields, but not for any other fields. On the other hand, you can specify a caption for any field, regardless of the data type.

Table 4-1 lists each general field property available in an Access table. The properties are compared to each data type. If the data type supports a property, an X appears beneath it. Note that the Lookup Wizard option is not included in the table. Although it is listed as a data type option when you create a field, it is actually a link that launches the wizard. The data type assigned to the field is based on the values created by using the wizard.

Property	Text	Memo	Number	Date/Time	Currency	AutoNumber	Yes/No	OLE Object	Hyper-link
Field Size	X		X			X			
Format	X	X	X	X	X	X	X		X
Input Mask	X			X					
Caption	X	X	X	X	X	X	X	X	X
Default Value	X	X	X	X	X		X		X
Validation Rule	X	X	X	X	X		X		X

Table 4-1 Properties Supported for Each Data Type

Property	Text	Memo	Number	Date/Time	Currency	AutoNumber	Yes/No	OLE Object	Hyper-link
Validation Text	X	X	X	X	X		X		X
Required	X	X	X	X	X		X	X	X
Allow Zero Length	X	X							X
Indexed	X	X	X	X	X	X	X		X
Unicode Compression	X	X							X
IME Mode	X	X		X					X
IME Sentence Mode	X	X		X					X
Smart Tags	X	X	X	X	X	X			X
Decimal Places			X		X				
Precision			X						
Scale			X						
New Values						X			

Table 4-1 Properties Supported for Each Data Type *(continued)*

X ? meaning

As you can see in Figure 4-1, Access provides default values for some of a data type's properties, while leaving other properties—the ones that don't require a value—blank. For example, a Text field is automatically configured with a field size of 50, but no default caption is provided, as shown in the figure. You can leave the field size as 50 or change the value, and you can add a caption.

To configure a field property, you must open the table in Design view, select the applicable field, and then click the property. For some properties, such as the Field Size and Caption properties in a Text field, you simply type in the setting. Other properties, such as the Required property, include a drop-down list. For these properties, select the property, click the down arrow, and then select the appropriate option.

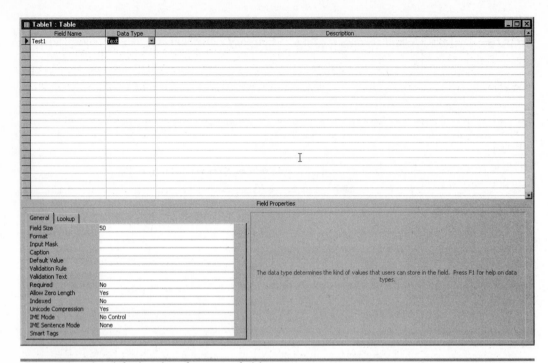

Figure 4-1 The default values for a Text field

TIP

If you highlight the text in a property's text box and then type in the first letter of the new property setting option, the option will be displayed. For example, if you type **n** in the text box for the Required property, the No option will be displayed (if the property includes a drop-down list).

Several properties also include a Build button that appears when you select the property. The Build button, which is shown with three dots (…), launches a utility that helps you configure a particular property. For example, if you click the Build button associated with the Input Mask property, the Input Mask wizard appears.

Now let's take a look at the individual properties. Most properties are covered in this section; however, I cover the properties related to validation rules and indexes in separate sections.

NOTE

This section covers only those properties that appear in the General tab in the lower portion of the Design view window. Properties listed on the Lookup tab are discussed in "Configure Lookup Field Properties," later in this module.

Setting the Field Size

The Field Size property allows you to configure the maximum size of Text, Number, and AutoNumber fields. If you're configuring the field size of a Text field, you simply type in the appropriate number, which represents the maximum number of characters that a value in that field can contain.

A Number field works a little differently. Rather than specifying the number of characters, you must select one of the following options:

- **Byte**   This choice stores integers (whole numbers) from 0 through 255.

- **Integer**   This option stores integers from –32,768 through +32,768.

- **Long Integer**   This stores integers from about –2 billion through +2 billion. This option is the default setting.

- **Single**   This choice stores numbers that can contain up to 7 decimal places.

- **Double**   This stores numbers that can contain up to 15 decimal places.

- **Replication ID**   This option stores globally unique identifiers (GUIDs), which are unique identifiers associated with specific objects.

- **Decimal**   This selection stores numbers that can contain up to 28 decimal places. This option makes the Precision and Scale properties available.

AutoNumber fields, like Number fields, require that you use a predefined property setting option. However, for AutoNumber fields, your options are limited to Long Integer and Replication ID.

Formatting the Field Data

The Format property allows you to configure how data is displayed for all data types except OLE Object. By using the Format property, you can specify the appearance of the data without affecting the data itself. The formatting settings that you configure in Design view are applied to the values as they appear in Datasheet view and to any new controls that are added to forms or reports. Controls added prior to the formatting change will be unaffected. (A *control* is an object that you add to a form or report that is used to display or manipulate data.)

The options that you can use when configuring the Format property depend on which data type is applied to the field. For many data types, the Format options are predefined, and you merely select the appropriate option from a drop-down list. For the other data types, you must specify a value.

Text and Memo Fields

The Format property for Text and Memo fields requires you to type in specific values if you want to apply special formatting to a field. Access defines a number of characters and symbols that you can use to format Text and Memo values. In addition, some of these symbols can be used to create custom formats for other fields, including Hyperlink fields. Table 4-2 describes several of the more common symbols.

Now let's look at an example that puts several of these symbols together. Suppose you are configuring a field that you just added to your table. You select the Text data type and then add the following setting to the Format property:

```
>;@;"Unknown value"[Red]
```

The greater-than (>) symbol indicates that all values should be displayed in uppercase. The at (@) symbol indicates that Access must display either a character or space in that field. The at symbol is required if you're going to include a literal value in quotes, which in this case is "Unknown value". A color is then specified after the literal value to indicate that the value should appear in red.

Number, Currency, and AutoNumber Fields

Number, Currency, and AutoNumber fields provide a set of predefined Format property settings that determine how numeric values are displayed. The settings can range from basic numbers to percentages and currency. Table 4-3 describes each of the predefined Format settings available for the Number, Currency, and AutoNumber fields.

Symbol	Description
"ABC"	If no entry is made in the field when a record is added to the table, the field will contain the text you specify in quotation marks. Note that ABC is just a placeholder. You can type any letters or numbers within the quotation marks.
!	This forces the left alignment of the values in the field.
[color]	This specifies a color for the values displayed in a field. Access supports the following color options: [Black], [Blue], [Green], [Cyan], [Red], [Magenta], [Yellow], and [White].
@	This symbol indicates that a space or a character is required.
&	This symbol indicates that a character is not required.
<	This displays all text in lowercase.
>	This displays all text in uppercase.
;	This symbol separates multiple commands.

Table 4-2 Formatting Symbols for the Text and Memo Fields

Setting	Description	Example
General Number	Displays numerical data as it was entered into the field. This is the default setting for Number and AutoNumber fields.	39567.429
Currency	Displays numerical data along with a currency symbol and a thousands separator. The display is based on the regional settings as they're configured in the operating system. This is the default setting for the fields configured with the Currency data type.	$39,567.43
Euro	Displays numerical data in the same manner as the Currency setting, but uses the Euro symbol.	€39,567.43
Fixed	Displays at least one digit, with a default setting of two decimal places.	39567.43
Standard	Displays numerical data along with a thousands separator. The display is based on the regional settings as they're configured in the operating system.	39,567.43
Percent	Displays numerical data as percentages.	3956742.90%
Scientific	Displays numerical data in scientific notation.	3.96E+04

Table 4-3 Format Settings for Number, Currency, and AutoNumber Fields

Date/Time Fields

When you configure the Format property for a Date/Time field, you have a number of options for how you can display data in that field. For example, you can display both dates and time, or you can display either one or the other. Table 4-4 describes each of the predefined settings available for Date/Time fields.

Yes/No Fields

A Yes/No field acts as a type of switch that indicates one of two settings. By default, a field supports either a Yes value or a No value. However, you can use the Format property to change these options to True and False or to On and Off. Yes, True, and On are considered equivalent values, and No, False, and Off are considered equivalent.

Providing an Input Mask

An *input mask* is a type of filter that determines how data is entered into a field. It is similar to the Format property in that it affects how data is displayed without affecting the data itself. But the Input Mask property is different because it provides users with a fill-in-the-blank type format that limits the way data can be entered. For example, you can create an input mask that

Setting	Description	Example
General Date	Displays a combination of date and time values. If only a date value is available, no time is displayed. If only a time value is available, no date is displayed. This is the default setting.	10/31/2004 10:30:27 PM
Long Date	Displays the day and date, as configured in the Long Date setting in the regional settings of the Windows operating system.	Sunday, October 31, 2004
Medium Date	Displays the date only.	31-Oct-04
Short Date	Displays the date only, as configured in the Short Date setting in the regional settings of the Windows operating system.	10/31/04
Long Time	Displays the hour, minutes, and seconds, as configured in the Time setting in the regional settings of the Windows operating system.	10:30:27 PM
Medium Time	Displays the hour and minutes only.	10:30 PM
Short Time	Displays the hour and minutes in military time.	22:34

Table 4-4 Format Settings for Date/Time Fields

requires data to conform to the format used for Social Security numbers (nine digits and two hyphens). With this input mask, users are automatically provided with the necessary hyphens and are limited to nine digits.

You can configure an input mask for Text fields and Date/Time fields. Access provides a number of predefined input masks for both field types. To configure a field with an input mask, select the field in Design view, click the Input Mask property, and then click the Build button. When the Input Mask wizard appears, select the appropriate input mask and follow the steps in the wizard to complete the property configuration.

If you're configuring an input mask for a Text field, you have five options from which to choose, as shown in Figure 4-2. The options are self-explanatory, and each includes an example of how the data will look.

You can also configure an input mask for Date/Time fields. However, the predefined input masks available for these fields are different from those available for Text fields. Access provides five predefined input masks for Date/Time fields, as shown in Figure 4-3.

Creating a Caption

The Caption property is available to all types of fields, regardless of the data type. The property allows you to define a display name for a field. The display name is used in Datasheet view in

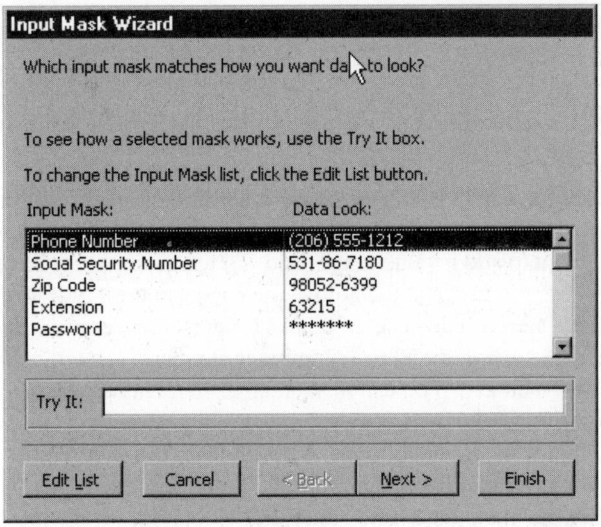

Figure 4-2 The Input Mask wizard for a Text field

place of the actual field name. You would configure a caption for a field if you think that the field name is not descriptive enough. The caption can be made up of letters, numbers, spaces,

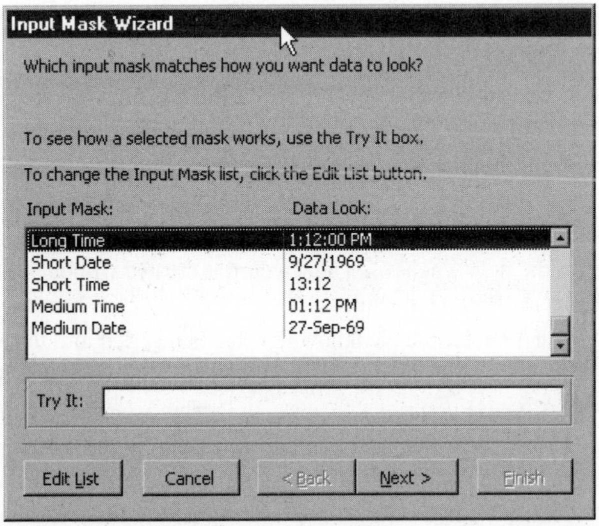

Figure 4-3 The Input Mask wizard for a Date/Time field

Ask the Expert

Q: **The Input Mask wizard includes a text box named Try It. What is this for?**

A: The Try It text box, which is located near the bottom of the wizard screen, allows you to test the input mask that you've selected. You'll see what the users will actually see when they attempt to add a value to the field. To test an input mask, select the input mask that you want to use, and then move the cursor to the Try It text box to make the text box active. Once you do, a set of blanks (underscores) appears and, if applicable, one or more hyphens. For the Phone Number input mask, a set of parentheses for the area code is also included. You can then enter test data into the text by filling in the blanks. Access automatically keeps the hyphens and parentheses in their correct positions and limits the number of characters to what is permitted by the input mask. This allows you to verify that the input mask works properly. If you discover that you want to modify the input mask, click the Edit List button, which opens the Customize Input Mask Wizard dialog box. You can then make the necessary changes. If you need help while editing the input mask, click the Help button.

and special characters, and it can contain up to 255 characters. To define a caption for a field, simply select the field in Design view and type in the new name in the Caption property. Once you save the table, Access will use the name in Datasheet view.

Providing a Default Value

There may be times when you want to ensure that a value is always entered into a field, even if the actual value is not known. For example, you might have a table that includes a field for a customer's home phone number. The field is configured so that a value must be added whenever a new record is inserted into the table. However, users who are entering data do not always know their customers' home phone numbers. To get around this, you can configure a default value that is added to the field whenever a new record is created without a home phone number. For example, you can configure a default value of "Unknown". Whenever a new record is added without a phone number, the "Unknown" value is inserted into that field.

Another use of default values is to insert a value that is more commonly used than other values. For example, suppose you run a business in Portland, Oregon. Your customers are made up primarily of Oregon residents, but some reside across the border in Washington. As a result, the State field in your Customers table might be configured with a default value of "OR". This way, "OR" will automatically be inserted into the field whenever a record is added to the table, unless you specify another state.

You can configure a default value for all fields except AutoNumber and OLE Object. To configure a default value for a field, select the field in Design view and type the default value in the Default Value property. Access will automatically add quotation marks around the information that you type. The default value will then be inserted into the field (without the quotation marks) whenever another value is not entered into that field.

NOTE

You may have discovered that the Default Value property includes a Build button, which opens the Expression Builder utility. Expression Builder allows you to create expressions that can be used in the Default Value property or the Validation Rule property. An *expression* is a combination of symbols that create a formula used to produce a specific result. For example, you can use an expression to add two numeric values together. For more information about expressions and Expression Builder, see Module 11.

Requiring Values and Allowing Blank Fields

For all field types except AutoNumber, you have the option of either requiring that the field always contain a value or allowing the field to be blank. To configure a field so that a value is always required, set the Required property to Yes. If you want to allow a field to be blank, set the property to No. Yes and No are the only options available for the Required property.

In addition to the Required property, Access provides the Allow Zero Length property for Text, Memo, and Hyperlink fields. The Allow Zero Length property also applies to blank values; however, this property distinguishes between null values and zero-length strings:

- A *null value* is a type of placeholder that Access (and other relational database management systems) uses to indicate a missing or unknown value. This is not the same as 0 but is actually a value stored in the database. When you set the Required property to No, null values will be used in the field if no other values are provided.

- A *zero-length string* is a string that contains no characters. It is used to indicate that no value exists. Unlike a null value, which indicates an unknown value, a zero-length string tells the database that there is no value for that field.

Let's take a look at an example to help clarify this. Suppose you have a field that lists customers' e-mail addresses. You might not know the e-mail addresses of some customers, or even whether they have e-mail at all. In these cases, you would want to use a null value for that field. However, you might know of some customers who definitely do not have e-mail accounts, in which case you would want to be able to use a zero-length string for the field.

If you want to configure a Text, Memo, or Hyperlink field to allow zero-length strings, set the Allow Zero Length property to Yes otherwise, set the property to No.

The Required property and Allow Zero Length property work together to allow different types of values:

- If you want to permit blanks in a field and don't care why the fields are blank, set both the Required property and the Allow Zero Length property to No.

- If you want to permit blanks in a field but want to be able to distinguish between null and zero-length values to tell why the fields are blank, set the Required property to No and the Allow Zero Length property to Yes.

- If you want to permit blanks in a field only for zero-length strings, set both the Required property and the Allow Zero Length property to Yes.

- If you want to always require a value in a field, set the Required property to Yes and the Allow Zero Length property to No.

Progress Check

1. Which field property is available for every field type?

2. How do you configure the Field Size property for a Text field?

3. You're configuring the Format property for a Text field, and you want all text to be uppercased. Which symbol should you use?

4. How should you configure a field's properties if you want to ensure that the field does not allow blanks?

Using Unicode Compression

In order to support the internationalization of its product, Access—along with a number of other products—provides for the use of *Unicode,* a character-encoding scheme that supports not only single-byte characters such as those found in English, Spanish, and German, but also double-byte characters such as those found in Chinese and Japanese. Because Unicode supports such a wide range of characters, each character requires two bytes, even if it is traditionally represented by a single byte.

---

1. Caption

2. In the Field Size property text box, type in a value that represents the maximum number of characters that a value in that field can contain.

3. The greater-than (>) symbol

4. Set the Required property to Yes and Allow Zero Length to No.

However, Access allows you to compress single-byte Unicode characters in order to minimize file size and optimize performance. If Unicode compression is enabled, the single-byte characters are compressed when the data is stored and uncompressed when it is retrieved.

Access allows you to compress Text, Memo, and Hyperlink fields. To apply Unicode compression to one of these fields, select the field in Design view and set the Unicode Compression property to Yes; otherwise, set the property to No. By default, Unicode compression is enabled for all three field types.

Configuring the IME Settings

Another way that Access supports the internationalization of its product is through the use of the Input Method Editor (IME). IME converts keystrokes into East Asian characters, such as those in the Chinese, Japanese, and Korean languages. You can think of IME as an alternative keyboard layout that enters East Asian text into a program.

Access includes two IME-related properties that can be applied to Text, Memo, Date/Time, and Hyperlink fields. The first property—IME Mode—provides a number of options that determine how Access will behave when the focus is moved to a particular field. The second property is IME Sentence Mode, which applies only to Japanese. The IME Sentence Mode property includes options that determine whether the language used is literary or conversational.

To configure either property, select the field in Design view, click the IME Mode or IME Sentence Mode property, and then select the appropriate option.

NOTE

A thorough discussion of the IME-related properties is beyond the scope of this book. However, you can learn more about IME at the Microsoft web site at http://microsoft.com.

Applying Smart Tags

Access allows you to associate smart tags with any field type except Yes/No and OLE Object. A *smart tag* is an object that contains a set of actions that you can associate with the values in a field. For example, suppose that you have a field that contains the names of all the employees in your company. You can associate the Person Name smart tag with that field. When you view a value (an employee name) in that field, you have the option of taking one of several actions offered by the smart tag. This can include scheduling a meeting with the employee or adding the employee as a contact.

Access provides three predefined smart tags that are installed on your system when you install Access. Table 4-5 shows the action options for each predefined smart tag.

Smart Tag	Action Options
Date	Schedule a Meeting Show my Calendar
Financial Symbol	Stock quote on MSN MoneyCentral Company report on MSN MoneyCentral Recent news on MSN MoneyCentral
Person Name	Send Mail Schedule a Meeting Open Contact Add to Contacts

Table 4-5 Actions Associated with the Predefined Smart Tags

To associate a smart tag with a field, take the following steps:

1. Select the field in Design view.

2. Select the Smart Tags property, and then click the Build button. The Smart Tags dialog box appears.

3. Select the check box next to the smart tag that you want to use.

4. Click OK.

You can also link to a Microsoft web site that allows you to download additional smart tags. To link to the site, click the More Smart Tags button in the Smart Tags dialog box.

Configuring Numerical Data

Access provides three field properties that are related to numerical data: Decimal Places, Precision, and Scale. The Decimal Places property is used to configure the number of digits to display to the right of the decimal point. It does not affect how data is stored, only how it appears when you view it. By default, the Decimal Places property is set to Auto, which means that the number of decimal places displayed depends on the Field Size option that has been selected. However, you can choose any number from 0 to 15 for the number of decimal places displayed.

The Decimal Places property is available to Number and Currency fields only. To configure the property, select the field in Design view, select the Decimal Places property, and then select a value from the drop-down list.

The two other numeric properties—Precision and Scale—are available only to Number (not Currency) fields, and only when the Field Size property is set to Decimal. The Precision property determines the total number of digits that can be entered into a Number field. The Scale property determines the total number of digits that can be entered to the right of the decimal point. For either property, you can enter a value from 0 to 28. The default for the Precision property is 18, and the default for the Scale property is 0.

To configure either property, select the Number field in Design view and then enter the appropriate setting in the property's text box.

Determining New Values

The New Values property applies only to fields configured with the AutoNumber data type. As you'll recall from Module 3, the AutoNumber data type allows Access to automatically assign a unique identifier to each record that is added to a table. You can use the New Values property to configure how Access will assign those numbers.

The New Values property includes two options: Increment and Random. Both of these options are available only if the Field Size property is set to Long Integer. As the option names suggest, Increment adds 1 to the previous field value for each new record that is added to the table. For example, the first record added will be assigned a value of 1, the second record will be assigned a value of 2, the third a value of 3, and so on. The Random option tells Access to assign a random number to each new record.

Progress Check

1. Which types of fields support Unicode compression?

2. What is a smart tag?

3. In what circumstances are the Precision and Scale properties available?

CRITICAL SKILL

4.2 Define Validation Rules

For those times when you need to restrict the data that can be entered into a field, Access allows you to define validation rules that limit a field's range of values. A *validation rule*

---

1. Text, Memo, and Hyperlink

2. A smart tag is an object that contains a set of actions that you can associate with the values in a field.

3. The Precision and Scale properties are available only to Number fields and only when the Field Size property is set to Decimal.

is an expression that is made up of operators, literal values, and other elements that together create a type of formula that defines the acceptable value range. You define a validation rule by entering the expression in the Validation Rule property for the specific field. The Validation Rule property can be configured for any field type except AutoNumber and OLE Object.

NOTE

You can also define a validation rule in the table's properties. This type of validation rule applies to the table as a whole, rather than only to one field. I discuss table validation rules in "Configure Table Properties," later in this module.

A validation can include a number of elements that can be combined to form an expression:

- **Operators**   An operator is used to calculate or compare data. Access supports five types of operators: arithmetic (+, −, *, and /), comparison (<, >, =, <=, >=, and <>), and logical (And, Or, and Not).

- **Functions**   A function is a predefined operation that you can use within an expression to perform a certain task. For example, the Date function retrieves the current date.

- **Literals**   A literal value is any character or set of characters that is included in the expression to be used exactly as typed. For example, a literal value might be a word such as "Book."

- **Identifier**   An identifier is the name of an Access database object, such as a table or field. For example, the identifier for the Customers table in the Northwind database is [Customers]. (Identifiers are enclosed in brackets when used in expressions.)

You can mix these elements together to form expressions that define exactly the type of value that can be entered into a field. In addition, you can use wildcards within your expressions. A wildcard is a placeholder that represents one or more characters in the value that will be entered into a field. The question mark (?) wildcard represents exactly one character, and the asterisk (*) wildcard represents any number of characters.

The best way to understand how to build expressions is to look at examples that are used to create validation rules. Table 4-6 provides a number of examples and describes how they restrict the data added to a field.

Keep in mind that the examples in Table 4-6 represent only a small portion of the types of expressions that you can create. Expressions are discussed in more detail in Module 11. You can also use the Expression Builder utility (which you access through the property's Build button) to create a variety of validation rules. Your best bet is to create a sample table and practice creating validation rules, using many of the different elements available for building expressions.

Validation Rule	Description
> Date( )	Date( ) is a function that returns the current date. The greater-than (>) comparison operator compares the value entered into the field to the current date. For the value to be valid, it must be a date later than the current date.
>= 10 And <= 20	The expression is made up of two conditions, which are joined by the And logical operator. The first condition (>= 10) uses the greater-than-or-equal-to (>=) comparison operator to compare the value entered into the field to 10, a literal value. The second condition (<= 20) uses the less-than-or-equal-to (<=) comparison operator to compare the field value to 20. Because the And logical operator is used, both conditions must be met in order for a value to be accepted. In other words, the value must fall within the range of 10 through 20 (including the values 10 and 20).
Like "A*" Or Like "B*"	The two conditions that make up this expression use the Like comparison operator to compare the field value to the literal values and wildcards. In the first condition, the value must begin with the letter A but can include any number of additional characters after the A. The second condition is like the first, only it is restricted to the letter B. The two conditions are joined by the Or logical operator, which means that one of the two conditions must be met. In other words, the value entered into the field must begin with the letter A or the letter B. (A value can start with an uppercase or lowercase A or B. Access ignores the case.) Note that Access automatically adds the quotation marks around the literal values.
Between 0 And 100	The Between comparison operator and the And logical operator are used together to define an acceptable range of values. In this case, the field value must fall within the range of 0 through 100 (including the values 0 and 100). This is the same as saying >= 0 And <= 100.
<> 0	The does-not-equal (<>) comparison operator indicates that the field value cannot equal 0.
>= #1/1/03# And < #1/1/04#	The first condition in this expression specifies that the date entered into the field must be the same as or later than January 1, 2003. The second condition specifies that the date must be earlier than January 1, 2004. The conditions are joined by the And logical operator, which means that both conditions must be met in order for the data to be valid. In other words, the date entered into the field must fall in 2003. Note that Access adds the number signs (#) around the date values.
Not "Unknown"	The Not logical operator specifies that the field value cannot equal the literal value. In other words, you cannot enter the word "Unknown" into this field.

Table 4-6 Examples of Field Validation Rules

Once you add the necessary expression to the Validation Rule property, you should configure the Validation Text property. Validation Text allows you to specify the message that users will receive if they enter data that violates the validation rule. The message should specify the range of values permitted in the field. To configure the Validation Text property, simply type in the information in the property's text box.

4.3 Create Field Indexes

When you query a field in a table, Access must sort through the records and return the requested information in the specified order. Each query requires the necessary processing power to search each record and return the data in the correct order. The more records there are in a table, the more processing power is necessary to fulfill the request. If the query requests data from multiple fields or multiple tables, even more processing power might be needed.

To streamline query processing—and subsequently optimize query performance—Access uses indexes in its databases to make finding and sorting data more efficient. An *index* is a set of pointers that reference data in a field. You can think of an index as you would an index in a book. A book index helps you locate information wherever it is located within the book's contents. In the same way, a field index helps you locate data in the field without having to search the entire contents of the field.

You can create an index on any field type except OLE Object. Access automatically creates an index on the primary key field. For all other fields, you must create the index manually. To do so, select the field in Design view and then select one of the following options in the Index property:

- Yes (Duplicates OK)

- Yes (No Duplicates)

As you can see, the only difference between the two options is that one permits duplicate values within the field and the other requires each value in the field to be unique. If after you create an index you want to remove it from the field, select the No option.

You should create an index on any field that you intend to query frequently or that you intend to use to create a relationship with another table. However, if a field contains many of the same values, an index provides little advantage and should not be created. For example, you might want to index a field that contains customers' last names, but you might not want to index a field that contains the states in which the customers reside.

When deciding which fields to index, you should keep in mind that indexes increase database size, so you might need to take storage needs into consideration when adding indexes to your tables.

Viewing Field Indexes

Once you've created the necessary indexes, you can view the indexes for the entire table. To view the indexes, open the table in Design view and then click the Indexes button on the Table Design toolbar. This causes the Indexes dialog box to appear, as shown in Figure 4-4. For each index, the index name, field name, and sort order are specified. The sort order can be either ascending or descending.

Each index includes three properties, which are shown in the bottom-left part of the Indexes dialog box. The Primary property indicates whether the indexed field is the primary key. (A key icon is also displayed on the row that contains the primary key field.) The Unique property indicates whether a field must contain unique values only, and the Ignore Nulls property indicates whether null values are excluded from the index. You can also use the Indexes dialog box to delete, modify, and add indexes.

CRITICAL SKILL
4.4 # Configure Lookup Field Properties

You might find that, for certain fields, you want to allow only values from a list that you have defined. For example, you might have a field that lists the titles used for various positions in your company, such as "manager," "sales clerk," etc. These positions can be listed in another table or you can create a list that contains them. The values are then available to choose from when data is being entered into the field.

A field that references values in a list or another table is referred to as a *lookup field*. You can create a lookup field by selecting the Lookup Wizard option in the Data Type column of the field that you're configuring. The option launches the wizard, which allows you to look for values in another table or to create a list.

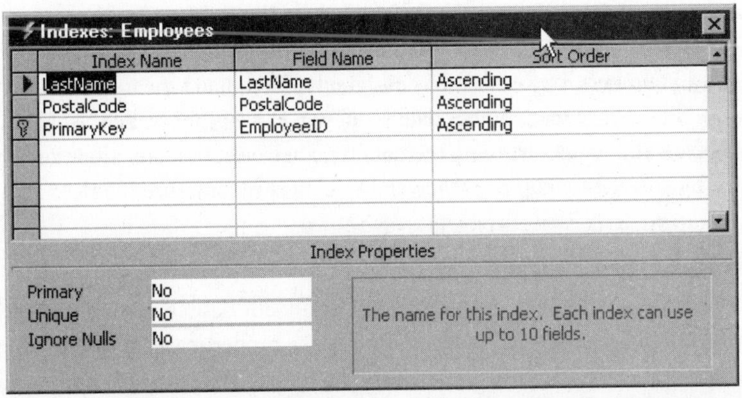

Figure 4-4 Viewing indexes for the Employees table in the Northwind database

Ask the Expert

Q: The indexes that you describe are defined on individual fields. Can you create an index on more than one field?

A: You can define indexes on multiple fields in the Indexes dialog box. If such an index is created, Access first sorts records in the first field. If duplicates are found, Access sorts the duplicates according to the next field, and so on. A multiple-field index can contain up to ten fields. To create a multiple-field index, take the following steps:

1. Click the Index Name column in the first empty row of the Indexes dialog box.

2. Enter an index name and then select a field and sort order.

3. In the row immediately beneath the row with the new index, select a field name and sort order, but do not name the index. The second row is automatically included with the index created in the first row.

To view the properties for the multiple-row index, you must select the first row of the index, the one that includes the index name.

Figure 4-5 shows the opening screen of the Lookup wizard. You should select one of the two options and click Next. The wizard will then step you through the process of creating the necessary list or table reference for your lookup field.

After you've run the Lookup wizard, Access automatically assigns a data type to the field based on the values that you added to your list or the data type of the source column. You might find that you want to change the data type once the field has been created. This would probably be necessary only if you've created a list. For example, you might have created a list that contains all numbers, but Access has assigned a Text data type to the field. If you decide that you would rather use the Number data type, you can simply make the change. However, you should be careful about changing the data type because, in many situations, changing the data type eliminates the lookup reference and you must reconfigure the field as a lookup field.

Setting Lookup Properties

When you create a lookup field, Access automatically configures a set of properties related to the lookup list or table reference. You can modify the properties as necessary to meet your specific needs. To access the properties, select the lookup field in Design view and then select the Lookup tab. Figure 4-6 shows the default properties for a field that references a list of values (referred to as a *value list*).

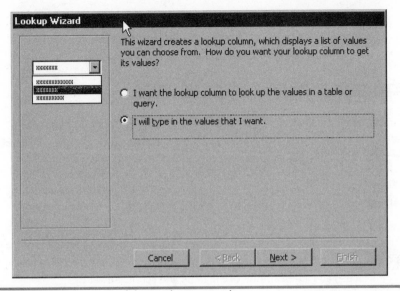

Figure 4-5 The opening screen of the Lookup wizard

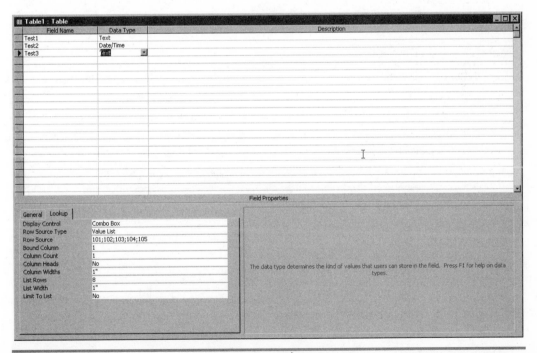

Figure 4-6 The Lookup tab in the Design view window

As you can see in Figure 4-6, a number of properties are associated with a lookup field. Table 4-7 provides a brief description of each of these properties.

Configure Table Properties

Up to this point, we've looked at configuring the properties for the fields in a table. However, you can configure properties for the table as a whole. Access allows you to configure two types of table properties: table object properties and table design properties.

Configuring Table Object Properties

Table object properties are those properties that apply to the general characteristics of the table as an object within the database. As you can see in Figure 4-7, the properties provide information such as the date that the table object was created, when it was modified, and who owns the table. You can also add a description of the table and set its attributes.

To access the table object properties, right-click the table in the database window and then select Properties from the shortcut menu. You can also select the table and then click the Properties button on the Database toolbar.

Property	Description
Display Control	Determines whether the lookup data will be displayed in a combo box, list box, or text box.
Row Source Type	Indicates whether the source of the data is a table or a list.
Row Source	Defines the lookup data. If the source type is a list, the values are listed here. If the source type is a table, the query used to extract data from that table is listed here.
Bound Column	Indicates the column that contains the value that a control is set to. The columns are numbered according to how they were selected in the Lookup wizard.
Column Count	Indicates the number of columns in the related table that are involved.
Column Heads	Determines whether field names, captions, or the first row of data is used for column headings.
Column Widths	Sets the column width in a multiple-column list.
List Rows	Indicates the maximum number of rows displayed in a list.
List Width	Sets the width of a control's drop-down list.
Limit To List	Prevents users from entering values that aren't on the list.

Table 4-7 The Lookup Field Properties

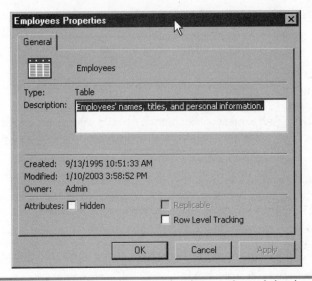

Figure 4-7 The Employees Properties dialog box for the Northwind database

Configuring Table Design Properties

Table design properties are those properties that you access through Design view and that are related to the table data. Unlike the field properties, which appear in the Design view window, you have to take an extra step to access the table properties. Once you've opened the table in Design view, click the Properties button on the Table Design toolbar to open the Table Properties dialog box, shown in Figure 4-8.

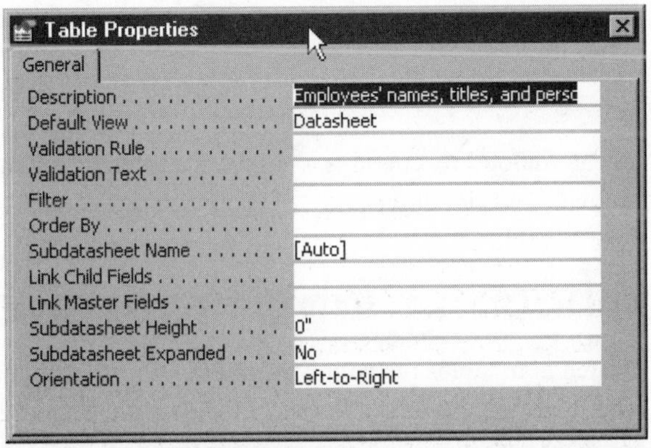

Figure 4-8 The Table Properties dialog box for the Employees table in the Northwind database

Property	Description
Description	The information that appears in the Description column of the database window when the window is in Details view.
Default View	The default view used to display the table's data. The default setting is Datasheet.
Validation Rule	An expression that restricts the data entered into a table. A table-level validation rule is used when the values in one column should be restricted by the values in another column.
Validation Text	Text used for the error message if data violates the validation rule.
Filter	A set of criteria applied to a table in order to display a subset of records from the table. Filters are discussed in Module 8.
Order By	The sort order used for records.
Subdatasheet Name	The name of the related table, if applicable. The default setting is [Auto].
Link Child Fields	Fields in the child table that link to the master table. A child table is the table that contains the foreign key (the child field) that is linked to the primary key (the master field) in the master table. The master table is the table that contains the primary key that is linked to the foreign key in the child table. The tables are linked together through a relationship. For information on relationships, see Module 5.
Link Master Fields	Fields in the master table that link to the child table.
Subdatasheet Height	Default height of the subdatasheets. The default setting is 0".
Subdatasheet Expanded	The setting that determines whether all subdatasheets are expanded when you open a table. The default setting is No.
Orientation	The direction in which fields are displayed in the table. The default setting is Left-to-Right.

Table 4-8 Table Properties in an Access Database

The Table Properties dialog box contains a number of properties that apply to the table as a whole. Table 4-8 provides a brief description of each table property that you can configure.

Project 4-1   Configuring Table Properties

In Module 3, you created nine tables for your consumer advocacy application. When you created the tables, you provided the field names, set the data types, and, in some cases, included descriptions. You also identified a primary key for each table. However, at the time that you defined the fields, you left the properties with their default values. You will now update many of the field properties to meet the needs of your application. In addition, you will configure properties that apply to the entire table. As you work though the steps in the project, you might want to refer back to the discussion in this module for a description of each property.

Step by Step

1. If they're not already opened, open Access and then open the ConsumerAdvocacy.mdb file.

2. Verify that the Tables object type is selected in the database window.

3. Select the Orders table, and click the Design button at the top of the database window. The Design view window opens and displays the definition for the Orders table.

4. Select the MemberID field, select the Field Size property, and change the value to 7. Change the Required property to Yes.

5. Select the PaymentID field, select the Field Size property, and change the value to 2. Change the Required property to Yes.

6. Select the OrderDate field, select the Format property, and select the Short Date option. Change the Required property to Yes.

7. Select the ShippedDate field, select the Format property, and select the Short Date option.

8. Select the Amount field, select the Required property, and select the Yes option.

9. In the OrderStatus field, select Lookup Wizard from the drop-down list in the Data Type column. The first screen of the Lookup wizard appears.

10. Select the I Will Type The Values That I Want radio button, and then click Next. The second screen of the wizard appears.

11. In the first row of the Col1 column, type **Ordered**.

12. In the second row of the Col1 column, type **Shipped**, and click Next. The next screen of the Lookup wizard appears.

13. Click Finish. The wizard closes, and the field is now configured with the Text data type.

14. Select the Lookup tab to view the lookup properties for the OrderStatus field.

15. Select the General tab, select the Field Size property, and change the value to 15. Change the Required property to Yes.

(continued)

4

Managing Table Properties

Project
4-1

Configuring Table Properties

16. Save the Orders table, but do not close it.

17. Click the Properties button on the Table Design toolbar. The Table Properties dialog box appears.

18. In the Validation Rule property text box, type **[ShippedDate]>=[OrderDate]**. This will ensure that the ship date is always the same as or later than the order date.

19. In the Validation Text property text box, type **The shipped date must be the same as or later than the order date.**

20. Close the Table Properties dialog box, save the Orders table, and close the table.

21. Open the Staff table in Design view.

22. Select the State field, select the Default Value property, and type **WA** in the property text box. Change the Field Size value to 2.

23. Select the StartDate field, select the Format property, and select the Short Date option.

24. Select the Validation Rule property, and type **>=1/1/1995** in the property text box. In the Validation Text property text box, type **The date must be the same as or later than 1/1/95.**

25. Select the PostalCode field and set the Field Size to 10. Then select the Input Mask property and click the Build button. Save the table if prompted. The Input Mask wizard appears.

26. Select the Zip Code input mask, and then click Finish. The input mask is added to the Input Mask property.

27. Select the HomePhone field, set the Field Size to 15, and configure the Input Mask property with the Phone Number input mask.

28. Select the NameLast field, select the Indexed property, and then select the Yes (Duplicates OK) option from the drop-down list. Change the Field Size property to 20.

29. Configure the Field Size property for the remaining fields in the Staff table as follows:

- StaffID = 7
- NameFirst = 20
- NameMI = 1
- City = 20
- PositionID = 3
- Supervisor = 7

30. Configure the properties in the remaining tables based on the settings listed in the following table:

Table	Field	Property
Products	ProductID	Field Size = **5**
Positions	PositionID	Field Size = **3**
ProductOrders	ProductID	Field Size = **5**
FormOfPayment	PaymentID	Field Size = **2**
NumberTypes	TypeID	Field Size = **2**
PhoneNumbers	TypeID	Field Size = **2**
PhoneNumbers	Number	Field Size = **25**
PhoneNumbers	MemberID	Field Size = **7**
Members	MemberID	Field Size = **7**
Members	NameFirst	Field Size = **20**
Members	NameMI	Field Size = **1**
Members	NameLast	Field Size = **20**
Members	City	Field Size = **20**
Members	State	Field Size = **2**
Members	PostalCode	Field Size = **10**
Members	PostalCode	Input Mask = **00000\-9999;;_** (Zip Code)
Members	BeginDate	Format = **Short Date**
Members	BeginDate	Validation Rule = **>=1/1/1995**
Members	BeginDate	Validation Text = **The date must be the same as or later than 1/1/95.**

Project Summary

As you have seen in this project, setting a table's properties can be a very involved process, and in all likelihood, we could have refined the property settings even more. And if this were a large database, the process would have been even more daunting, so you can see why setting these properties when you create the table will make property configuration a less difficult task. Despite the complexities of the properties, Access makes them relatively straightforward to configure and modify. Keep in mind, however, that when modifying properties, you must be aware of any data that is stored in the table. Some changes could adversely affect that data. For this reason, you must plan carefully when working with properties, and give careful consideration to any potential changes to the property configuration.

Module 4 Mastery Check

1. Which properties are available for every field type except OLE Object?

   A. Default Value

   B. Format

   C. Indexed

   D. Validation Rule

2. What is the default value assigned to the Field Size property of a Text field?

   A. 25

   B. 50

   C. 75

   D. 100

3. You're configuring the Field Size property of a Number field. You want to store whole numbers ranging from 10 through 100. Which Field Size option should you use?

   A. Byte

   B. Integer

   C. Single

   D. Double

4. You're configuring a Text field for your table. You want all the values to be displayed in lowercase and printed in red. What setting should you use for the Format property?

5. You're configuring the Format property for a Number field. You want the numbers to be displayed with a thousands separator and you want the display to be based on the regional settings as they're configured in the operating system. Which Format option should you use?

   A. General Number

   B. Currency

   C. Fixed

   D. Standard

6. A(n) _____ is a type of filter that determines how data is entered into a field. It provides users with a fill-in-the-blank type format that limits the way data can be entered.

7. For which fields can you define a default value?

A. Hyperlink

B. Currency

C. AutoNumber

D. OLE Object

8. How should you configure a Text field's properties if you want to allow zero-length stings in that field?

9. Which language's characters will be compressed if you set the Unicode Compression property to Yes?

A. Chinese

B. English

C. Japanese

D. German

10. You're configuring a Number field, and you set the Field Size property to Decimal. Which property should you configure to set the total number of digits in the field?

A. Format

B. Precision

C. Required

D. Scale

11. A(n) _____ is an expression that is made up of operators, literal values, and other elements that together create a formula that defines the acceptable value range.

12. You're creating an expression that limits numerical values to the range of 100 through 200, inclusive. Which expression should you use?

A. 100 Between 200

B. 100 <> 200

C. >= 100; <= 200

D. >= 100 And <= 200

13. On what fields should you create an index?

14. How do you create a lookup field?

15. Which lookup field property indicates whether the source of the data is a table or a list?

    A. Row Source

    B. Row Source Type

    C. List Rows

    D. Limit To List

16. What is the difference between table object properties and table design properties?

Module 5

Managing Table Relationships

CRITICAL SKILLS

5.1 Work with Relationships in an Access Database

5.2 Create Relationships Between Tables

5.3 Modify Existing Relationships

As you'll recall from Module 2, one of the most important functions of the relational database is to ensure the integrity of data. Access provides a number of configuration options that limit the values that can be entered into a field. For example, you can use data types to define the kind of values that are allowed in a field and the operations that can be performed on those values. Or you can use validation rules to limit the values to a specific range or to apply other conditions. However, none of these methods keep data in sync with data in other tables. For this, you must define relationships between tables that establish logical connections between related fields. In fact, relationships are critical to the process of ensuring the integrity of data. In this module, we'll review the different types of relationships supported in an Access database and how those relationships are used to enforce referential integrity. We'll then look at the process of creating relationships between tables and modifying those relationships.

CRITICAL SKILL
5.1 # Work with Relationships in an Access Database

The types of relationships supported by an Access database are consistent with the principles of the relational model, as they apply to the enforcement of referential integrity. For this reason, before I discuss how to create a relationship, we'll review the various types of relationships and how they're implemented in an Access database. We'll then take a look at the Relationships window, which is the Access tool used to view, define, and modify relationships.

Understanding Access Relationships

In Module 2, I discussed the types of relationships that can exist between tables. In fact, part of the process of creating a data model is to identify the relationships between tables. As you'll recall, a relationship is an association between tables that links the data in those tables in a meaningful way. A data model can include three types of relationships:

- **One-to-one** A record in the first table is related to only one record in the second table, and a record in the second table is related to only one record in the first table.

- **One-to-many** A record in the first table is related to one or more records in the second table, but a record in the second table is related to only one record in the first table.

- **Many-to-many** A record in the first table is related to one or more records in the second table, and a record in the second table is related to one or more records in the first table.

NOTE

A many-to-many relationship is physically implemented by adding a third table between the two related tables. The third table, known as a junction table, creates a one-to-many relationship with each of the two original tables. *Many-to-many*

The purpose of identifying these relationships—and subsequently configuring them in your database—is to enforce referential integrity from one table to the next. *Referential integrity* refers to the state of the database in which data in one or more fields in one table is kept consistent with data in one or more fields in another table (or sometimes the same table). The data in the first table references data in the second table, and it is the rules of referential integrity that keep the data consistent.

You enforce referential integrity in your database by configuring relationships between participating tables. A relationship is established between fields in a parent table and a child table. The parent table, also referred to as the master table, is the table in the relationship that contains one or more fields that are configured as the primary key or with a unique index and that participate in the relationship. The primary key or unique index ensures that the values are unique. The child table is the table in the relationship that contains one or more fields that are configured as a foreign key. A *foreign key* is a referencing set of fields that contain data consistent with the parent fields. The foreign key in the child table references the primary key in the parent table. The foreign key ensures that every value in a foreign key field matches a value in the related parent field.

TIP

The child fields in the foreign key, like the parent fields, should be indexed to improve query performance. The index acts as a pointer to the values in the foreign key fields. For more information on setting up an index on a field, see Module 4.

Once a relationship has been configured, referential integrity prevents users from taking the following actions:

- Adding records to the child table if a foreign key field contains a value that does not exist in the related parent field

- Deleting a record in the parent table if a related record exists in the child table

- Changing a value in the primary key or unique index field of the parent table if a record in the child table will be left without an associated record in the parent table

- Changing a value in the foreign key field of a child table if that change results in the record not being associated with a record in the parent table

Let's take a look at an example of a one-to-many relationship to help illustrate the point. Suppose that you have two tables: Publishers and Books. The Publishers table contains the PublisherID field, which is the table's primary key. The Books table also includes a PublisherID field. In this case, the field is configured as a foreign key that references the PublisherID field in the Publishers table. As a result, a relationship exists between the two tables, as shown in Figure 5-1.

In this relationship, the Publishers table is the parent table, and the Books table is the child table. You cannot add a record to the Books table if the PublisherID value does not exist in the PublisherID field of the Publishers table. In addition, you cannot delete a record from the Publishers table if a Books record contains a PublisherID value that references the record you want to delete. You also cannot change a record in either table if that change would result in a Books record referencing a publisher that doesn't exist in the Publishers table. As you can see, a relationship can provide a valuable means for ensuring that the publisher-related data in the Books table is always consistent with the data in the Publishers table.

Navigating the Relationships Window

To allow you to view, create, and modify relationships, Access provides the Relationships window, a graphical interface that shows the tables and relationships in a database. The Relationships window, like a data model, displays tables and their fields as individual objects. The tables are connected by lines that represent the relationships between tables. Figure 5-2 shows the Relationships window as it appears when you open it for the Northwind database.

As you can see in Figure 5-2, each table is represented by its own object. You can scroll through the list of fields within the table, or you can resize the table to display all the fields at once. You can also move the tables around to whatever positions are most convenient for viewing the tables and their relationships. Keep in mind, however, that the relationship lines move with the tables, so you want to be aware of the relationships as you reposition the tables.

Although the Relationships window displays information similar to that of a data model, the symbols used to represent the types of relationships are different from what you've seen in this book. The "one" side of a relationship is represented by the number 1, and the "many" side is represented by the infinity (∞) symbol.

As you'll notice in Figure 5-2, the relationship lines attach to the tables at the fields that participate in the relationship. For example, a one-to-many relationship exists between the Orders table and the Customers table. The "one" side of the relationship is the CustomerID

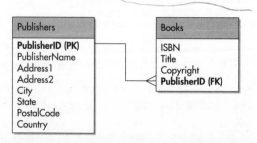

Figure 5-1 A one-to-many relationship between a parent and a child table

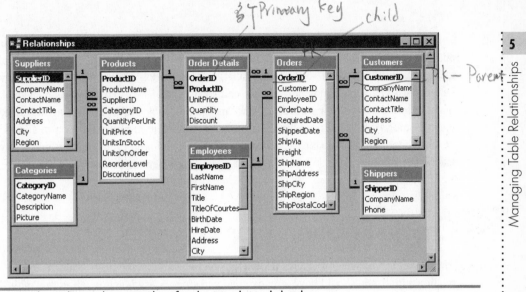

Figure 5-2 The Relationships window for the Northwind database

field in the Customers table. This field is the primary key for that table and, like all primary keys in the Relationships window, uses bold type. The "many" side of the relationship is the CustomerID field in the Orders table. This field is the foreign key, which means that it can contain only values that are included in the primary key of the Customers table. In other words, you cannot add a record to the Orders table without a valid customer ID.

To open the Relationships window, first open the appropriate database file and then click the Relationships button on the Database toolbar. (You can also select Relationships from the Tools menu.) If any relationships already exist in the database, the Relationships window opens immediately, displaying only the tables participating in the relationships. If no relationships exist, the Show Table dialog box appears (shown in Figure 5-3), and you must add tables to the window.

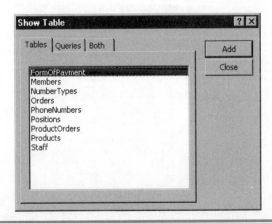

Figure 5-3 The Show Table dialog box for the ConsumerAdvocacy.mdb database file

Once the Relationships window is opened, you can add other tables from the database by clicking the Show Table button on the Relationship toolbar. (The Relationship toolbar replaces the Database toolbar when you open the Relationships window.) When you click the Show Table button, the Show Table dialog box appears, and you can add tables to the table relationship layout diagram in the Relationships window. You can also hide tables by right-clicking the table and then selecting Hide Table from the shortcut menu. The Relationships window also allows you to create and modify relationships as necessary. (Creating and modifying relationships is discussed later in the module, in the sections "Create Relationships Between Tables" and "Modify Existing Relationships.")

CRITICAL SKILL
5.2 Create Relationships Between Tables

The Relationships window makes it easy for you to create one-to-many and one-to-one relationships. (You should have already created the necessary junction tables to handle many-to-many relationships.) When you create a relationship, you'll need to configure the settings related to referential integrity and those related to how data is returned when the two tables are queried. Once you finish configuring the relationships, you can save the table relationship layout as it appears in the Relationships window.

Defining a Table Relationship

The process of creating a relationship in Access is almost as simple as drawing a line. You connect the primary key (or unique index field) in the parent table to the foreign key in the child table, and then you set the necessary options. For example, suppose you want to create a relationship between the Suppliers table and the Products table in the Northwind database. (Assume for a moment that a relationship doesn't already exist). The two tables, without a relationship, would appear as they do in Figure 5-4.

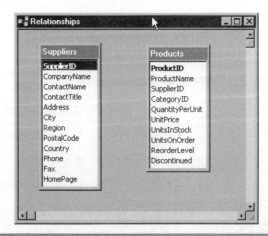

Figure 5-4 Creating a relationship between the Suppliers and Products tables

To create a relationship between the tables, select the SupplierID field in the Suppliers table, drag it to the Products table, and drop it on the SupplierID field in that table. This is the field that will be configured as the foreign key. When you drop the field, the Edit Relationships dialog box appears, as shown in Figure 5-5. The Edit Relationships dialog box contains details about the relationship, including the tables and fields participating in the relationship and the relationship type.

TIP

If you're creating a one-to-one relationship, drag the primary key field of one table to the primary key field of the other table. It doesn't matter which table you start with because the records in either table can match only one record in the other table.

When you click the Create button, the Edit Relationships dialog box closes and a line connects the two tables. If you take a look at Figure 5-6, you'll see that the line doesn't include any symbols that indicate the type of relationship. This is because the relationship has not yet been configured to enforce referential integrity. When you enforce referential integrity, the line will include the number 1 symbol and the infinity symbol that you saw in Figure 5-2.

Enforcing Referential Integrity

To enforce referential integrity in your relationships, you must select the Enforce Referential Integrity check box in the Edit Relationships dialog box. Normally you would select this option when you first create the relationship, but you can add referential integrity at any time simply by double-clicking the relationship line to open the Edit Relationships dialog box. When the dialog box appears, select the Enforce Referential Integrity check box, and then click OK. The dialog box will close and the number 1 symbol and the infinity symbol will be added to the diagram.

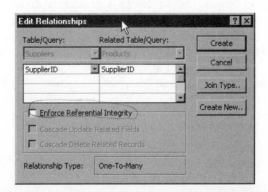

Figure 5-5 The Edit Relationships dialog box that appears when a relationship is created

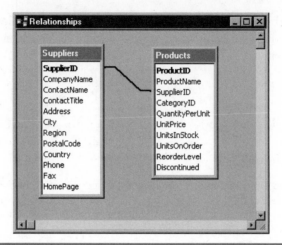

Figure 5-6 A relationship that does not enforce referential integrity

Ask the Expert

Q: There might be times when you want to modify a table definition while you're creating a relationship. Can you modify tables in the Relationships window?

A: Access makes it fairly easy to modify your table definitions when you're using the Relationships window. If there is a specific table definition that you want to modify, right-click the table in the Relationships window and then select the Table Design option from the shortcut menu. This will open the table in Design view. You can then modify the table definition and save it as you normally would. When you close the Design view window, you're returned to the Relationships window, where you can continue defining and editing the necessary relationships.

You can also add a table to the database from the Relationships window. From the Relationship toolbar, select Table from the New Object drop-down list. You're then presented with the New Table dialog box, which allows you to choose a method for creating a table. The table creation process is the same as you learned in Module 3. Once you have created the new table, click the Show Table button on the Relationship toolbar to open the Show Table dialog box. You can then add the new table to your layout in the Relationships window.

When you select the Enforce Referential Integrity check box, two more options become available that allow you to perform actions that would normally not be allowed:

- **Cascade Update Related Fields**   This option allows you to change values in the primary key that are then cascaded to the foreign key. The values in the foreign key are updated so that referential integrity is maintained between the two tables.

- **Cascade Delete Related Records**   This option allows you to delete records in the parent table that have associated records in the child table. The child records are then deleted so that referential integrity is maintained between the two tables.

Although these options are available, you should be very careful when using them. One of the advantages of enforcing full referential integrity is to ensure that no changes are made that could adversely affect the data.

When you enforce referential integrity on a relationship, there are several guidelines that should be followed:

- Although the field names do not have to match, the data types must be the same for the primary key and the foreign key, except in the case of the AutoNumber data type.

- An AutoNumber primary key must be linked to a Number foreign key that has its field size set to Long Integer.

- For Number fields, the Field Size property must be the same for the primary key and the foreign key.

Configuring the Join Properties

queries

In addition to setting the referential integrity options when creating a relationship, you can set the join properties for that relationship. The join properties are concerned with the way queries retrieve data from the two tables in the relationship. These types of queries, referred to as *joins*, match the values in the related fields (the primary key and the foreign key) in order to return results that combine data from the tables. The results of those queries can depend on the join operation that you select when configuring the relationship.

To configure the join properties for a relationship, click the Join Type button in the Edit Relationships dialog box. When the Join Properties dialog box appears (shown in Figure 5-7), select the appropriate option.

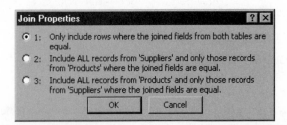

Figure 5-7 The Join Properties dialog box

The join option that you select depends on the type of information that you want to include in your query results. Because a join matches values in the primary key field with values in the foreign key field, your query results will include—at the very least—rows in which the values match. For example, if you were to query the Products table and the Suppliers table in Figure 5-6, your query results would include those rows with a SupplierID value that is the same in both tables.

NOTE

The query might specify other conditions that must be met, which would affect the query results, but the join condition would still require that the SupplierID values be the same. Queries are discussed in more detail in Modules 10 and 11.

By configuring the join properties, you can specify that the query results include additional data from the left or the right table. The *left table* is the table that appears first in the join condition defined in your query, and the *right table* is the one that appears second in your join condition. As you can see in Figure 5-7, you can select one of three options:

● The first option is the default. Your query results will include only those records with matching values in the joined fields (the primary key from the parent table and the foreign key from the child table).

● The second option indicates that your query results will include those records with matching values in the joined fields, plus all the records from the table at the left of the query join condition.

● The third option indicates that your query results will include those records with matching values in the joined fields, plus all the records from the table at the right of the query join condition.

No matter which option you select, the underlying data and table structure will be unaffected.

Saving the Relationships Layout

Once you've created your relationships, you might want to save the table relationship layout that you created in the Relationships window. Access provides several methods that you can use to save the layout:

● Click the Save button on the Relationship toolbar.

● Select Save from the File menu.

● Press CTRL-S.

● Right-click anywhere in the Relationships window (except on a table) and then select Save Layout from the shortcut menu.

You do not have to provide a filename when you save the relationship layout. The layout is specific to the opened database file. Whenever you open the Relationships window, it displays the layout as it appeared the last time it was saved.

Progress Check

1. What are the three types of relationships that can be included in a data model?

2. What is referential integrity?

3. What information is displayed in the Relationships window?

4. What symbols are used in the Relationships window to represent a one-to-many relationship?

CRITICAL SKILL
5.3 Modify Existing Relationships

As you saw earlier in this module, you can use the Relationships window to view relationships and configure them in your database. However, you can also use the Relationships window to edit the relationships and delete them from the database.

Editing Relationships

To edit a relationship, you must open the Relationships window and then open the Edit Relationships dialog box. Access provides three methods for opening the dialog box:

● Double-click the relationship line.

● Right-click the relationship line and then select Edit Relationship from the shortcut menu.

● Select the relationship line and then select Edit Relationship from the Relationships menu.

---

1. One-to-one, one-to-many, and many-to-many

2. Referential integrity refers to the state of the database in which data in one or more fields in one table is kept consistent with data in one or more fields in another table.

3. The Relationships window, like a data model, displays tables and their fields as individual objects. The tables are connected by lines that represent the relationships between tables.

4. The "one" side of a relationship is represented by the number 1, and the "many" side is represented by the infinity (∞) symbol.

Once the dialog box is opened, you can change fields, add fields, and set the referential integrity options. You can also create new relationships or modify the join type. To create a new relationship, click the Create New button and enter the appropriate table names and field names. To configure the join type, click the Join Type button and select the appropriate join option.

Deleting Relationships

You can delete a relationship at any time without affecting the underlying data. However, once you've deleted the relationship, referential integrity can no longer be enforced on the participating fields, although you can re-establish the relationship. To delete a relationship, right-click the relationship line as it appears in the Relationships window, and then select Delete from the shortcut menu. You can also delete a relationship by selecting the relationship line and then selecting Delete from the Edit menu.

Project 5-1 Creating Table Relationships

In Module 3, you created tables in the ConsumerAdvocacy.mdb database file. You based these tables on the data model that you developed in Module 2. As you'll recall from the process of creating that model, one of the steps that you took was to identify the relationships that existed between the tables. All the relationships that you identified were one-to-many relationships, including a self-referencing relationship in the Staff table. You will now use that data model to physically implement those relationships in your Access database. (Refer to Project 3-1 in Module 3 to view the current data model.)

Step by Step

1. Open Access and then open the ConsumerAdvocacy.mdb file, if they are not already open.

2. Click the Relationships button on the Database toolbar. The Show Table dialog box appears, displaying a list of all the tables in your database.

3. Select all the tables in the list, and then click Add. You can select all the tables by clicking the name of the table at the top of the list (FormOfPayment), pressing and holding SHIFT, and then clicking the last table name in the list (Staff).

4. Click Close to close the Show Table dialog box. The Relationships window appears, displaying all the table objects.

5. Arrange the table objects so that they're laid out in a manner similar to the data model. This will make drawing relationships between the tables easier, and it will make the diagram clearer, once you've created the relationships. Also expand the tables so that all fields are showing and so you can read all table and field names.

6. Select the OrderID field (primary key) in the Orders table (parent table), drag it to the ProductOrders table (child table), and drop it on the OrderID field (foreign key) in the ProductOrders table. The Edit Relationships dialog box appears.

7. Select the Enforce Referential Integrity check box, and then click Create. A relationship line is added between the two tables. The number 1 is shown at the Orders end of the line, and the infinity symbol is shown at the ProductOrders end of the line.

8. Use the same method as above to create a relationship for each of the following table pairs:

Parent Table	Primary Key	Child Table	Foreign Key
Products	ProductID	ProductOrders	ProductID
FormOfPayment	PaymentID	Orders	PaymentID
Members	MemberID	Orders	MemberID
Members	MemberID	PhoneNumbers	MemberID
NumberTypes	TypeID	PhoneNumbers	TypeID
Positions	PositionID	Staff	PositionID

9. The final relationship to configure is the self-referencing one on the Staff table. However, Access does not allow you to drag a field to another field in the same table. You must configure such relationships manually. To do so, select Edit Relationship from the Relationships menu. The Edit Relationships dialog box appears.

10. Click the Create New button. The Create New dialog box appears.

11. Select Staff from the Left Table Name drop-down list and from the Right Table Name drop-down list.

12. Select StaffID from the Left Column Name drop-down list.

13. Select Supervisor from the Right Column Name drop-down list, and then click OK. The Create New dialog box closes, and the Edit Relationships dialog box reappears, displaying the new relationship.

14. Select the Enforce Referential Integrity check box, and then click Create. A relationship line is added to the table.

15. Right-click anywhere in the Relationships window except on a table object, and then select the Show All option in the shortcut menu. A table object named Staff_1 has been added to the diagram. The table is added to show the self-referencing relationship that you just created. No new table has been added to the database, only to the diagram. Unfortunately, the original relationship line does not disappear until you close and re-open the Relationships window.

(continued)

16. Press CTRL-S to save the table relationship layout. Then close the Relationships window and re-open it by clicking the Relationships button on the Database toolbar. When the Relationships window appears, the Staff_1 table and relationship are displayed correctly. Your table relationship layout should now look similar to the following illustration:

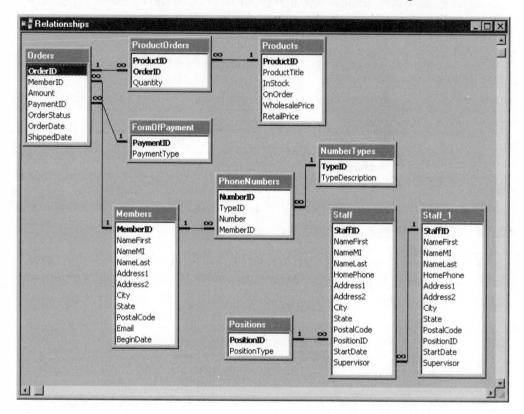

Project Summary

Your database should now be configured with all the necessary relationships, which means that your database should now be complete. In the next module, you will learn how to configure security on the database, but that will not affect the underlying structure or impact how data is stored. As a result, you can begin to add data to the database. Because relationships have been configured, referential integrity will be enforced and you will not be able to add or change data that violates those relationships.

Module 5 Mastery Check

1. Which type of relationship requires the creation of a junction table to form two relationships of another type?

    A. One-to-one

    B. One-to-many

    C. Many-to-one

    D. Many-to-many

2. _____ refers to the state of the database in which data in one or more fields in one table is kept consistent with data in one or more fields in another table.

3. You're configuring a one-to-many relationship between two tables. What is the name of the field in the child table that references a field in the parent table?

    A. Primary key

    B. Unique index

    C. Foreign key

    D. Junction

4. Which actions are prevented when referential integrity is enforced?

    A. Adding records to the child table if a foreign key field contains a value that does not exist in the related parent field

    B. Deleting a record in the child table if a related record exists in the parent table

    C. Changing a value in the primary key or unique index field of the parent table if a record in the child table will be left without an associated record in the parent table

    D. Changing a value in the foreign key field of a child table if that change results in the record not being associated with a record in the parent table

5. How are primary key fields represented in the Relationships window?

6. How do you add tables to the Relationships window?

7. You're creating a relationship between the Publishers table and the Books table. You want to create a one-to-many relationship, with the Publishers table as the parent table and the Books table as the child table. Both tables contain a PublisherID field, which is the primary key in the Publishers table. What should you do first?

   A. Select the foreign key in the Publishers table, drag it to the Books table, and drop it on the primary key in the Books table.

   B. Select the primary key in the Publishers table, drag it to the Books table, and drop it on the PublisherID field in the Books table.

   C. Select the primary key in the Books table, drag it to the Publishers table, and drop it on the PublisherID field in the Publishers table.

   D. Select the foreign key in the Books table, drag it to the Publishers table, and drop it on the primary key in the Publishers table.

8. How do you enforce referential integrity in a relationship?

9. You're creating a new relationship between two tables in your database. You want any changes made to the primary key of the parent table to be cascaded down to the foreign key of the child table. Which option or options should you select?

   A. Cascade Delete Related Records

   B. Related Table/Query

   C. Cascade Update Related Fields

   D. Enforce Referential Integrity

10. You're creating a relationship between two tables. The parent table includes a primary key that is made up of one AutoNumber field. How should the foreign key field be configured?

11. A(n) _____ is a type of query that matches the values in the related fields of two tables in order to return results that combine data from the tables.

12. How are the join properties configured by default?

13. What methods can you use to save the table relationship layout in the Relationships window?

14. What actions can you take in the Edit Relationships dialog box?

15. How do you delete a relationship?

Module 6

Managing Database Security

CRITICAL SKILLS

6.1 Password-Protect Your Database File

6.2 Apply User-Level Security

6.3 Encode and Decode Your Database File

U p to this point in the book, you have learned about a number of ways in which you can protect data. These methods—such as configuring data types, setting validation rules, and establishing relationships—have focused on preventing users from entering or modifying data in ways that would violate the integrity of the data. However, Access supports other methods for protecting the database and its data. For example, you can configure database security so that users must use a password to open a database file. In addition, you can encode a file so that it can't be read by a word processor or utility program. Access also allows you to create security accounts so that you can grant specific types of access permissions to specific users. In this module, you'll learn how to configure the various types of security options within Access. You'll learn how to password-protect your database file, apply user-level security to a database, and encode and decode the database.

 CRITICAL SKILL 6.1 Password-Protect Your Database File

When you protect your database with a password, you're requiring users to enter a password when they open the file. This method of security is most appropriate when there is only one person using the database or when there are only a few users, rather than multiple users accessing the database over a network. However, although a database might be password-protected, the password itself is stored in an unencrypted form, so the security of the database can be compromised. In addition, database password protection applies to the file as a whole. Once the user has opened the database, he or she can access any of the objects within the database, unless user-level security has also been configured.

CAUTION

You should not password-protect your database file if you will be replicating the database. You cannot synchronize a database that is protected by a password.

Despite the limitations of password-protecting your database file, there might be times when you'll want to implement this type of security. The process of setting up the database for password-protection is relatively straightforward; however, you must first open the database in exclusive mode. *Exclusive mode* is a particular state in which you can open a database file. When you open a database in exclusive mode, other users are prevented from opening the file while you're using it.

To open a database file in exclusive mode, you must use the Open dialog box to access the file. You can access the Open dialog box by clicking the Open button on the Database toolbar or by clicking the More link on the Getting Started task pane. Once the Open dialog box is open, navigate to the folder that contains the file, select the file, and then select Open Exclusive from the Open drop-down list (which you access by clicking the down arrow on the Open button). Once the database is opened in exclusive mode, you can set the password.

Figure 6-1 The Set Database Password dialog box

To password-protect the database file, click the Tools menu, point to Security, and then select Set Database Password. When the Set Database Password dialog box appears (shown in Figure 6-1), enter the password in the Password text box and again in the Verify text box, and then click OK. The next time that you try to open the file, you'll be prompted for the password.

At some point, you might decide that you want to cancel password protection on your database file. To do so, you must again open the database in exclusive mode. Once the database is opened, click the Tools menu, point to Security, and then select Unset Database Password. You'll then be prompted for the password, even though you had to supply the password to open the file. You'll then be able to open the file without supplying a password.

CRITICAL SKILL
6.2 Apply User-Level Security

Access provides a system for securing your database that is far more effective than password-protecting the database file. This system—user-level security—allows you to control which users have access to which data objects and what type of operations they can perform on those objects. For example, you can configure your Access database so that some users can view and modify the data in a table, other users can only view the data, and the remaining users cannot access the data at all.

To set up user-level security, you must take a number of steps, which can include creating a workgroup, creating user and group accounts, and assigning permissions to those accounts on specific data objects. However, before I explain how to perform each of these tasks, I want to provide you with a brief definition of each of the primary components that make up the Access security model:

- **Workgroup**   A set of users who access the databases in the same instance of Access. Each workgroup is associated with its own *workgroup information file* (WIF), a file that contains information about the users in the workgroup.

- **User account**   A type of security account in an Access workgroup that represents a user who can access data objects and data in a database. Permissions are assigned to the user account to allow that user specific types of access to data objects. A user account is often referred to simply as a *user*.

- **Group account**   A type of security account in an Access workgroup that contains a set of user accounts. The user accounts are grouped together so that permissions can be assigned to the group account rather than to each user account. The user account is then granted the same permissions as those granted to the group account. A group account is often referred to simply as a *group*.

- **Permission**   A type of access right that is granted to a specific user or group account for access to a data object. For example, you can grant the Read Data permission to a specific user account on the Employees table (in the Northwind database). That user will then be able to view the data in the Employees table but not modify the data unless that user is granted additional permissions.

- **Object**   Any data object in an Access database on which permissions can be assigned. Data objects include not only the database object itself but also tables, queries, forms, reports, and macros.

Workgroups, user and group accounts, permissions, and objects work together to allow you to set up an effective security strategy that you can use to protect your Access databases.

NOTE

In addition to manually configuring user-level security, which is the approach I take in this module, you can use the Security wizard to set up security. The wizard steps you through the process of creating a workgroup, creating user and group accounts, and assigning permissions. To access the Security wizard, click the Tools menu, point to Security, and then select User-Level Security Wizard. Despite the availability of the wizard, I recommend that you learn how to configure security manually. This process will give you a better understanding of how security is implemented and what steps you need to take to modify the current settings.

Managing Access Workgroups

The process of managing an Access workgroup is essentially the process of managing the WIF. Each workgroup is associated with exactly one WIF, and Access can be associated with only one WIF at any one time. As a result, Access is associated with exactly one workgroup whenever it is opened. For all practical purposes, you can think of a workgroup and a WIF as one and the same thing.

The information in a WIF includes the user account names, their passwords, and the group accounts of which the users are members. By default, a WIF is created when you install Access on your computer. This file (System.mdw) contains the initial account information necessary to allow you to begin to use Access.

When you set up user-level security on your system, you can use the existing workgroup as it is defined in the System.mdw file, you can create a new workgroup and WIF, or you can use another WIF that has already been created. If you use the System.mdw WIF, there is nothing more that you need to do with workgroup in terms of configuring Access security. However, it is generally a good idea to create a new workgroup and WIF prior to setting up new user and group accounts. That way, you will preserve the original workgroup and WIF with their default settings.

If you decide to create a new workgroup or join an existing one, you must use the Workgroup Administrator utility, which is shown in Figure 6-2. To access the Workgroup Administrator, click the Tools menu, point to Security, and then click Workgroup Administrator. The Workgroup Administrator provides information about the current WIF and contains the buttons necessary to create a workgroup or join an existing workgroup.

Creating a Workgroup

When you click the Create button in the Workgroup Administrator dialog box, the Workgroup Owner Information dialog box appears, as shown in Figure 6-3. In the dialog box, you should enter your name, the name of your organization, and a workgroup ID, which is a case-sensitive alphanumeric value that uniquely identifies the workgroup. The workgroup ID must be 4 to 20 characters long.

CAUTION

Be sure to write down the name, organization, and workgroup ID exactly as you enter them into the Workgroup Owner Information dialog box. If for any reason you must re-create the WIF, you will need to use the information exactly as you entered it originally.

Once you've entered the necessary information into the Workgroup Owner Information dialog box, click OK. The Workgroup Information File dialog box appears (shown in Figure 6-4) and displays a path and filename based on the default WIF. Type in a new name for the WIF, and if necessary, change the path where you want the new WIF located.

```
┌─ Workgroup Administrator ──────────────────────── [?][X] ─┐
│                                                            │
│   Name:          WIF_owner                                 │
│   Company:       WIF_org                                   │
│   Workgroup:     C:\Documents and Settings                 │
│                  \Administrator.DOMAIN01\Application Data   │
│                  \Microsoft\Access\System.mdw              │
│                                                            │
│   Your workgroup is defined by the workgroup information   │
│   file that is used at startup. You can create a new       │
│   workgroup by creating a new information file, or join an │
│   existing workgroup by changing the information file      │
│   that is used at startup.                                 │
│                                                            │
│          [ Create... ] [ Join... ]    [  OK  ]             │
└────────────────────────────────────────────────────────────┘
```

Figure 6-2 The Workgroup Administrator dialog box

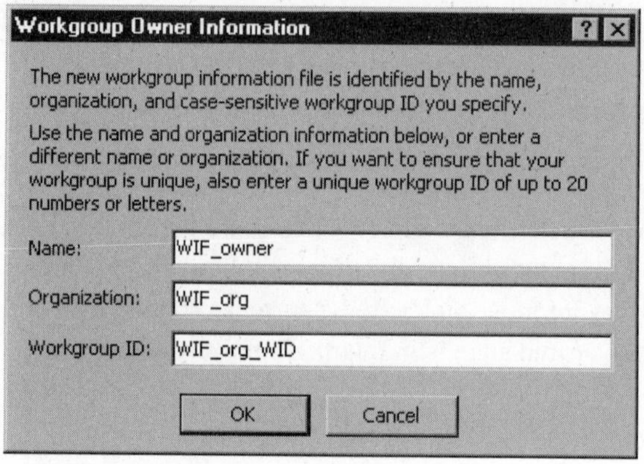

Figure 6-3 The Workgroup Owner Information dialog box

After you've entered the correct path and filename, click OK. The Confirm Workgroup Information dialog box appears, displaying the information that you entered into the previous dialog boxes. The Confirm Workgroup Information dialog box is shown in Figure 6-5. Notice that it displays your name, the name of your organization, the workgroup ID, and the path and filename for the new WIF. If any of this information is incorrect, click the Change button and make the necessary modifications.

After you've verified that all the information in the Confirm Workgroup Information dialog box is correct, click OK. You'll receive a message saying that the new workgroup has been created. Click OK to close the message box. The Workgroup Administrator dialog box reappears, displaying the new workgroup information. Close the Workgroup Administrator dialog box by clicking OK.

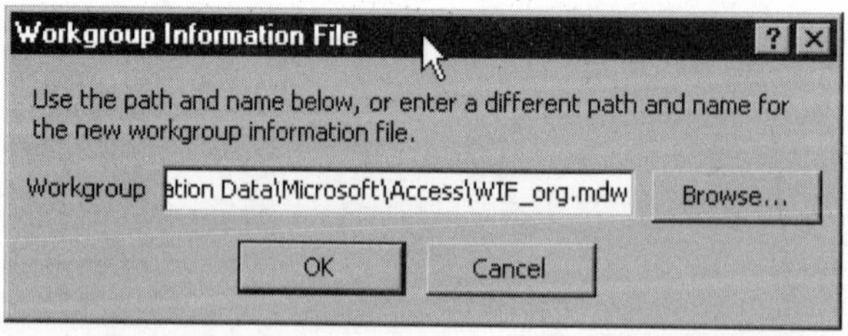

Figure 6-4 The Workgroup Information File dialog box

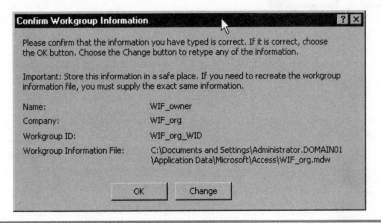

Figure 6-5 The Confirm Workgroup Information dialog box

Joining a Workgroup

The process of joining a workgroup is actually the process of associating Access with a WIF different from the current one. To join an existing workgroup, click the Join button in the Workgroup Administrator dialog box in order to open the Workgroup Information File dialog box. This is the same dialog box that you saw in Figure 6-4 when you were creating a workgroup. You can enter the path and filename of the WIF, or you can navigate to where the file is located by clicking the Browse button.

After you've entered the correct path and filename, click OK. You'll receive a message saying that you have successfully joined the workgroup. Click OK to close the message box. The Workgroup Administrator dialog box reappears, displaying the new workgroup information. Close the Workgroup Administrator dialog box by clicking OK.

Managing Security Accounts

Access supports two types of security accounts: users and groups. You can add and delete both types of accounts, add users to groups, and set the password for the current user. To configure user and group accounts, you must use the User And Group Accounts dialog box, which you can access by clicking the Tools menu, pointing to Security, and then clicking User And Group Accounts. By default, the Users tab is selected when you open the dialog box, as shown in Figure 6-6.

Ask the Expert

Q: You state that Access can be associated with only one WIF at a time. Is there a way to associate a specific database with a WIF without joining a different workgroup?

A: Yes, you can associate a database with a WIF when you open the database file. This can be helpful when you want to apply a different set of security configurations to a specific database, without joining a different workgroup. This saves you the trouble of having to join one workgroup before you open the database and then rejoin the original workgroup after you finish the database. This can be especially useful when you have multiple databases and want to use one workgroup for one database and another workgroup for the rest of the databases.

To associate a database with a WIF, you must open the database through a shortcut or a command-line utility, rather than through the Access interface. Whenever you open a database file through the interface, the database will be associated with the WIF currently configured for Access. To associate a WIF with a specific database in Windows XP, take the following steps:

1. If necessary, create the WIF that you want to use with the database file.

2. After you create the WIF, verify that Access is still associated with the correct WIF. Creating a WIF will associate Access with the new WIF, which might not be what you want. Once you verify that you have the correct WIF, close Access.

3. Create a shortcut to the database file, and then open the shortcut properties and select the Shortcut tab. In the Target text box, type the path and filename of the Access executable file (Msacces.exe) before the path and filename of the Access database file. At the end of the entire entry, type **/wrkgrp**, and then type the path and filename of the WIF. Each path/filename combination must be enclosed in double quotes. For example, your shortcut entry might look like the following:

    "C:\Program Files\Microsoft Office\Office11\Msaccess.exe" "C:\Program Files\Microsoft Office\Office11\Samples\ConsumerAdvocacy1.mdb" /wrkgrp "C:\Documents and Settings\Administrator.Domain01\Application Data\Microsoft\Access\Test1.mdw"

    The process for configuring the shortcut might vary from one operating system to the next, but the important point to remember is to use the /wrkgrp switch and to include the WIF path and filename. When you open the file, the database will be associated with the specific WIF. However, when you open the same file through the Access interface, the primary WIF will be used.

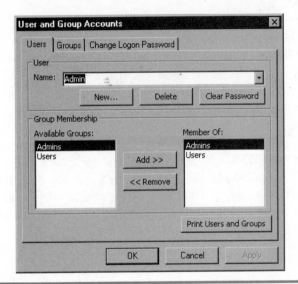

Figure 6-6 The Users tab of the User And Group Accounts dialog box

Administering User Accounts

To configure user accounts in Access, select the Users tab in the User And Group Accounts dialog box. The Users tab allows you to add and delete user accounts, clear the password for the current user (the user signed into Access), and add users to and remove users from any of the groups configured in Access.

The first time that you open the User And Group Accounts dialog box, you'll notice that one account already exists in the workgroup: the Admin account. If you select the down arrow in the Name drop-down list, you'll see that no other user accounts exist. However, as you can see in the Available Groups list, two group accounts also exist: Admins and Users. By default, all users are added to the Users group, and the Admin user account is added to the Admins group.

The Admin user account has full access to all objects in all databases. When you first open Access, you're logging on as the Admin user. Any actions taken prior to configuring user-level security are done through the Admin account. Because no password is required when you initially set up Access, you're not prompted for a user name or password when you open an Access database or try to change the security configurations. However, if you were to configure a password for the Admin account, you would be prompted for the logon information.

To add a user to the workgroup, you must be a member of the Admins group. On the Users tab of the User And Group Accounts dialog box, click the New button. When the New User/Group dialog box appears, enter a name for the user and a personal ID. The name and personal ID must be unique within the workgroup. The name can contain up to 20 characters, including letters, numbers, spaces, and some symbols. The personal ID, which is used by Access to uniquely identify the account, is a case-sensitive alphanumeric value that can be 4 to 20 characters long. The personal ID is not the same as a password. Assigning a password to an account is a separate process. If a user logs onto Access before a password has been assigned, no password is required, only the user name.

Once you've entered the name and personal ID in the New User/Group dialog box, click OK. The new user account is then added to the list of users in the Users tab of the User And Group Accounts dialog box. The new user is also added to the Users group. You can tell which groups a user belongs to by looking at the Member Of list.

To add a user to a group, select the user from the Name drop-down list, select the group from the Available Groups list, and then click the Add button. To remove a user from a group, select the user from the Name drop-down list, select the group from the Member Of list, and then click the Remove button.

NOTE

You cannot remove a user from the Users group. All user accounts are always included in this group.

You can also delete a user from a workgroup. Simply select the user from the Name drop-down list and then click the Delete button. You'll receive a message asking if you're sure that you want to delete the user account. Click Yes, and the account is removed from the workgroup.

Administering Group Accounts

Adding and deleting group accounts is as easy as adding and deleting user accounts. To add and delete groups, select the Groups tab in the User And Group Accounts dialog box, shown in Figure 6-7. To add a group to a workgroup, click the New button. When the New User/Group dialog box appears, enter a name for the group and a personal ID. The group name and personal ID follow the same conventions as the name and personal ID you use when creating a new user account. Once you've entered the name and personal ID, click OK. The new group account is added to the list of groups, and it is included in the list of groups in the Available Groups list on the Users tab.

To delete a group from a workgroup, select the group from the Name drop-down list on the Groups tab and then click the Delete button. You'll receive a message asking if you're sure that you want to delete the group account. Click Yes, and the account is removed from the workgroup.

Changing the Logon Password

You can set a password or change the existing password of the user who is currently logged on to Access. You cannot change the password of any user other than the current one. However, if no password has been assigned to a user or if you know the password of a user, you can log on

Figure 6-7 The Groups tab of the User And Group Accounts dialog box

as that user and assign or change the password yourself. You might want to do this if you've just created a user account and you want to assign a password to that account immediately, before giving that user access to the databases. In that case, you must close Access, log on as the new user, and then assign the password.

To assign an initial password or change an existing one, select the Change Logon Password tab of the User And Group Accounts dialog box, as shown in Figure 6-8. Enter the old password in the Old Password text box. If no password was assigned to the user, leave the text box blank. Then type in the new password in the New Password text box and again in the Verify text box. After you've entered the password, click OK or Apply.

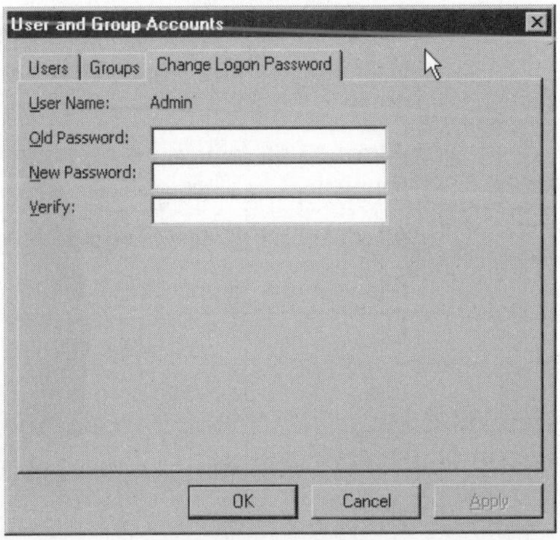

Figure 6-8 The Change Logon Password tab of the User And Group Accounts dialog box

NOTE

You must assign a password to the Admin account in order to implement user-level security. If you do not assign a password, Access does not prompt a user for logon credentials when opening a database, even if a user account has been created and a password assigned. Instead, the database automatically opens under the Admin account.

Assigning Permissions to Security Accounts

Once you have created a user or group account, you can assign permissions to that account so that the user or group of users can access specific objects in a database. When you assign permissions, you're granting access rights to the objects in a specific database, rather than to all databases within Access.

For each object in the database, you can select the type of access that you want to grant to the user or group account. Each object type supports certain types of permissions. In other words, the permissions that you can set for table objects are not all the same as those that you can set for a form, although many are the same. Table 6-1 describes the various permissions that you can set for an object.

Permission	Description
Open/Run	Allows a user to run a macro or to open a database, form, or report.
Open Exclusive	Allows a user to open a database in exclusive mode.
Read Design	Allows a user to open the specified object in Design view in order to view the object definition. This property does not apply to the database object.
Modify Design	Allows a user to open the specified object in Design view in order to modify the object definition. This property does not apply to the database object.
Administer	Allows a user to have full access to the object and to assign permissions to other users.
Read Data	Allows a user to view the data in a table or query.
Update Data	Allows a user to update the data in a table or query.
Insert Data	Allows a user to insert data into in a table or query.
Delete Data	Allows a user to delete data from a table or query.

Table 6-1 Object Permissions in an Access Database

Each object type supports a subset of the permissions listed in Table 6-1. You can see which object types support which permissions by viewing the permissions in the User And Group Permissions dialog box. However, for your convenience, Table 6-2 maps out which permissions are supported for which object types. An X is used to indicate that a permission can be configured for an object type.

Configuring Object Permissions

To assign permissions to a user, you must use the Permissions tab of the User And Group Permissions dialog box, shown in Figure 6-9. The Permissions tab displays the permissions that are available for each object type. Those permissions not available are either grayed out or not displayed.

To access the User And Group Permissions dialog box, click the Tools menu, point to Security, and then select User And Group Permissions. When the User And Group Permissions dialog box appears, the Permissions tab is selected by default. On this tab, you can assign permissions to the individual user or group account. To set permissions, take the following steps:

1. Select the Users radio button or Groups radio button to display the appropriate accounts in the User/Group Name list.

2. In the User/Group Name list, select the user or group account whose permissions you want to configure.

3. From the Object Type drop-down list, select the object type to display those objects in the Object Name list.

Permission	Database	Table	Query	Form	Report	Macro
Open/Run	X			X	X	X
Open Exclusive	X					
Read Design		X	X	X	X	X
Modify Design		X	X	X	X	X
Administer	X	X	X	X	X	X
Read Data		X	X			
Update Data		X	X			
Insert Data		X	X			
Delete Data		X	X			

Table 6-2 Permissions Supported for Each Object Type

Figure 6-9 The Permissions tab of the User And Group Permissions dialog box

4. In the Object Name list, select the object whose permission you want to set. To select more than one object at a time, select the first object, press and hold down CTRL, and then select the other objects.

5. In the Permissions section at the bottom of the Permissions tab, select the type of permissions that you want to apply to that account, or clear the permissions that you do not want applied to the account.

6. Click Apply.

7. Select other objects and object types as appropriate to set the desired permissions.

You can set or modify the permissions for any user or group account as long as you're logged on as the Admin account. If you log on as another user, your ability to set permissions might be limited, depending on the type of access granted to that account.

NOTE

By default, when you create a database, the Admin user account and the Admins and Users group accounts are granted all available access permissions on all objects. New user accounts, on the other hand, are granted no permissions. However, because all new users are automatically added to the Users group (and cannot be removed), they are granted all permissions implicitly, which means that they have full access to all objects. If you want to limit the access of the Users group, you must modify the permissions for that group.

Changing Object Ownership

Whenever an object is created in an Access database, the user who creates the object becomes the owner of the object. For example, if User1 creates a table in the Northwind database, User1 automatically becomes the owner of that object. As a result, that user has full control over the object and can modify the object's definition, view data contained in the object, or configure permissions on the object. However, Access allows you to change the owner of an object in the Change Owner tab of the User And Group Permissions dialog box, as shown in Figure 6-10.

To change an object's owner, take the following steps:

1. Select the Groups radio button or Users radio button to display the appropriate accounts in the New Owner drop-down list, and then select the new owner from that list.

2. In the Object Type drop-down list, select the object type to display a list of applicable objects in the Object list.

3. Select the object whose ownership you want to modify from the Object list.

4. Click the Change Owner button, and then click OK to close the User And Group Permissions dialog box.

   Once you change the owner of the object, the new owner has full control over that object.

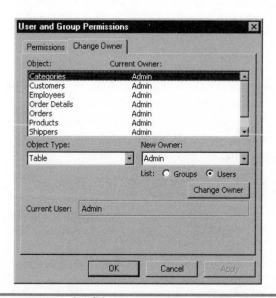

Figure 6-10 The Change Owner tab of the User And Group Permissions dialog box

Progress Check

1. In what mode must you open a database when setting up password protection on the database file?

2. What are the primary components that make up the Access security model?

3. What information is included in a workgroup information file?

4. For which users can you change the password?

Encode and Decode Your Database File

Another form of security that you can consider when working with Access is to encode your database files. Encoding a file compacts the file and prevents word processing and utility programs from being able to read the file. However, any Access users can still open the file and access the database objects if no other security is configured on the database, as long as those users can access the network share where the file resides. Despite the limitations, encoding a file can be useful when you want to transmit the database electronically or store it on certain media.

Encoding the Database File

To encode (or decode) a database file, you must be the owner of the database object, be a member of the Admins group, or be logged in with the Admin user account. The last two requirements apply only if user-level security is configured on the database. You can encode a database file by using the Encode Database As dialog box, shown in Figure 6-11.

To encode a database file, take the following steps:

1. Open the database file.

2. Click the Tools menu, point to Security, and then click Encode/Decode Database. The Encode Database As dialog box appears.

---

1. Exclusive mode
2. Workgroups, user accounts, group accounts, permissions, and objects
3. User account names, their passwords, and the group account of which the users are members
4. Only the current user

Figure 6-11 The Encode Database As dialog box

3. Navigate to the desired folder, and then, in the File Name text box, type a name for the encoded database file. You can use the same name as the original file—which replaces the file—or you can use a new name.

4. Click Save.

The database file is encoded, and you can open it the same way you do any other file. When you open an encoded file, it is decoded until you close the file again.

NOTE
If you encode the database file with a name different from the original name, be sure that the drive has plenty of storage space for both files.

Decoding the Database File

At some point, you might decide that you no longer want the database file to be encoded. You can decode the file as simply as you encoded it. To do so, you must use the Decode Database As dialog box, shown in Figure 6-12.

To decode an encoded database file, take the following steps:

1. Open the encoded database file.

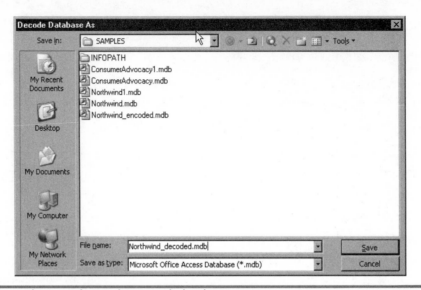

Figure 6-12 The Decode Database As dialog box

2. Click the Tools menu, point to Security, and then click Encode/Decode Database. The Decode Database As dialog box appears.

3. Navigate to the desired folder, and then, in the File Name text box, type a name for the decoded database file. You can use the same name as the encoded file—which replaces the file—or you can use a new name.

4. Click Save.

You can now open the file at any time and work with the database in its decoded form, as you would with any other database file.

Project 6-1 Configuring User-Level Security

The process of configuring user-level security, when setting up only a few security accounts, is relatively straightforward. However, as the number of users and groups increases, so does the complexity of security configurations. To introduce you to user-level security, this project walks you through the basic steps necessary to set up security in Access. You will create a workgroup in the ConsumerAdvocacy.mdb file, add a user to the workgroup, change the logon password for the Admin account, and configure permissions for the new user. You will then delete the user from the workgroup and rejoin the default workgroup. Once you've completed this process, you should have a basic understanding of user-level security. You can then add the necessary user and group accounts to your workgroups and configure permissions according to the needs of your organization.

Step by Step

1. Open Access if it is not already open, and then open the ConsumerAdvocacy.mdb file.

2. Click the Tools menu, point to Security, and then click Workgroup Administrator. The Workgroup Administrator dialog box appears, displaying information about the current WIF.

3. Click Create. The Workgroup Owner Information dialog box appears.

4. In the Name text box, type **TestOwner**; in the Organization text box, type **TestOrg**; and in the Workgroup ID text box, type **TestOrgWID**. Then click OK. The Workgroup Information File dialog box appears.

5. In the Workgroup text box, leave the path as is, but change the filename to TestOrg.mdw, and then click OK. The Confirm Workgroup Information dialog box appears, displaying the settings that you just configured.

6. Confirm that the information is correct, and then click OK. You'll receive a message box saying that the new workgroup has been created.

7. Click OK to close the message box. You're returned to the Workgroup Administrator dialog box, which is displaying the new WIF information.

8. Click OK.

9. Click the Tools menu, point to Security, and then click User And Group Accounts. The User And Group Accounts dialog box appears, with the Users tab selected.

10. Click New. The New User/Group dialog box appears.

11. In the Name text box, type **User1**; in the Personal ID text box, type **User1PID**; and then click OK. The new user account is added to the list of users in the Name drop-down list on the Users tab.

12. Select the Change Logon Password tab. In the New Password text box and the Verify text box, type **password** (all lowercase), and then click OK.

13. Click the Tools menu, point to Security, and then click User And Group Permissions. The User And Group Permissions dialog box appears, with the Permissions tab selected.

14. Select User1 from the User/Group Name list, and then select the Orders table from the Object Name list.

15. In the Permissions section, select the Administer check box, and then click Apply. All permissions are automatically selected because the Administer permission grants full access to an object.

(continued)

6

Managing Database Security

Project
6-1

Configuring User-Level Security

16. Select Products from the Object Name list, select the Read Data permission, and then click Apply. The Read Design permission is automatically selected when you select the Read Data permission.

17. Select ProductOrders from the Object Name list, select the Read Data, Update Data, Insert Data, and Delete Data permissions, and then click OK.

18. Close and re-open Access, and then open the ConsumerAdvocacy.mdb file. When you try to open the file, you're prompted for a name and password (through the Logon dialog box).

19. Type **User1** in the Name text box, but do not type anything in the Password text box because no password has been assigned to this user account. Then click OK. The Consumer Advocacy database opens.

20. Close and re-open Access, and then open the ConsumerAdvocacy.mdb file. The Logon dialog box appears.

21. In the Name text box, type **Admin**, in the Password text box, type **password**, and then click OK. The Consumer Advocacy database opens.

22. Click the Tools menu, point to Security, and then click User And Group Accounts. The user And Group Accounts dialog box appears.

23. Select User1 from the Name drop-down list, and then click Delete. A message box appears, asking you to confirm whether you want to delete this account.

24. Click Yes. The User1 account is removed from the Name drop-down list. The only user account should now be Admin.

25. Click Clear Password to clear the Admin account password, and then click OK. You'll no longer prompted for a name and password when you open a database file, and user-level security will no longer be in effect.

26. Click the Tools menu, point to Security, and then click Workgroup Administrator. The Workgroup Administrator dialog box appears.

27. Click Join. The Workgroup Information File dialog box appears.

28. Click Browse. The Select Workgroup Information dialog box appears.

29. If you're not already in the folder that contains the System.mdw file (the default WIF), navigate to that folder, select the System.mdw file, and then click Open. You're returned to the Workgroup Information File dialog box.

30. Click OK. You'll receive a message saying that you've successfully joined the new workgroup.

31. Click OK to close the message box. You're returned to the Workgroup Administrator dialog box, which should now be displaying information about the default WIF.

32. Click OK.

Project Summary

In this project, you configured user-level security. However, by the time you completed the project, you returned your database to the state it was in at the beginning of the project, though you now have a WIF named TestOrg.mdw that is currently not being used. You can use the WIF at a later time and modify the security settings to meet your specific needs, or you can create a new WIF.

User-level security is the most effective method that you can use to secure a database in Access. It provides the most flexibility in terms of which objects you can protect and the type of protection that you can apply. I recommend that you create a copy of the ConsumerAdvocacy.mdb file with which to practice, and then create users and groups and configure various permissions for the new database. Once you've configured the permissions, be sure to test access to the different data objects to see what level of protection exists on the database.

✔

Module 6 Mastery Check

1. What security concerns should you be aware of when password-protecting a database file?

2. Which component in the Access security model is a type of access right that is granted to a specific user?

   A. User account

   B. Workgroup

   C. Permission

   D. Object

3. _____ mode is the state in which you can open a database file that prevents any other users from opening the file while you're using it.

4. What is the difference between a workgroup and a group account?

5. How many workgroups can Access be associated with at any one time?

   A. Exactly one

   B. One for each WIF that has been created

C. One for each database object

D. As many as necessary

6. What is the name of the default WIF that is created when you install Access?

7. Which types of security accounts does Access support?

A. Workgroups

B. Users

C. Groups

D. Objects

8. What is the name of the default user account that is created automatically by Access?

9. Which group are all users added to by default?

A. Admin

B. Admins

C. Security

D. Users

10. What type of access does the Admin account have?

11. How do you add a user account to a workgroup?

12. How must you configure the Admin account in order to implement user-level security?

13. You created a user account in a workgroup, and you want to allow the user to view the data in the database but not make any changes. Which permission should you assign?

A. Open Exclusive

B. Administer

C. Read Data

D. Read Design

14. Which object type supports the Open Exclusive permission?

A. Database

B. Table

C. Form

D. Macro

15. What does encoding a file accomplish?

Part II

Data Access and Modification

Module 7

Modifying Data in an Access Database

CRITICAL SKILLS

7.1 Insert Data into a Table

7.2 Update Data in a Table

7.3 Delete Data from a Table

In Part I, you learned how to create an Access database and the tables necessary to support that database. As part of this process, you configured table properties, established relationships between tables, and set up user-level security on the database and table objects. You are now ready to add data to the database, modify that data, and query the data for specific information. In this module, you will learn how to insert data into a table, update that data, and then delete the data. Later in Part II, you will learn how to find, sort, and filter data; import, export, and link data; and retrieve specific types of information from the database. Once you have a foundation in how to access and manipulate data, you'll be ready to create the other objects that will be used in your data-driven application.

Insert Data into a Table

Before you can manipulate data in a database in any way, the tables of the database must, of course, contain data. So you should know how to add records to a table before you learn how to manipulate information in those records. As you'll recall from Module 2, each field within a record must contain only one value, and each record must contain the same number of values, even if some fields contain null values. In addition, the data in the record must conform to the constraints placed on the fields by the data types and the table properties. However, before we get into the details of value limitations, let's take a look at the methods used to create a new record.

Creating a New Record

You can add new records to a table in a number of ways: by importing the data, by entering the data through a form, or by accessing the table directly through Datasheet view and entering the new data there. Importing data is discussed in Module 9, and using forms is discussed in Module 12. In this section, I'll focus on how to create a new record in the Datasheet view window.

The Datasheet view window, as you've seen in earlier modules, displays the data in a table in a column/row structure. Each field is represented by a column, and each record is represented by a row. For example, Figure 7-1 shows the Employees table from the Northwind database, as the table appears in Datasheet view. As you can see, the table includes a number of fields, such as Employee ID, Last Name, First Name, and Title. When you add a new record to the table, you are essentially adding a new row that contains a value in each field.

Access provides several methods that you can use to add a new record to a table in Datasheet view:

- Click the Insert menu and then click New Record. (You can also click the Edit menu, point to Go To, and then click New Record.)

- Click the New Record button on the Table Datasheet toolbar.

- Click the New Record navigation button at the bottom of the Datasheet view window.

- Press the CTRL-= key combination.

Employees : Table								
	Employee ID	Last Name	First Name	Title	Title Of C	Birth Date	Hire Date	Address
	1	Bishop	Scott	Sales Representative	Mr.	08-Dec-1968	01-May-1992	507 - 20th Ave. E.
	2	Fuller	Andrew	Vice President, Sales	Dr.	19-Feb-1952	14-Aug-1992	908 W. Capital Way
	3	Leverling	Janet	Sales Representative	Ms.	30-Aug-1963	01-Apr-1992	722 Moss Bay Blvd.
	4	Peacock	Margaret	Sales Representative	Mrs.	19-Sep-1958	03-May-1993	4110 Old Redmond Rd.
	5	Buchanan	Steven	Sales Manager	Mr.	04-Mar-1955	17-Oct-1993	14 Garrett Hill
	6	Suyama	Michael	Sales Representative	Mr.	02-Jul-1963	17-Oct-1993	Coventry House
	7	King	Robert	Sales Representative	Mr.	29-May-1960	02-Jan-1994	Edgeham Hollow
	8	Callahan	Laura	Inside Sales Coordinator	Ms.	09-Jan-1958	05-Mar-1994	4726 - 11th Ave. N.E.
	9	Dodsworth	Anne	Sales Representative	Ms.	02-Jul-1969	15-Nov-1994	7 Houndstooth Rd.
*	(AutoNumber)							

Record: |◄| ◄ | 1 | ► | ►| | ►* | of 9

Figure 7-1 The Employees table in the Northwind database, as seen in Datasheet view

(right margin, vertical text) Modifying Data in an Access Database

When you use any of these methods to create a new record, your cursor is moved to the first field of the first empty row beneath the last record, and you can begin to enter data into each field in the record.

TIP

When you're viewing a table in Datasheet view, you can tell the status of a record by the symbol that appears at the beginning of that record. For example, an arrow is used for the record that is currently selected. In the last row of the table, which is where you would insert a new record, an asterisk is used. If you're currently inserting or modifying data in a record, a pencil is used.

Inserting Data into a Field

When adding a record to a table, you should enter a value into each field, unless the field should be left blank. You can move from one field to the next by using one of several methods:

● Click on the field that you want to move to.

● Press TAB or ENTER to move from one field to the next.

● Use the appropriate arrow key to move to the field above, below, to the right, or to the left of the current field.

Regardless of how you move from one field to the next, you must conform to the restrictions applied to inserted values by the field's data type. The type of data that you can add and the way in which you can add it varies from one data type to the next.

NOTE

See Module 3 for information about the restrictions placed on data by each data type. See Appendix B for information about shortcut keys that you can use to navigate through the fields.

Character Fields

Character data fields are fields that are configured with the Text or Memo data type. You can enter letters (uppercase or lowercase), numbers, and many symbols, such as dashes (-) and number signs (#). For Text data, the size of the value cannot exceed the size specified in the Field Size property, which itself cannot exceed 255 characters. A Memo field is not restricted by the Field Size property; however, Access places a 65,535-character limitation on Memo fields.

Access does not allow you to enter a value in a Text or Memo field that exceeds the maximum size allowed. For example, if a Text field is limited to five characters, you will be able to type only five characters. Otherwise, there are few restrictions on the type of characters that you can enter into a Text or Memo field.

Numerical Fields

Fields that are configured with the Number or Currency data type can accept numerical values only. By default, both types of fields are automatically assigned a value of 0 when you create a new record, and you can replace the 0 with an appropriate value. If the value is a fraction and requires a decimal, you must include the decimal point, assuming that the current configuration supports decimals. However, if the Field Size property is configured as an integer, fractions are rounded to the nearest whole number, so be certain that this is what you want when entering values into these types of fields. For numerical fields that do support decimals, you do not have to include a decimal point if the value is a whole number. Access will automatically add the decimal point and the necessary zeros to make the data within the field consistent.

A third type of numerical field is AutoNumber. A field configured with this data type is automatically assigned a numerical value whenever a new record is added to a table. You cannot enter a value in this type of field or change an existing value.

NOTE

When you first create a record that contains an AutoNumber field, the field includes an entry that reads "(AutoNumber)." A number is not assigned to the record until you insert data into one of the other fields. Once a number has been assigned to a record, it will not be used in the field again, even if you delete the original record.

Date/Time Fields

As the name implies, a Date/Time field is limited to date and time data. The information that is displayed in this type of field depends on how the Format property for the field has been configured. The format property determines whether dates, times, or both are displayed and determines how that information is displayed.

Regardless of how the Format property is set for a Date/Time field, Access is somewhat flexible on how you can enter data into that field. For example, suppose the Format property is configured with the Short Date option. You can enter a value of 10/12/04 or 10-12-04 and Access will display it as 10/12/2004. In addition, if the data applies to the current year, you need to enter only 10/12 or 10-12, and Access will add the correct year. If the Format property is configured with the Long Date option, you can enter 8/15/04 or 8-15-04, and Access will convert it to Sunday, August 15, 2004.

Yes/No Fields

A Yes/No field is made up of one bit of data and is represented by a check box. To indicate a value of Yes, True, or On, select the check box. For a value of No, False, or Off, the check box should be clear.

OLE Object Fields

For most field types, except AutoNumber, you enter data into the field simply by typing, pasting, or selecting a value. However, the method that you use to insert data into an OLE object field is very different from that for other fields. As you'll recall from Module 3, an OLE Object field can contain an embedded object or a link to an object such as an Excel spreadsheet or a Word document. (*OLE* refers to *object linking and embedding*.)

To insert an object or an object link into an OLE Object field, you must use the Microsoft Office Access dialog box, shown in Figure 7-2. The dialog box allows you to embed a new object or to embed an existing file or a link to that file.

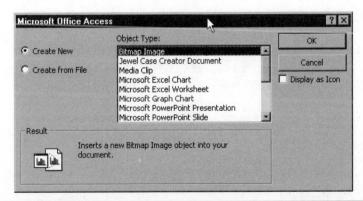

Figure 7-2 The Microsoft Office Access dialog box, with the Create New option selected

You can use one of two methods to open the Microsoft Office Access dialog box. In both cases, you must move the cursor to the applicable OLE Object field and then take one of the following steps:

● Right-click the field, and then click Insert Object in the shortcut menu.

● Click the Insert menu, and then click Object.

If you want to create a new object to embed, select the type of object from the Object Type list, and then click OK. This will launch the appropriate application in which you can create the embedded document. Once you create the object, close the application. The object will automatically be embedded in the appropriate field.

You might decide that you want to embed an existing file or a link to that file. To do so, select the Create From File option in the Microsoft Office Access dialog box. When you select this option, the dialog box changes, as shown in Figure 7-3.

Once you select this option, browse to the appropriate file or enter the path and filename in the File text box. Rather than embedding the file in the Access table, you can create a link from the table to the file by selecting the Link option. That way, the file always remains separate from the Access table.

Whether you create a new file or use an existing file, you can display the object as an icon in forms and reports, rather than as the object itself. For example, rather than displaying an actual picture, you can display an icon that links to the picture.

Hyperlink Fields

A Hyperlink field allows you to enter a link to a file or web page on the Internet or an intranet. You can enter a Uniform Resource Locator (URL), such as http://www.osborne.com, or a Universal Naming Convention (UNC) path and filename, such as C:\WordDocuments\Names.doc.

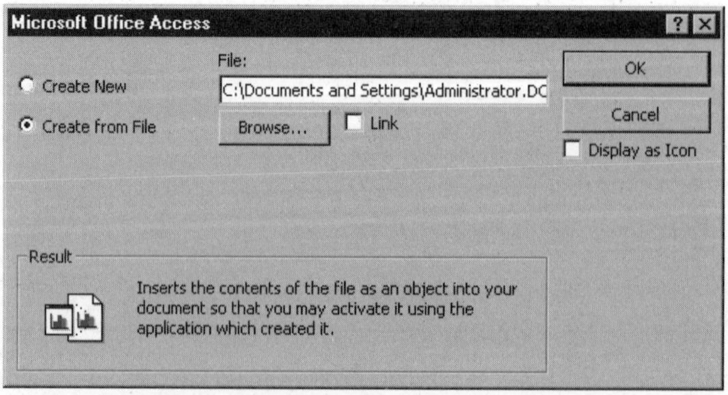

Figure 7-3 The Microsoft Office Access dialog box, with the Create From File option selected

In addition to the actual URL or UNC link, you can include several other elements in the value that you enter into a Hyperlink field, with each element separated by a pound sign:

DisplayText#URL/UNC#Subaddress#ScreenTip

As you can see, a Hyperlink value can include four elements:

- **DisplayText**   The information that you want to have appear in the field instead of the URL or UNC. If you don't specify any display text, the actual URL or UNC is displayed.

- **URL/UNC**   The link to the web page or file.

- **Subaddress**   A location within the object targeted by the URL or UNC. For example, you can jump to a bookmark within a Word document or to a cell within an Excel worksheet.

- **ScreenTip**   The information that you want to have appear when the mouse is passed over the hyperlink.

Let's take a look at an example to help illustrate how to create a value for a Hyperlink field. The following hyperlink opens a Word document named Book.doc:

Book Document#C:\WordDocuments\Books.doc#Authors#Click Here!

When you enter this value into the a Hyperlink field, the field will display "Book Document" and will link to the Books.doc file in the C:\WordDocuments folder. When you click the link, the document will open at the Authors bookmark. If you pass your cursor over the hyperlink, you'll see the message "Click Here!"

If you want to enter a value that does not include all four elements, you should still use the pound sign as a placeholder for each element. For example, if you wanted to display only the UNC and the screen tip, you would enter #C:\WordDocuments\Books.doc##Click Here! In addition, if you want the field to contain only the hyperlink and no other elements, you can enter the UNC or URL without any pound signs.

Working with Property Restrictions

As you have seen so far, the values that you can enter into a field are limited by the data type that is configured for that field. However, there are several table properties that can also affect the values that can be entered into a field.

The Input Mask Property

An input mask acts as a filter that determines how data can be entered into a field. It provides users with a fill-in-the-blanks kind of format that limits the way a value can be entered. Consider, for example, an input mask that is used for Social Security numbers. When the input mask is applied, you can enter only nine digits into that field. In addition, you're provided with the necessary dashes to properly format the Social Security number.

The Required Property and Allow Zero Length Property

For all fields except those configured with the AutoNumber type you have the option of requiring the field to contain a value. If the Required property is set to Yes, you must provide a value according to the restrictions of the data type and the other properties. If the property is set to No and the field is left blank, a null value is inserted into the field.

For Text, Memo, and Hyperlink fields, you also have the option of configuring the Allow Zero Length property, which indicates whether zero-length strings are permitted. If the field is configured to allow zero-length strings and you want to enter one as a value in a field, enter two consecutive quotation marks (" ").

Lookup Properties

When lookup properties are configured on a field, the values that are inserted into the field must come from a predefined list or another table. When you enter data into a field that is associated with a lookup list, you must select the values from a drop-down list that is available for the specific field. For example, the Employees table in the Northwind database includes a field named Title Of Courtesy. The field is linked to a lookup list that contains several values that can be used for that field. When you create a new record in the Employees table, you must choose from one of the values that appears in the drop-down list that is associated with the Title Of Courtesy field, as shown in Figure 7-4.

If you know the value that you want to enter into the field, you do not have to select it from the list. Instead, you can type the first letter or several letters, and Access will complete the value with one of the values from the list. However, you must be certain that a similar value is not mistakenly inserted into the field.

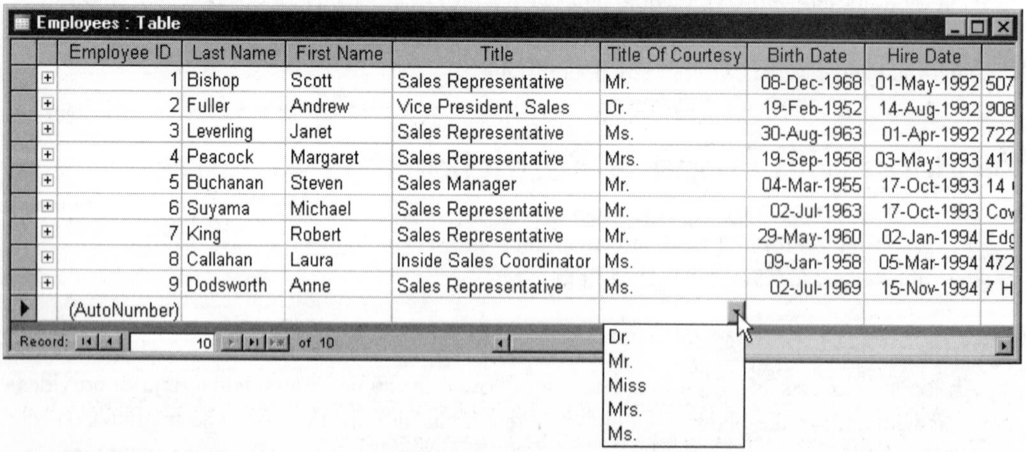

	Employee ID	Last Name	First Name	Title	Title Of Courtesy	Birth Date	Hire Date	
+	1	Bishop	Scott	Sales Representative	Mr.	08-Dec-1968	01-May-1992	507
+	2	Fuller	Andrew	Vice President, Sales	Dr.	19-Feb-1952	14-Aug-1992	908
+	3	Leverling	Janet	Sales Representative	Ms.	30-Aug-1963	01-Apr-1992	722
+	4	Peacock	Margaret	Sales Representative	Mrs.	19-Sep-1958	03-May-1993	411
+	5	Buchanan	Steven	Sales Manager	Mr.	04-Mar-1955	17-Oct-1993	14
+	6	Suyama	Michael	Sales Representative	Mr.	02-Jul-1963	17-Oct-1993	Cov
+	7	King	Robert	Sales Representative	Mr.	29-May-1960	02-Jan-1994	Edg
+	8	Callahan	Laura	Inside Sales Coordinator	Ms.	09-Jan-1958	05-Mar-1994	472
+	9	Dodsworth	Anne	Sales Representative	Ms.	02-Jul-1969	15-Nov-1994	7 H
▶	(AutoNumber)							

Record: 10 of 10

Dr.
Mr.
Miss
Mrs.
Ms.

Figure 7-4 The Title Of Courtesy field in the Employees table of the Northwind database

Copying and Moving Data

You might find that, when adding new records to a table, you want to copy or move data from another location—either within the same table or from a different table. Once you insert the copied or moved data, you can modify the data or use the information as is, as long as the new records do not violate any of the constraints placed on the fields.

NOTE

In addition to copying entire records, you can copy individual fields from one record to another. This is particularly handy if you have a field that requires duplicate values in multiple records.

Access provides several methods for copying or moving records. Regardless of the method you use, the basic steps are the same:

1. Select the record to be copied or moved.

2. Cut or copy that record.

3. Paste the record into its new location.

You can copy or move one or more records at a time. To select consecutive records in a table, click the first record in the group of records that you want to select, press and hold down SHIFT, and then click the last record in that group. You can also select the first record, hold down the left mouse button, and highlight the consecutive records to select all of them. Note that you cannot select more than one record if the records are not consecutive.

Copying Records

To copy a record, select the record and then use one of the following methods to copy the data:

- Press CTRL-C.

- Click the Copy button on the Table Datasheet toolbar.

- Click the Edit menu, and then click Copy.

The copied data is then added to the clipboard, which you can view in the Clipboard task pane, as shown in Figure 7-5.

Once you've copied the record to the clipboard, select the empty row at the bottom of the table (in Datasheet view) and take one of the following actions:

- Press CTRL-V.

- Click the Paste button on the Table Datasheet toolbar.

- Click the Edit menu, and then click Paste.

- In the Clipboard task pane, point to the clipboard data that you just copied or cut, click the down arrow, and then click Paste.

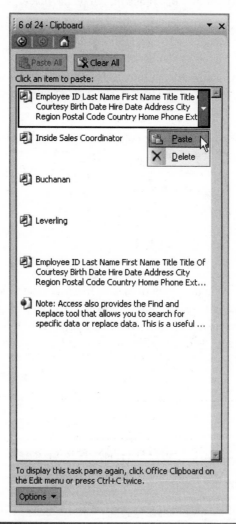

Figure 7-5 The Clipboard task pane

If you're pasting multiple records into a table, you'll be prompted for verification that you want to insert these records.

Moving Records

Moving records is very similar to copying records. The only significant difference is that when you first move a record, you're essentially deleting it from the table, copying it to the clipboard, and then pasting it into its new location. To move a record, first select the record and then take one of the following actions:

● Press CTRL-X.

● Click the Cut button on the Table Datasheet toolbar.

● Click the Edit menu, and then click Cut.

After the original record has been removed from the table and copied to the clipboard, you can paste it into its new location, just as you did when you were copying a record.

Progress Check

1. In what ways can records be added to a table?

2. What default value is initially assigned to a Number or Currency field?

3. What type(s) of address link can you include in a Hyperlink field?

4. How many records can you copy or move at one time?

---

1. You can add new records to a table by importing the data, by entering the data through a form, or by accessing the table directly through Datasheet view and entering the new data there.

2. 0

3. A URL or UNC

4. One or more

CRITICAL SKILL
7.2 # Update Data in a Table

After data has been entered into a table, you might find that you want to edit that data. You can edit data through the Datasheet view window, as long as you've been granted the permissions necessary to update the table. When editing data, you'll often have to move from field to field and row to row. Access allows you to configure keyboard options that determine how certain keys will behave when you move the cursor. This section explains how to edit data in Datasheet view and then describes how to configure keyboard options that will help you when editing data.

NOTE

Access also provides the Find And Replace tool, which allows you to search for specific data or replace data. This is a useful tool if you need to update numerous instances of the same value. The Find And Replace tool is discussed in Module 8.

Editing Field Data

To a great degree, the process of changing the data in a field is similar to entering the data for the first time when you first create a record. You must still adhere to the constraints placed on values by data types and table properties. For example, if the Field Size property of a Text field is set to 5, you cannot enter more than five characters into that field.

For many field types (Text, Memo, Number, Date/Time, and Currency), the process of updating a value is as simple as selecting the value within the field and then entering the new value. Once you've entered the new value, press ENTER or TAB, or move your cursor to another field or row.

For other field types, the process of editing a value varies. For example, to edit a Yes/No field, simply select or clear the check box. Fields configured with the OLE Object or Hyperlink data type are a little more complicated to edit.

NOTE

You cannot edit an AutoNumber field. The values are assigned by Access and cannot be changed.

Editing an OLE Object Field

To modify an OLE Object field, right-click the field, point to the *ObjectType* Object option, and then click Edit or Edit Package, whichever option appears. The Edit Package option is used only if the object is a package, such as a .jpg file.

Ask the Expert

Q: When I move the cursor to a field by using TAB or the arrow keys, the cursor usually highlights the value, but if I move the cursor by clicking on the field, an insertion point is placed within the field. Why does Access do this?

A: When you are manipulating data in a table in Datasheet view, Access operates in one of two modes: Navigation mode or Edit mode. By default, the cursor operates in *Navigation mode,* which means that the cursor's insertion point isn't visible and an entire field is selected at the cursor's location. However, the cursor can also operate in *Edit mode,* which allows you to move from character to character within a field. As a result, the insertion point is visible and the field is no longer selected. To switch between Navigation mode and Edit mode, press F2. You can also switch to Edit mode by clicking within a field. However, if you use the TAB key or arrow keys to move to another field, you're returned to Navigation mode. Then, as soon as you start typing in that field, you switch back to Edit mode.

The *ObjectType* placeholder refers to the type of object that is embedded or linked to the field. For example, if the embedded object is an Excel worksheet, the *ObjectType* Object option will appear as "Worksheet Object."

When you select Edit, the embedded or linked object opens in its associated program. For example, suppose a field contains the Bitmap Image value, which means that a bitmap is embedded in or linked to that field. When you go to edit that field, the file will open in Microsoft Paint, and you can make the necessary corrections to the image. Once you've made the modifications, close the application.

Editing a Hyperlink Field

As you'll recall from earlier in the module, a Hyperlink field can contains four elements, with each element separated by a pound sign:

DisplayText#URL/UNC#Subaddress#ScreenTip

To edit a value in a Hyperlink field, you must use the Edit Hyperlink dialog box, as shown in Figure 7-6. To access this dialog box, right-click the field, point to Hyperlink, and then click Edit Hyperlink. When the Edit Hyperlink dialog box appears, make the necessary corrections.

To edit the display text, modify the value in the Text To Display text box. To edit the URL or UNC, as well as the subaddress, modify the value in the Address text box. If a subaddress is included, you must separate it from the main address with a pound sign. To edit the ScreenTip, click the ScreenTip button and make the necessary changes in the Set Hyperlink ScreenTip dialog box.

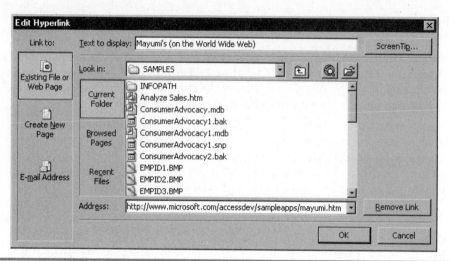

Figure 7-6 The Edit Hyperlink dialog box

Setting Keyboard Options

When editing the data in a table, you might find that you must maneuver through the various records and fields in order to make the required changes. Access allows you to modify the default actions of several keys to facilitate this task. To change these settings, click the Tools menu and then click Options. When the Options dialog box appears, select the Keyboard tab, as shown in Figure 7-7. The Keyboard tab contains three main sections: Move After Enter, Behavior Entering Field, and Arrow Key Behavior.

The Move After Enter section is concerned with the behavior of the ENTER key when it is pressed within a field:

- **Don't Move**   The insertion point stays in the current field.

- **Next Field**   The insertion point moves to the next field. This is the default option.

- **Next Record**   The insertion point moves to the next record.

The Behavior Entering Field section specifies what happens to the cursor when it is moved into a field:

- **Select Entire Field**   The entire value within the field is selected. This is the default option.

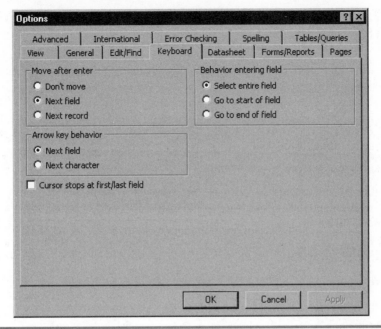

Figure 7-7 The Keyboard tab of the Options dialog box

● **Go to Start of Field**   The cursor's insertion point is placed at the beginning of the field, before the first character.

● **Go to End of Field**   The insertion point is placed at the end of the field, after the last character.

The Arrow Key Behavior section is related to the actions of the RIGHT ARROW key and the LEFT ARROW key:

● **Next Field**   The cursor moves to the next field when you press RIGHT ARROW, and moves to the previous field when you press LEFT ARROW. This is the default option.

● **Next Character**   The cursor's insertion point moves to the next character when you press RIGHT ARROW and moves to the previous character when you press LEFT ARROW.

In addition to the options in the three sections, the Keyboard tab includes the Cursor Stops At First/Last Field check box. If this option is checked, the cursor's insertion point is locked within the current record, and the LEFT ARROW and RIGHT ARROW are prevented from moving the cursor to the previous or next record.

CRITICAL SKILL
7.3 Delete Data from a Table

Updating a table might involve deleting individual characters from a field, deleting an entire field, or deleting entire records.

- To delete an individual character, click in the field right before or right after the character that you want to delete. If you want to delete the previous character, press BACKSPACE. If you want to delete the next character, press DELETE. For consecutive characters, you can highlight those characters and then press BACKSPACE or DELETE.

- To delete an entire value in a field, use TAB or the arrow keys to move the cursor to that field, which highlights the entire field, and then press BACKSPACE or DELETE. If you're in Edit mode (in which the cursor's insertion point is displayed and the value is not highlighted), press F2 to switch to Navigation mode, which will highlight the entire field, and then press BACKSPACE or DELETE.

- To delete a record, select the record and then take one of the following steps:
  - Click the Delete Record button on the Table Datasheet toolbar.
  - Right-click the record and then click Delete Record in the shortcut menu.
  - Click the Edit menu and then click the Delete option or the Delete Record option.

You can delete multiple records at one time simply by selecting those records and then clicking the Delete Record button on the Table Datasheet toolbar or clicking one of the options in the Edit menu. However, you cannot use the Delete Record option in the shortcut menu to delete multiple records.

Whenever you try to delete a record or records, you're prompted to confirm whether you actually want to delete the selected record(s). Click Yes if you're certain that the deletion is correct.

Project 7-1 Manipulating Data in the Consumer Advocacy Database

In Module 5, you defined the relationships among the tables in the Consumer Advocacy database. By establishing those relationships, you ensured that data must exist in certain fields in order for that data to be valid in the referencing fields. In this project, you will begin to add data to the database. However, because of the relationships that exist, you will first add data to those tables that supply fixed values to other tables through the relationships. Specifically, you will add the necessary data to the FormOfPayment, NumberTypes, and Positions tables. From there, you'll be able to add data to the related tables in the database.

Step by Step

1. Open Access (if it is not already open) and then open the ConsumerAdvocacy.mdb database file.

2. Ensure that the Tables object type is selected in the database window, and then double-click the FormOfPayment table. The table will open in Datasheet view.

3. In the PaymentID field of the first row (which is the new record), type **CK**, and then press TAB. The cursor moves to the PaymentType field.

4. Type **Check**, and then press TAB. The cursor moves to the PaymentID field in the next row. The first record is now created, and you're ready to create the next record.

5. In the new record, type **VI**, and then press TAB. The cursor moves to the PaymentType field.

6. Type **Visa**, and then press TAB to move to the next row.

7. For the next record, type **MC** in the PaymentID field, and type **MasterCard** in the PaymentType field. Press TAB after you've entered the appropriate value in each field.

8. For the last record, type **AX** in the PaymentID field, and type **American Express** in the PaymentType field.

9. Close the Datasheet view window.

10. In the database window, double-click the NumberTypes table to open the table in Datasheet view.

11. You will create seven records in the NumberTypes table. Use the values in the following table to create the necessary records:

TypeID Value	TypeDescrip Value
H1	Home (1)
H2	Home (2)
B1	Business (1)
B2	Business (2)
C1	Cell (1)
F1	Fax (1)
F2	Fax (2)

Once you've created the seven records, close the Datasheet view window.

12. In the database window, double-click the Positions table to open the table in Datasheet view.

(continued)

13. You will create four records in the Positions table. Use the values in the following table to create the necessary records:

PositionID Value	PositionType Value
DIR	Director
SUP	Supervisor
EMP	Employee
VOL	Volunteer

Once you've created the four records, close the Datasheet view window.

14. Double-click the NumberTypes table to modify the records in that table.

15. Click the New Record button on the Table Datasheet toolbar. The cursor is moved to the TypeID field of the last row (the new record).

16. Type **C2** in the TypeID field, and type **Cell (2)** in the TypeDescrip field.

17. Select the record that has a TypeID value of F2.

18. Click the Delete Record button on the Table Datasheet toolbar. You're prompted to confirm the deletion.

19. Click Yes. The row is deleted from the table.

20. For the record that contains a TypeID value of F1, click the TypeID field, and then press F2 to change to Navigation mode. This highlights the entire value.

21. Change the value by typing **FX**.

22. Close the Datasheet view window.

Project Summary

By adding values to the FormOfPayment, NumberTypes, and Positions tables, you made it possible to add the necessary values in other tables. For example, now that the NumberTypes table contains the necessary data, you can add TypeID values to the PhoneNumbers table. Keep in mind, however, that before you can add MemberID values to the PhoneNumbers table, those values must exist in the Members table. Whenever you add data to a table, you must take into account the relationships that exist among tables, as well as the constraints placed on the data by data types and table properties.

Module 7 Mastery Check

1. What information is displayed in the Datasheet view window?

2. What methods can you use to move from one field to the next?

3. Which types of fields does character data apply to?

    A. Number

    B. Text

    C. Memo

    D. Currency

4. How are fractions handled in a numerical field if the Field Size property is configured as an integer?

5. What type of value can you enter into an AutoNumber field?

6. Your field is configured with the Date/Time data type, and the Format property is configured with the Long Date option. Which values will the field accept?

    A. 815

    B. 8/15

    C. 0815

    D. 8-15

7. How do you insert a new object into an OLE Object field?

8. What are the four elements that can be included in a value in a Hyperlink field?

9. How do you enter data in a field that is configured with a lookup list?

10. How do you select consecutive records in a table?

11. Which type of field contains a check box that you can select or clear?

    A. Hyperlink

    B. AutoNumber

    C. Memo

    D. Yes/No

12. Which key can you use to switch between Navigation mode and Edit mode in the Datasheet view window?

    A. F2

    B. INSERT

    C. ENTER

    D. F10

13. How do you edit a value in a Hyperlink field?

14. You're working in Datasheet view and you're entering values into various fields. You want to change the behavior of the keyboard when you press ENTER so that the insertion point moves to the next record. What should you do?

15. How do you delete an entire value in a field?

Module 8

Finding, Sorting, and Filtering Data

CRITICAL SKILLS

8.1 Find Data in a Table

8.2 Sort Data in a Table

8.3 Filter Data in a Table

When accessing data in an Access database, you'll often find that a table contains so many records that it can be difficult to sort through those records to find the information that you need. This can be a problem, particularly when you're viewing table data in Datasheet view and all the records are displayed at one time. In order to facilitate your efforts to locate specific records in Datasheet view, Access provides a number of methods that you can use to find, sort, and filter data. In this module, I explain how you can use these methods to locate exactly the type of data that you're looking for.

As you continue to work your way through this book, you'll find that there are other ways to access the data that you need. For example, you can use queries to request specific types of information from one or more tables, or you can use forms to present the information that users need to access; however, when you're viewing data in Datasheet view, you are essentially working with all records in a table at one time, so Access makes this process easier and allows you to get at the information that you want to see.

CRITICAL SKILL
8.1 Find Data in a Table

Access provides a valuable tool for locating records in a database. The Find And Replace tool allows you to search for records based on a value within those records. For example, suppose that you want to find records in the Products table (in the Northwind database) that contain a value of Beverages in the Category field. You can use the Find And Replace tool to locate all those records that contain the Beverages value. You can even use the tool to replace that value with another value. In addition, you can search an entire table for a value, regardless of the field that contains the value.

NOTE

Access also allows you to move to specific records by using the navigation keys at the bottom of the Datasheet view window. You can use the navigation keys to move to the first record, the previous record, the next record, the last record, or the new record. You can also use the Go To commands in the Edit menu to move to the same records.

Finding Values in a Table

The Find And Replace tool is a dialog box that contains two tabs: the Find tab and the Replace tab. The Find tab, shown in Figure 8-1, provides the functionality that you need to search for records that contain a specified value. You can search for that value either within a field or within the entire table. You can also decide whether the value that you enter must match part of a field, an entire field, or only the beginning of a field.

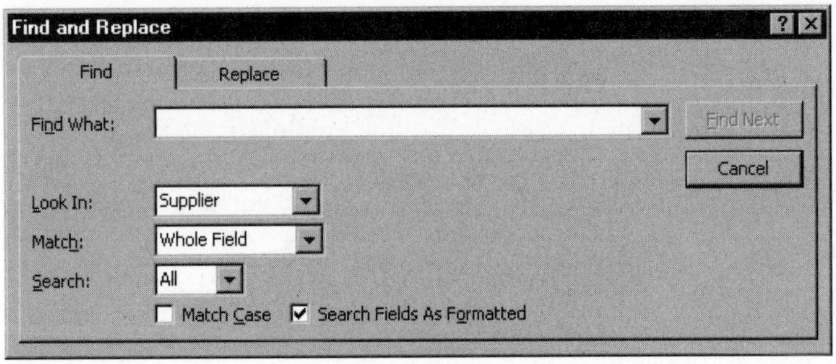

Find and Replace | ? | X

| Find | Replace |

Find What: [   ] ▼ | Find Next |

| Cancel |

Look In: Supplier ▼

Match: Whole Field ▼

Search: All ▼

☐ Match Case   ☑ Search Fields As Formatted

Figure 8-1 The Find tab of the Find And Replace dialog box

To access the Find And Replace dialog box and search for a record, you must first open the table in Datasheet view. Then select the field that you want to search (unless you plan to search the entire table) and take one of the following steps:

- Press CTRL-F

- Click the Find button on the Table Datasheet toolbar

- Click the Edit menu and then click Find

By default, the Find And Replace dialog box appears with the Find tab displayed. However, if you open the dialog box by pressing CTRL-H, the Replace tab will be displayed.

To find a specific record or records, first type the value that you're searching for in the Find What text box. When you open the Find And Replace dialog box, the Find What text box contains the value in the field (of the current record) that is selected in the Datasheet view window. If no value is selected, the last value searched for since opening Access will be displayed. If no searches were conducted since opening Access, no value is displayed.

TIP

As you can see, the Find What text box also has a drop-down list associated with it. The drop-down list contains those values that you searched for since opening Access. The most recently searched value is listed first, and the oldest searched value is listed last. You can select any value from the list for your searches, rather than having to retype a particular value.

The Look In drop-down list contains two options: the selected field (which is displayed by default) and the name of table (which allows you to search the entire table). You should select whichever option best fits your needs.

The Match drop-down list contains three options:

- **Any Part Of Field** The specified value can exist in any part of the field. For example, suppose you're searching the Title field of the Employees table in the Northwind database. If you specify the value "sales," your search will find records that contain the values Sales Manager, Sales Representative, Inside Sales Coordinator, and Vice President, Sales.

- **Whole Field** The specified value must match the entire field value. For example, if you search for the value "sales" in the Title field of the Employees table, your search will not find any records.

- **Start Of Field** The specified value must be at the beginning of the field value. For example, a search for "sales" in the Title field of the Employees table will return only rows that contain the values Sales Manager and Sales Representative.

The Search drop-down list allows you to search all records, only those records that are below the cursor's position in the table, or only those above the cursor's position. You can also select the Match Case check box if you want to search only for values that match the case of the value that you specified in the Find What text box.

One other option on the Find tab of the Find And Replace dialog box is the Search Fields As Formatted check box. You should select this option if you want to search records with values based on how they're displayed, rather than how they're actually stored in the database. For example, suppose a Date/Time value is stored as 8/10/2004 but is displayed as Tuesday, August 10, 2004. If the Search Fields As Formatted check box is selected, your search would find the value "August;" otherwise, it would not.

Locating Null and Zero-Length String Values

In most cases, when you're searching for records, your search will be based on specific values, as you saw earlier in this module. However, there might be times when you want to search for records that contain null or zero-length string values. For example, your database might include a table that tracks customer data. One field in the table might include the customers' e-mail addresses; however, the table does not contain e-mail addresses for all customers. As a result, you might decide that you want to locate those records that do not include an e-mail address. You can use the Find And Replace dialog box to locate null and zero-length string values.

To find a null value, type **null** or **is null** in the Find What text box. To find a zero-length string value, type empty double-quotes ("") in the text box. In both cases, the Search Fields As Formatted check box must be cleared, and the Match option must be set to Whole Field. You can then search for the records as you would search for any other values.

Using Wildcards in Your Searches

Up to this point, most of the Find operations that we've looked at have searched for an exact value. Even when you search on only part of the field (by setting the Match option to Any Part Of Field or to Start Of Field), the value that you specify must still be an exact match within the limitations of that Match option. However, there might be times when you want even more flexibility in your searches than the Match option provides. For example, suppose that you want to search for records that contain last names that begin with "Sch" and end with "t." You can use wildcards in your search string to locate these records.

A *wildcard* is a symbol that you can use along with other characters in a search value to find similar values. Access supports a number of wildcards that can be used individually in your search string or mixed together to add even more flexibility to your search. Table 8-1 describes each of the wildcards that you can use in the Find And Replace dialog box and provides examples of each.

To use any of the wildcards in a search, enter the search string in the Find What text box. The wildcards should be used along with regular characters in the search string, as you can see in the examples in Table 8-1. You can set the other options in the Find And Replace dialog box as you would for a search that doesn't use wildcards.

Finding and Replacing Values in a Table

Up to this point, I've discussed only the Find tab of the Find And Replace dialog box. However, the Replace tab (shown in Figure 8-2) builds on the functionality found in the Find tab by allowing you to replace values identified by your search. (If you've used the Find And Replace tool in any Office product, you should already be familiar with how the process works.)

Most of the features on the Replace tab are identical to those you saw in the Find tab. You can search for records that contain the value identified in the Find What text box. Like the Find tab, the Replace tab also allows you to identify null and zero-length string values

Wildcard	Description	Example of Search String	Example of Search Results
Asterisk (*)	Represents zero or more characters.	mix*	mix, mixed, mixing, mixture
Question mark (?)	Represents a single alphabetic character.	b?g	bag, beg, big, bog, bug
Number sign (#)	Represents a single numeric character.	13##	1301, 1345, 1399
Brackets ([ ])	Used to match the characters within the brackets.	b[ae]g	bag, beg
Exclamation point (!)	Used to match any character except those within the brackets.	b[!ae]g	big, bog, bug
Hyphen (-)	Used to designate the range of characters within the brackets. Ranges must be defined in ascending order.	a[b-d]e	abe, ace, ade

Table 8-1 Using Wildcards When Searching for Data

Ask the Expert

Q: You state that you can use wildcards in your search string to find records with values that are not an exact match. However, it's possible for some values to contain characters that Access recognizes as wildcards. How do you search for these types of values?

A: You can search for characters that would otherwise be interpreted as wildcards by enclosing those characters in brackets. This is the only way to search for most of these characters, such as the asterisk, question mark, number sign, opening bracket, and hyphen. For example, if the value that you're searching for ends in a question mark, your search string might read, "Where are you going[?]" When Access sees this search string, it ignores the brackets and searches only for the words and the question mark. You can also enclose the exclamation point and closing bracket within brackets, but it's not necessary. However, if you're searching for a set of opening and closing brackets that are together, you must enclose both of them in a set of brackets, like this: [[ ]].

and use wildcards to broaden your searches. The only options that the Replace tab includes that are not included in the Find tab are the Replace With text box, the Replace button, and the Replace All button.

The Replace With text box allows you to specify a new value for your records. For example, suppose you have a table that lists the e-mail addresses of your customers. You have decided that you no longer want the E-mail field to support null values and would rather use a default value that reads "Unknown". To make this change, simply type **null** or **is null** in the Find What text box and then type **Unknown** in the Replace With text box. If you click the Replace All button, all null values in the E-mail field will be replaced with the new value.

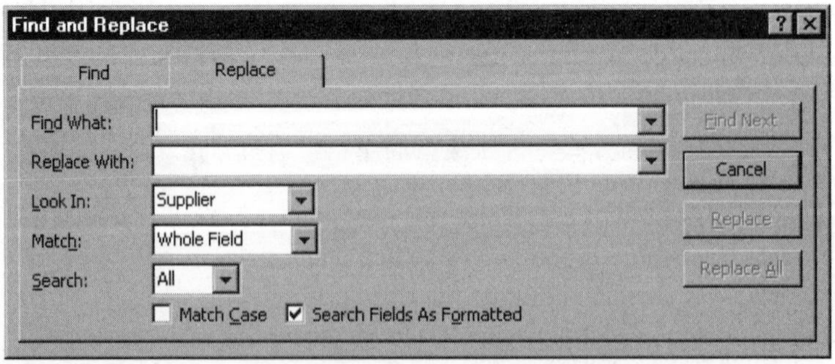

Figure 8-2 The Replace tab of the Find And Replace dialog box

You can also use the Find Next button to search for the first instance of a null value, and then you can use the Replace button to update one record at a time, rather than updating all the applicable records at once. Each time you click Replace, the selected value is replaced by the new value and the cursor moves to the next instance of null in the E-mail field.

CAUTION

Keep in mind that the Replace tab is a very powerful tool that makes it easy to update data. As a result, you can change critical data with a click of a button. Use great care when replacing a value, especially if you are using the Replace All feature. Be sure to verify the values that you enter in both the Find What text box and the Replace With text box.

Progress Check

1. What two tabs are available in the Find And Replace dialog box?

2. What methods can you use to open the Find And Replace dialog box?

3. What should you type in the Find What text box if you want to locate a null value?

CRITICAL SKILL
8.2 Sort Data in a Table

By default, records in a table are automatically sorted according to the primary key. If the primary key is a AutoNumber field, the records are sorted from the 1 value on up. If another type of field is used as the primary key, the values are sorted in ascending order (A through Z if the field is alphabetical; 1 and up if it is numerical). However, Access allows you to sort records in a table based on values in fields other than the primary key. In fact, you can sort records based on the values in one or more fields, and you can sort those values in ascending order or descending order. You can sort any fields except those configured with the OLE Object data type.

---

1. The Find tab and the Replace tab

2. You can open the dialog box by pressing CTRL-F or CTRL-H, clicking the Find button on the Table Datasheet toolbar, or clicking the Edit menu and then clicking Find.

3. You should type **null** or **is null**.

Sorting Values in a Single Field

Access makes sorting a single field very easy. Simply open the table in Datasheet view and then take one of the following actions:

- Select the field or move the cursor anywhere in the field and then click the Sort Ascending button or the Sort Descending button on the Table Datasheet toolbar.

- Select the field or move the cursor anywhere in the field, click the Records menu, point to Sort, and then click Sort Ascending or Sort Descending.

- Right-click anywhere in the field and then click Sort Ascending or Sort Descending in the shortcut menu.

Once the field has been sorted, you can simply move through the records and modify data as you have always done.

Now let's take a look at an example of a table whose records have been sorted. Figure 8-3 shows the Products table in the Northwind database. The table has been sorted according to the Supplier field. Notice that the suppliers are listed in alphabetical order (in ascending order). This means that the records are no longer listed according to the Product ID values, as they would have been by default because the Product ID field is the primary key. However, you can still scroll through the records and modify the data as you did before sorting the records.

Product ID	Product Name	Supplier	Category	Quantity Per Unit	Unit Price	Units In
39	Chartreuse verte	Aux joyeux ecclésiastiques	Beverages	750 cc per bottle	$18.00	
38	Côte de Blaye	Aux joyeux ecclésiastiques	Beverages	12 - 75 cl bottles	$263.50	
35	Steeleye Stout	Bigfoot Breweries	Beverages	24 - 12 oz bottles	$18.00	
34	Sasquatch Ale	Bigfoot Breweries	Beverages	24 - 12 oz bottles	$14.00	
67	Laughing Lumberjack Lager	Bigfoot Breweries	Beverages	24 - 12 oz bottles	$14.00	
11	Queso Cabrales	Cooperativa de Quesos 'Las Cabras'	Dairy Products	1 kg pkg.	$21.00	
12	Queso Manchego La Pastora	Cooperativa de Quesos 'Las Cabras'	Dairy Products	10 - 500 g pkgs.	$38.00	
58	Escargots de Bourgogne	Escargots Nouveaux	Seafood	24 pieces	$13.25	
2	Chang	Exotic Liquids	Beverages	24 - 12 oz bottles	$19.00	
3	Aniseed Syrup	Exotic Liquids	Condiments	12 - 550 ml bottles	$10.00	
1	Chai	Exotic Liquids	Beverages	10 boxes x 20 bags	$18.00	
62	Tarte au sucre	Forêts d'érables	Confections	48 pies	$49.30	
61	Sirop d'érable	Forêts d'érables	Condiments	24 - 500 ml bottles	$28.50	
31	Gorgonzola Telino	Formaggi Fortini s.r.l.	Dairy Products	12 - 100 g pkgs	$12.50	
32	Mascarpone Fabioli	Formaggi Fortini s.r.l.	Dairy Products	24 - 200 g pkgs.	$32.00	
72	Mozzarella di Giovanni	Formaggi Fortini s.r.l.	Dairy Products	24 - 200 g pkgs.	$34.80	
60	Camembert Pierrot	Gai pâturage	Dairy Products	15 - 300 g rounds	$34.00	
59	Raclette Courdavault	Gai pâturage	Dairy Products	5 kg pkg.	$55.00	
53	Perth Pasties	G'day, Mate	Meat/Poultry	48 pieces	$32.80	
52	Filo Mix	G'day, Mate	Grains/Cereals	16 - 2 kg boxes	$7.00	
51	Manjimup Dried Apples	G'day, Mate	Produce	50 - 300 g pkgs.	$53.00	
8	Northwoods Cranberry Sauce	Grandma Kelly's Homestead	Condiments	12 - 12 oz jars	$40.00	
7	Uncle Bob's Organic Dried Pears	Grandma Kelly's Homestead	Produce	12 - 1 lb pkgs.	$30.00	
6	Grandma's Boysenberry Spread	Grandma Kelly's Homestead	Condiments	12 - 8 oz jars	$25.00	
26	Gumbär Gummibärchen	Heli Süßwaren GmbH & Co. KG	Confections	100 - 250 g bags	$31.23	
25	NuNuCa Nuß-Nougat-Creme	Heli Süßwaren GmbH & Co. KG	Confections	20 - 450 g glasses	$14.00	
27	Schoggi Schokolade	Heli Süßwaren GmbH & Co. KG	Confections	100 - 100 g pieces	$43.90	
76	Lakkalikööri	Karkki Oy	Beverages	500 ml	$18.00	
49	Maxilaku	Karkki Oy	Confections	24 - 50 g pkgs.	$20.00	

Record: 1 of 77

Figure 8-3 The Products table sorted according to the Supplier field

8

Finding, Sorting, and Filtering Data

NOTE
You can save the sort order of a table simply by saving the table. Whenever you save a table, you're preserving the most current sort order. However, if you don't want to preserve the sort order, don't save the table. If you want to save the table for other reasons, simply re-sort on the primary key field in ascending order and the table will be returned to its default sort order.

Sorting Values in Multiple Fields

Access also allows you to sort a table based on more than one field. Sorting values in multiple fields will work only if the fields are adjacent in the table. In addition, the fields are always sorted from left to right. This means that the first field selected is sorted first, and the next field is then sorted based on the first column. Let's take a look at Figure 8-4 for an example of how this works.

The table has been sorted based on the Supplier field and the Category field. The Supplier field is sorted first. As you can see, the values are listed in ascending alphabetical order. The Category field is then sorted. For example, if you take a look at the rows that contain a Supplier value of Exotic Liquids, you can see that the Category values are grouped together for the Beverages value and the Condiments value.

Product ID	Product Name	Supplier	Category	Quantity Per Unit	Unit Price	Units In
39	Chartreuse verte	Aux joyeux ecclésiastiques	Beverages	750 cc per bottle	$18.00	
38	Côte de Blaye	Aux joyeux ecclésiastiques	Beverages	12 - 75 cl bottles	$263.50	
35	Steeleye Stout	Bigfoot Breweries	Beverages	24 - 12 oz bottles	$18.00	
34	Sasquatch Ale	Bigfoot Breweries	Beverages	24 - 12 oz bottles	$14.00	
67	Laughing Lumberjack Lager	Bigfoot Breweries	Beverages	24 - 12 oz bottles	$14.00	
11	Queso Cabrales	Cooperativa de Quesos 'Las Cabras'	Dairy Products	1 kg pkg.	$21.00	
12	Queso Manchego La Pastora	Cooperativa de Quesos 'Las Cabras'	Dairy Products	10 - 500 g pkgs.	$38.00	
58	Escargots de Bourgogne	Escargots Nouveaux	Seafood	24 pieces	$13.25	
2	Chang	Exotic Liquids	Beverages	24 - 12 oz bottles	$19.00	
1	Chai	Exotic Liquids	Beverages	10 boxes x 20 bags	$18.00	
3	Aniseed Syrup	Exotic Liquids	Condiments	12 - 550 ml bottles	$10.00	
61	Sirop d'érable	Forêts d'érables	Condiments	24 - 500 ml bottles	$28.50	
62	Tarte au sucre	Forêts d'érables	Confections	48 pies	$49.30	
31	Gorgonzola Telino	Formaggi Fortini s.r.l.	Dairy Products	12 - 100 g pkgs	$12.50	
32	Mascarpone Fabioli	Formaggi Fortini s.r.l.	Dairy Products	24 - 200 g pkgs.	$32.00	
72	Mozzarella di Giovanni	Formaggi Fortini s.r.l.	Dairy Products	24 - 200 g pkgs.	$34.80	
60	Camembert Pierrot	Gai pâturage	Dairy Products	15 - 300 g rounds	$34.00	
59	Raclette Courdavault	Gai pâturage	Dairy Products	5 kg pkg.	$55.00	
52	Filo Mix	G'day, Mate	Grains/Cereals	16 - 2 kg boxes	$7.00	
53	Perth Pasties	G'day, Mate	Meat/Poultry	48 pieces	$32.80	
51	Manjimup Dried Apples	G'day, Mate	Produce	50 - 300 g pkgs.	$53.00	
8	Northwoods Cranberry Sauce	Grandma Kelly's Homestead	Condiments	12 - 12 oz jars	$40.00	
6	Grandma's Boysenberry Spread	Grandma Kelly's Homestead	Condiments	12 - 8 oz jars	$25.00	
7	Uncle Bob's Organic Dried Pears	Grandma Kelly's Homestead	Produce	12 - 1 lb pkgs.	$30.00	
26	Gumbär Gummibärchen	Heli Süßwaren GmbH & Co. KG	Confections	100 - 250 g bags	$31.23	
25	NuNuCa Nuß-Nougat-Creme	Heli Süßwaren GmbH & Co. KG	Confections	20 - 450 g glasses	$14.00	
27	Schoggi Schokolade	Heli Süßwaren GmbH & Co. KG	Confections	100 - 100 g pieces	$43.90	
76	Lakkalikööri	Karkki Oy	Beverages	500 ml	$18.00	
50	Valkoinen suklaa	Karkki Oy	Confections	12 - 100 g bars	$16.25	

Record: 1 of 77

Figure 8-4 The Products table sorted according to the Supplier and Category fields

To sort multiple fields in a table, open the table in Datasheet view and then select the participating fields. To select the fields, click the first field name at the top of the column, keep the left mouse button depressed, slide the mouse over to the next column or columns that you want to include in the sort, and then release the mouse button. After you've selected the fields, take one of the following actions:

● Click the Sort Ascending button or the Sort Descending button on the Table Datasheet toolbar.

● Click the Records menu, point to Sort, and then click Sort Ascending or Sort Descending.

NOTE

You cannot sort multiple columns by right-clicking one of the fields. When you right-click a field, only that field is selected, so only that field will be sorted.

Experiment with selecting multiple columns and sorting the values in ascending and descending order. Because you're affecting the sort order only, your changes have no impact on the data stored in the database.

Progress Check

1. How are records in a table sorted by default?

2. How many adjacent fields can you sort in a table?

CRITICAL SKILL
8.3 Filter Data in a Table

When you use the Find And Replace tool to locate a specific value in a table, you're searching through all the records to find that value. Even when you sort field data, you're still working with all the records in the table. However, Access allows you to filter data so that you can view only a subset of the records. This is particularly useful in large tables in which you want to view records that contain specific information.

For example, suppose that you have a table that tracks customer information. This information includes the city in which the customer resides. If you want, you can filter the

---

1. By default, records in a table are automatically sorted according to the primary key.
2. Two or more

records so that you're viewing only the records of customers who live in a specific city, thus removing all other records from view. Filtering data does not affect the data stored in the table, but it does make it easier to view specific data.

Access provides several methods for filtering data:

- Filtering by selection, in which you simply select a value in a field
- Filtering by excluded selection, in which you select the value to be filtered out
- Filtering by form, in which you identify field values that will be returned

In addition to these options, you can create an advanced filter that provides more flexibility than the other types of filters, allowing you to refine your filters to an even greater degree so that you can view records with very specific data.

Filtering by Selection

The easiest way to filter data is to filter by selection. When using this method to filter data, you simply select the value on which you want to base your filter and then take one of the following steps:

- Click the Filter By Selection button on the Table Datasheet toolbar.
- Right-click the value and then click Filter By Selection in the shortcut menu.
- Click the Records menu, point to Filter, and then click Filter By Selection.

The filter is immediately applied to the table. As a result, only those records that meet the filter criteria are displayed, although all the records still exist in the table.

Let's take a look at an example to demonstrate how this works. Suppose that you want to filter data in the Products table of the Northwind database. When you open the table in Datasheet view, all records are included. If you want to view only those records that include a Category value of Beverages, you would select one of the Beverages values in the Category field. It does not matter which record you select. Once you select the field and apply the filter, only the Beverages records are displayed, as shown in Figure 8-5.

TIP

When you're viewing filtered data in Datasheet view—as opposed to viewing the data without a filter—the Datasheet view window displays "FLTR" at the bottom of the window, and the navigation bar adds the word "(Filtered)" to the display. In addition, the Apply Filter button on the Table Datasheet toolbar changes to the Remove Filter button.

	Product ID	Product Name	Supplier	Category	Quantity Per Unit	Unit Price	U
	1	Chai	Exotic Liquids	Beverages	10 boxes x 20 bags	$18.00	
	2	Chang	Exotic Liquids	Beverages	24 - 12 oz bottles	$19.00	
	24	Guaraná Fantástica	Refrescos Americanas LTDA	Beverages	12 - 355 ml cans	$4.50	
	34	Sasquatch Ale	Bigfoot Breweries	Beverages	24 - 12 oz bottles	$14.00	
	35	Steeleye Stout	Bigfoot Breweries	Beverages	24 - 12 oz bottles	$18.00	
	38	Côte de Blaye	Aux joyeux ecclésiastiques	Beverages	12 - 75 cl bottles	$263.50	
	39	Chartreuse verte	Aux joyeux ecclésiastiques	Beverages	750 cc per bottle	$18.00	
	43	Ipoh Coffee	Leka Trading	Beverages	16 - 500 g tins	$46.00	
	67	Laughing Lumberjack Lager	Bigfoot Breweries	Beverages	24 - 12 oz bottles	$14.00	
	70	Outback Lager	Pavlova, Ltd.	Beverages	24 - 355 ml bottles	$15.00	
	75	Rhönbräu Klosterbier	Plutzer Lebensmittelgroßmärkte AG	Beverages	24 - 0.5 l bottles	$7.75	
	76	Lakkalikööri	Karkki Oy	Beverages	500 ml	$18.00	
*	(AutoNumber)					$0.00	

Record: 1 of 12 (Filtered)

Figure 8-5 The Products table filtered by selection

Once you've applied a filter, you can sort and modify records as you normally would in the Datasheet view window. When you no longer want the data filtered, you can take one of the following steps to remove the filter:

- Click the Remove Filter button on the Table Datasheet toolbar.
- Right-click any value and then click Remove Filter/Sort in the shortcut menu.
- Click the Records menu and then click Remove Filter/Sort.

After you remove a filter, you can re-apply that filter at any time. The most recent filter created is always the one that is applied to a table. To re-apply a filter, do one of the following:

- Click the Apply Filter button on the Table Datasheet toolbar.
- Click the Records menu and then click Apply Filter/Sort.

By using the Apply Filter and Remove Filter options, you can toggle back and forth between viewing filtered records and viewing all records.

Filtering by Excluded Selection

The process of filtering by excluding a selection is similar to filtering by selection. The main difference is that you're identifying the records (based on the specified value) that should be excluded from view, rather than included. To filter by excluding a selected value, select the value that you want to base your filter on, and then do one of the following:

- Right-click the value and then click Filter Excluding Selection in the shortcut menu.
- Click the Records menu, point to Filter, and then click Filter Excluding Selection.

Your view will now include only those records that do not contain the excluded value. For example, if you excluded the Beverages value from the Category field in the Products table (of the Northwind database), your table view would be similar to what is shown in Figure 8-6.

Ask the Expert

Q: You state that, when creating a filter by selection in Datasheet view, you must select the value on which you want to base your filter. What happens if you select only part of the value, rather than the entire value?

A: Normally, when you select a value, you select the entire value (in Navigation mode) or place the cursor's insertion point somewhere within the value (in Edit mode). As a result, the filter criteria is based on an exact match with that value. However, if you select only part of that value, the filter criteria changes. For example, if the part of the value that you select includes the first character, the values returned must begin with the selected character. This would be similar to setting the Match option in the Find And Replace dialog box to Start Of Field. However, if the part of the selected value does not include the first character, the values returned can have matching characters anywhere within those fields, as you saw with the Any Part Of Field setting in the Match option of the Find And Replace dialog box.

	Product ID	Product Name	Supplier	Category	Quantity Per Unit	Unit Price	U
	3	Aniseed Syrup	Exotic Liquids	Condiments	12 - 550 ml bottles	$10.00	
	4	Chef Anton's Cajun Seasoning	New Orleans Cajun Delights	Condiments	48 - 6 oz jars	$22.00	
	5	Chef Anton's Gumbo Mix	New Orleans Cajun Delights	Condiments	36 boxes	$21.35	
	6	Grandma's Boysenberry Spread	Grandma Kelly's Homestead	Condiments	12 - 8 oz jars	$25.00	
	7	Uncle Bob's Organic Dried Pears	Grandma Kelly's Homestead	Produce	12 - 1 lb pkgs.	$30.00	
	8	Northwoods Cranberry Sauce	Grandma Kelly's Homestead	Condiments	12 - 12 oz jars	$40.00	
	9	Mishi Kobe Niku	Tokyo Traders	Meat/Poultry	18 - 500 g pkgs.	$97.00	
	10	Ikura	Tokyo Traders	Seafood	12 - 200 ml jars	$31.00	
	11	Queso Cabrales	Cooperativa de Quesos 'Las Cabras'	Dairy Products	1 kg pkg.	$21.00	
	12	Queso Manchego La Pastora	Cooperativa de Quesos 'Las Cabras'	Dairy Products	10 - 500 g pkgs.	$38.00	
	13	Konbu	Mayumi's	Seafood	2 kg box	$6.00	
	14	Tofu	Mayumi's	Produce	40 - 100 g pkgs.	$23.25	
	15	Genen Shouyu	Mayumi's	Condiments	24 - 250 ml bottles	$15.50	
	16	Pavlova	Pavlova, Ltd.	Confections	32 - 500 g boxes	$17.45	
	17	Alice Mutton	Pavlova, Ltd.	Meat/Poultry	20 - 1 kg tins	$39.00	
	18	Carnarvon Tigers	Pavlova, Ltd.	Seafood	16 kg pkg.	$62.50	
	19	Teatime Chocolate Biscuits	Specialty Biscuits, Ltd.	Confections	10 boxes x 12 pieces	$9.20	
	20	Sir Rodney's Marmalade	Specialty Biscuits, Ltd.	Confections	30 gift boxes	$81.00	
	21	Sir Rodney's Scones	Specialty Biscuits, Ltd.	Confections	24 pkgs. x 4 pieces	$10.00	
	22	Gustaf's Knäckebröd	PB Knäckebröd AB	Grains/Cereals	24 - 500 g pkgs.	$21.00	
	23	Tunnbröd	PB Knäckebröd AB	Grains/Cereals	12 - 250 g pkgs.	$9.00	
	25	NuNuCa Nuß-Nougat-Creme	Heli Süßwaren GmbH & Co. KG	Confections	20 - 450 g glasses	$14.00	
	26	Gumbär Gummibärchen	Heli Süßwaren GmbH & Co. KG	Confections	100 - 250 g bags	$31.23	
	27	Schoggi Schokolade	Heli Süßwaren GmbH & Co. KG	Confections	100 - 100 g pieces	$43.90	
	28	Rössle Sauerkraut	Plutzer Lebensmittelgroßmärkte AG	Produce	25 - 825 g cans	$45.60	
	29	Thüringer Rostbratwurst	Plutzer Lebensmittelgroßmärkte AG	Meat/Poultry	50 bags x 30 sausgs.	$123.79	
	30	Nord-Ost Matjeshering	Nord-Ost-Fisch Handelsgesellschaft mbH	Seafood	10 - 200 g glasses	$25.89	
	31	Gorgonzola Telino	Formaggi Fortini s.r.l.	Dairy Products	12 - 100 g pkgs	$12.50	
	32	Mascarpone Fabioli	Formaggi Fortini s.r.l.	Dairy Products	24 - 200 g pkgs.	$32.00	
	33	Geitost	Norske Meierier	Dairy Products	500 g	$2.50	

Products : Table

Record: 1 of 65 (Filtered)

Figure 8-6 The Products table filtered by exclusion of the selected value

Filtering by Form

When filtering by form, you can include more than one field in your filter criteria. To apply this type of filter, you must use the Filter By Form window, shown in Figure 8-7. The Filter by Form window allows you to select a value from each field in a table.

To open the Filter By Form window, first open the table in Datasheet view, and then take one of the following steps:

- Click the Filter By Form button on the Table Datasheet toolbar.
- Click the Records menu, point to Filter, and then click Filter By Form.

When the Filter By Form windows appears, you're ready to create your filter. In some cases, if a filter was previously defined for the table, the filter criteria will be displayed in the appropriate fields. If necessary, click the Clear Grid button on the Filter/Sort toolbar to remove the previous criteria. You can also remove any of the previous filter elements simply by deleting them.

When the Filter By Form window is ready, select a value for each field that you want to include in the filter criteria. For example, suppose you first select the Beverages value in the Category field, and you then want to select the Exotic Liquids value for the Supplier field. Click the down arrow associated with that field (as shown in Figure 8-7), and then select the value. Repeat this process for any necessary additional fields.

Once you've defined the filter criteria, click the Apply Filter button on the Filter/Sort toolbar. This closes the Filter By Form window and displays the table data in Datasheet view. However, only the records that meet the filter criteria are displayed, as shown in Figure 8-8. The filter is based on the Exotic Liquids value in the Supplier field and the Beverages value in the Category field.

You can use expressions in your search criteria to further refine your filter. As you'll recall from Module 4, an expression is a combination of symbols that create a formula used to produce a specific result. For example, your criteria for a number field can be >10, which means that any records included in the view must have a value greater than 10 for that specific field. (For a complete discussion of expressions, see Module 11.)

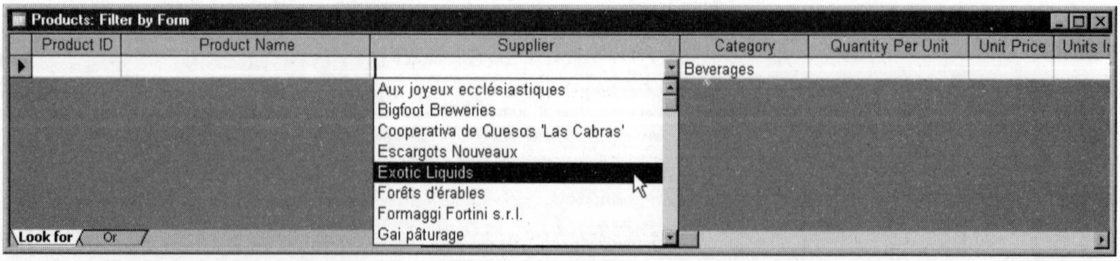

Figure 8-7 The Filter By Form window for the Products table in the Northwind database

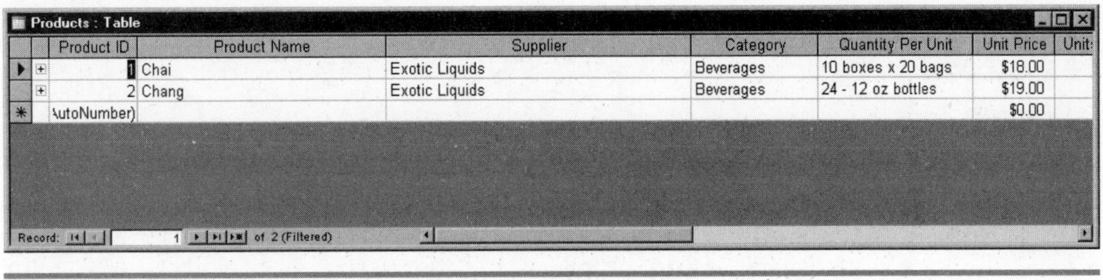

Product ID	Product Name	Supplier	Category	Quantity Per Unit	Unit Price	Unit:
1 Chai		Exotic Liquids	Beverages	10 boxes x 20 bags	$18.00	
2 Chang		Exotic Liquids	Beverages	24 - 12 oz bottles	$19.00	
AutoNumber)					$0.00	

Record: 1 of 2 (Filtered)

Figure 8-8 The Products table filtered with the Filter By Form window

In addition to expressions, you can use wildcards in Text and Memo fields, just as you use wildcards in the Find And Replace dialog box.

TIP

A simple way to create a filter on one field is to use the Filter For option in the shortcut menu. In this case, you simply right-click the field, enter the appropriate value to the right of the Filter For option in the shortcut menu, and then press ENTER. The filtered data is automatically displayed. You can then view the filter that you created in the Filter By Form window.

Creating Advanced Filters

Although the types of filters that we've looked at so far should meet most of your needs, there might be times when you want to refine your filters even further. Access allows you to create filters that are more flexible and comprehensive than those created by selection or form. To create advanced filters, you must use the Filter window, shown in Figure 8-9, and define the filter and sort criteria for each applicable field.

NOTE

If you applied any filters to the table before saving the table, the Filter window might also display associated lookup tables, depending on the filter criteria and the configuration of the table when it was last saved.

To access the Filter window, click the Records menu, point to Filter, and then click Advanced Filter/Sort. When the Filter window appears, you'll see a graphical representation of the table and a grid that is used to define the criteria for the participating fields. In some cases, if a filter or sort order has already been specified for the table, the criteria will be displayed in the grid. Before you enter new criteria, click the Clear Grid button on the Filter/Sort toolbar to

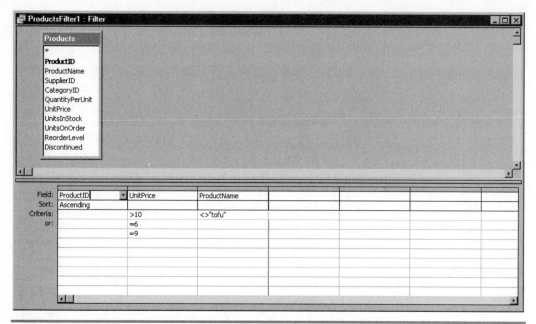

Figure 8-9 Using the Filter window to filter the Products table

clear the previous criteria. You can also delete the criteria elements individually, which is useful if you want to preserve part of the filter.

Once the Filter window is ready, you can begin to define the new filter and sort criteria for each participating field. To create the criteria, you must first identify the participating field within the grid. There are several methods that you can use to define a field:

● Drag the field from the table to the Field cell of the first available column.

● Select the Field cell in the first available column and then double-click the field in the table.

● Select the down arrow in the Field cell of the first available column and then click the appropriate field.

Once you've identified the participating field, you can define a sort order for the values in that field. As you saw earlier in the module, a sort order can be ascending or descending. To define a sort order, click the down arrow for the Sort cell in the participating field, and then click Ascending or Descending in the drop-down list. If you want to clear a defined sort order, click the (not sorted) option in the drop-down list or simply delete the current sort order. You can define a sort order whether or not you define filter criteria. In addition, you can define filter criteria without defining a sort order.

As you would expect, defining filter criteria is more complex than defining a sort order. Unlike filtering by selection or form, filtering in the Filter window provides no values to choose from. You must type in the values that you want included in your criteria. In addition, the Filter window allows you to define more than one condition for each field. For example, in Figure 8-9, three conditions are defined for the UnitPrice field. For a record to be included in the table view when the filter is applied, the UnitPrice value for that record must meet one of three conditions. In other words, the unit price must be greater than $10.00, equal to $6.00, or equal to $9.00. In addition, based on the criteria defined for the ProductName field (also shown in Figure 8-9), records with a UnitPrice value greater than 10 cannot include a ProductName value of Tofu. Also, when the filter is applied, the records in the view are sorted in ascending order according to the ProductID field.

The view that the filter shown in Figure 8-9 would generate is shown in Figure 8-10. Notice that the view does not include a row for the record that contains a Product ID value of 14. This is because that record contains a Product Name value of Tofu. In addition, no records are included that have a UnitPrice value that is not greater than 10, unless the value is equal to 6 or 9, as is the case with the records that have Product ID values of 13 and 23, respectively.

As you can see, the Filter window allows you to create complex filters that are useful in many different situations. Keep in mind, however, that not all filters need to be this extensive (although some may be far more extensive). In most cases, creating a filter by selection or by form will be the easiest solution.

Product ID	Product Name	Supplier	Category	Quantity Per Unit	Unit Price	Units
1	Chai	Exotic Liquids	Beverages	10 boxes x 20 bags	$18.00	
2	Chang	Exotic Liquids	Beverages	24 - 12 oz bottles	$19.00	
4	Chef Anton's Cajun Seasoning	New Orleans Cajun Delights	Condiments	48 - 6 oz jars	$22.00	
5	Chef Anton's Gumbo Mix	New Orleans Cajun Delights	Condiments	36 boxes	$21.35	
6	Grandma's Boysenberry Spread	Grandma Kelly's Homestead	Condiments	12 - 8 oz jars	$25.00	
7	Uncle Bob's Organic Dried Pears	Grandma Kelly's Homestead	Produce	12 - 1 lb pkgs.	$30.00	
8	Northwoods Cranberry Sauce	Grandma Kelly's Homestead	Condiments	12 - 12 oz jars	$40.00	
9	Mishi Kobe Niku	Tokyo Traders	Meat/Poultry	18 - 500 g pkgs.	$97.00	
10	Ikura	Tokyo Traders	Seafood	12 - 200 ml jars	$31.00	
11	Queso Cabrales	Cooperativa de Quesos 'Las Cabras'	Dairy Products	1 kg pkg.	$21.00	
12	Queso Manchego La Pastora	Cooperativa de Quesos 'Las Cabras'	Dairy Products	10 - 500 g pkgs.	$38.00	
13	Konbu	Mayumi's	Seafood	2 kg box	$6.00	
15	Genen Shouyu	Mayumi's	Condiments	24 - 250 ml bottles	$15.50	
16	Pavlova	Pavlova, Ltd.	Confections	32 - 500 g boxes	$17.45	
17	Alice Mutton	Pavlova, Ltd.	Meat/Poultry	20 - 1 kg tins	$39.00	
18	Carnarvon Tigers	Pavlova, Ltd.	Seafood	16 kg pkg.	$62.50	
20	Sir Rodney's Marmalade	Specialty Biscuits, Ltd.	Confections	30 gift boxes	$81.00	
22	Gustaf's Knäckebröd	PB Knäckebröd AB	Grains/Cereals	24 - 500 g pkgs.	$21.00	
23	Tunnbröd	PB Knäckebröd AB	Grains/Cereals	12 - 250 g pkgs.	$9.00	
25	NuNuCa Nuß-Nougat-Creme	Heli Süßwaren GmbH & Co. KG	Confections	20 - 450 g glasses	$14.00	
26	Gumbär Gummibärchen	Heli Süßwaren GmbH & Co. KG	Confections	100 - 250 g bags	$31.23	
27	Schoggi Schokolade	Heli Süßwaren GmbH & Co. KG	Confections	100 - 100 g pieces	$43.90	
28	Rössle Sauerkraut	Plutzer Lebensmittelgroßmärkte AG	Produce	25 - 825 g cans	$45.60	
29	Thüringer Rostbratwurst	Plutzer Lebensmittelgroßmärkte AG	Meat/Poultry	50 bags x 30 sausgs.	$123.79	
30	Nord-Ost Matjeshering	Nord-Ost-Fisch Handelsgesellschaft mbH	Seafood	10 - 200 g glasses	$25.89	
31	Gorgonzola Telino	Formaggi Fortini s.r.l.	Dairy Products	12 - 100 g pkgs	$12.50	
32	Mascarpone Fabioli	Formaggi Fortini s.r.l.	Dairy Products	24 - 200 g pkgs.	$32.00	
34	Sasquatch Ale	Bigfoot Breweries	Beverages	24 - 12 oz bottles	$14.00	
35	Steeleye Stout	Bigfoot Breweries	Beverages	24 - 12 oz bottles	$18.00	

Record: 1 of 64 (Filtered)

Figure 8-10 The Products table filtered according to the Unit Price and Product Name fields

NOTE

Though filters can be fairly sophisticated, queries are an even more flexible and comprehensive method for viewing data in a table. Queries allow you to link data with other tables and can be very specific, allowing you to focus on exactly the type of data that you want to view. In addition, a query is an object separate from the table, so you can create as many queries as necessary to provide you with exactly the type of information you need. In fact, you can save a form filter or an advanced filter as a query simply by clicking the Save As Query button on the Filter/Sort toolbar. Queries are discussed in more detail in Modules 10 and 11.

Project 8-1 Finding, Sorting, and Filtering Data

In this module, you learned how to find and replace data, sort the records in a table based on one or more fields, and filter data so that you can view a specific subset of records. You will now perform many of these functions on the Products table of the Northwind database. (You'll be using a Northwind table, rather than a table from the consumer advocacy database, because so far you've added very little data to the consumer advocacy tables.) You won't be changing any data in the Products table, but you will search for specific values, sort data, and create several filters.

Step by Step

1. If they're not already open, open Access and then open the Northwind.mdb database file.

2. Verify that the Tables object is selected in the database window, and then double-click the Products table. The Datasheet view window appears and displays the records in the Products table.

3. Select one of the values in the Category field. You can tab to the value or click within the value.

4. Click the Find button on the Table Datasheet toolbar. The Find And Replace dialog box appears, with the Find tab selected.

5. In the Find What text box, type **Produce**, and then click Find Next. The first occurrence of Produce is selected, and the record that contains that value becomes the current record, as indicated by the arrow at the beginning of the record.

6. Click Find Next once more. The next instance of Produce is selected, and that record becomes the current record.

7. Delete or highlight the value in the Find What text box, and then type **queso**. In the Look In drop-down list, click Products : Table. In the Match drop-down list, click Any Part Of Field.

8. Click Find Next. The first instance of Queso is selected, and the record with a Product ID value of 11 becomes the current record.

9. Click Find Next once more. The next instance of Queso is selected, which is in the same record but a different field.

10. Click Cancel to close the Find And Replace dialog box. You're returned to the Datasheet view window.

11. Select the Supplier field, and then click the Sort Ascending button on the Table Datasheet toolbar. The records are sorted according to the supplier names.

12. Select both the Supplier field and the Category field, and then click the Sort Ascending button on the Table Datasheet toolbar. The records are first sorted by the Supplier field and then by the Category field.

13. Sort the table in ascending order by the Product ID field.

14. Select the Produce value in the Category field of any record.

15. Click the Filter By Selection button on the Table Datasheet toolbar. The filter is applied, and only records with a Category value of Produce are displayed.

16. Click the Remove Filter button on the Table Datasheet toolbar. The filter is removed and all records are displayed.

17. Select the Beverages value in the Category field of any record.

18. Click the Records menu, point to Filter, and then click Filter Excluding Selection. The filter is applied and all records that contain a Category value of Beverages are removed from view.

19. Click the Remove Filter button on the Table Datasheet toolbar. The filter is removed and all records are displayed.

20. Click the Filter By Form button on the Table Datasheet toolbar. The Filter By Form window appears.

21. Click the down arrow in the Supplier field to open the drop-down list, and then click Exotic Liquids.

22. Click the down arrow in the Category field to open the drop-down list, and then click Beverages.

23. Click the Apply Filter button on the Filter/Sort toolbar. The Filter By Form window closes, and two records are displayed.

(continued)

24. Click the Remove Filter button on the Table Datasheet toolbar. The filter is removed and all records are displayed.

25. Click the Records menu, point to Filter, and then click Advanced Filter/Sort. The Filter window appears, displaying the Products table and two related lookup tables.

26. Resize the Filter window so that the entire Products table and criteria grid are displayed. Do not worry about the lookup tables at this time.

27. Click the Clear Grid button the Filter/Sort toolbar. The grid is cleared of any criteria elements that were previously defined.

28. Select the UnitPrice field from the Products table and drag it to the Field cell in the first row of the first column.

29. In the Criteria cell of that column, type **<10**.

30. Select the UnitsInStock field from the Products table and drag it to the Field cell in the first row of the second column.

31. In the Criteria cell of that column, type **>20**.

32. Select the ProductName field from the Products table and drag it to the Field cell in the first row of the third column.

33. In the Sort cell of that column, click Ascending in the drop-down list.

34. Click the Apply Filter button on the Filter/Sort toolbar. Records with a unit price less than $10.00 and a unit amount greater than 20 are displayed. The records are also sorted by the name of the product.

35. Click the Remove Filter button on the Table Datasheet toolbar. The filter is removed and all records are displayed.

36. Close the Products table, without saving changes to the table.

Project Summary

In this project, you searched the Products table for records that contained specific values. You also sorted that table based on the values in one field and in two fields. You then created four filters, one based on selection, one on exclusion, one by form, and one with advanced settings. You can use any of these methods for any table in an Access database. The more data that a table contains, the more useful these tools become.

Module 8 Mastery Check

1. What option should you select in the Find And Replace dialog box if you want to search the entire table, rather than one field?

2. What options are available in the Match drop-down list in the Find And Replace dialog box?

3. In what circumstances should you select the Search Fields As Formatted check box in the Find And Replace dialog box?

4. What should you type in the Find What text box of the Find And Replace dialog box if you want to find a zero-length string value?

   A. Null

   B. Is Null

   C. Single-quotes ('')

   D. Double-quotes ("")

5. You're using the Find And Replace dialog box to search for a customer name. You know the first three letters of the last name (Bur) but do not know the full last name or how many letters are in the name. What should you type in the Find What dialog box?

   A. Bur?

   B. Bur#

   C. Bur*

   D. Bur!

6. What is the purpose of the Replace With text box on the Replace tab of the Find And Replace dialog box?

7. How is a table sorted by default if the primary key is not an AutoNumber field?

8. Which types of fields does Access allow you to sort?

   A. Text

   B. Number

   C. AutoNumber

   D. OLE Object

9. You're creating a filter on the Employees table in the Northwind database. You want to filter out all records except those records with a Last Name value of Fuller. Which filter method is the easiest to use in this situation?

   A. Filter by excluded selection

   B. Filter by selection

   C. Filter by using advanced options

   D. Filter by form

10. How do you remove a filter from a table?

11. How does filtering by selection differ from filtering by excluding a selection?

12. You're using the Filter By Form window to create a filter on a table. How do you define the filter criteria for that table?

13. In addition to field values, what other elements can you include in your criteria in the Filter By Form window?

14. What information is included in the Filter window that is used for advanced filters?

15. What information can you define for each field in the Filter window?

Module 9

Importing, Exporting, and Linking Data

CRITICAL SKILLS

9.1   Import Data into Your Database

9.2   Link Data to an External Data Source

9.3   Export Data out of Your Database

A s you have learned, one of the main functions of an Access database—and the data-driven application that supports the database—is to allow you to store and manipulate data in a way that ensures the integrity of that data. Regardless of where that data originates, how the data is used, or where the data is sent, the information within the database must be reliable and consistent.

In some cases, the Access application is a self-contained unit in that data is added directly to the tables through the Datasheet view window or through a form and retrieved directly from the database without the use of outside applications and files. However, in many cases, you will need to use data from outside the database or send data to outside sources. For this reason, Access supports the ability to add data to your database by importing from or linking to various data sources. In addition, you can export data to a number of types of external files and data sources, depending on how you want to export that data. In this module, you'll learn how to import into, link to, and export from various types of data sources. The data sources include not only other Access databases, but dBase databases, Excel spreadsheets, text files, and Extensible Markup Language (XML) files.

Import Data into Your Database

The process of importing data can often be essential to your application. If it is done properly, it will allow you to easily and accurately populate the tables in your database. When you import data, you're copying the data from an outside source into a table in your database. Often a new table must be created during the import process in order to accommodate the imported data, but in some cases you can copy the data into an existing table, depending on the source of that data.

Access allows you to import data from a number of different types of data sources, including other Access databases. (For a complete list of the supported data source types, see Access Help.) In this section, we'll look at how to import data from several of those data sources. The import process is, for the most part, similar from one data source to the next, although there are some differences. However, Access carefully walks you through the process of importing data, so once you learn how to import data from one data source, you can usually adapt easily to other data sources.

Importing Data from an Access Database

There is probably no easier type of data to import than Access data. In fact, when you perform an import operation with an external Access database, you're actually importing a data object. For example, if you were to import customer data from the Northwind database into your database, you would be importing the entire Customers table, not just the data within the table. As a result, you would end up with a table named Customers in your database.

NOTE

If you were to import the Customers table and your database already included a table named Customers, the imported table would be assigned a new name, such as Customers1.

You can import any data object from an Access database, including tables, queries, forms, reports, pages, macros, and modules. If you import a table and want to use that data in another table that already exists in your database, you can run a query that adds the data from the imported table to the original table. You can then delete the imported table. (Queries are discussed in detail in Modules 10 and 11.)

To import an object from an Access database into your database, take the following steps:

1. Open your database file.

2. Click the File menu, point to Get External Data, and then click Import. The Import dialog box appears, as shown in Figure 9-1. The Import dialog box allows you to specify the type of data source and to navigate to the appropriate file. By default, Microsoft Office Access is selected as the data source, unless you have imported data from another type of data source since opening Access.

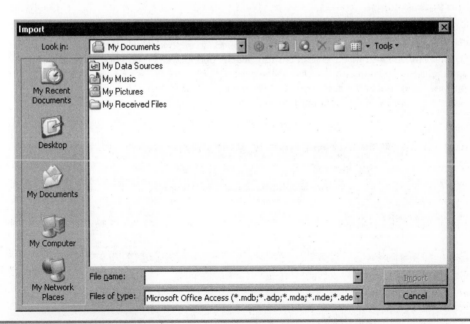

Figure 9-1 The Import dialog box

Importing, Exporting, and Linking Data

3. Locate and select the file, and then click Import. The Import Objects dialog box appears, as shown in Figure 9-2. The Import Objects dialog box lists all the objects in the target database. The objects are organized according to object types, one object type for each tab.

4. For each object type, select the objects that you want to import into your database. You can select any object from any tab. For example, you can select the Customers table and Employees table from the Tables tab and the Employee Sales By Country query from the Queries tab.

5. After you select all the objects that you want to import, click OK. The objects are added to your database. You can then modify the object properties and data as you would for any other object in your database.

If you import a table that contains a lookup field or a foreign key to another table, you will need to import the applicable tables as well as the referencing table itself, otherwise you'll receive an error message when you try to open the table in Datasheet view. However, if you do not plan to import any supporting tables, you can simply modify the table properties to eliminate the dependencies on external data.

TIP

You can modify the import settings when you import an Access object. When the Import Objects dialog box appears, click the Options button to expand the dialog box. You can then set options related to relationships, menus and toolbars, and import/export specifications. You can also determine whether to import a table definition and data, or only the definition. In addition, you can determine whether to import a query object as a query or as a table that contains the results of running that query.

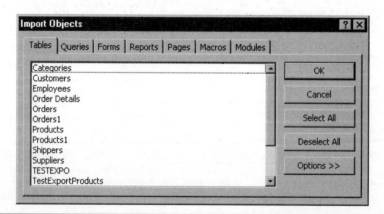

Figure 9-2 The Import Objects dialog box

Importing Data from a dBase Database

You might find that a database from a source other than Access contains information that you want to import into your database. Fortunately, Access allows you to import data from a variety of data files, including dBase, Lotus, and Paradox. The process used to import data from each data source is very similar, although we'll be looking specifically at importing data from a dBase file. When you import data from one of these types of database, you must identify the data source and navigate to the correct file. Just as with importing from Access, the data is added to the database as a table object. Access automatically assigns a name to the new table, based on the name of the database file.

Many of the steps that you use to import data from a dBase file are basically the same as those for importing a table from an Access database. To import dBase data, take the following steps:

1. Open your database file.

2. Click the File menu, point to Get External Data, and then click Import. The Import dialog box appears (the same dialog box as is shown in Figure 9-1).

3. In the Files Of Type drop-down list, select dBASE 5 (*.dbf), navigate to the dBase file, and select that file.

4. Click Import. A message box appears saying that the new data has been imported.

5. Click OK, and then close the Import dialog box. You can see in the database window that a new table has been added to the table objects.

Once you import the data from the dBase file into the new table, you can modify the table properties and the data as you would in any other Access table.

Importing Data from an Excel Spreadsheet

Many organizations rely on Excel spreadsheets to track and calculate information. As a result, you might find that you want to store some of the information in a spreadsheet in one of the tables in your database. Because Excel organizes a spreadsheet into a column/row structure, just like a table in Access, the process of importing data from an Excel file is usually not a problem. In fact, you begin the import process just as you do when importing data from a database. However, once you've identified an Excel data source, you must take a couple of additional steps that are different from importing from a database.

To import data from an Excel spreadsheet into an Access database table, take the following steps.

1. Open your database file.

2. Click the File menu, point to Get External Data, and then click Import. The Import dialog box appears.

Ask the Expert

Q: You state that you can import data from a variety of databases, including dBase, Lotus, and Paradox. What about databases such as SQL Server or Oracle?

A: Access allows you to import data from databases such as SQL Server, Visual FoxPro, Oracle, or other Structured Query Language (SQL) databases. However, the process of importing data from these databases is a little different from that for the other data sources. To begin with, you must create an Open Database Connectivity (ODBC) connection between your computer and the data source. The ODBC connection is created within the operating system. For example, in Windows XP, you can create and configure ODBC connections by using the Data Sources (ODBC) utility in the Control Panel. When you launch this utility, the ODBC Data Source Administrator dialog box appears, allowing you to create a new connection. When you create an ODBC connection, you must identify the type of data source and the location of that source, and you must provide a name for the connection. Refer to the online help in your operating system for further instructions on how to create an ODBC connection.

Once you've created an ODBC connection, open the Import dialog box as you do for any other data source. In the Files Of Type drop-down list, select ODBC Databases. This opens the Select Data Source dialog box, which allows you to select the ODBC connection that you just created. Once you select the connection, you'll be prompted to select the table in the database that you want to import. The table is then imported into your Access database and provided with the same name that it had in the target database.

3. In the Files Of Type drop-down list, select Microsoft Excel (*.xls), navigate to the Excel file, and then select that file.

4. Click Import. The first screen of the Import Spreadsheet wizard appears, as shown in Figure 9-3. The screen allows you to select the worksheet or range that you want to import. It also displays sample data so that you can see how the data will be imported into your Access table.

5. Select the appropriate worksheet or range, and then click Next. The next screen of the wizard appears, as shown in Figure 9-4. This screen allows you to determine whether the first row contains the column headings that should be used as field designations when the data is imported. The screen also displays a data sample to allow you to determine whether headings should be used.

6. Select the First Row Contains Column Headings check box if appropriate, and then click Next. The third screen of the Import Spreadsheet wizard appears, as shown in Figure 9-5. When you are importing data from a spreadsheet (as opposed to a database), you can designate

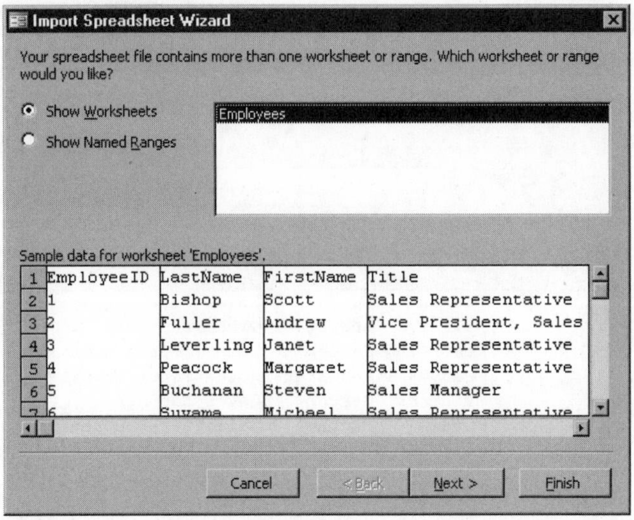

Figure 9-3 The first screen of the Import Spreadsheet wizard

whether you want to create a new table to hold the imported data or whether you want the data inserted into an existing table. If you insert the data into an existing table, you will be presented with only one more screen. If you insert the data into a new table, you will be presented with three more screens. In either case, the last screen is the same.

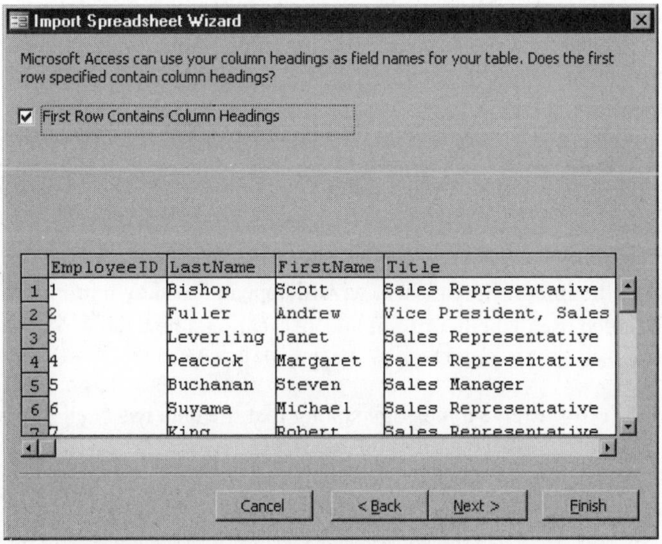

Figure 9-4 The second screen of the Import Spreadsheet wizard

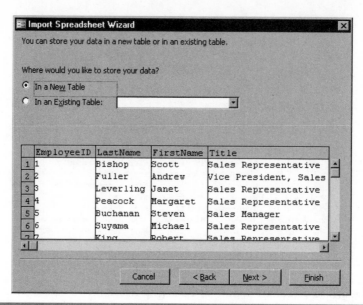

Figure 9-5 The third screen of the Import Spreadsheet wizard

7. Select the In a New Table option or the In An Existing Table option. If you select the second option, you must also select the table from the drop-down list. Once you've made your selection, click Next. The fourth screen of the Import Spreadsheet wizard appears, as you can see in Figure 9-6. This screen appears only if you selected the In A New Table option. The screen allows you to configure individual fields within the new table. You can also choose not to include a field in the imported data.

8. Configure the fields as necessary, and then click Next. The next screen of the Import Spreadsheet wizard (shown in Figure 9-7) appears, allowing you to configure a primary key for the new table.

9. Configure a primary key (or choose not to use a primary key), and then click Next. The final screen of the Import Spreadsheet wizard appears, as shown in Figure 9-8. This screen is the same screen used whether or not you're creating a new table. You can rename the table, have Access analyze the data, or display Help.

10. Click Finish. You'll receive a message stating that the data has been imported.

11. Click OK to close the message box. You're returned to the database window.

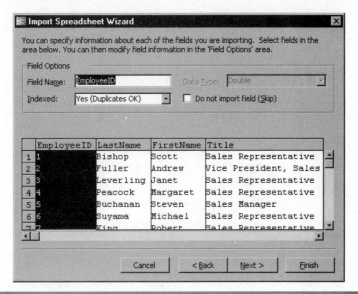

Figure 9-6 The fourth screen of the Import Spreadsheet wizard

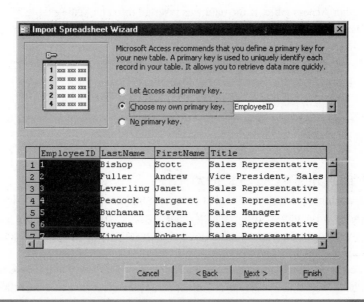

Figure 9-7 The fifth screen of the Import Spreadsheet wizard

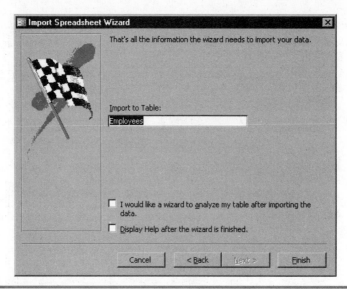

Figure 9-8 The final screen of the Import Spreadsheet wizard

If you created a new table when you imported the data, you can manage that table as you would any other Access table. If the data was inserted into an existing table, you can open that table and view and manipulate the new data.

NOTE

You cannot import data into an existing table if the data in any way conflicts with the primary key or any other constraints that exist on the table. Be certain that you know exactly what you're importing before you begin the import process.

Importing Data from a Text File

Text files are often used to store data that must be transferred to and from various data sources. Text files provide a neutral medium that is easily accessed by a variety of programs, including text editors and word processing applications. As a result, you will no doubt commonly run into situations in which you will want to import data from a text file.

The process of importing text data is very straightforward. Many of the steps that you use to import text data you've already seen. To import data from a text file, take the following steps:

1. Open your database file.

2. Click the File menu, point to Get External Data, and then click Import. The Import dialog box appears.

3. In the Files Of Type drop-down list, select Text Files (*txt;*.csv;*.tab;*.asc), navigate to the text file, and then select that file.

4. Click Import. The first screen of the Import Text wizard appears, as shown in Figure 9-9. The screen allows you to determine whether the file is delimited (that is, the values are separated by a character such as a tab) or fixed width (the values are evenly aligned). Delimited is the most commonly used format. The screen also displays a sample of the imported data.

5. Select the Delimited option or the Fixed Width option, and then click Next. The second screen of the Import Text wizard appears. If you selected Delimited, the screen appears as it does in Figure 9-10. The screen allows you to determine what character is used to delimit the values in each row. You can also configure whether the first row contains field names. If you selected the Fixed Width option in the first screen, the second screen would be a little different. It would allow you to set the spacing for the columns.

6. Configure the settings on the second screen, and then click Next. The remaining screens are similar to what you saw in the Import Spreadsheet wizard. You can determine whether to import the data into a new table or an existing table, configure individual fields, set a primary key, and name the table.

Once you complete the Import Text wizard, the imported data is added to your Access database. You can then take the necessary steps to work with that data or, if applicable, manage the new table.

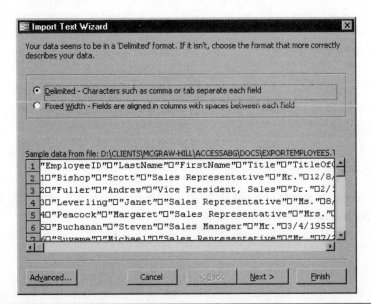

Figure 9-9 The first screen of the Import Text wizard

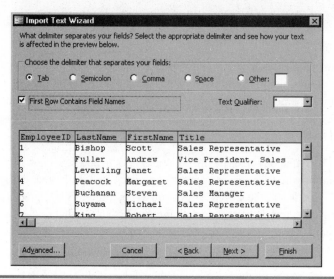

Figure 9-10 The second screen of the Import Text wizard

Importing Data from an XML File

XML is a language standard that is used describe and deliver data in various environments. It has gained wide acceptance primarily by supporting data exchange in web environments; however, it is fast becoming a standard used for exchanging information in other environments. Access allows you to import that data into your database. To import XML data, take the following steps:

1. Open your database file.

2. Click the File menu, point to Get External Data, and then click Import. The Import dialog box appears.

3. In the Files Of Type drop-down list, select XML (*.xml;*.xsd), navigate to the XML file, and then select that file.

4. Click Import. The Import XML dialog box appears, as shown in Figure 9-11. The dialog box lists the available tables in the file.

5. Select the table that you want to import, and then click OK. You'll receive a confirmation message that the XML data has been imported. Click OK to close the message box.

A new table is added to your Access database. The table is assigned a name based on the XML table that you imported. You can rename the table, modify the table properties, or manipulate the data within the table, as you would with any Access table.

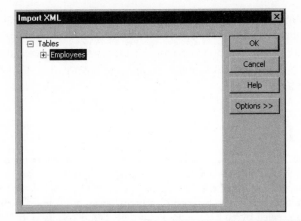

Figure 9-11 The Import XML dialog box

Progress Check

1. Which data objects can you import from an Access database?

2. How is data from a dBase file added to an Access database?

3. How can data from an Excel spreadsheet be added to an Access database?

4. How are values separated in a delimited text file?

CRITICAL SKILL
9.2 Link Data to an External Data Source

In the previous section, we looked at how to import data into an Access database. In most cases, this means creating a new table in your database and copying the data into that table. However, you also have the option of *linking* to an external data source. Instead of copying the data into your database, you create a link that allows you to view and manipulate an image of that data. The actual data remains in the external data source, which can be an Access database, another type of database, an Excel spreadsheet, a text file, or any one of the other supported data sources.

1. Tables, queries, forms, reports, pages, macros, and modules

2. The data is added to the database as a table object.

3. You can add Excel data to an Access database by inserting the data into an existing table or by creating a new table.

4. Values are separated by a character such as a tab.

The steps that you take to link data to an external data source are similar for most data sources. In fact, these steps are very close to the same steps you took when you were importing data. In this section, we'll look at how to link data to an Access table, a dBase file, an Excel spreadsheet, and a text file. For information on how to link to other types of data sources, see Access online Help.

TIP

When you link a table in an Access database, an arrow is added before the object icon that precedes the table name in the database window. In addition, the icon used to represent the table object might change, depending on the type of link. For example, a link to a dBase file is represented by a dBase icon, whereas a link to an Excel spreadsheet is represented by an Excel icon. Regardless of the icon used, an arrow always precedes it.

Linking to an Access Database

When you create a link to an Access database, you're actually linking to a table within that database. A copy of the table structure is stored in your database, so it appears as though the actual table and its data are part of your database. Although you can work with the data as though it were stored in your table, you cannot configure many of the table properties. In addition, you must have the proper permissions to access the external data, even though the link was created within your database.

Linking to a table in an Access database is similar to importing a table. The main difference is that, while you can import any data object from an Access database, you can create links only to tables. To create a link to a table in an external Access database, take the following steps:

1. Open your database file.

2. Click the File menu, point to Get External Data, and then click Link Tables. The Link dialog box appears, as shown in Figure 9-12. The Link dialog box allows you to specify the type of data source and to navigate to the appropriate file. By default, Microsoft Office Access is selected as the data source type.

3. Locate and select the file, and then click Link. The Link Tables dialog box appears, as shown in Figure 9-13. This dialog box allows you to select the table or tables that you will be linking to.

4. Select one or more tables, and then click OK. The linked tables are added to your database.

The tables are automatically assigned names based on the tables to which they are linked. You can change the table name and some of the table properties; however, many properties cannot be changed because of the linked data.

Figure 9-12 The Link dialog box

Linking to a dBase Database

Access allows you to link to dBase and Paradox files. However, though you can import data from a Lotus file, you can't link to it, although you can link to a variety of SQL databases that support ODBC connectivity. The process of linking to a dBase file and that for linking to a Paradox file are nearly the same. However, linking to an ODBC data source requires different steps, and you should consult Access online Help for details.

Figure 9-13 The Link Tables dialog box

As with most data sources, the steps that you take to link to a dBase file are nearly the same as importing data from that file. To link to dBase data source, take the following steps:

1. Open your database file.

2. Click the File menu, point to Get External Data, and then click Link Tables. The Link dialog box appears (the same dialog box as was shown in Figure 9-12).

3. In the Files Of Type drop-down list, select dBASE 5 (*.dbf), navigate to the dBase file, and select that file.

4. Click Link. A message box appears saying that the new data has been linked.

5. Click OK to close the message box, and then close the Link dialog box. You can see in the database window that a linked table has been added to the table objects.

When you link to a dBase file, the table created in your database is assigned the same name as the file. You can change the table name and some of the table properties; however, as with all linked tables, many properties cannot be modified.

Linking to an Excel Spreadsheet

Linking to an Excel spreadsheet requires many of the same steps as importing a spreadsheet. You must identify the file and follow the steps outlined in the wizard. As with other types of links, a table is created in your database and the data is displayed as though it were stored in your database. To link data from your Access database to an Excel spreadsheet, take the following steps.

1. Open your database file.

2. Click the File menu, point to Get External Data, and then click Link Tables. The Link dialog box appears.

3. In the Files Of Type drop-down list, select Microsoft Excel (*.xls), navigate to the Excel file, and then select that file.

4. Click Link. The first screen of the Link Spreadsheet wizard appears. The wizard includes screens that are nearly identical to screens in the Import Spreadsheet wizard. Follow the steps as outlined in the Link Spreadsheet wizard.

Once you complete the wizard, the linked table is added to your database, and you can work with the data as you would with any other type of linked data.

Linking to a Text File

If you know how to import data from a text file, you'll have no problem linking to a text file. To create a link to a text file, take the following steps:

1. Open your database file.

2. Click the File menu, point to Get External Data, and then click Link Tables. The Link dialog box appears.

3. In the Files Of Type drop-down list, select Text Files (*txt;*.csv;*.tab;*.asc), navigate to the text file, and then select that file.

4. Click Link. The first screen of the Link Text wizard appears. The wizard includes screens that are nearly identical to screens in the Import Text wizard. Follow the steps as outlined in the Link Text wizard.

Once you complete the wizard, the linked table is added to your database, and you can work with the data as you would with any other type of linked data.

NOTE

Depending on the indexed sequential access method (ISAM) configuration on your system, you may not be able to update or delete data that's linked to a text data source. However, you should be able to insert a row into the linked table. (ISAM is the architecture used by most desktop relational database systems. For more information about ISAM, see Access online Help.)

Project 9-1 Importing and Linking Data to the Consumer Advocacy Database

> Members.txt, Products.xml, Staff.xls

As you have seen, Access allows you to import data directly into your database or link to data in other data sources. In some cases, you can import data directly into a table. You can also create a new table to store the imported data. When you link to a data source, you must always view that data through a linked table. In this project, you will import data from a text file, an XML file, and an Excel file into the consumer advocacy database. In addition, you will create a link within that database to a table in the Northwind database. To perform the steps related to importing data, you will need to download the following three files from the McGraw-Hill/Osborne web site (http://www.osborne.com): Members.txt, Products.xml, and Staff.xls. (Note that the names used in the Members.txt and Staff.xls files were originally exported from the Northwind database.) Because we will be linking to a table in the Northwind database, you do not have to take any special actions to prepare for performing the steps related to linking data (assuming that the Northwind sample database is already installed on your system).

(continued)

Step by Step

1. If they're not already open, open Access and then open the ConsumerAdvocacy.mdb file.

2. The first set of data that you'll import will be taken from the Staff.xls file. Click the File menu, point to Get External Data, and then click Import. The Import dialog box appears.

3. In the Files Of Type drop-down list, select Microsoft Excel (*.xls), navigate to the Staff.xls Excel file, and then select that file.

4. Click Import. The first screen of the Import Spreadsheet wizard appears, with the Staff worksheet selected.

5. Click Next. The second screen of the Import Spreadsheet wizard appears.

6. Select the First Row Contains Column Headings option, and then click Next. The next screen of the wizard appears.

7. Select the In An Existing Table option, select Staff from the drop-down list, and then click Next. The final screen of the wizard appears.

8. Click Finish. A message box appears stating that the data has been imported to the Staff table.

9. Click OK to close the message box. The Staff table is populated with data from the Staff.xls file.

10. The next set of data that you'll import will be taken from the Member.txt file. Click the File menu, point to Get External Data, and then click Import. The Import dialog box appears.

11. In the Files Of Type drop-down list, select Text Files (*.txt;*.csv;*.tab;*.asc), navigate to the Members.txt file, and then select that file.

12. Click Import. The first screen of the Import Text wizard appears. The Delimited option is selected by default. Leave this option selected.

13. Click Next. The second screen of the Import Text wizard appears, with the Tab option selected. The First Row Contains Field Names option is not selected. Leave these options as they are.

14. Click Next. The third screen of the wizard appears.

15. Select the In An Existing Table option, select Members from the drop-down list, and then click Next.

16. The final screen of the wizard appears.

17. Click Finish. A message box appears stating that the data has been imported to the Members table.

18. Click OK to close the message box. The Members table is populated by data from the Members.txt file.

19. The next set of data that you'll import will be taken from the Products.xml file. Click the File menu, point to Get External Data, and then click Import. The Import dialog box appears.

20. In the Files Of Type drop-down list, select XML (*.xml;*.xsd), navigate to the Products.xml file, and then select that file.

21. Click Import. The Import XML dialog box appears.

22. Select the Products table, and then click OK. A message box appears stating that data has been imported from the Products.xml file.

23. Click OK to close the message box. The Products1 table is added to your database. The new table contains the data from the Products.xml table. The table was named Products1 because a table named Products already existed in your database. In Modules 10 and 11, you will learn how to create queries that will allow you to copy the data from the Products1 table to the Products table.

24. Now you will create a link to a table in the Northwind database. Click the File menu, point to Get External Data, and then click Link Tables. The Link dialog box appears.

25. Ensure that the Microsoft Office Access (*.mdb;*.mda;*.mde), option is selected in the Files Of Type text box, and navigate to the folder that contains the Northwind.mdb file.

26. Select the Northwind.mdb file, and then click Link. The Link Tables dialog box appears.

27. Select the Employees table, and then click OK. The Employees table is added to your database. Notice that the table icon is preceded by an arrow to indicate that this is a linked table.

28. Select the Employees table, and then click the Delete button at the top of the database window. The link to the Employees table in the Northwind database is removed.

Project Summary

As you have seen, the steps for importing data from a text file, XML file, and Excel file share many similarities. Now that you have practiced importing these three types of files, you should be able to import data from nearly any type of data source. In addition, you have also seen that the steps necessary to link data are very similar to those for importing data, so linking data from other types of data sources should be fairly straightforward. Linking data can be useful if you want users to be able to update that data in their source programs. However, if you plan to use the data only in Access, you should import it, rather than link to it. Access is more efficient when it's working with data within the structure of its own tables, rather than relying on an external program.

9.3 Export Data out of Your Database

As you have seen, when you import data, you're bringing data into your database. However, there will no doubt be times when you want to copy data out of the database into formats that other users can take advantage of. To this end, Access allows you to export data into a number of different file types. For example, you can export data to another Access database or to text and XML files. Access supports a wide range of export file types. In this section, we'll look specifically at exporting data into Access and dBase databases, as well as into Excel, text, and XML files. Although the process for exporting data into these formats is similar, there are some differences among them, so we'll look at the process of exporting each of these types in detail so that you have a better understanding of how the process for each one works.

NOTE

The type of data source that you can export a data object to depends on the type of object that you're exporting. For example, you can export a module to an Access database file or to a text file, but you can export a macro only to an Access file. On the other hand, you can export a table to nearly all the supported data source types. For this reason, this section focuses primarily on exporting tables.

Exporting Data to an Access Database

As long as you know where the target Access database file is located, exporting a table into that database is a relatively straightforward process. In fact, you can export any data object to another Access database file. This can be handy if you're creating a new database, sharing information, or simply preserving data from a database that is no longer in production.

To export a table from one Access database to another, take the following steps:

1. Open your database file, select the Tables object type, and then select the table.

2. Click the File menu and then click Export. The Export Table '*TableName*' To dialog box appears, as shown in Figure 9-14. The dialog box allows you to name the file, identify the data source that you will be importing data to, and identify the folder that will contain the new file. By default, Microsoft Office Access is selected as the data source type.

3. Navigate to the folder that contains the Access database file, select the file, and then click Export. The Export dialog box appears, as shown in Figure 9-15. The dialog box allows you to change the default name provided to the exported table. You can also choose to export only the table definition, rather than the definition and data, which is the default.

4. Click OK. The exported table is added to the Access database.

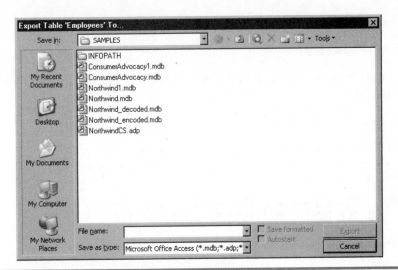

Figure 9-14 The Export Table '*TableName*' To dialog box

There are no other steps that you need to take. If you go into the target database, you'll see that the table has been added. You can then manipulate the table as you would any other table within that database.

Exporting Data to a dBase Database

Exporting a dBase file is even simpler than exporting an object to an Access database. One thing to note, however, is that dBase, like Paradox, limits the filename to 11 characters, as seen in the old DOS standard. This means that the actual filename can be only eight characters. The remaining three characters are reserved for the .dbf file extension. If you type in more than eight characters for the filename, only the first eight are used.

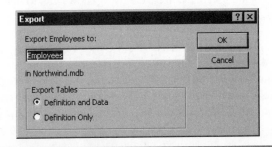

Figure 9-15 The Export dialog box

To export data from an Access table to a dBase file, take the following steps:

1. Open your database file, select the Tables object type, and then select the table.

2. Click the File menu, and then click Export. The Export Table '*TableName*' To dialog box appears.

3. In the Save As Type drop-down list, select the appropriate dBase option.

4. In the File Name text box, type in a filename if necessary, navigate to the appropriate folder, and then click Export. The new file is added to the folder.

Exporting Data to an Excel Spreadsheet

The process for exporting data to an Excel spreadsheet is similar to exporting to a dBase file. To export to an Excel file, take the following steps:

1. Open your database file, select the Tables object type, and then select the table.

2. Click the File menu, and then click Export. The Export Table '*TableName*' To dialog box appears.

3. In the Save As Type drop-down list, select the appropriate Excel option.

4. In the File Name text box, type in a filename if necessary, navigate to the appropriate folder, and then click Export. The new file is added to the folder.

Ask the Expert

Q: You talk about exporting and linking data to an Excel spreadsheet. However, the Database toolbar contains a button named OfficeLinks, with a Word logo on the button. What are these tools for?

A: The OfficeLinks button on the Database toolbar allows you to link and export data in an Access table to a Word document or an Excel spreadsheet. The OfficeLinks button offers three tools: Merge It With Microsoft Office Word, Publish It With Microsoft Office Word, and Analyze it With Microsoft Office Excel. Merge It With Microsoft Office Word links data in the table to a Word document, either an existing one or one you can create at the time. Publish It With Microsoft Office Word exports the data in the Access table to a rich text format (RTF) document in Word. The text is added as a table to the Word document, and you can manipulate the table and data as necessary. Analyze It With Microsoft Office Excel exports the data directly to an Excel spreadsheet. You can manipulate the spreadsheet and the data as necessary. For a more thorough explanation of these tools, be sure to check the Microsoft Office System documentation.

Exporting Data to a Text File

Exporting to a text file is a little more complicated than exporting to other types of files. When you export data to a text file, you must determine whether the data will be delimited or fixed width. If it will be delimited, you must decide what character will be used to separate the values. If it will be fixed width, you must decide how to space the columns. In addition, you must also determine whether to include field names in the text file. Despite these extra steps, exporting to a text file is still relatively easy.

To export data from an Access table to a text file, take the following steps:

1. Open your database file, select the Tables object type, and then select the table.

2. Click the File menu and then click Export. The Export Table '*TableName*' To dialog box appears.

3. In the Save As Type drop-down list, select Text Files (*txt;*.csv;*.tab;*.asc).

4. In the File Name text box, type in a filename if necessary, navigate to the appropriate folder, and then click Export. The first screen of the Export Text wizard appears, as shown in Figure 9-16. In this screen, you must determine whether the data will be saved as delimited or as fixed width.

5. Select the Delimited option or the Fixed Width option, and then click Next. The next screen of the Export Text wizard appears. If you configured the file as delimited, the screen will appear as it does in Figure 9-17. From there, you can choose the delimiter type and determine whether the top row contains field names. If you configured the file as Fixed Width, the screen allows you to adjust the column width.

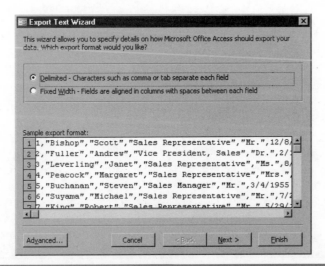

Figure 9-16 The first screen of the Export Text wizard

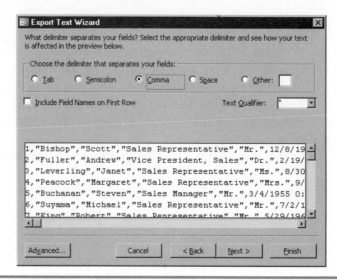

Figure 9-17 The second screen of the Export Text wizard

6. Configure the file as necessary, and then click Next. The final screen of the Export Text wizard appears, as shown in Figure 9-18. This is the final screen for both the delimiter option and the fixed width option.

7. Provide a path and filename for the text file if necessary, and then click Finish. You'll receive a message saying that the data has been exported. Click OK to close the message box.

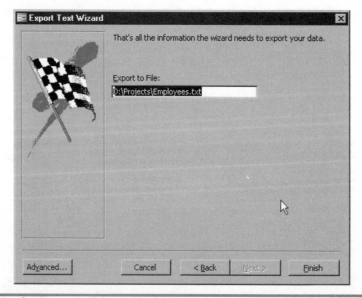

Figure 9-18 The final screen of the Export Text wizard

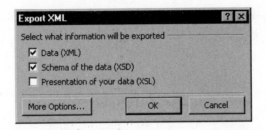

Figure 9-19 The Export XML dialog box

Exporting Data to an XML File

The main decision that you have to make when you export data to an XML file is what type of additional files you want to create. When exporting data to XML, you have the option of creating three types of files: .xml, .xsd, and .xsl. Data is saved in an .xml file, the data schema is saved in an .xsd file, and the data presentation is saved in an .xsl file. By default, .xml and .xsd file types are created when you export the data, but you can choose to create any of the three types of files. However, you can create an .xsl file only if you've also created an .xml file.

To export data to any of the XML-related files, take the following steps:

1. Open your database file, select the Tables object type, and then select the table.

2. Click the File menu and then click Export. The Export Table '*TableName*' To dialog box appears.

3. In the Save As Type drop-down list, select XML (*.xml).

4. In the File Name text box, type in a filename if necessary, navigate to the appropriate folder, and then click Export. The Export XML dialog box appears, as shown in Figure 9-19. The dialog box allows you to determine what types of XML-related files will be created.

5. Select the appropriate file type options, and then click OK. The new files are created in the designated folder.

Project 9-2 Exporting Data out of the Consumer Advocacy Database

Exporting data is a handy way of making that data available to users who want to view information in formats other than an Access database file. You can export the same data in a variety of formats. In this project, you will copy data out of the Staff table in the consumer advocacy database into Excel, text, and XML files. You'll create these files by using the export functionality within Access. Once the files are created, you can use them in whatever manner you want.

(continued)

You can even delete them. However, after you've exported the data, you might want to view that data to see how it is formatted when it is exported out of Access.

Step by Step

1. If they're not already open, open Access and then open the ConsumerAdvocacy.mdb database file.

2. Ensure that the Tables object type is selected, and then select the Staff table. You will export the data in the table to an Excel spreadsheet.

3. Click the File menu and then click Export. The Export Table 'Staff' To dialog box appears.

4. In the Save As Type drop-down list, select the Microsoft Excel 97-2003 (*.xls) option.

5. If necessary, type **Staff** in the File Name text box, navigate to the folder where you want to locate the Excel file, and then click Export. An Excel file is created and stored in the target location.

6. You'll now export the data in the Staff table to a text file. Verify that the Staff table is selected.

7. Click the File menu and then click Export. The Export Table 'Staff' To dialog box appears.

8. In the Save As Type drop-down list, select Text Files (*txt;*.csv;*.tab;*.asc).

9. In the File Name text box, type in **Staff** if necessary, navigate to the appropriate folder, and then click Export. The first screen of the Export Text wizard appears, with the Delimited option selected. Leave this option selected.

10. Click Next. The second screen of the Export Text wizard appears.

11. Select the Tab option, and then click Next. The final screen of the wizard appears.

12. Click Finish. A message box appears stating that the data was exported to the new text file.

13. Click OK to close the message box.

14. Now you will export the Staff table to an XML file. Be sure that the Staff table is still selected in the database window.

15. Click the File menu and then click Export. The Export Table 'Staff' To dialog box appears.

16. In the Save As Type drop-down list, select XML (*.xml).

17. In the File Name text box, type in **Staff** if necessary, navigate to the appropriate folder, and then click Export. The Export XML dialog box appears, allowing you to determine what types of XML-related files will be created. By default, .xml and .xsd files are created.

18. Click OK. The new files are created in the designated folder.

Project Summary

In this project, you exported data from the Staff table into three different types of files: Excel, text, and XML. The process of exporting the Staff data has no impact on the data that is stored in the table. The exporting process simply copies the data to an external source. You can now use these files as you would any other Excel, text, or XML file. You can view them directly or import them into an Access database. You can even import them into other data sources, depending on what functionality is supported by that source.

✓ Module 9 Mastery Check

1. You're importing data from another Access database into your Access database. Which data objects can you import into your database?

   A. Macros

   B. Forms

   C. Reports

   D. Tables

2. What database file can you import into an Access table, but not link to?

   A. dBase

   B. Lotus

   C. Paradox

   D. SQL Server

3. Which data sources allow you to insert imported data directly into a table?

   A. Access tables

   B. dBase files

   C. Excel spreadsheets

   D. Text files

4. What would prevent you from inserting Excel data into an existing table?

5. What is the difference between a delimited text file and a fixed width text file?

6. What is XML?

7. What is the difference between importing data and linking data?

8. What is the main difference between importing an object from an Access database and linking to an object in an Access database?

9. What name is provided by default to a table that is linked to a dBase file?

10. To which file type can you export a module?

   A. XML file

   B. Access database file

   C. Text file

   D. dBase file

11. Which data object types in an Access database can you export to another Access database?

12. You're exporting data to a dBase file. How long can the filename be?

13. You're exporting data into a text file. During the export process, you determine that the file will be formatted as a delimited file. What other decision must you make if the file is delimited?

14. Which XML-related file stores the data presentation?

   A. .xml

   B. .xsd

   C. .xsl

   D. .xls

15. What is the difference between importing and exporting data?

Module 10

Querying an Access Database

CRITICAL SKILLS

10.1 Create a Select Query

10.2 Create a Crosstab Query

10.3 Create an Action Query

Once data has been added to a database, you must be able to view and modify that data in a way that allows you to target specific records and values. As you have seen, you can open a table in Datasheet view and modify data directly. You can also sort the data and apply various types of filters. However, rather than use these methods to view and update data, you can create queries that allow you to define a precise set of criteria that can be used to retrieve specific records and fields and display them in Datasheet view. You can also use queries to add, update, and delete records in a table.

Access supports a number of different types of queries. Select queries and crosstab queries retrieve records from your database, and the action queries (make-table, update, append, and delete) allow you to modify that data. In this module, you will learn about all six types of queries and how they can be used to view and modify data.

CRITICAL SKILL
10.1 Create a Select Query

A *query* is a data object in an Access database that contains a defined set of criteria that can be used to retrieve or update records in a database. The most common type of query is the *select query*, which is a type of query that retrieves and displays a subset of data from one or more tables. The process used to create a select query is basically the same whether you're creating a single-table query or a multiple-table query. However, it's important for you to understand how to use both types of select query, so we'll take a look at them individually.

Creating a Single-Table Select Query

The simplest type of query to create is one that is based on only one table. In this type of query, all values returned come from a single table. For example, you can create a select query in the Northwind database that retrieves records from the Products table. The query can be defined to retrieve only the ProductName, SupplierID, and UnitPrice fields for those products with a UnitPrice value greater than $20.00. When you run the query, the results are displayed in the Datasheet view window, as shown in Figure 10-1.

As you can see, the query retrieves only the three fields and displays only those records with a UnitPrice value greater than $20.00. In a select query, you can retrieve any record and any field, depending on how you define the criteria in the query definition.

To define any type of query, you must use either the Design view window or a wizard. In order to provide you with a comprehensive foundation in the query creation process, this module will focus on using Design view. Keep in mind, however, that Access provides several wizards that you can use to create queries. Even if you choose to use these wizards, you should still learn how to create queries in Design view so that you have a better understanding of the various components that make up a query.

Product Name	Supplier	Unit Price
Alice Mutton	Pavlova, Ltd.	$39.00
Camembert Pierrot	Gai pâturage	$34.00
Carnarvon Tigers	Pavlova, Ltd.	$62.50
Chef Anton's Cajun Seasoning	New Orleans Cajun Delights	$22.00
Chef Anton's Gumbo Mix	New Orleans Cajun Delights	$21.35
Côte de Blaye	Aux joyeux ecclésiastiques	$263.50
Fløtemysost	Norske Meierier	$21.50
Gnocchi di nonna Alice	Pasta Buttini s.r.l.	$38.00
Grandma's Boysenberry Spread	Grandma Kelly's Homestead	$25.00
Gravad lax	Svensk Sjöföda AB	$26.00
Gudbrandsdalsost	Norske Meierier	$36.00
Gumbär Gummibärchen	Heli Süßwaren GmbH & Co. KG	$31.23
Gustaf's Knäckebröd	PB Knäckebröd AB	$21.00
Ikura	Tokyo Traders	$31.00
Ipoh Coffee	Leka Trading	$46.00
Louisiana Fiery Hot Pepper Sauce	New Orleans Cajun Delights	$21.05
Manjimup Dried Apples	G'day, Mate	$53.00
Mascarpone Fabioli	Formaggi Fortini s.r.l.	$32.00
Mishi Kobe Niku	Tokyo Traders	$97.00
Mozzarella di Giovanni	Formaggi Fortini s.r.l.	$34.80
Nord-Ost Matjeshering	Nord-Ost-Fisch Handelsgesellschaft mbH	$25.89
Northwoods Cranberry Sauce	Grandma Kelly's Homestead	$40.00
Pâté chinois	Ma Maison	$24.00

ProductsGreaterThan$20 : Select Query

Record: 1 of 37

Figure 10-1   Running a select query that retrieves data from the Products table in the Northwind database

Access supports a number of methods for opening the Design view window that is used to create a query:

- Select the Queries object type in the database window and double-click Create Query In Design View.

- Select the Queries object type in the database window, click the New button at the top of the database window, and then double-click Design View in the New Query window.

- Click the Insert menu, click Query, and then double-click Design View in the New Query window.

Once the Design view window is open, you're ready to create a select query. When you open the Design view window, the Query Design toolbar replaces the Database toolbar.

NOTE

The Design view window allows you to create any type of query. By default, the window is set up to create a select query. You can change the query type by clicking the down arrow on the Query Type button on the Query Design toolbar and then selecting the type.

When you first open the Design view window, the Show Table dialog box appears, as shown in Figure 10-2. The dialog box lists all the tables and queries in the database. You can base a query on tables, other queries, or both. Regardless of whether you base your query on tables or on other queries, the purpose of the query is the same: to extract a subset of data from the source data. You might choose to base a query on another query to simplify the new query. That way, you can leverage off the criteria already defined in the source query. However, if you base a query on another query, you must be certain that the source query is not going to change, otherwise the new query can be affected.

The Show Table dialog box allows you to select the initial tables and queries that you might want to use in your query. By default, the Tables tab is selected in the dialog box, but you can select objects from any tab. You should select the objects that you want to include in your query, click Add, and then close the dialog box.

The tables and queries that you selected in the Show Table dialog box are added as objects to the Design view window. If more than one table has been added and relationships exist between those tables, the relationships are shown as connecting lines, as you'll find in the Relationships window. (See Module 5 for information about relationships.) You can add or remove table and query objects from the Design view window at any time. Once the correct table and query objects are displayed, you're ready to start defining the criteria.

In order to demonstrate how to define the criteria, let's return to the query that was used to return the results shown in Figure 10-1. The query results include three fields: ProductName, SupplierID, and UnitPrice. This means that your query is based, at the very least, on those three fields. In addition, the values in the ProductName field are sorted in ascending order, and only records with a UnitPrice value over $20.00 are displayed. The definition for this query, as it appears in Design view, is shown in Figure 10-3.

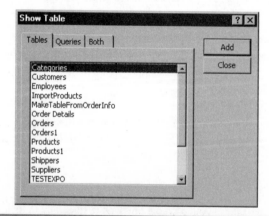

Figure 10-2 The Tables tab of the Show Table dialog box

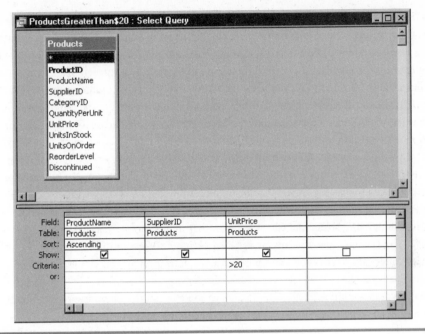

Figure 10-3 The definition for the ProductsGreaterThan$20 query

As you can see, the Design view window for queries is very similar to the window used for creating filters. The window includes the Products table object and the design grid, which contains the query definition. In this case, the ProductName field is sorted in ascending order. The SupplierID field is included, but no sort order is defined for that field. In addition, no criteria is defined for either field. However, the UnitPrice field includes an expression in the criteria that specifies that values in the field must be greater than 20.

The process of creating a query such as this one begins with adding the field names to the design grid. To do so, you merely drag the field name from the table object to the Field cell of the appropriate column. You can also select the field name from the drop-down list associated with the Field cell. Another alternative for adding a field to a Field cell is to double-click the field name in the table object. The name will be added to the next available Field cell.

TIP

You can drag multiple field names to Field cells at the same time. Simply select the field names from the table object and drag them to the first available Field cell. Access will automatically add each field to a Field cell, in the order that the fields appear in the table object.

For each field that you include, you must include the table name. You can also define a sort order and criteria. The Criteria cells can contain field names, field values, wildcards, expressions, operators, and functions. You saw examples of criteria elements when learning about how to filter data. (Filters were discussed in Module 8. Expressions, operators, and functions will be discussed in Module 11.) Notice that for each column in the design grid you can select or clear the Show option. By default, all fields defined in the criteria are displayed in the query results (which means that the Show option is selected). However, there might be times when you want to base your query on a field but do not want to show that field. In that case, you simply clear the Show option.

Once you have defined a query, you can view the results of that query by clicking the View button on the Query Design toolbar. The retrieved data is displayed in the same way that table data is displayed in Datasheet view. (You might have to click the down arrow on the View button and select Datasheet View, rather than simply clicking the button.) You can return to the Design view window by again clicking the View button. After you're satisfied that your query is correct, you can save the query definition as you would any other data object in your database.

After you have created and saved a query, you can run it at any time by double-clicking the query in the database window. You can also run the query by selecting it and then clicking

Ask the Expert

Q: The select query shown in this section contains only fixed criteria, which means that a new query has to be created if any of the criteria elements change. Is it possible to create a query that allows you to enter a changing value so that you don't have to redefine the entire query?

A: Access allows you to create a type of query that defines a parameter within the query definition. The parameter acts as a placeholder that allows you to specify a value whenever you run that query. For example, suppose that you want to create a query that retrieves data from the Products table in the Northwind database, and you want the query to retrieve the product name and supplier for whichever product ID you specify. To do this, you would create a query that is based on the ProductID, ProductName, and SupplierID fields. For the ProductID field, you would type the following value as the criteria: **[Enter the Product ID:]**. By enclosing the value in brackets, you'd be telling Access to treat this value as a parameter. As a result, when you ran this query, the Enter Parameter Value dialog box would appear and display a message that says, "Enter the Product ID:" You would then enter the appropriate value and click OK. The query would run, using the value that you supplied, and the results would display the product ID, product name, and supplier for the product ID that you entered.

Open. In addition, you can run the query from the Design view window by clicking the Run button on the Query Design toolbar. You can run the current query from the Design view window without having first saved it.

Creating a Multiple-Table Query

Although querying a single table can often be useful, a far more powerful use of queries is to retrieve data from multiple tables. This can be very effective when relationships exist between tables and you want to present the data in a way that is most useful to the end user. Suppose, for example, that you want to create a query in the Northwind database that returns information about orders. The query should include the name of the company that placed the order, the order ID of each order, the name of the products that shipped, and the date that they were shipped. In addition, the query should return only those records with a ship date after December 31, 1997.

The challenge here is that the information that you want to retrieve exists in different tables. However, Access allows you to create queries that join the tables together so that you can retrieve exactly the information you're looking for. Your definition for this query would be similar to the one shown in Figure 10-4.

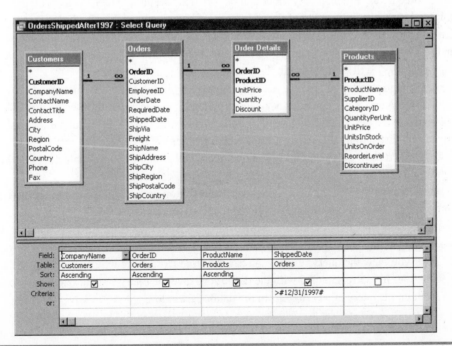

Figure 10-4 A query definition that returns order information from the Northwind database

Let's first take a look at the table objects that are displayed in the Design view window. Notice that customer name information is included in the Customers table, order information is included in the Orders and Order Details tables, and product names are included in the Products table. Because all these tables include information necessary to perform the query, they should all be included in the Design view window.

NOTE

In actuality, you do not have to include the Order Details table object in the Design view window because no fields are actually selected from the field. However, because the table acts as a junction table between the Orders table and the Products table, it is included here to better demonstrate the relationships that exist between the tables. Regardless of whether you include the Order Details table, Access uses the table in the underlying SQL statement that is defined by the query.

As you can see from the query, four fields are included in the definition. The first three columns in the design grid simply identify three of the fields that should be included in the query results: the CompanyName field from the Customers table, the OrderID field from the Orders table, and the ProductName field from the Products table. There is no criteria specified for the three fields, although they should all be sorted in ascending order. As a result, the records in the query results will be sorted first by CompanyName values, then by OrderID values, and then by ProductName values. The fourth column in the design grid is the only field that actually qualifies which records are returned. In this case, only records with a ShippedDate value later than 12/31/1997 will be included in the query results.

For the most part, you create a multiple-table query in the same way that you create a single-table query. After you add the necessary tables and queries to the Design view window, you populate the design grid by identifying the participating fields, optional sort orders, and any criteria that should be used to specify which records are returned. The main difference between this type of query and a single-table query is that in a multiple-table query definition, you can include fields from different tables in the same design grid.

Once you've defined the query, click the View button on the Query Design toolbar to view your results. The query results are displayed in a Datasheet view window. If you were to view the results from the query definition shown in Figure 10-4, the Datasheet view window would look similar to the one displayed in Figure 10-5.

After you view the query results, you can return to Design view by again clicking the View button. If you're satisfied with the definition, save the query to your database. You can then run the query at any time from the database window.

Company Name	Order ID	Product Name	Shipped Date
Alfreds Futterkiste	10835	Original Frankfurter grüne Soße	21-Jan-1998
Alfreds Futterkiste	10835	Raclette Courdavault	21-Jan-1998
Alfreds Futterkiste	10952	Grandma's Boysenberry Spread	24-Mar-1998
Alfreds Futterkiste	10952	Rössle Sauerkraut	24-Mar-1998
Alfreds Futterkiste	11011	Escargots de Bourgogne	13-Apr-1998
Alfreds Futterkiste	11011	Fløtemysost	13-Apr-1998
Ana Trujillo Emparedados y helados	10926	Konbu	11-Mar-1998
Ana Trujillo Emparedados y helados	10926	Mozzarella di Giovanni	11-Mar-1998
Ana Trujillo Emparedados y helados	10926	Queso Cabrales	11-Mar-1998
Ana Trujillo Emparedados y helados	10926	Teatime Chocolate Biscuits	11-Mar-1998
Antonio Moreno Taquería	10856	Chang	10-Feb-1998
Antonio Moreno Taquería	10856	Singaporean Hokkien Fried Mee	10-Feb-1998
Around the Horn	10793	Filo Mix	08-Jan-1998
Around the Horn	10793	Jack's New England Clam Chowder	08-Jan-1998
Around the Horn	10864	Laughing Lumberjack Lager	09-Feb-1998
Around the Horn	10864	Steeleye Stout	09-Feb-1998
Around the Horn	10920	Valkoinen suklaa	09-Mar-1998
Around the Horn	10953	Gorgonzola Telino	25-Mar-1998
Around the Horn	10953	Sir Rodney's Marmalade	25-Mar-1998
Around the Horn	11016	Gorgonzola Telino	13-Apr-1998
Around the Horn	11016	Inlagd Sill	13-Apr-1998
Berglunds snabbköp	10837	Boston Crab Meat	23-Jan-1998
Berglunds snabbköp	10837	Konbu	23-Jan-1998
Berglunds snabbköp	10837	Lakkalikööri	23-Jan-1998
Berglunds snabbköp	10837	Zaanse koeken	23-Jan-1998

Record: 1 of 661

Figure 10-5 Orders in the Northwind database shipped after 1997

Project 10-1   Adding a Select Query to the Consumer Advocacy Database

A select query allows you to retrieve data from one or more tables in your database. In this project, you will create a select query that retrieves information from the Staff table and the Positions table in the consumer advocacy database. The query will retrieve the first name, last name, and start date from the Staff table. You will also retrieve the PositionType values from the Positions table; however, these values will not be displayed in the query results. In addition, your query will return only those records whose StartDate value is later than 1996 and whose PositionType value is Employee.

Step by Step

1. If they're not already open, open Access and then open the ConsumerAdvocacy.mdb file.

2. Select the Queries object type in the database window, and then double-click Create Query In Design View. The Design view window opens with the Show Table dialog box active and the Tables tab selected.

(continued)

3. Select the Positions table and the Staff table, and then click Add. The table objects are added to the database window, with a relationship line connecting the two tables.

4. Close the Show Table dialog box. The Design view window is now active.

5. Resize the Design view window and the table objects if necessary so that the design grid and table objects are fully visible.

6. Double-click the NameLast field in the Staff table object. The field is added to the first column in the design grid, and the Staff table is added to the Table cell.

7. In the Sort cell of the first column in the design grid, select Ascending from the drop-down list.

8. Drag the NameFirst field from the Staff table object to the Field cell of the second column. The Staff table is added to the Table cell.

9. In the Field cell of the third column in the design grid, select Staff.StartDate from the drop-down list. The Staff table is added to the Table cell.

10. In the first Criteria cell of the third column, type **>12/31/96**, and then click another cell to complete the entry. Number signs are added around the date value.

11. Double-click the PositionType field in the Positions table object. The field is added to the Field cell in the fourth column, and the Positions table is added to the Table cell.

12. Clear the Show check box in the fourth column.

13. In the first Criteria cell of the fourth column, type **employee**, and then click another cell to complete the entry. Quotation marks are added around the value.

14. Click the View button on the Query Design toolbar. The results of the query are displayed in a Datasheet view window. The query results include four records. Each record contains a NameLast value, a NameFirst value, and a StartDate value, and the records are sorted in ascending order by the NameLast field.

15. Click the View button on the Query Datasheet toolbar. The Design view window reappears.

16. Click the Save button on the Query Design toolbar. The Save As dialog box appears.

17. In the Query Name text box, type **EmployeesHiredAfter1996**, and then click OK. The query is saved to the consumer advocacy database.

18. Close the Design view window.

19. Verify that the Queries object type is selected in the database window, and then double-click EmployeesHiredAfter1996. The query results are displayed in the Datasheet view window.

Project Summary

As you saw in this project, you can include fields from one or more tables in your select query. In addition, you can add criteria to the definition that specifies which records are included in the query results. Once you create a select query and save it to your database, you can run that query at any time to view the specified data. You can also modify the query definition. Running the query does not affect the data in the participating tables. However, if the data in the tables changes, if new data is added, or if data is deleted, the query results might change.

CRITICAL SKILL
10.2 Create a Crosstab Query

When working with data in an Access database, you might find that there are times when you want to summarize some of the data in the tables. These summaries can provide the basis for reports that supply meaningful data to database users. In order to facilitate this functionality, Access allows you to create the *crosstab query,* which is a type of query that groups together related data and summarizes values associated with that data.

Let's take a look at an example. Suppose that you want to know how much each Northwind customer is spending on each product that the customer has ordered. If you were to create a regular select query to retrieve this information, your query results would appear to include duplicate rows for each order that was placed by the same company for the same product, as shown in Figure 10-6.

Notice that there are two rows that contain the CompanyName value of Alfreds Futterkiste and a ProductName value of Rössle Sauerkraut and that you have to add the totals manually. In addition, a row is returned for each product that the company has ordered. If this information were summarized through a crosstab query, the results would include only one row per company name and one column per product name, and the unit price would be summarized for each product, as shown in Figure 10-7.

In the case of the crosstab query shown in Figure 10-7, the summarized values are added together, but you can also summarize the values in other ways to provide you with the data that you need. For example, you can find the average unit price for each product or identify the highest or lowest price per product.

As with select queries, you create a crosstab query by first opening the Design view window and selecting the appropriate tables and queries that should be included in the new query. However, before you can fully define a crosstab query, you must set up the design grid to support this type of query. To do so, click the down arrow in the Query Type button on the Query Design toolbar and then click Crosstab Query. When you do this, two rows—Total and Crosstab—are added to the design grid, as shown in Figure 10-8.

ProductPrices-SelectQuery : Select Query

Company Name	Product Name	Unit Price
Alfreds Futterkiste	Aniseed Syrup	$10.00
Alfreds Futterkiste	Chartreuse verte	$18.00
Alfreds Futterkiste	Escargots de Bourgogne	$13.25
Alfreds Futterkiste	Fløtemysost	$21.50
Alfreds Futterkiste	Grandma's Boysenberry Spread	$25.00
Alfreds Futterkiste	Lakkalikööri	$18.00
Alfreds Futterkiste	Original Frankfurter grüne Soße	$13.00
Alfreds Futterkiste	Raclette Courdavault	$55.00
Alfreds Futterkiste	Rössle Sauerkraut	$45.60
Alfreds Futterkiste	Rössle Sauerkraut	$45.60
Alfreds Futterkiste	Spegesild	$12.00
Alfreds Futterkiste	Vegie-spread	$43.90
Ana Trujillo Emparedados y helados	Camembert Pierrot	$34.00
Ana Trujillo Emparedados y helados	Gudbrandsdalsost	$28.80
Ana Trujillo Emparedados y helados	Konbu	$6.00
Ana Trujillo Emparedados y helados	Mascarpone Fabioli	$32.00
Ana Trujillo Emparedados y helados	Mozzarella di Giovanni	$34.80
Ana Trujillo Emparedados y helados	Outback Lager	$12.00
Ana Trujillo Emparedados y helados	Queso Cabrales	$21.00
Ana Trujillo Emparedados y helados	Singaporean Hokkien Fried Mee	$14.00
Ana Trujillo Emparedados y helados	Teatime Chocolate Biscuits	$9.20
Ana Trujillo Emparedados y helados	Tofu	$23.25
Antonio Moreno Taquería	Alice Mutton	$39.00
Antonio Moreno Taquería	Boston Crab Meat	$18.40
Antonio Moreno Taquería	Chang	$19.00

Record: |◄| ◄ | 1 | ► | ►| | ►* | of 2155

Figure 10-6 Retrieving order information through a select query

ProductPrices-CrosstabQuery : Crosstab Query

Company Name	Alice Mutton	Aniseed Syrup	Boston Crab Meat	Camembert Pie	Carnarvon Tigers	Chai	Chang
Alfreds Futterkiste		$10.00					
Ana Trujillo Emparedados y helados				$34.00			
Antonio Moreno Taquería	$39.00		$18.40				$19.00
Around the Horn				$34.00			$19.00
Berglunds snabbköp	$31.20	$10.00	$36.80	$61.20		$18.00	$19.00
Blauer See Delikatessen				$34.00	$62.50		
Blondel père et fils	$31.20				$62.50	$18.00	
Bólido Comidas preparadas	$39.00						
Bon app'	$39.00		$36.80		$100.00		
Bottom-Dollar Markets	$70.20	$10.00	$14.70	$68.00		$18.00	
B's Beverages		$8.00	$14.70				
Cactus Comidas para llevar							
Centro comercial Moctezuma							
Chop-suey Chinese				$34.00		$14.40	$19.00
Comércio Mineiro							
Consolidated Holdings							$15.20
Die Wandernde Kuh			$14.70			$14.40	$19.00
Drachenblut Delikatessen							
Du monde entier	$39.00					$18.00	
Eastern Connection				$34.00		$18.00	
Ernst Handel	$148.20	$20.00	$18.40	$68.00	$50.00		$34.20
Familia Arquibaldo			$14.70	$34.00			
Folies gourmandes					$125.00		
Folk och fä HB							$49.40

Record: |◄| ◄ | 1 | ► | ►| | ►* | of 89

Figure 10-7 Retrieving order information through a crosstab query

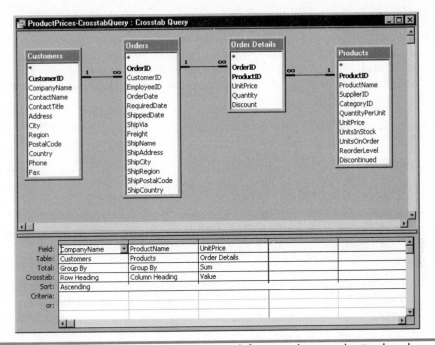

Figure 10-8 The design grid for a crosstab query definition, showing the Total and Crosstab rows

The Total row allows you to specify various actions that support the process of summarizing data. Most of the options available to the Total row are functions that perform a predefined set of actions. For example, you can use the Sum function to add together the values in a specific field. (Functions are discussed in Module 11.) In addition to providing functions, the Total row provides options that relate to other types of actions that are associated with the specified fields. One particularly useful option for creating a crosstab query is the Group By option, which is used to specify that the values in the designated field are to be grouped together. Notice that, in Figure 10-8, the first and second columns use the Group By option in the Total row for both fields. This indicates that the two fields form the foundation for the summarized data; the values from these fields are grouped together to allow you to summarize the data from the UnitPrice field.

The Crosstab row in the design grid works in conjunction with the Total row. The Crosstab row provides four options:

● **Row Heading**   The values from this field are grouped together to form a row for each column. The first field in each row contains the grouped value from the designated field. Examples of row headings in Figure 10-7 are Alfreds Futterkiste, Ana Trujillo Emparedados y helados, and Antonio Moreno Taquería, all of which are values in the CompanyName field in the Customers table. This is the first column in the design grid shown in Figure 10-8.

- **Column Heading**   The values from this field are grouped together to form a heading for each column except for the first column. Each column heading represents a grouped value from the designated field. Examples of column headings in Figure 10-7 are Alice Mutton, Aniseed Syrup, and Boston Crab Meat, all of which are values in the ProductName field in the Products table. This is the second column in the design grid shown in Figure 10-8.

- **Value**   The values from this field are summarized according to the Row Heading and Column Heading fields and the function selected in the Total row.

- **(not shown)**   This option is used when you're including a field in your crosstab query that is not a Row Heading, Column Heading, or Value field. The (not shown) option allows you to create fields that help to further define which rows are included in the query results. For example, you can add another column to the design grid for the UnitPrice column. This new column might contain an expression that limits the results to only those totals that exceed a particular unit price.

The Row Heading and Column Heading options must be used with the Group By option in the Total row. The Value option must be used with one of the functions (such as Sum or Avg) in the Total row. Each crosstab query must have one or more Row Heading fields, one Column Heading field, and one Value field.

When you create a crosstab query, you can specify criteria in the Row Heading and Column Heading fields, but not in the Value field. If you want to define criteria for the Value field, add that field to a new column in the design grid, select the Where option for the Total row, select the (not shown) option for the Crosstab row, and then enter the expression in the Criteria cell, as shown in Figure 10-9.

As you can see, a new column has been added to the design grid. The column uses the same field as the Value field. The expression added to the criteria specifies that the total values returned must exceed $100.00. In addition, an expression has been added to the criteria of the Row Heading field. Now all values in this field must begin with the letter *m* or later. If you run this query, your results will look similar to those in Figure 10-10. Notice that the results include only summarized values that exceed $100.00 and only those companies whose names begin with the letter *m* or later.

NOTE

When you specify only the first letter as part of the expression, as in >"m", any value that begins with m and has more than one character is considered greater than the specified value. For example, "ma" and "mb" are both greater than m, as are "na" and "oa."

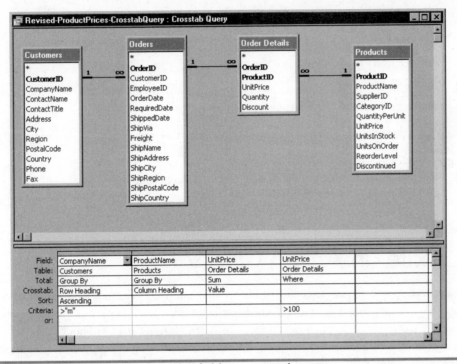

Figure 10-9 Adding criteria to the Value field in a crosstab query

Company Name	Côte de Blaye	Thüringer Rostbratwurst
Mère Paillarde	$210.80	
Piccolo und mehr	$210.80	
Princesa Isabel Vinhos		$123.79
Queen Cozinha	$210.80	
QUICK-Stop	$527.00	$123.79
Rancho grande	$263.50	
Rattlesnake Canyon Grocery	$474.30	
Richter Supermarkt		$123.79
Santé Gourmet	$263.50	
Save-a-lot Markets		$247.58
Simons bistro	$210.80	
Spécialités du monde	$263.50	
Split Rail Beer & Ale	$210.80	
The Big Cheese	$263.50	
The Cracker Box		$123.79
Tortuga Restaurante	$263.50	
Tradição Hipermercados		$123.79
Wartian Herkku		$123.79
White Clover Markets	$263.50	

Record: 1 of 19

Figure 10-10 Query results from the revised crosstab query

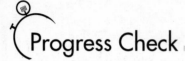

Progress Check

1. What is a query?

2. What dialog box appears when you first open the Design view window when the Queries object type is selected in the database window?

3. What types of criteria elements can you include in the Criteria cells of the design grid in the Design view window?

4. What two rows are added to the design grid for a crosstab query?

Create an Action Query

As you've seen so far, the select query and crosstab query are effective ways to view specific data stored in an Access database. You can make the queries as simple or as complicated as you like and run them as often as you want, and the underlying data will not be affected. However, there is another type of query, known as the *action query,* that allows you to update data in the tables participating in the query. Access supports four types of action queries: make-table, update, append, and delete. In this section, we'll look at each one of these queries and explain how they're used to modify data in your Access database.

CAUTION

Because an action query updates data, you must be very careful when you create and run these queries. Each time you run the query, the changes defined by the query are implemented. As a result, you should never run an action query unless you're certain that the query will make the changes that you want to make. Before saving any query to the database, view the results of the query by clicking the View button on the Query Design toolbar. Viewing the query results in this way will not affect the data.

---

1. A query is a data object in an Access database that contains a defined set of criteria that can be used to retrieve or update records in a database.

2. The Show Table dialog box

3. The Criteria cells can contain field names, field values, wildcards, expressions, operators, and functions.

4. The Total row and the Crosstab row

Creating a Make-Table Query

The first type of action query that we'll look at is the make-table query. As the name suggests, the *make-table query* is a type of query that creates a table based on the results generated from that query. In most respects it is just like a select query, except that rather than displaying the query results in a Datasheet view window, the query creates a table that contains the results.

When you first create a make-table query, you must provide a name for the new table. After the query has been created, the table will be created each time you run the query. You can view and modify the data in the table just as in any other table in an Access database. The data in that table is not linked to the data in the originating tables that were used to define the query. If the data in the underlying tables changes, you must run the query again in order to re-create the table and populate it with the changed data.

Because creating a make-table query is similar to creating a select query, the processes used to create the two types of queries are also similar, except for the fact that you must provide a name for the new table. To create a make-table query, open the Design view window, and add the necessary tables and queries to the window. After you close the Show Table dialog box, click the down arrow on the Query Type button on the Query Design toolbar, and then click Make-Table Query. The Make Table dialog box appears (shown in Figure 10-11). You must enter a table name and, optionally, the path and name of the Access database file if you want to create the table in a database other than the current one. By default, the new table is created in the current database.

Once you've identified the name of the table that will be created when you run the query, you can create the query definition as you would any other type of select query. The definition can be based on one or more tables, the fields can be sorted, and criteria can be defined on any fields. After you create the definition, you can view the results of your query by clicking the View button on the Query Design toolbar. This displays the results in a Design view window without actually creating the table. To create the table, click the Run button on the Query Design toolbar or run the query from the database window.

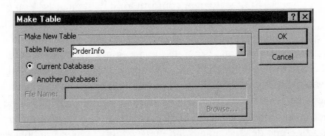

Figure 10-11 The Make Table dialog box used to create a make-table query

When you first run the query, you'll receive a message asking you to confirm whether you want to run this query, and then you'll receive a second message notifying you that you're about to paste the rows from the query result into a new table. (You won't receive the first message if you run the query from within the Design view window.) If you run the query again after the table has been created, you'll also receive a message telling you that the existing table will be deleted before the query is run. In each case, click Yes to continue. Once the table has been created, you can view and modify the data or the table definition as you would any other table.

TIP

Each query listed in the database window is accompanied by an icon that is different for each query type. The icons used for action queries include an exclamation point to indicate that it is an action query so that you're aware that, by running the query, you're about to modify data in the database.

Ask the Expert

Q: You state that you can use the View button on the Query Design toolbar to view the results of a query when you're working with that query in Design view. When I click the down arrow on the View button, I also see an option that says SQL View. What is this view for?

A: SQL View allows you to view the actual SQL statement underlying the query. Whenever you create a query in Design view, an SQL statement is generated. The SQL statement defines the tables and fields that participate in the query and includes clauses that determine which records are returned in the query results. Access uses a special form of SQL designed specifically for Access databases, although many of the elements in an Access SQL statement conform to SQL standards. You can modify the SQL statement directly in the SQL view window; however, this might change the way the query results display the data. For most SQL queries, you can use the Design view window to define the query and generate the necessary SQL statements. As a result, you will rarely need to use the SQL View window. However, some SQL statements must be created directly in the SQL View window. These statements include the *union query,* which combines fields from one or more tables into one table; the *pass-through query,* which sends commands to an ODBC database; the *data-definition query,* which creates, modifies, and deletes tables; and the *subquery,* which is a query embedded inside another query. For a complete explanation of each type of query and SQL in general, see Access online Help.

Creating an Update Query

When you run a make-table query, you're adding data to a new table, so you're not affecting any of the existing data or tables, unless you're simply re-running the make-table query and replacing that table. However, the other three types of action queries can directly affect data or tables that already exist. The first of these types of action queries that we'll look at is the update query. An *update query* is a type of query that modifies existing data in a table. In the query definition, you identify which records in a table should be modified and what the new values should be. Each time you run your query, the values are changed.

Let's take a look at an example of an update query to show you how it works. Figure 10-12 shows a query definition that is based on the Products table in the Northwind database. As with any other query that you create in the Design view window, you must first identify the participating tables. After that, you must select the query type. To do so, click the down arrow on the Query Type button on the Query Design toolbar, and then click Update Query. The design grid is modified by the removal of the Sort and Show rows and the addition of the Update To row.

The Update To row is used to identify the new value for a particular field. Notice in Figure 10-12 that the first column contains the UnitsOnOrder field and an expression in the Update To cell. The expression deducts 10 from whatever the current value is in that field. For example, if there are currently 47 units on order for a particular record, the new value will be 37.

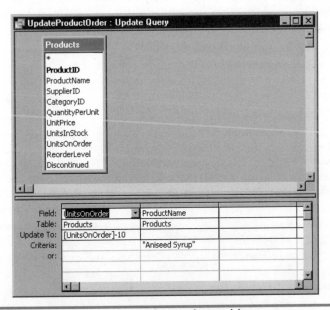

Figure 10-12 Creating an update query on the Products table

In addition to identifying any new values, you should identify which records will be updated, unless you want every record in a table updated. If you do not specify which records should be updated, then all records will be updated. For example, if you were to use only the first column shown in Figure 10-12 in your query definition, 10 units would be deducted from the current UnitsOnOrder value for each record. However, you can specify which records will be updated by including a column that defines a field value for the records to be updated. In the case of the query definition shown in Figure 10-12, the second column contains the ProductName field and specifies that only records that have a ProductName value of Aniseed Syrup should be updated with a new UnitsOnOrder value. As a result, only one record would be updated in the table because only one record has a ProductName value of Aniseed Syrup.

Once you've defined your update query, you should view it (by clicking the View button on the Query Design toolbar) before you actually run the query. When you view the query in Datasheet view, what you're actually seeing is a table that contains the values that will be updated. In many cases, all you will see is a single value. For example, if you view the query shown in Figure 10-12, you will see only a single value, which is the value in the single Aniseed Syrup record that will be modified when you run the query. The Datasheet view window displays only the data as it currently exists, not what it will look like after you run the query. As you can see in Figure 10-13, the current UnitsOnOrder value for the Aniseed Syrup record is 70. When you run the query, it will be changed to 60.

Once you're satisfied that your query definition is correct, you can save the query and then run it from the Design view window (by clicking the Run button on the Query Design toolbar) or from the database window. When you run the query, you will receive one or two messages, depending on which method you use to run the query. You will first receive a message asking whether you're sure that you want to run this type of query, and you will then receive a message providing you with the number of rows that will be updated. In each case, click Yes to continue.

CAUTION

Each time you run an update query, the values are updated in the participating table. For example, when you run the query shown in Figure 10-12 the first time, it changes the UnitsOnOrder value from 70 to 60. However, the second time that you run the query the value will be changed from 60 to 50, and so on. Do not re-run an update query unless you're certain that you want the data updated once again.

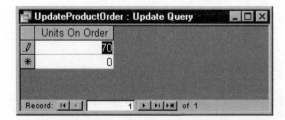

Figure 10-13 Viewing the data that will be updated in the Products table

Progress Check

1. What is an action query?

2. When is a table created in a make-table query?

3. How do you view the results of a make-table query without creating a table?

4. What is an update query?

Creating an Append Query

The next action query that we'll look at is the append query. The *append query* is a type of query that takes the records returned by the query and inserts them into an existing table. You can think of an append query as a cross between a select query and a make-table query. As in a select query, you identify fields, specify sort orders, and define criteria. And, as in a make-table query, you must identify a target table when you're first creating the query. However, unlike the make-table query, the append query does not create a new table; instead, it adds data to a table that already exists in the current database or in another Access database.

The process of creating an append query is similar to that for creating a make-table query. After you've added the necessary tables to the Design view window, you must identify the target table and set up the design grid to accommodate this type of query. To do so, click the down arrow on the Query Type button on the Query Design toolbar, and then click Append Query. This will launch the Append dialog box (shown in Figure 10-14), which allows you to identify the target table. You can select the target table from the Table Name drop-down list. The list will contain the names of the tables in the current database or the remote database, depending on which database you've selected.

Figure 10-14 The Append dialog box used to identify the target table

1. An action query is a type of query that allows you to update data in the tables participating in the query.
2. The table is created whenever you run the query.
3. You can view the results of a make-table query by clicking the View button on the Query Design toolbar.
4. An update query is a type of query that modifies existing data in a table.

After you've identified the target table, you can define the rest of the query. When you selected the Append Query option, the Show row in the design grid was replaced by the Append To row. The Append To row identifies the field of the target table into which a value will be inserted. For example, the query shown in Figure 10-15 shows a value of ProductID in the Append To cell of the first column. This means that the value from the ImportProductID field in the ImportProducts table will be inserted into the ProductID field of the Products table.

NOTE

The query definition shown in Figure 10-15 includes one column in the design grid for every field in the ImportProducts table. Because every field is included, you could have set up the design grid differently. Instead of using a column for each field, you could have used only one column that contained values that represented every field in the table. In this case, you would have used the ImportProducts.* value in the Field cell and the Products.* value in the Append To cell.

Other than the Append To row replacing the Show row, the design grid is identical to the grid used for select queries, so you simply create the query as you would any select or make-table query. Keep in mind that you need to match each field that you add to the Field cell in a column to the corresponding Append To cell in that column so that Access knows where to insert the value.

Once you've created your query, you can then view the data that will be inserted into the table by clicking the View button on the Query Design toolbar. Viewing the table in this manner allows you to see exactly what data will be inserted into the target table without actually running the query. When you do finally run the query, the query results will be inserted into the table,

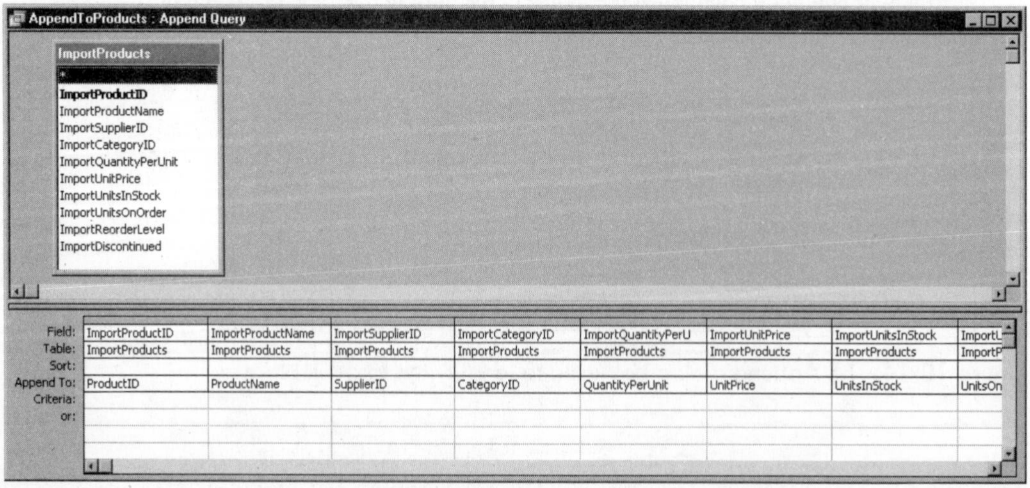

Figure 10-15 Using an append query to insert data into the Products table

and each time you run the query, the results will again be inserted into the table. As with other types of action queries, Access will prompt you with the necessary warning messages to let you know that you're about to add data to the database.

Creating a Delete Query

The last type of action query that we'll look at is the delete query. As you would expect, a *delete query* is used to delete data from a table. To create a delete query, you must first set up the design grid in the Design view window to support this type of query. After you've identified the participating tables, click the down arrow on the Query Type button on the Query Design toolbar, and then click Delete Query. The Sort and Show rows are removed from the design grid and the Delete row is added, as shown in Figure 10-16.

The Delete row supports two options: From and Where. The correct option is selected automatically depending on what field you select from the table object. If you select the asterisk, which represents all fields, the From option is used, as shown in the first column of the figure. If you select an individual field from the table object, as shown in the second column, the Where option is used. The From option indicates that the table identified by the asterisk option contains the data to be deleted. Because you can delete only entire records from a table, and not individual fields, the From option and the asterisk option must be used together. On the other hand, the Where option must be used when an individual field is specified. The Where option refines the query by indicating that a particular condition must be met for a record to be deleted. If you were to define a From field without defining a Where field, all records would be deleted from the table.

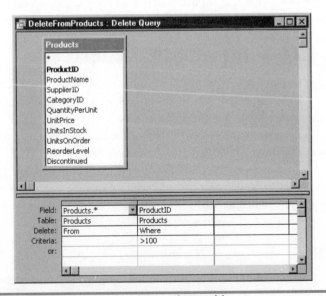

Figure 10-16 Defining a delete query on the Products table

If you refer again to Figure 10-16, you can see how the From option identifies the Products table as the table that contains the data to be deleted. Notice that the Field cell uses the Products.* value, which is what is displayed if you drag the asterisk from the table object to the Field cell. This indicates that all fields are included in this column. Notice also that the From option is used in the Delete cell. However, if you take a look at the second column, which identifies the ProductID field, the Where option is used, along with an expression in the criteria that limits the query to a ProductID value greater than 100. In other words, only records with a ProductID value greater than 100 will be deleted from the table.

Once you've set up your delete query, you should view it in Datasheet view by clicking the View button on the Query Design toolbar. This allows you to view the records that will be deleted from the table without actually deleting the records. Once you're satisfied with your query, you can run it to actually delete the records. However, keep in mind that, once you do run the query, the records are permanently deleted from the table, and you cannot undo that deletion. In addition, if you run the query again, more records are deleted from the table, if they meet the criteria defined in the query definition.

TIP

You should consider making a backup copy of any table from which you plan to delete records. That way, if you run into a problem with the deletion, you'll have a backup copy to fall back on so that you can retrieve the lost data.

When you run a delete query, you'll receive two messages, one telling you that you are about to take an action that will affect data and one telling you the number of rows that you are about to delete. In both cases, simply click Yes to continue with the deletion.

Project 10-2 Creating Action Queries

As you've seen in this module, Access supports four different types of action queries: make-table, update, append, and delete. In this project, you will create and run an append query and then an update query. For the append query, you will be retrieving data from the Products1 table in the consumer advocacy database and inserting that data into the Products table. The Products1 table is a table that you created in Project 9-1 in Module 9, when you imported data into your database. You will now transfer that imported data into the Products table. After you run the append query, you will create an update query that will modify some of the data that you just copied into the Products table. You will run the update query one time and then verify that the records have been correctly updated.

Step by Step

1. If they're not already open, open Access and then open the ConsumerAdvocacy.mdb database file.

2. Select the Queries object type in the database window, and then double-click Create Query In Design View. The Design view window and the Show Table dialog box appear, with the dialog box active.

3. Double-click the Products1 table and then click Close. The Products1 table object is added to the Design view window, and the Show Table dialog box closes.

4. Resize the Design view window and the Products1 table object so that you can see the entire table.

5. Click the down arrow on the Query Type button on the Query Design toolbar, and then click Append Query. The Append dialog box appears.

6. In the Table Name drop-down list, select Products, and then click OK. The query will now append records to the Products table.

7. Double-click the asterisk in the Products1 table object. The first column in the design grid is populated with field and table information about the source table and the target table.

8. Click the View button on the Query Design toolbar. The rows that will be added to the Products table are displayed in a Datasheet view window.

9. Click the View button again to return to the Design view window.

10. Click the Save button on the Query Design toolbar. The Save As dialog box appears.

11. In the Query Name text box, type **AppendProducts**, and then click OK. The Save As dialog box closes and you're returned to the Design view window.

12. Close the Design view window.

13. Double-click the AppendProducts query in the database window. A message box appears stating that you are about to run an append query.

14. Click Yes. A second message box appears stating that you are about to append eight rows.

15. Click Yes.

16. Select the Tables object type in the database window, and then double-click the Products table. The Products table opens in Datasheet view and displays the records that have just been inserted into the table.

17. Close the Datasheet view window.

18. Select the Queries object type in the database window, and then double-click Create Query In Design View. The Design view window and Show Table dialog box appear, with the dialog box active.

(continued)

19. Double-click the Products table, and then click Close. The Products table object is added to the Design view window, and the Show Table dialog box closes.

20. Resize the Design view window and the Products table object so that you can see the entire table.

21. Click the down arrow on the Query Type button on the Query Design toolbar, and then click Update Query. The Sort and Show rows are removed from the design grid, and the Update To row is added.

22. Double-click the OnOrder field in the table object. The field and table names are added to the first column in the design grid.

23. In the Update To cell of the first column, type **[OnOrder]-5**.

24. Double-click the ProductTitle field in the table object. The field and table names are added to the second column in the design grid.

25. In the first Criteria cell of the second column, type **hat***, and then select another cell to complete the expression. The value is changed to the Like "hat*" expression.

26. Click the View button on the Query Design toolbar. Two values (both 30) are displayed in the Datasheet view window. These are the two values that will be modified.

27. Click the View button again to return to the Design view window.

28. Click the Save button on the Query Design toolbar. The Save As dialog box appears.

29. In the Query Name text box, type **UpdateProducts**, and then click OK. The Save As dialog box closes and you're returned to the Design view window.

30. Close the Design view window.

31. Double-click the UpdateProducts query in the database window. A message box appears stating that you are about to run an update query.

32. Click Yes. A second message box appears stating that you are about to update two rows.

33. Click Yes.

34. Select the Tables object type in the database window, and then double-click the Products table. The Products table opens in Datasheet view. The OnOrder values for the two hat products should now be 25.

Project Summary

In this project, you created and ran an append query and an update query. In each case, you ran the query only one time. If you were to run the append query a second time, you would receive a message warning you that you could not add the records to the table because you violated one of the constraints on the table. This is because the primary key on the table requires unique values, so you cannot add records that have already been added. However, you could run the update query repeatedly. Whenever you do so, five units will be subtracted from the OnOrder value of the applicable records. Regardless of what type of action query you're running, you should be careful that you are correctly updating data. If necessary, make backup copies of your tables to ensure that you can recover any lost data.

✓

Module 10 Mastery Check

1. Which type of query retrieves and displays a subset of data from one or more tables?

   A. Make-table

   B. Append

   C. Select

   D. Crosstab

2. In what window are the results of a select query displayed?

3. Which rows are included by default in the design grid of the Design view window for a select query?

   A. Sort

   B. Total

   C. Append To

   D. Show

4. How do you view the results of a query when in Design view without actually running the query?

5. What is the main difference between a single-table query definition and a multiple-table query definition?

6. A(n) _____ query is a type of query that groups together related data and summarizes values associated with that data.

7. You're creating a crosstab query in the Design view window. For one of the fields, you want the values grouped together to form a row for each unique value. Which option should you use in the Crosstab cell?

   A. Row Heading

   B. Column Heading

C. Value

D. (not shown)

8. You're creating a crosstab query in the Design view window. One of the fields is configured with the Column Heading option. Which option should you use in the Total row of the design grid?

   A. Where

   B. Sum

   C. Group By

   D. Count

9. What are the four types of action queries?

10. What is the difference between an update query and an append query?

11. A(n) _____ query is a type of query that creates a table based on the results generated from that query.

12. Which types of action queries directly affect data or tables that already exist in a database?

   A. Make-table

   B. Update

   C. Append

   D. Delete

13. What information do you identify in an update query definition?

14. What is the main difference between an append query and a make-table query?

15. You're creating a delete query in the Design view window. You drag the asterisk from the table object to the Field cell of the column in the design grid. Which option is added the Delete cell of that column?

   A. Value

   B. From

   C. Group By

   D. Where

Module 11

Adding Expressions to Your Queries

CRITICAL SKILLS

11.1 Work with Expressions

11.2 Add Expressions to Your Queries

11.3 Use Expression Builder to Create Expressions

239

Throughout this book, you have seen expressions used in a number of places—in validation rules, as parts of different types of filters, and in the criteria of query definitions. Expressions provide a great deal of flexibility when you need to define conditions that can be applied to data in a specific environment. Expressions can play a critical role in creating a query that can span multiple tables while limiting the data returned to only the essential information. The more detailed the expression, the more useful the data returned by the query. In this module, we will look at how expressions are used in query definitions to determine which records are included in the query results and to return calculated data. Although this module focuses specifically on how expressions are defined in queries, much of what you learn here can be applied to filters, validation rules, default values, and anywhere else expressions can be used.

CRITICAL SKILL
11.1 # Work with Expressions

In Module 4, you were introduced to expressions when you learned how to configure default values and validation rules. As you'll recall from that module, an expression is a combination of symbols and values that create a formula used to produce a specific result. The result is a value or range of values that specify a condition that must be met in whatever environment the expression is used. For example, if a field validation rule is configured with an expression, any values entered into that field must meet the condition specified by the expression, otherwise the value is not permitted.

Expressions are not limited to default values and validation rules. As you saw in Module 8, expressions can be used extensively in filters to refine those filters so that you can view exactly the information that you want to see. The same is true for queries. Expressions can be pivotal to creating robust, intricate queries that allow you to view or modify specific records in your Access tables. You saw a number of examples of expressions in Module 10, where the expressions were defined as part of the query's criteria. However, you can also use expressions to create fields in your query results that contain calculations based on the data that exists in your tables.

Before we look at the various ways in which expressions can be used in a query, let's take a look at the components that make up an expression. As I have mentioned, an expression is a formula, and as such it is made up of parts that allow you to define one or more conditions that must be met by the applicable values. An expression can consist of any of the following elements:

- **Operators** Operators are symbols or words that are used to compare or calculate data. They serve a purpose similar to the symbols used in mathematical calculations. In fact, in some cases the symbols are the same, such as the plus (+) sign or the equal (=) sign.

- **Functions** A function is a predefined operation that returns a specific value that is used within the expression. For example, the Date function returns the current date.

- **Identifiers** These are the names of Access database objects, such as tables or fields. For example, the identifier for the Customers table in the Northwind database is [Customers]. (Identifiers are enclosed in brackets when used in expressions.)

- **Literals** Literals are values that are used exactly as typed into an expression. For example, the literal ABC could be used to compare to values in the database that contain ABC.

For a statement to qualify as an expression, it must include at least one operator and one of the other three elements. In addition, each expression can be made up of multiple conditions. A *condition* is basically an expression. The term "condition" is used when multiple expressions are linked together into one statement. When this occurs, the individual expressions are referred to as "conditions," and the conditions are linked together to form one "expression." I'll be discussing how conditions are linked together later in the module, in the section "Logical Operators." Now let's take a closer look at the four components that make up an expression.

NOTE

In addition to the four components, Access supports the use of wildcards in an expression. As you'll recall from Module 4, a wildcard is a placeholder that represents one or more characters in a value. The question mark (?) wildcard represents exactly one character, and the asterisk (*) wildcard represents any number of characters.

Using Operators in an Expression

Access supports four types of operators that can be used in an expression: comparison, arithmetic, logical, and concatenation. In this section, I'll explain each type and provide examples that demonstrate how they're used.

Comparison Operators

The first type of operator that we'll look at is the comparison operator. A comparison operator compares a value in a field to an element that defines another value. For example, you might want to use a comparison operator to return values in a field that are greater than 100. To do this, you would use the greater than (>) comparison operator and the 100 literal to produce the >100 expression.

Access supports ten comparison operators that can be used in an expression. Table 11-1 provides examples of each comparison operator and describes how those examples are used to compare data.

As you can see, comparison operators provide you with a wide range of actions. You can use them with literals, functions, and identifiers to create expressions that restrict and calculate values. If no comparison operator is specified in an expression, Access uses the equal (=) operator, unless a wildcard is used, in which case the Like operator is used. For example, if

Operator	Example	Field Value Restriction
>	>30	The returned value must be a numerical value greater than 30.
>=	>=#1/1/99#	The returned value must be a date/time value that is the same as or later than January 1, 1999.
<	<301	The returned value must be a numerical value less than 301.
<=	<=0	The returned value must be a numerical value less than or equal to 0.
=	="Unknown"	The returned value must be a character string value that equals Unknown.
<>	<>#12/31/2001#	The returned value must be a date/time value that does not equal December 31, 2001.
Like	Like "D*"	The returned value must begin with the letter D but can include any number of characters after the D.
Between	Between 10 And 20	The returned value must fall within the range of 10 through 20, inclusive.
Is	Is Null	The returned value must be null. The Is operator can also be used with Not Null to return values that are not null.
In	In ("WA", "CA")	The returned value must equal WA or CA.

Table 11-1 The Comparison Operators Used in Access Queries

you specify Unknown, in a query's criteria, Access creates the ="Unknown" expression. If you specify Un*, Access creates the Like "Un*" expression.

NOTE

Access requires quotation marks around text values (as in ="beverages") and number signs around date/time values (as in <>#12/31/2001#). If you do not add the quotation marks or number signs, Access adds them automatically.

Arithmetic Operators

The primary arithmetic operators that you'll use in Access expressions are the same as those that you'll see in basic mathematical formulas. By using arithmetic operators, you can add, subtract, multiply, and divide the value represented by the functions, literals, and identifiers in an expression. Table 11-2 provides examples of the primary arithmetic operators and describes how those examples are used to manipulate numerical values.

Operator	Example	Action
+	[InStock]+10	Adds 10 to the value in the InStock field
-	[InStock]-19	Subtracts 19 from the value in the InStock field
*	[InStock]*3	Multiplies the value in the InStock field by 3
/	[InStock]/2	Divides the value in the InStock field by 2

Table 11-2 The Arithmetic Operators Used in Access Queries

You can use arithmetic operators on numerical values only. Whenever you create a condition that uses an arithmetic operator, you must include two other expression components (functions, literals, or identifiers) in the condition. The only exception to this is the minus (-) sign, which can be used to change the sign of a numerical value. For example, you can change a positive numerical value to a negative value.

Logical Operators

Logical operators are used primarily to compare two or more conditions within an expression. The operators determine which conditions in the expression must be met. The most commonly used logical operators used in Access are And, Or, and Not:

- **And**   The conditions on both sides of the operator must evaluate to true. In other words, a value must conform to any two conditions that are connected by And.

- **Or**   At least one of the conditions on either side of the operator must evaluate to true. This means that the value can conform to either of the two conditions that are connected by the Or operator.

- **Not**   This operator negates the condition that follows it, which means that a value must *not* conform to the condition.

Logical operators are used extensively in query expressions to connect multiple conditions. For example, suppose that you have two conditions that contain comparison operators that define an acceptable range of values:

>=100 And <=200

The And logical operator is used to connect the two conditions. Because the And condition is used, both conditions must be met. (The conditions must evaluate to true.) As a result, a value must be greater than or equal to 100 *and* less than or equal to 200 in order to be returned by a query.

Now suppose that you use an Or logical operator to compare two conditions that each contain comparison operators:

="Beverages" Or ="Condiments"

In this expression, either the first condition must be met *or* the second condition must be met. As a result, the value returned by the query must be Beverages or Condiments.

Now let's take a look at an example that uses the Not operator in two conditions that are connected by an And operator:

Not "Beverages" And Not "Condiments"

Because both conditions must be met, the values returned cannot be Beverages and cannot be Condiments, but can be any other acceptable value.

NOTE

When you use a Not operator in an expression, Access changes the operator to a not equal to (<>) comparison operator when you save and close the query.

The Concatenation Operator

Access supports the use of a concatenation operator that allows you to combine multiple text values in order to create one character string. The ampersand (&) operator is used along with the appropriate functions, literals, or identifiers to join together the represented values. For example, the following expression joins together values from the FirstName field with values from the LastName field:

[FirstName]&" "&[LastName]

Notice that a space is added (between the quotation marks) so that when the values are concatenated, the first name and last name are not strung together. The space is considered a text literal and as such requires the quotations marks. Now the names will be displayed in one column in a readable format.

Using Functions in an Expression

Functions are useful for taking an action on a value returned by an expression. For example, you can use a function to specify that an expression must return a value in a specific data type, as shown in the following example:

CCur([UnitPrice]*[Quantity])

In this example, the expression enclosed in the function's parentheses ([UnitPrice]*[Quantity]) multiplies the value in the UnitPrice field by the value in the Quantity field for each record returned by the query. The fields, as you would probably guess, are configured with different data types. The CCur function converts the value returned by this expression into the Currency data type. So your query results will display the totals as currency, which is how you would want to view this sort of data, even though the values are derived from fields with different data types.

In addition to using a function to perform an action on an expression, you can use a function directly in an expression:

>Date()

In this example, the Date function is used to return today's date. The greater than (>) operator is then used to compare the field value to today's date. If the value is later than today's date, the value is returned.

Access supports more than 150 functions. The easiest way to view a list of all of the available functions is through Expression Builder, an Access tool that helps you create expressions. Once in Expression Builder, you can see a list of all of the functions, sorted into 14 categories, and you can view the related Help files for each type of function. (I'll be discussing Expression Builder later in the module, in the section "Using Expression Builder to Create Expressions.")

For most functions, you must supply one or more arguments. An *argument* is a value that is included with the function and that is used to process that function. The arguments are enclosed in a set of parentheses after the function name. If more than one argument is used, the arguments are separated by commas. For example, the DateAdd function adds a specified amount of time to a date:

DateAdd("d",28,#9/10/2001#)

The DateAdd function takes three argument. Notice that the arguments are separated by commas. The first argument determines the interval that will be used. In this case, "d" is used to indicate days. The second argument indicates the number of days that will be added to the specified date. The third argument is the base date that will be added to. In other words, 28 days will be added to September 10, 2001. The function will return a new date value based on the function's calculation.

For some functions, an argument is not required. However, in these cases you must still use the parentheses. For example, the Date function does not require an argument, but when you use the function in an expression, you must include parentheses, as shown in the following example:

>=Date()

For many functions, an argument can take the form of an expression. You saw an example of this type of argument earlier in this section when the CCur function was used to convert the value returned by the expression to the Currency data type. In that case, the argument was the expression enclosed in the parentheses ([UnitPrice]*[Quantity]). The function uses the value returned by the expression in the same way that it would use a literal value.

Generally, the most common types of functions that you'll be using in your queries are those related to date and time, those used to manipulate data, and those used to convert data to a particular data type. In addition, you will often use aggregate functions to help you summarize and calculate data.

Using Aggregate Functions

In Module 10, you learned how to create a crosstab query, which is a type of query that groups together related data and summarizes values associated with that data. As you'll recall from that discussion, one of the rows in the design grid that you configured was the Total row, which allows you to select from a number of options. Many of the options available to the Total row are functions. These functions, known as *aggregate functions,* apply summary calculations to groups of data. For example, you can find the average of a set of values (by using the Avg function) or add the values together (by using the Sum function).

In addition to being able to use aggregate functions for crosstab queries, you can use them in expressions as you would any other function. You can also use them through the Total row of any query definition. By default, the Total row is not included in the design grid of a query unless it is a crosstab query. However, you can add the Total row to any query by clicking the Totals button on the Query Design toolbar. Once the Total row has been added, you can select the aggregate function from the cell's drop-down list. I'll be discussing how to use aggregate functions and the Total row in more detail later in this module, in the section "Creating Queries with Aggregate Functions."

Using Identifiers in an Expression

As you have learned, an identifier is the name of an Access data object. Identifiers are used not only for tables and fields, but also for queries, forms, reports, and any other type of Access object. You have already seen identifiers used in expressions in Module 10 and in this module. In these cases, field identifiers were used to represent the values that the fields contain. In this way, field values can be calculated in the same way as literal values or the values returned by functions.

When you use an identifier in an expression, you should enclose it in brackets. If you are referencing parent and child objects (such as a table and one of its fields), you must use an exclamation mark (!) to separate the identifiers, as in [Products]![UnitPrice]. UnitPrice is a field in the Products table. Notice that both identifiers are enclosed in brackets and separated by an exclamation point. When you refer to the parent object and child object together, the child object name is considered to be *qualified*.

Using Literals in an Expression

Access allows you to use three different types of literals in your expressions: numerical, text, or date/time. For numerical literals, simply type in the number in the appropriate place in your expression, as in the following example:

[InStock]>100

In this case, the literal is 100 and it is added directly to the expression.

Text literals must be enclosed in quotation marks. For example, the following expression uses Unknown as a text literal:

="Unknown"

As a result, all values returned for that field must equal Unknown.

For date/time values, enclose the value in number signs. In the following example, the value returned must be later than October 1, 1972.

>#10/1/72#

Progress Check

1. What are the four components that can be included in an expression?

2. What is a comparison operator?

3. How can a function be used in a query?

4. How would you represent the Employees table and the LastName field of that table in an expression?

---

1. Operators, functions, identifiers, and literals

2. A comparison operator is a type of operator that compares a value from a field to an element that defines another value.

3. A function can be used to take an action on a value returned by an expression, or it can be used directly in the expression to represent a value. In addition, aggregate functions can be used in the Total row of the design grid to summarize and calculate data.

4. [Employees]![LastName]

Add Expressions to Your Queries

Now that you have an understanding of all of the components that make up an expression, you're ready to create your own expressions. Of course, you've already seen examples of a number of different expressions, and you've even created a few of your own in the projects in previous modules. However, now we'll look at the expression creation process a little more closely and discuss how these expressions fit into a query.

The examples of query expressions that you've seen so far were those that you create in the criteria section of the design grid (in the Design view window). However, you can also create expressions in the Field row of the design grid, and you can use aggregate functions in the Total row, which essentially creates an expression based on the aggregate function that you select.

Creating Criteria Expressions

In Module 10, you learned how to create a select query in the Design view window. As you'll recall from that discussion, the Design view window displays objects for the participating tables and includes a design grid that you use to identify the fields that are included in the query results. In addition, the design grid allows you to specify a sort order, determine which fields will be displayed in the query results, and define the criteria that establishes which records are included.

As you have already seen, you define a query's criteria by using expressions to establish which values are acceptable in the query results. For each participating field, you can define one or more expressions, and for each expression, you can define one or more conditions, depending on the context of that expression. Let's take a look at examples of different expressions so that you can see how they're used to determine which records are returned by a query.

Using Operators and Literals

All expressions must include at least one operator and at least one function, literal, or identifier. In the first query example that we'll look at, the expressions are made up of operators and literals, as shown in Figure 11-1. The query includes three expressions, each one in a separate column of the Criteria row.

The first expression (Between 10300 And 11000) is defined on the OrderID field of the Orders table. The expression uses the Between comparison operator to limit the values permitted in this field to the range of 10300 through 11000, inclusive. The numerical values 10300 and 11000 are both literals. Only records with an OrderID value that falls within this range are returned by the query.

The second expression (<> "Alice Mutton" And <> "Geitost") is defined on the ProductName field in the Products table. The expression uses the not equal to (<>) comparison operator in

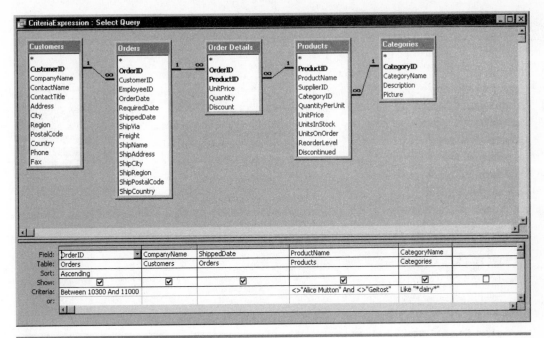

Figure 11-1 Operators and literals in query criteria expressions

two conditions that are connected by the And operator. Each condition includes a literal enclosed in quotation marks. The quotation marks must be used for text literals. Because the conditions are connected by the And operator, both conditions must evaluate to true. In other words, the records returned by the query must *not* include a ProductName value of Alice Mutton or Geitost.

The third expression (Like "*dairy*") is defined on the CategoryName field in the Categories table. In this expression, the Like operator is used to indicate that the returned value must be similar to the literal defined in the expression. In this case, the text literal (dairy) includes asterisk (*) wildcards on either side to indicate that any characters can appear before or after the literal. This means that the returned value must include the word "dairy" but that the word can appear anywhere in the value.

Now let's take a look at the results that are generated by the query. Figure 11-2 shows the records that are returned. Notice that the first Order ID value to be listed is 10304, which falls within the acceptable range. Also notice that the Product Name values do not include Alice Mutton or Geitost and that all the Category Name values include the word "dairy." As you can see, each record conforms to the restrictions defined by the query's expression.

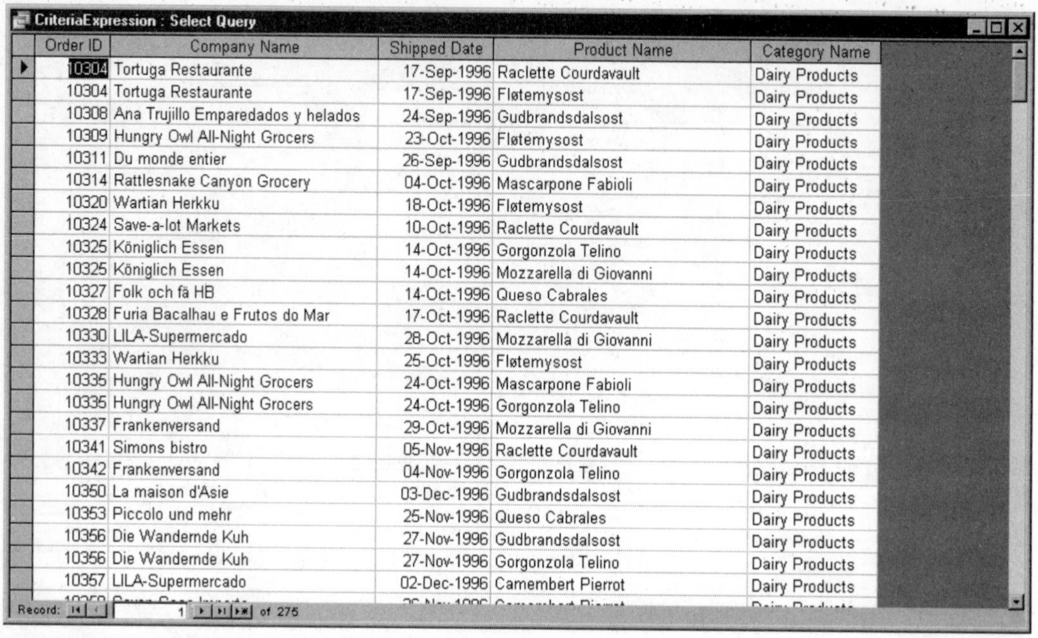
CriteriaExpression : Select Query

Order ID	Company Name	Shipped Date	Product Name	Category Name
10304	Tortuga Restaurante	17-Sep-1996	Raclette Courdavault	Dairy Products
10304	Tortuga Restaurante	17-Sep-1996	Fløtemysost	Dairy Products
10308	Ana Trujillo Emparedados y helados	24-Sep-1996	Gudbrandsdalsost	Dairy Products
10309	Hungry Owl All-Night Grocers	23-Oct-1996	Fløtemysost	Dairy Products
10311	Du monde entier	26-Sep-1996	Gudbrandsdalsost	Dairy Products
10314	Rattlesnake Canyon Grocery	04-Oct-1996	Mascarpone Fabioli	Dairy Products
10320	Wartian Herkku	18-Oct-1996	Fløtemysost	Dairy Products
10324	Save-a-lot Markets	10-Oct-1996	Raclette Courdavault	Dairy Products
10325	Königlich Essen	14-Oct-1996	Gorgonzola Telino	Dairy Products
10325	Königlich Essen	14-Oct-1996	Mozzarella di Giovanni	Dairy Products
10327	Folk och fä HB	14-Oct-1996	Queso Cabrales	Dairy Products
10328	Furia Bacalhau e Frutos do Mar	17-Oct-1996	Raclette Courdavault	Dairy Products
10330	LILA-Supermercado	28-Oct-1996	Mozzarella di Giovanni	Dairy Products
10333	Wartian Herkku	25-Oct-1996	Fløtemysost	Dairy Products
10335	Hungry Owl All-Night Grocers	24-Oct-1996	Mascarpone Fabioli	Dairy Products
10335	Hungry Owl All-Night Grocers	24-Oct-1996	Gorgonzola Telino	Dairy Products
10337	Frankenversand	29-Oct-1996	Mozzarella di Giovanni	Dairy Products
10341	Simons bistro	05-Nov-1996	Raclette Courdavault	Dairy Products
10342	Frankenversand	04-Nov-1996	Gorgonzola Telino	Dairy Products
10350	La maison d'Asie	03-Dec-1996	Gudbrandsdalsost	Dairy Products
10353	Piccolo und mehr	25-Nov-1996	Queso Cabrales	Dairy Products
10356	Die Wandernde Kuh	27-Nov-1996	Gudbrandsdalsost	Dairy Products
10356	Die Wandernde Kuh	27-Nov-1996	Gorgonzola Telino	Dairy Products
10357	LILA-Supermercado	02-Dec-1996	Camembert Pierrot	Dairy Products

Record: 1 of 275

Figure 11-2 Query results generated the operators and literals used in Figure 11-1

Using Functions and Identifiers

The next example that we'll look at builds on the previous example by defining an expression on the ShippedDate field, as shown in Figure 11-3. The new expression combines all four components (function, identifier, operator, and literal) in one expression.

The expression uses the Year function to extract only the year from the ShippedDate field. Because ShippedDate is a field object (and as such is used here as an identifier), it is enclosed in brackets, all of which are enclosed in the function's parentheses. The value returned by the Year function is then compared to the literal 1997. The greater than or equal to (>=) comparison operator is used to compare the data. As a result, the function's value must be greater than or equal to 1997, or that record is not returned.

You may have noticed that, when working with a long expression in the grid, you cannot view the entire expression at once. To remedy this, you can expand the column within the grid, which often takes care of this problem. However, there might be times when the expression is so long that resizing the column becomes cumbersome. Another method that you can use to view the entire expression is to *zoom* in on the expression. To do this, right-click the cell and then click Zoom in the shortcut menu. The Zoom dialog box appears (shown in Figure 11-4), and you can view and edit the expression in its entirety.

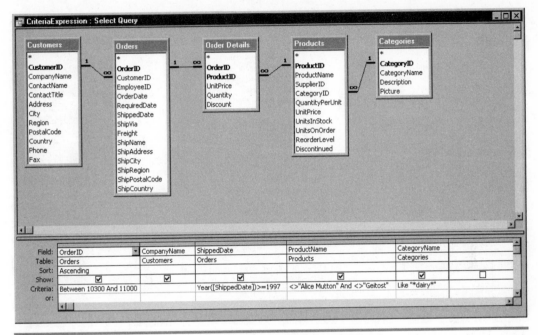

Figure 11-3 Using all four components in an expression

Now let's return to our query example. When you view the query, the results will include only those records with a Shipped Date value that contains the year 1997 or later, as shown in Figure 11-5. Notice that, even though the entire date is displayed, you were able to base your

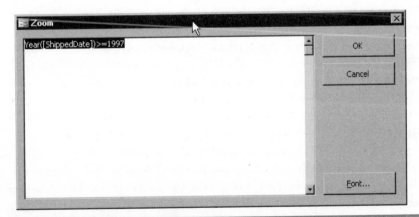

Figure 11-4 Using the Zoom dialog box to view an entire expression

Order ID	Company Name	Shipped Date	Product Name	Category Name
10380	Hungry Owl All-Night Grocers	16-Jan-1997	Camembert Pierrot	Dairy Products
10392	Piccolo und mehr	01-Jan-1997	Gudbrandsdalost	Dairy Products
10393	Save-a-lot Markets	03-Jan-1997	Gorgonzola Telino	Dairy Products
10395	HILARIÓN-Abastos	03-Jan-1997	Gudbrandsdalost	Dairy Products
10396	Frankenversand	06-Jan-1997	Mozzarella di Giovanni	Dairy Products
10396	Frankenversand	06-Jan-1997	Fløtemysost	Dairy Products
10399	Vaffeljernet	08-Jan-1997	Fløtemysost	Dairy Products
10401	Rattlesnake Canyon Grocery	10-Jan-1997	Fløtemysost	Dairy Products
10407	Ottilies Käseladen	30-Jan-1997	Fløtemysost	Dairy Products
10407	Ottilies Käseladen	30-Jan-1997	Gudbrandsdalost	Dairy Products
10407	Ottilies Käseladen	30-Jan-1997	Queso Cabrales	Dairy Products
10410	Bottom-Dollar Markets	15-Jan-1997	Raclette Courdavault	Dairy Products
10411	Bottom-Dollar Markets	21-Jan-1997	Raclette Courdavault	Dairy Products
10419	Richter Supermarkt	30-Jan-1997	Gudbrandsdalost	Dairy Products
10419	Richter Supermarkt	30-Jan-1997	Camembert Pierrot	Dairy Products
10423	Gourmet Lanchonetes	24-Feb-1997	Gorgonzola Telino	Dairy Products
10423	Gourmet Lanchonetes	24-Feb-1997	Raclette Courdavault	Dairy Products
10430	Ernst Handel	03-Feb-1997	Raclette Courdavault	Dairy Products
10434	Folk och få HB	13-Feb-1997	Queso Cabrales	Dairy Products
10435	Consolidated Holdings	07-Feb-1997	Mozzarella di Giovanni	Dairy Products
10439	Mère Paillarde	10-Feb-1997	Queso Manchego La Pastora	Dairy Products
10442	Ernst Handel	18-Feb-1997	Queso Cabrales	Dairy Products
10443	Reggiani Caseifici	14-Feb-1997	Queso Cabrales	Dairy Products
10446	Toms Spezialitäten	19-Feb-1997	Gorgonzola Telino	Dairy Products

Record: 1 of 232

Figure 11-5 Query results generated by the expressions in Figure 11-3

expression on only the year because you used the Year function, and that this did not affect the way that the values are displayed, nor did it affect the underlying data.

Using Multiple Lines of Criteria

The last two query examples that we looked at included several expressions in the definition's criteria. As you'll recall, the expressions were all defined on the in the same Criteria row. However, Access allows you to define multiple rows of criteria, which allows you to create queries that are even more specific than queries where only one row of criteria is used.

Each row of criteria is treated as one unit, and the rows are separated by using "or" logic, just as the Or operator is used to separate conditions in an expression. In other words, for a query to return a record, the record must meet the restrictions specified in any one of the configured criteria rows. Let's take a look at an example to help clarify this.

Figure 11-6 shows a query that contains two rows of criteria. The first row is configured with the same expressions as the last example that you looked at. The second row is different from the first row in two ways. First, an expression is not defined for the ShippedDate field. Second, values returned by the CategoryName field must contain the word "meat," rather than "dairy."

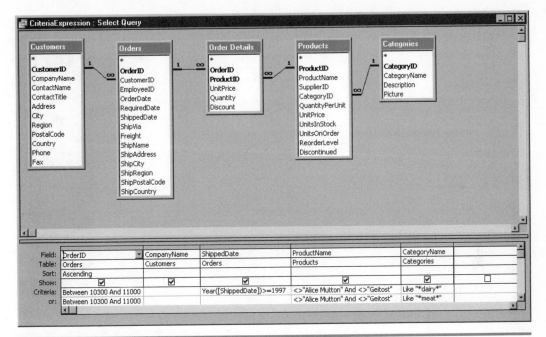

Figure 11-6 Using a second row of criteria in the design grid

When you run the query, the records returned must meet the conditions specified in the first criteria row *or* the conditions specified in the second criteria row. As a result, the same records are returned as were returned in the last example. In addition, any record that meets the second row of conditions is also returned. This means that, in addition to the records that were previously returned, records that include "meat" in the CategoryName field are also returned, regardless of the ShippedDate value, as shown in Figure 11-7.

Notice that the results now show records with a Shipped Date value that includes 1996. Also notice that these records all include a Category Name value of Meat/Poultry, but not Dairy Products. Not until 1997 do records with a Dairy Products value appear. As you can see, all the records in the query results meet the conditions specified in one of the two criteria rows in the query definition.

Creating Calculated Field Expressions

So far, you've seen how expressions can be added to the criteria of a query definition. However, you can also use expressions in the Field row of the design grid in order to create calculated fields in your query results. For example, the query definition shown in Figure 11-8 includes two field expressions— one in the second column of the design grid and one in the sixth column.

Order ID	Company Name	Shipped Date	Product Name	Category Name
10305	Old World Delicatessen	09-Oct-1996	Thüringer Rostbratwurst	Meat/Poultry
10306	Romero y tomillo	23-Sep-1996	Perth Pasties	Meat/Poultry
10306	Romero y tomillo	23-Sep-1996	Tourtière	Meat/Poultry
10312	Die Wandernde Kuh	03-Oct-1996	Perth Pasties	Meat/Poultry
10331	Bon app'	21-Oct-1996	Tourtière	Meat/Poultry
10342	Frankenversand	04-Nov-1996	Pâté chinois	Meat/Poultry
10349	Split Rail Beer & Ale	15-Nov-1996	Tourtière	Meat/Poultry
10352	Furia Bacalhau e Frutos do Mar	18-Nov-1996	Tourtière	Meat/Poultry
10354	Pericles Comidas clásicas	20-Nov-1996	Thüringer Rostbratwurst	Meat/Poultry
10356	Die Wandernde Kuh	27-Nov-1996	Pâté chinois	Meat/Poultry
10360	Blondel père et fils	02-Dec-1996	Thüringer Rostbratwurst	Meat/Poultry
10360	Blondel père et fils	02-Dec-1996	Tourtière	Meat/Poultry
10362	Bon app'	28-Nov-1996	Tourtière	Meat/Poultry
10367	Vaffeljernet	02-Dec-1996	Tourtière	Meat/Poultry
10369	Split Rail Beer & Ale	09-Dec-1996	Thüringer Rostbratwurst	Meat/Poultry
10375	Hungry Coyote Import Store	09-Dec-1996	Tourtière	Meat/Poultry
10380	Hungry Owl All-Night Grocers	16-Jan-1997	Perth Pasties	Meat/Poultry
10380	Hungry Owl All-Night Grocers	16-Jan-1997	Camembert Pierrot	Dairy Products
10382	Ernst Handel	16-Dec-1996	Thüringer Rostbratwurst	Meat/Poultry
10388	Seven Seas Imports	20-Dec-1996	Perth Pasties	Meat/Poultry
10389	Bottom-Dollar Markets	24-Dec-1996	Pâté chinois	Meat/Poultry
10392	Piccolo und mehr	01-Jan-1997	Gudbrandsdalsost	Dairy Products
10393	Save-a-lot Markets	03-Jan-1997	Gorgonzola Telino	Dairy Products
10395	HILARIÓN-Abastos	03-Jan-1997	Perth Pasties	Meat/Poultry

Record: 1 of 347

Figure 11-7 Query results generated by the multiple lines of criteria shown in Figure 11-6

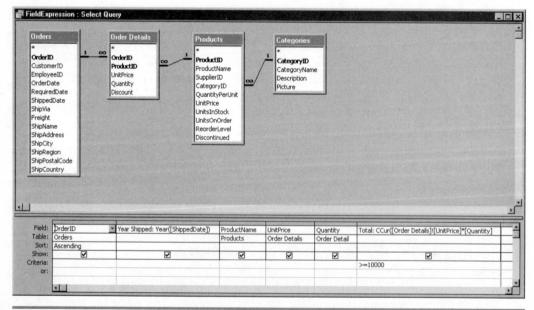

Figure 11-8 Using field expressions in a query

Let's take a look at each field expression to give you a better idea of how this works. The first field expression (Year Shipped: Year([ShippedDate])) is made up of a field name, a function, and an identifier. The field name is an identifier that will be assigned to the new field returned by the query. In this case, the field will be assigned the name Year Shipped. The colon following the field name separates the name from the rest of the expression. The Year function follows the field name. The ShippedDate field identifier—along with the brackets that surround it—is enclosed in the function's parentheses. The function extrapolates the year from the ShippedDate value and displays it in the query results.

In the second field expression (Total: CCur([Order Details]![UnitPrice]*[Quantity])), the UnitPrice value is multiplied with the Quantity value for each record returned by the query. The CCur function then converts the calculated value into the Currency data type, and the converted values are inserted into the Total field. Because two tables in the query contain a UnitPrice field, you must qualify the field identifier by including the table identifier and by separating the identifiers with an exclamation point (!).

If you were to run this query, your results would appear as shown in Figure 11-9. Notice that the Year Shipped field contains only the year and that the Total field contains the calculated values, returned as Currency values.

You may have noticed that the query definition also included a criteria expression in the Total calculated field. As a result, only records with a Total value greater than $10,000 are included in the query results. You can use criteria expressions in your query along with field expression.

Creating Queries with Aggregate Functions

When you create a crosstab query, you must select values for the Total row of the design grid. The Total row is added to the grid when you configure it for crosstab queries. However, you can use the Total row in other types of queries to summarize data, as mentioned previously. Most of the options in the Total row are aggregate functions, but the row includes other options necessary to summarizing data.

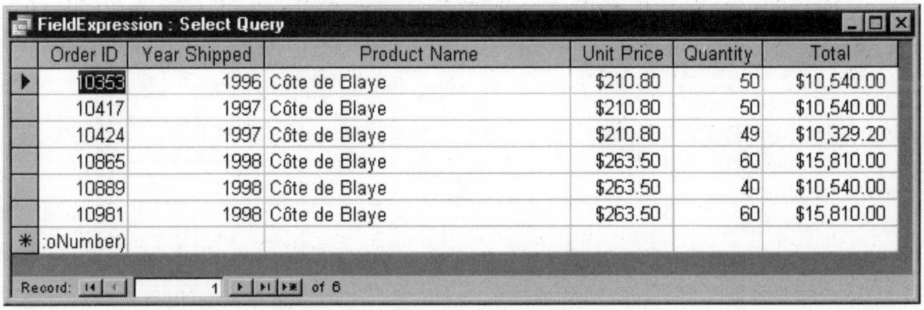

Order ID	Year Shipped	Product Name	Unit Price	Quantity	Total
10353	1996	Côte de Blaye	$210.80	50	$10,540.00
10417	1997	Côte de Blaye	$210.80	50	$10,540.00
10424	1997	Côte de Blaye	$210.80	49	$10,329.20
10865	1998	Côte de Blaye	$263.50	60	$15,810.00
10889	1998	Côte de Blaye	$263.50	40	$10,540.00
10981	1998	Côte de Blaye	$263.50	60	$15,810.00

FieldExpression : Select Query

Record: 1 of 6

Figure 11-9 Query results generated by the field expressions

If you take a look at Figure 11-10, you'll see that the Total row is used in the query definition. Notice that the Total option is different for each column. Only the fields configured with the aggregate functions (Count, Avg, and Sum) actually summarize data. The other two fields use the Group By and Where options to determine which records are returned.

Let's take a look at each column in the design grid to better understand how the data is summarized. The first column is configured for the OrderID field. Because the Group By option is selected for this field, the query results will be grouped together based on the OrderID values. The second column is configured for the OrderDate field. In this case, the Where option is selected. The Where option allows you to define an expression in the Criteria row for fields that are not summarized. However, because they're not summarized, the values cannot be displayed in the query results. By default, the Show option is cleared when you select the Where option. (You can also add criteria expressions to summarized fields.)

The last three columns identify which fields will be summarized and how they will be summarized. The summaries are based on the Group By column. In other words, each group of OrderID values will be summarized. The query results will include the number of records being summarized, the average UnitPrice value for the grouped records, and the sum of the UnitPrice values, as shown in Figure 11-11.

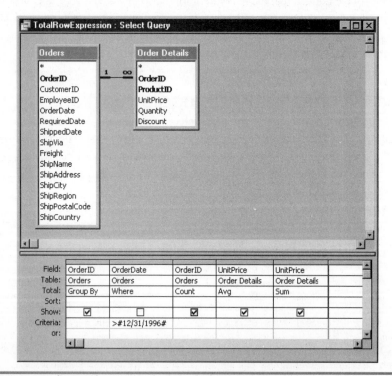

Figure 11-10 Using the Total row to calculate and summarize data

Order ID	CountOfOrderID	AvgOfUnitPrice	SumOfUnitPrice
10400	3	$43.13	$129.40
10401	4	$21.28	$85.10
10402	2	$21.15	$42.30
10403	2	$12.05	$24.10
10404	3	$17.37	$52.10
10405	1	$8.00	$8.00
10406	5	$17.74	$88.70
10407	3	$20.93	$62.80
10408	3	$22.03	$66.10
10409	2	$13.30	$26.60
10410	2	$23.00	$46.00
10411	3	$22.40	$67.20
10412	1	$18.60	$18.60
10413	3	$22.73	$68.20
10414	2	$4.65	$9.30
10415	2	$16.60	$33.20
10416	3	$16.37	$49.10
10417	4	$60.20	$240.80
10418	4	$13.40	$53.60
10419	2	$28.00	$56.00
10420	4	$26.60	$106.40
10421	4	$17.20	$68.80
10422	1	$24.90	$24.90
10423	2	$27.00	$54.00

Record: 1 of 679

Figure 11-11 Query results generated by the Total row in the design grid

As you can see, summary values are provided for each group of unique Order ID values. For example, the first row returned is for Order ID 10400. In this case, three records have been summarized (as reported in the CountOfOrderID field). The average UnitPrice value for the three records is $43.13 (shown in the AvgOfUnitPrice field), and the total UnitPrice value for the three records is $129.40 (as shown in the SumOfUnitPrice field). By grouping together records in this way, you can generate useful summary information based on your data.

TIP

Access automatically assigns names to summarized fields, as in the SumOfUnitPrice field. You can assign your own names to summarized fields by modifying the field's properties. In the Design view window, place the cursor somewhere within the field's column in the design grid, and then click the Properties button on the Query Design toolbar to open the Field Properties dialog box. In the Caption text box, type the name you want displayed for the field.

Ask the Expert

Q: **The expression examples that you have shown us in this module have all been part of select queries. Can you use expressions in action queries?**

A: You can use expressions in any type of query in much the same way you would use them in a select query. For example, you can create a delete query that deletes only those rows that meet the condition specified in the definition's criteria. As with select queries, the type of expressions that you use and the extent to which you use them depends on what data you're trying to modify. In addition, you can use expressions in the Update To row of an update query. For example, your update query might be based on an expression that adds a fixed quantity to a field value, such as [InStock]+10. This expression adds 10 to the value in the InStock field for each record that is returned by the query. As with any type of action query, be sure to view the rows affected by the query before you actually run it.

CRITICAL SKILL
11.3 # Use Expression Builder to Create Expressions

So far, the expressions that we've looked at have been created manually; they were simply typed into the correct cells in the design grid of the Design view window. For simple expressions, this is the easiest method to use. However, for more complex expressions, Access provides Expression Builder, a tool that (as the name suggests) allows you to create any type of expression wherever expressions are supported.

To access Expression Builder, select the cell in which you're creating the expression and then click the Build button on the Query Design toolbar. You can also right-click the cell and then click Build in the shortcut menu. You can create the entire expression from the Expression Builder window, which is shown in Figure 11-12.

The top part of the Expression Builder window is a large text box in which you create the expression. Beneath the text box are buttons that insert various types of operators into the expression. Simply click the appropriate button to add the operator.

The bottom two-thirds of the Expression Builder window is made up of three panes. The left pane lists all available objects in a hierarchical format. For example, you can expand the Tables node to list all the tables in your database. The middle pane lists the child objects associated with the parent objects in the left pane. If you select a table in the left pane, the table's fields are displayed in the middle pane.

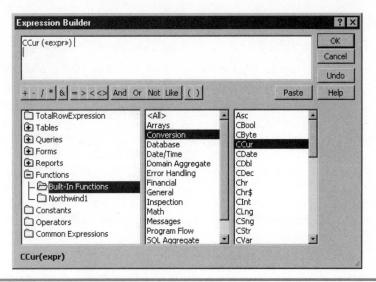

Figure 11-12 Using Expression Builder to identify a function

If the objects in the middle pane can be broken down further, their child objects are displayed in the right pane. For example, if you refer again to Figure 11-12, you'll see that the Functions node in the left pane contains two subnodes. Because the Built-In Functions subnode is selected, a list of function categories is displayed in the middle pane. In addition, because the Conversion category is selected in the middle pane, all conversion-related functions are displayed in the right pane.

To insert an object into your expression, double-click the object. You can also select the object and then click Paste. The object is inserted into the text box along with the *<<expr>>* placeholder, if appropriate, which indicates that this is where you can insert an expression or object. To add an expression, select the placeholder and insert the necessary operations, functions, identifiers, or literals. In addition to pasting objects and operations into the text box, you can type expression components directly into the box.

As you add components to your expression, it continues to be built, as shown in Figure 11-13. Notice that the expression now includes not only the CCur function, but also a qualified identifier ([Products]![UnitPrice]) and the multiplication (*) arithmetic operator. In addition, another *<<expr>>* placeholder has been inserted. At this point, you can add other components as necessary.

Once you've built your expression, click OK. The Expression Builder window closes, and the expression is added to the cell. You can then view and edit the expression as you would any other expression. If you open Expression Builder and the cell already contains an expression, that expression is displayed in the text box. You can then modify the expression as necessary.

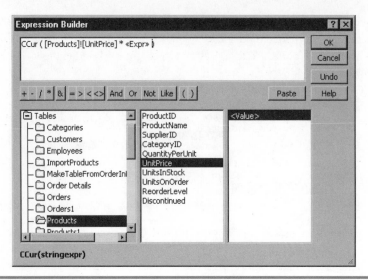

Figure 11-13 Creating an expression in Expression Builder

Project 11-1 Creating Expressions in a Query

In the projects in Module 10, you created several queries that allowed you to view and modify data in the consumer advocacy database. One of the queries that you created was an append query that added data to the Products table. You will now create a query that retrieves information from the Products table. The query will include criteria and field expressions. You will then view the query results and save the query to your database.

Step by Step

1. If they're not already open, open Access and then open the ConsumerAdvocacy.mdb database file.

2. If necessary, select the Queries object type in the database window, and then double-click Create Query In Design View. The Design view window and the Show Table dialog box appear, with the dialog box active.

3. Double-click the Products table to add the Products table object to the Design view window, and then click Close. The Show Table dialog box closes and the Design view window becomes active.

4. Resize the Design view window and the Products table object as necessary so that all fields in the table are displayed.

5. Select the ProductTitle, InStock, OnOrder, and WholesalePrice fields in the Products table object, and drag the fields to the Field cell in the first column of the design grid. Each field name is added to a column, in the order that the fields are listed in the table object. The table name is also added to the Table row for each field.

6. In the Criteria row of the ProductTitle field, type **t-shirt***, and then click another part of the design grid to complete the expression. The Like operator and quotation marks are added to the expression.

7. Click the Field cell of the fifth column in the design grid, and then click the Build button on the Query Design toolbar. The Expression Builder window appears.

8. In the text box at the top of the window, type **Total Cost:** (including a space after the colon).

9. Double-click the Functions node in the left pane, and then click the Built-In Functions subnode. A list of function types appears in the middle pane, and a list of functions appears in the right pane.

10. Click the Conversion function type in the middle pane, and then double-click the CCur function in the right pane. The CCur function and two <<*expr*>> placeholders are added to the text box.

11. Delete the first <<*expr*>> placeholder, and then place the cursor to the left of the remaining <<*expr*>> placeholder.

12. Click the Open Parentheses button to add an opening parenthesis to the expression, and then select the <<*expr*>> placeholder.

13. Double-click the Tables node in the left pane, and then click the Products subnode. The fields for the Products table appear in the middle pane.

14. Double-click the InStock field in the middle pane. The qualified field name is added to the expression in the text box.

15. Click the Plus button to add the operator to the expression, and then select the <<*expr*>> placeholder.

16. Double-click the OnOrder field in the middle pane. The qualified field name is added to the expression in the text box.

17. Click the Close Parentheses button to add a closing parenthesis to the expression.

18. Click the Multiply button to add the multiplication operator to the expression, and then select the <<*expr*>> placeholder.

(continued)

19. Double-click the WholesalePrice field in the middle pane. The qualified field name is added to the expression. Your expression should now look like the following:

    Total Cost: CCur((([Products]![InStock]+[Products]![OnOrder])
    *[Products]![WholesalePrice])

20. Click OK to close the Expression Builder window. The expression is added to the design grid cell that you selected earlier.

21. Right-click the cell that contains the new expression, and then click Zoom in the shortcut menu. The expression is displayed in the Zoom dialog box.

22. Click OK to close the Zoom dialog box and return to the Design view window.

23. Click the View button on the Query design toolbar. The query results are displayed in the Datasheet view window. Notice that the results include the Total Cost field, which reports the total price for the t-shirts in stock and on order.

24. Click the View button on the Query Datasheet toolbar to return to the Design view window.

25. Click the Save button on the Query Design toolbar. The Save As dialog box appears.

26. In the Query Name text box, type **TShirtCosts**, and then click OK. The query is saved to your database.

27. Close the Design view window.

Project Summary

In the project, you created a select query that included two expressions. The first expression was a simple criteria query that used the Like operator to return records with a ProductTitle value that started with t-shirt. The second expression was a field query that calculated the values of the InStock, OnOrder, and WholesalePrice fields. In the expression, you first added the values of the InStock and OnOrder fields and then multiplied that total by the WholesalePrice field. The result was then converted to a currency data type and displayed in the Total Cost field. You could have included other expressions in your query, additional rows of criteria, or additional calculated fields. Because this was a select query, no data in the underlying table was affected.

Module 11 Mastery Check

1. Which component of an expression is used to compare or calculate data?

   A. Operator

   B. Function

   C. Identifier

   D. Literal

2. How is an identifier different from a literal?

3. What components must be included in a statement for that statement to be considered an expression?

4. Which type of operator should you use if you want to compare two conditions in an expression?

   A. Comparison

   B. Arithmetic

   C. Logical

   D. Concatenation

5. Which expression should you use if you want to return a date/time value that is the same as or later than January 1, 1999?

6. Which expression should you use if you want to add a value of 25 to the OnOrder field?

7. Which operator should you use to connect two conditions in which at least one of those conditions must evaluate to true?

   A. In

   B. Or

   C. Like

   D. And

8. Which expression should you use if you want to join the FirstName field and the LastName field into one field in your query results?

9. You are defining a select query, and you want to return only those records whose OrderDate value is after the current date. Which expression should you use?

   A. Between [OrderDate] and Date( )

   B. <Date( )

   C. Date( )+[OrderDate]

   D. >Date( )

10. What symbol should you use in an expression to separate a parent object from a child object?

11. Which type of literals must be enclosed in quotation marks?

   A. Text

   B. Object

   C. Numerical

   D. Date/Time

12. Which type of query expression allows you to include a calculated field in your query results?

   A. Criteria

   B. Field

   C. Aggregate

   D. Multiple row

13. What is an aggregate function?

14. You want to extract the year out of the DateDelivered field, which is configured as a Date/Time field. Which function should you use?

15. Which row in the design grid of the Design view window includes options that are aggregate functions?

Part III

Access Data Objects

Module 12

Creating and Configuring Forms

CRITICAL SKILLS

12.1 Navigate the Design View Interface

12.2 Add Controls to a Form

12.3 Configure Control Properties

12.4 Create Special Forms

267

In the first two parts of the book, you learned how to create a database and its tables. You also learned how to access and modify the data within those tables. In Part III, your focus will shift away from the database itself to the data objects that help transition the database to a data-driven application. Access supports several types of data objects, including forms, reports, data access pages, macros, and modules. We begin by focusing on the first of these data objects—forms. In this module, you will be introduced to forms and you will learn how to create and modify them so that you can create an effective and robust data-driven application. Forms provide the vehicle in which users can view and access data in the underlying database. By using forms, you can present the data in a way that is not only easier for the user to work with, but that also protects the underlying data structure. Forms define how users interact with the database and, as such, determine the effectiveness of the user experience.

CRITICAL SKILL
12.1 Navigate the Design View Interface

When using a desktop application, you usually access the information and tools within the application through a graphical user interface (GUI). For example, Microsoft Office Word allows you to view and modify documents, format text within those documents, and use various tools to perform such tasks as checking spelling or merging documents. All of these actions are conducted through the Word GUI. A *form* provides a similar type of interface between a user and the data within the database. By using a form, a user can view and modify data without having to access the database directly or know how the database is structured.

A form can be based on a table or query. For example, the Customers form (shown in Figure 12-1) in the Northwind database is based on the Customers table. The form displays the data one record at a time. The user can view and modify the data as necessary simply by locating the correct record.

As you can see in Figure 12-1, a form can display more than just the data that appears in the table. You can add labels to the form to identify that data or to provide other types of information, such as titles or instructions. You can also add lines, rectangles, or command buttons that allow users to take specific types of actions. In addition, you can add pictures either as background or as individual objects that you can position anywhere within the form. Access provides a great deal of flexibility for designing forms, allowing you to create forms that meet your exact needs.

Opening a New Form in Design View

You can create a form either directly in Design view or by using the Form wizard or one of the AutoForm tools. The wizard and the AutoForm tools simplify the process of creating a form. However, as with other objects in the database, my discussion focuses on using Design view to create a form, rather than any of the other methods. Once you learn how to create a form in

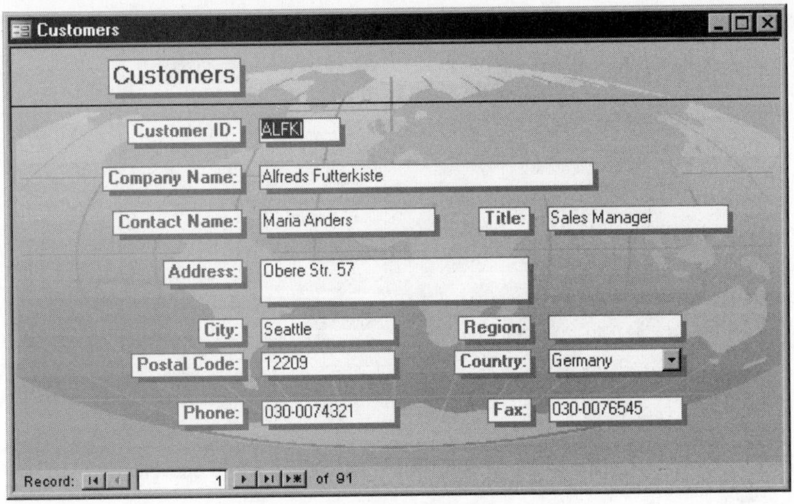

Figure 12-1 The Customers form in the Northwind database

Design view, you can use any of the other methods to create a form and then use Design view to modify the form. Learning to create a form in Design view will provide you with a strong foundation in the form-creation process, making it easier for you to use any of the other methods.

To open a new form in Design view, you must first select the Forms object type in the database window. From there, take one of the following steps:

- Double-click Create Form In Design View.

- Click the New button at the top of the database window.

- Click the Insert menu, and then click Form. (For this method, you do not have to select the Forms object type first.)

If you're creating a form that is linked to data in the database (which is the most common type of form), you must associate the new form to a table or query, so you should use the second or third option to open the new form. When you select one of these two options, the New Form dialog box appears, as shown in Figure 12-2. In this dialog box, you can select the method that you want to use to create the form and, optionally, you can select the table or query on which the form will be based.

To create a form in Design view, select the Design View option from the list box, select the table or query from the drop-down list at the bottom of the dialog box, and then click OK. When the new form opens in Design view, three windows appear: the Form window, the Toolbox, and the Field List.

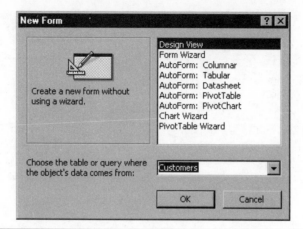

Figure 12-2 The New Form dialog box with the Customers table selected

NOTE

The Field List appears only if you select a table or query from the New Form dialog box when you first open the new form.

If you choose to open a new form by double-clicking the Create Form In Design View option, you can still associate a table or a query with a form by modifying the form's properties. To access the form's properties, click the Properties button on the Form Design toolbar. When the Form dialog box appears, select the Data tab. From the drop-down list for the Record Source property, select the table or query that you want to associate with the form.

Working with the Design View Windows

In Design view, you use the Form window, the Toolbox, and the Field List to add objects that interface with the data in the database or that perform other types of functions. In addition to opening the three windows in Design view, Access replaces the Database toolbar with the Form Design toolbar and the Formatting (Form/Report) toolbar. The Form Design toolbar contains options that allow you to perform such tasks as saving the form definition, changing views, accessing properties, or displaying the Toolbox and Field List. The Formatting (Form/Report) toolbar contains options that allow you to perform such tasks as changing the font size and color, formatting the text, and aligning the labels.

Using the Form Window

When you first open a new form in Design view, the Form window displays nothing but the design grid, as shown in Figure 12-3. The design grid allows you to place objects on the form and resize or reposition them as necessary. You can also resize the design grid, add fill color to the form background, or add a background picture, just as you saw in Figure 12-1.

The Form window also includes a ruler along the top of the window and one along the left side. You can use these rulers to align the objects that you place on the design grid. If you press and hold down the left mouse button while pointing to a ruler, a guide line appears. You can move that guideline by moving the mouse along the ruler. When you release the mouse button, the guideline disappears.

Using the Toolbox

The Toolbox is displayed whenever you open a form in Design view, unless the Toolbox was closed the last time you opened a form in Design view. If the Toolbox is not displayed, simply click the Toolbox button on the Form Design toolbar. You can also use this method to close the Toolbox. The Toolbox, which is shown in Figure 12-4, is made up of a collection of buttons that are used to add controls to the design grid. A *control* is an object that displays data, performs an action, or enhances the appearance of a form. For example, a text box is an example of a control.

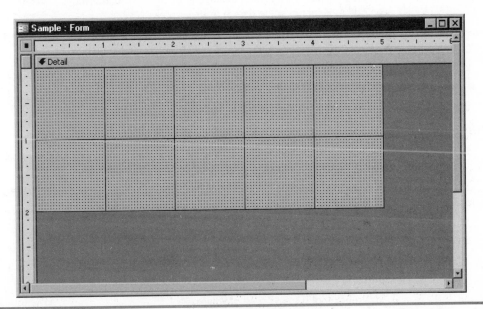

Figure 12-3 The Form window as it appears in Design view

Figure 12-4 The Toolbox as it appears in Design view

The Toolbox contains buttons for the most common types of controls that can be added to a form. In addition, the Toolbox includes a few buttons that allow you to take actions related to adding controls. Table 12-1 describes the buttons that are included in the Toolbox by default. The table describes the buttons as they appear, left to right, in the Toolbox. The table also indicates whether a wizard is available for a particular control type.

Button	Description	Wizard?
Select Objects	Used to indicate that a control button can be selected so that you can add that control to the design grid.	N/A
Control Wizards	Used to launch a wizard related to the selected control button. If a wizard is associated with the button, it will be launched when you click that button if the Control Wizards button is selected.	N/A
Label	Adds descriptive text, such as a title.	No
Text Box	Adds a control that displays data from the database.	No
Option Group	Groups together a set of option buttons, toggle buttons, or check boxes so that only one of the options can be selected.	Yes
Toggle Button	Adds a button that supports an on or off setting. The button represents a Yes/No value in the database.	No
Option Button	Adds a button that supports a selected or deselected setting. The button represents a Yes/No value in the database.	No
Check Box	Adds a check box that supports a selected or deselected setting. The button represents a Yes/No value in the database.	No
Combo Box	Adds a control that combines a text box with a drop-down list.	Yes
List Box	Adds a box that displays a list of values.	Yes
Command Button	Adds a button that initiates an action.	Yes

Table 12-1 Control-Related Buttons Available in the Toolbox

Button	Description	Wizard?
Image	Adds a picture to the form.	No
Unbound Object Frame	Adds a container that displays an OLE object that is not tied to an underlying table.	No
Bound Object Frame	Adds a container that displays an OLE object that is tied to an underlying table.	No
Page Break	Creates an additional page in the form.	No
Tab Control	Creates a form with multiple tabs.	No
Subform/ Subreport	Embeds a table, query, form, or report into the parent form.	Yes
Line	Adds a straight line to the form.	No
Rectangle	Adds a rectangle to the form.	No
More Controls	Allows you to access additional controls that are installed on your computer.	N/A

Table 12-1 Control-Related Buttons Available in the Toolbox *(continued)*

To add a control to a form without using a wizard, first verify that the Control Wizards button is not selected. If it is selected, deselect it. Next, click the Select Objects button if it is not already selected, click the applicable control button and click within the design grid where you want to locate the control. Depending on the control, you might want to resize it as you're adding it to the form. If a wizard is available for a control and you want to use that wizard, click the Control Wizards button, then click the control button, and then click within the design grid. When you click within the design grid, the wizard will be launched and you can follow the steps defined in the wizard to add the control.

As you can see in Table 12-1, Access allows you to add a variety of controls to a form. Figure 12-5 shows you what some of these controls might look like. The controls were labeled within the form (with Label controls) to indicate the type of control. In addition, the Combo Box control is expanded so that you can see how values are made available to a particular control. The sample form shown in this figure demonstrates many of the typical controls that you will add to a form. Although there are a number of other types of controls available, the ones shown here will give you a good sense of how data can be displayed and modified through a form.

Using the Field List

The final window to consider in Design view is the Field List. As the name implies, the Field List displays the fields that are contained in the table or query that is associated with the form.

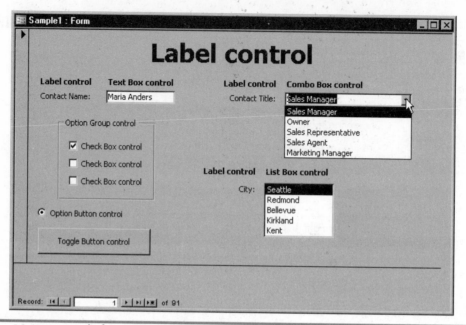

Figure 12-5 A sample form containing multiple controls

Figure 12-6 shows the Field List for the Customers table from the Northwind database. The Field List is similar to the table objects that you saw in the Design view window used to create queries and filters. The Field List allows you to add a bound Text Box control that is already associated with a field. If you were to use the Toolbox to add the Text Box control, you would

Figure 12-6 The Field List as it appears in Design view

have to first add the control and then manually associate the field with that control. This task will be covered later in this module, in the section "Adding a Bound Control to a Form."

Progress Check

1. On what database objects can you base a form?

2. Which toolbars appear when you open a form in Design view?

3. What is displayed in the Form window when you first open a new form in Design view?

4. What is contained in the Toolbox?

CRITICAL SKILL
12.2 Add Controls to a Form

Now that you have an overview of the windows that are included in Design view when you create a form, let's take a look at how you actually create that form. In addition to adding the various types of controls to a form, you can create option groups, you can format controls, and you can apply conditional formatting to specific controls.

Adding a Control to a Form

To create a usable form, you must add controls to the design grid in the Form window. To do this, you use the Toolbox or the Field List to populate the grid. You can then manipulate the controls on the grid to ensure that the form looks and behaves as desired.

If you refer once more to Figure 12-5, you'll see a sample form that contains various controls. Now let's take a look at what that form looks like in Design view. Figure 12-7 shows the Form window as it appears for the sample form. Notice that each control is positioned within the design grid. The controls can be moved, resized, and reformatted. In addition, you can remove controls or add controls.

---

1. You can base a form on a table or query.
2. The Form Design toolbar and the Formatting (Form/Report) toolbar
3. The design grid
4. The Toolbox is made up of a collection of buttons that are used to add controls to the design grid.

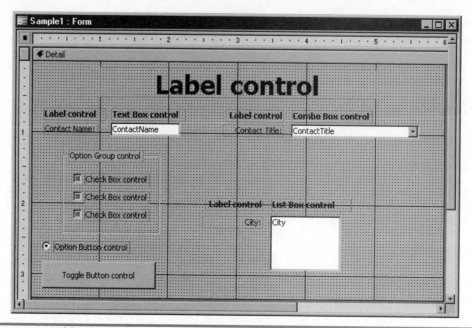

Figure 12-7 Adding multiple controls to a form in Design view

Although the methods used for adding controls are generally the same, there are a few differences, depending on the type of control that you're adding. Access supports three types of controls:

- **Bound controls** A bound control receives its value from the underlying table. If the value in the table changes, the value displayed through the control changes. A Text Box control is an example of a bound control.

- **Unbound controls** An unbound control is not tied to any values in a table. The control retains whatever value you enter. Label and Image controls are examples of unbound controls.

- **Calculated controls** A calculated control displays a value that is calculated, based on values in an underlying table. A calculated control receives its values through an expression. As a result, if the underlying values change, the value displayed in the control will change.

Now let's take a look at adding each type of control to a form.

TIP

After you add a control to a form, you can view how the control will appear in the actual form by clicking the View button on the Form Design toolbar. This switches the form to Form view. You can then view and test the control to make sure that it does what you want it to do. When you are finished, click the View button again to return to Design view.

Adding a Bound Control to a Form

The simplest type of bound control to add to a form is the Text Box control. To add this control, drag a field from the Field List to the design grid. When you create a Text Box control, you actually create two controls: one Text Box control and one Label control. The Label control is linked to the Text Box control. Although you can reformat the controls independently, they are still bound together.

You can add more than one Text Box control at a time. Simply select all the fields in the Field List that you want to add as bound controls and drag them at one time to the design grid. To select multiple fields, click the first field, press and hold down CTRL, and then click any additional fields that you want to include. If you want to select fields that are in consecutive order, click the first field, press and hold down SHIFT, and then click the last field. Once you select all the fields, drag them as a unit to the design grid. One control is added for each selected field, in the order that they appear in the Field List.

Adding a bound Combo Box control or List Box control is a little more complicated than adding a bound Text Box control. In both cases, you must use the Toolbox to add the control, and once the control is added, you must configure the control's properties. To add a Combo Box or List Box control, first verify that the Control Wizards button is deselected. Next, if necessary, click the Select Objects button in the Toolbox, and then click the Combo Box or List Box button. Finally, click the place in the design grid where you want to locate the control. Once you've placed the control, click the Properties button on the Form Design toolbar, which will launch the properties dialog box for that control.

NOTE

You must make sure that the control is selected when you click the Properties button. When you click the Properties button, the properties open for the selected control or form.

On the Data tab of the properties dialog box (shown later in this module in Figure 12-11), you must configure the Control Source property with the name of the participating field. This property binds the control to the specified field. Next, you must verify that the Table/Query option is selected for the Row Source Type property. Finally, you must create a query for the Row Source property. To create a query, click the Build button to the right of the Row Source property. This launches Query Builder, which follows a process similar to that for creating a query in Design view, as discussed in Module 10. In most cases, you will be creating a control that extracts a list of values from a related table.

Let's take a look at an example to help clarify this. Suppose that you're creating a form for the Products table and you want to add a bound Combo Box control that is based on the SupplierID field. However, you want to be able to display the actual company name rather than the supplier's ID. A one-to-many relationship exists between the SupplierID field in the Suppliers table and the SupplierID field in the Products table. Therefore, you plan to pull the related CompanyName values out of the Suppliers table. To do this, you would create a query that's based on the SupplierID field and the CompanyName field of the Suppliers table, as shown in Figure 12-8.

After you create the query, the SQL statement that is generated by the query will be displayed as the Row Source property. In the case of the example above, the statement would be the following:

```
SELECT Suppliers.SupplierID, Suppliers.CompanyName
FROM Suppliers ORDER BY Suppliers.CompanyName;
```

The statement is then used to generate the values that will be available in the Combo Box that you create for the form. You must include the SupplierID field in your query to match up the values with the SupplierID values in the Products table, even though the SupplierID values are not displayed.

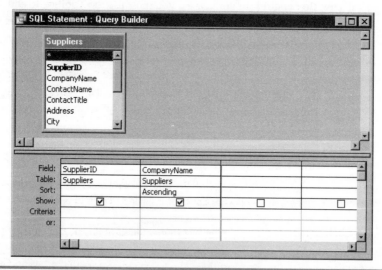

Figure 12-8 Creating a query for the Row Source property

Once you have configured the properties on the Data tab, you must configure at least two properties on the Format tab (shown later in this module in Figure 12-10). First, you should set the Column Count property to 2. This is because you're returning two fields in your query. Second, you should set the Column Widths property to 0";2" (for two columns). You must specify 0 for the first column so that only the second column is displayed, which in this case is the CompanyName field. Once you've set these properties, your Combo Box control will be ready to use.

NOTE

Properties are discussed in more detail later in this module, in the section "Configure Control Properties." For information about creating expressions, see Module 11. For information about relationships, see Module 5.

Adding an Unbound Control to a Form

Unbound controls are useful for providing information and enhancing the layout of your form. You can add lines, rectangles, pictures, and text to improve not only the form's appearance but its usability. To add an unbound control, click the Select Objects button in the Toolbox and then click the control's button. Next click the place in the design grid where you want to locate the control. After you've placed the control, you can resize it and move it as necessary.

Adding a Calculated Control to a Form

A calculated control is one in which an expression is used to define the value that is displayed in the form. The expression is created just like any other expressions that you've seen and can include a combination of functions, identifiers, literals, and operators. To create a calculated control, use the Toolbox to add a Text Box control to the design grid. Once you've placed the control, open its properties dialog box and add the expression to the Control Source property on the Data tab. The calculated value will be displayed on the form just as any other Text Box control value is; however, users will be unable to change that value.

Creating an Option Group

Access provides three types of controls that can be bound to a Yes/No field: the Check Box control, the Option Button control, and the Toggle Button control. If the control is selected on a form, the value evaluates to Yes. If the control is not selected, the value evaluates to No. For example, the Products table in the Northwind database includes a Yes/No field named Discontinued. You can add a Check Box control to your form to indicate whether a particular product has been discontinued. If the check box is selected, the product has been discontinued.

TIP

To add a Yes/No-related control to the design grid, click the Select Objects button in the Toolbox, then click the applicable control button, and finally click in the design grid where you want the control located. Once the control is added, configure the Control Source property on the Data tab with the Yes/No field that you want bound to the control.

In addition to using Yes/No controls individually, you can group them together within an Option Group control. When you group controls together, the Option Group control is bound to a field. In addition, each Yes/No control is configured with a value that can be inserted into the field, and only one of those controls can be selected. When a user selects a control, the value associated with the control is inserted into the field that is bound to the Option Group control.

If you refer back to Figure 12-7, you'll see an example of an Option Group control that includes three Check Box controls. When using the form, the viewer can select only one of those check boxes at a time. To add an Option Group control to a form, click the Select Objects button in the Toolbox, click the Option Group button, and then click in the design grid where you want the Option Group control located. Once you have added the control and positioned it as necessary, open the properties for that control and select the Data tab. In the Control Source property, select the field that the control will be bound to.

After you've configured the Option Group control, add a Yes/No control for each option that you want to include in the group. For example, if you want users to pick one of three colors, add a control for each of those colors. Make sure that you add the Yes/No controls within the box created by the Option Group control. Once you've added the controls, you must configure their properties. For each control, open the properties and select the Data tab. In the Option Value property, type in the value that you want to assign to that control. Each Yes/No control within the option group must be configured with a unique value.

Formatting a Control

Once you have added a control to the design grid, you can take a number of steps to change the appearance of that control. In most cases, you can move, resize, and change the appearance of the borders, fonts, and background. To make many of these changes, you can use the Formatting (Form/Report) toolbar. Simply select the control in the design grid and then select the appropriate options from the toolbar. In addition, you can also change the formatting through the Format tab of the control's properties. (We will be looking at control properties in more detail later in this module, in the section "Configure Control Properties.")

The best way to learn how to format the different controls is to try out the various options available on the Formatting (Form/Report) toolbar or in the control's properties dialog box. You should create a test form and try out the many ways that you can enhance the look of your form. To get you started in this process, let's take a look at formatting a Text Box control.

After you add a Text Box control to the design grid, you can select the actual Text Box control or the Label control that is linked to the Text Box control. Once you select the object, you can resize it by dragging the appropriate side or corner. The top-left corner of a control acts as the control's anchor, so any resizing that you do should be away from that corner.

In addition to resizing the Text Box control, you can format the control itself. For example, to change the background color within the control, select the control and then select a color from the Fill/Back Color option on the Formatting (Form/Report) toolbar. You can also change the color of the font by selecting a color from the Font/Fore Color option on the toolbar. In addition, you can change the size and typeface of the font used to display the value, and you can apply bold, italic, or an underline to the value.

Of course, after you have added a control to the design grid, you will want to change the default name that is assigned to that control to a name that applies to the value being displayed. To change the text in a Label control, select the object, click on the value within the object, and type in a new name. Remember to resize the Label object if necessary when you change the text or apply other formatting.

Again, the best way to learn how to format a control is to try out the various options. Experiment with changing colors and sizes, repositioning the controls, and adding lines and rectangles. View the forms in the Northwind database in Design view to see how those controls are formatted. Experiment with different options and different controls until you're comfortable changing the format of any control.

Applying Conditional Formatting

Access allows you to apply conditional formatting to Text Box and Combo Box controls. Conditional formatting is used to apply specific types of formatting to the control under special conditions. In addition to the default formatting that you can set up on the control, you can apply up to three conditional formats under the following conditions:

- When the field value equals a specified value or is within a range of values

- When an expression defined for the conditional formatting evaluates to true

- When the field has focus (is active)

To configure conditional formatting, add the Text Box or Combo Box control to the design grid, right-click the control, and then click Conditional Formatting to open the Conditional Formatting dialog box. When you first open the dialog box, only one of the conditions appears, but you can display up to three conditions by clicking the Add button. When all three conditions are displayed, the dialog box appears as it is shown in Figure 12-9.

When configuring the conditions, you can select one of three options: Field Value Is, Expression Is, and Field Has Focus. The Field Has Focus option is available only for the first condition. If you select this option, simply configure the formatting as necessary. If you select the Field Value Is option, you must configure the condition by specifying an operator option and the applicable values. For example, you can define a condition that is between 10 and 20.

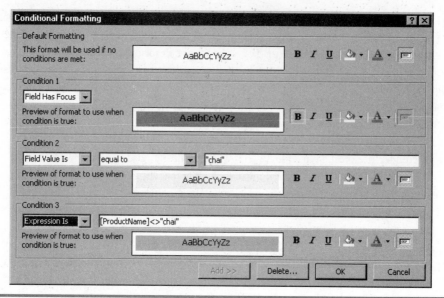

Figure 12-9 The Conditional Formatting dialog box

Once you specify the condition, you can configure the desired format. If you select the Expression Is option, you must enter an expression and then configure the desired formatting. Whenever any of the conditions defined in the Conditional Formatting dialog box are met, the formatting is applied to the control.

Progress Check

1. What are the three types of controls supported in Access?

2. How do you add a bound Text Box control to a form?

3. What is a calculated control?

4. What three types of Yes/No controls can you add to a form?

---

1. Bound controls, unbound controls, and calculated controls
2. Drag a field from the Field List to the design grid.
3. A calculated control is one in which an expression is used to define the value that is displayed in the form.
4. Check Box, Option Button, and Toggle Button

CRITICAL SKILL
12.3 Configure Control Properties

Earlier in the module, I mentioned some of the properties that you can configure for a control. Each control is configured with a set of properties that can be modified as necessary. To access a control's properties, take one of the following steps:

- Double-click the control in the Form window.

- Right-click the control in the Form window and then click Properties.

- Select the control in the Form window and then click the Properties button on the Form Design toolbar.

The dialog box that contains all the properties is named according to the type of control selected and the name used to identify the control. For example, the properties dialog box for a Text Box control that is named ProductName is assigned the name Text Box: ProductName.

The properties dialog box contains five tabs: Format, Data, Event, Other, and All. Each tab contains a set of properties related to the specific tab. The All tab lists all the properties. The properties that are listed on each tab vary according to control type. However, many of the control types share the same properties. In this section, we'll look at the properties for a Text Box control, but keep in mind that each control type is a little different.

Ask the Expert

Q: You state that you can configure the properties for each individual control. Can you configure properties for the form itself?

A: Yes, you can configure the form's properties. To access the form's properties, you should first select the form. A form is selected if a small black box appears in the upper-left corner of the Form window. This is the place to the left of the top ruler and above the left ruler. If the form is not selected (the black box isn't displayed), click the upper-left corner. Once the form is selected, click the Properties button on the Form Design toolbar. You can also open the form's properties by double-clicking the upper-left corner. Once the properties dialog box appears, you can configure the necessary settings. The dialog box includes the same tabs as the dialog box used for an object's properties; however, the properties listed in the form's dialog box are specific to the form as a whole.

Configuring Format Properties

The Format tab contains many of the same properties that you can set via the Formatting (Form/Report) toolbar. As you can see in Figure 12-10, you can format such characteristics as the border style and color, the font type and size, and the background style and color. You can even set the exact size of the control. All the formatting that you can do with the toolbar you can do in the Format tab, and much more.

To change a property setting, either type in a new setting or select an option from the drop-down list associated with that particular property. If the property contains a drop-down list, you must use one of the options in that list. Some of the properties contain a Build button to the right of the property text box. (If a drop-down list or Build button is available for a property, it is not visible until you select that property.) In the case of the properties on the Format tab, the Build button opens the Color dialog box, which allows you to select a color for the associated property.

After you have set all the properties that you want to configure, close the properties dialog box. The settings will be applied to the control.

TIP

You can configure the properties of more than one control at a time. Select the controls in the design grid and then open the properties dialog box. The dialog box displays only those properties that can be configured for all of the controls.

Configuring Data Properties

The properties on the Data tab are primarily related to source data that contains the values that will be displayed in the form. The properties apply primarily to bound controls and are critical to effectively providing data that can be viewed and modified. Figure 12-11 shows what the Data tab looks like for a Text Box control. Notice that it includes the Control Source property. As you learned earlier in this module, this property allows you to specify the field that will be bound to the control. You can also use this property to create a calculated control. For Combo Box and List Box controls, the Data tab also includes properties related to identifying the specific values that will be listed in the control.

You might have noticed that the Data tab includes properties that are the same as properties that you configured when you defined the fields in a table. For example, the tab includes the Input Mask, Default Value, and Validation Rule properties. As with field definitions, you can define these properties to limit the text that is entered into a field. However, the properties that you define in the form have no effect on the field itself. If you define a validation rule on a form, it applies only to data that is entered through the form, not to data entered into a field through any other method. In general, you should configure these sorts of properties directly in the

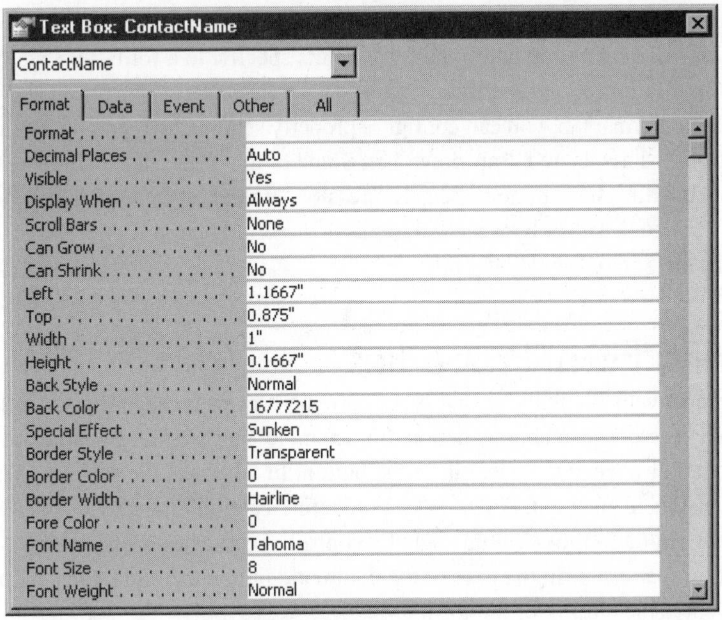

Figure 12-10 The Format tab of a control's properties

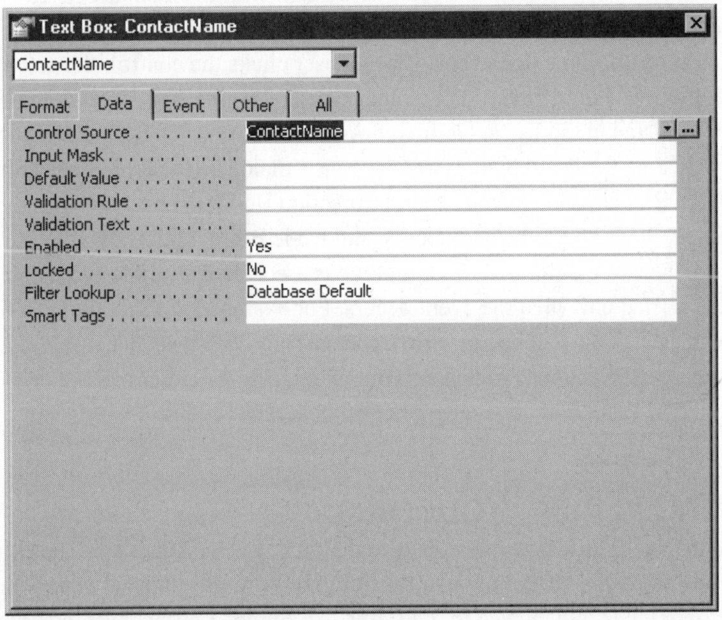

Figure 12-11 The Data tab of a control's properties

table in order to ensure consistency across all forms and to ensure the integrity of the data. If you find that you want to add additional constraints specific to a form, you can define those constraints in the control's properties.

As with the Format tab, you can configure property settings by typing in a value or selecting an option from the associated drop-down list. Some of the properties include a Build button. For the Data tab, the Build button opens Expression Builder or Query Builder, depending on the property selected. The only exception to this is the Build button for the Smart Tags property, which opens the Smart Tags dialog box.

Configuring Event Properties

One of the most valuable features that is supported by forms is the ability to define actions that will be taken in response to another action. For example, you can add a Command Button control that closes the form when the user clicks the button. In this case, the process of clicking the button is considered an event. An *event* is a predefined action that is associated with a control. When the user initiates the event through the control, Access performs an action that is configured for that event. In the case of the command button example, the action associated with the event is the closing of the form.

For nearly every control that can be added to a form, Access supports a set of predefined events specific to the control type. Each of these events can be configured with an action. For example, a Text Box control has 17 events associated with it, which are listed on the Events tab of the properties dialog box, as shown in Figure 12-12. Many of the events are self-explanatory. Take, for instance, the On Click event. When a user clicks the control, the action defined for the event will occur. For information on other types of events, see Access online Help.

Each event listed in the Event tab includes a Build button. To define an action for an event, you start by clicking the Build button, which opens a dialog box that provides links to Expression Builder, Macro Builder, and Code Builder. Expression Builder allows you to create expressions, Macro Builder allows you to create macros, and Code Builder allows you to build modules. Once created, the expression, macro, or module is associated with the event and becomes the action that is carried out when the event occurs. For example, if a module is defined on the On Change event, the module will be run when a change is made to the value displayed by the control.

In most cases, the actions defined on your events will be either macros or modules. For more information about how to create either of these, see Module 15.

Configuring Other Properties

The last tab that we'll look at in the properties dialog box is the Other tab. The Other tab contains miscellaneous properties that allow you to configure settings related to such things as the name of the control or the text displayed in the status bar. Figure 12-13 shows the properties that are available on this tab. You configure these properties as you would any of the other properties

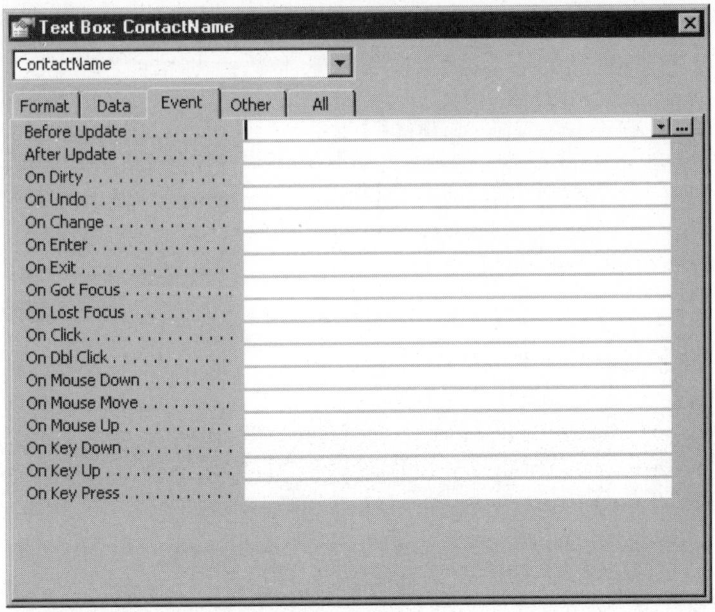

Figure 12-12 The Event tab of a control's properties

that we've looked at. Either enter a value or select an option from the drop-down list. The only property that includes a Build button is Tab Index. When you click the Build button, the Tab Order dialog box appears, which allows you to specify the order in which the user tabs from one control to the next.

Ask the Expert

Q: **Whenever I add a new control to a form, the control is configured with a default set of properties. Is there a way to modify the default property settings?**

A: Yes, you can configure the default settings for a control type. To do so, select the button in the Toolbox for the control type that you want to configure, and then click the Properties button on the Form Design toolbar. When the properties dialog box appears, configure the properties as you would for an individual control. Keep in mind, however, that you cannot configure all properties for a control type. For example, you cannot configure event properties for any control type other than Text Box and Combo Box, and you can configure few Data properties for the most of the controls. The best way to determine which properties are available for which control type is to view the properties for the specific control type.

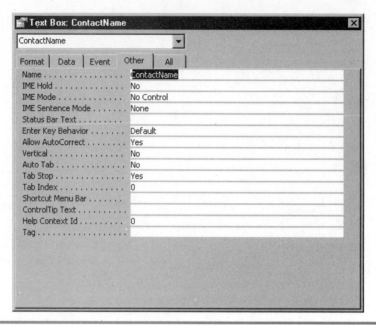

Figure 12-13 The Other tab of a control's properties

CRITICAL SKILL
12.4 Create Special Forms

The forms that we've looked at so far were very straightforward. They each consisted of controls that were arranged on the design grid. However, you can create forms that include other elements as well. For example, you can create a form that includes two or more tabs, or you can create a form that contains a subform. You can even create a form that is made up primarily of control buttons that allow you to open other forms. In this section, you'll learn how to create tabs, add subforms to a form, and create a switchboard, which is a type of form that directs the user to other objects in the application.

Creating Forms with Multiple Tabs

You have no doubt used applications that contained windows or dialog boxes with tabs. You've seen examples of tabs in the properties dialog boxes in the previous sections. Because tabs provide a useful way to organize information, Access allows you to add two or more tabs to your forms. This allows you to present the controls in a way that is easier for the users to work with. For example, suppose you're creating a form that is based on the Customers table in the Northwind database. You can separate the contact information from the address information, as shown in Figure 12-14.

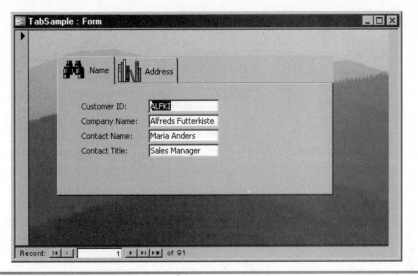

Figure 12-14 A form that contains two tabs, as seen in Form view

If you plan to use tabs in your form, you should add the Tab control to the design grid before adding any other controls. To add a Tab control, click the Select Objects button in the toolbox and then click the Tab Control button. Click somewhere within the design grid to place the Tab object, and then resize the object so that it is large enough for the controls that you plan to add. By default, the tab control includes two tabs, as shown in Figure 12-15.

After you've placed and resized the Tab object, you then add the controls to each tab. This is done in the same way as adding them without a tab. Once they're placed on the Tab control, you can move the Tab control as necessary, and the other controls will also be moved. However, you can still move the individual controls on the tab.

To add another tab to the Tab control, right-click anywhere on the control and then click Insert Page in the shortcut menu. A new tab will be added after the tabs that already existed. If you need to change the order of the tabs, right-click anywhere on the control and then click Page Order. This launches the Page Order dialog box, which allows you to arrange the order in which the tabs appear. You can also configure the Tab control properties by right-clicking the tab and then clicking Properties in the shortcut menu.

Creating Subforms

In Module 3, you were introduced to subdatasheets. As you'll recall, a subdatasheet is a window in a datasheet that displays records from one table that are related to the selected record in the datasheet. Subdatasheets are available by default for tables that have an established relationship with other tables. Access supports a similar functionality for forms. You can add a Subform/Subreport control to a form that allows you to view information in a table that is related to the record data displayed in the form.

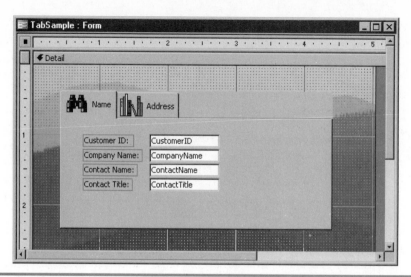

Figure 12-15 A form that contains a Tab control, as seen in Design view

Let's take a look at an example that will help explain this. The form shown in Figure 12-16 is based on the Suppliers table in the Northwind database. Because the Suppliers table is related to the Products table, you can add a Subform/Subreport control to the form that displays information from the Products table. For each record from the Suppliers table that is displayed in the form, the related data in the Products table is also displayed.

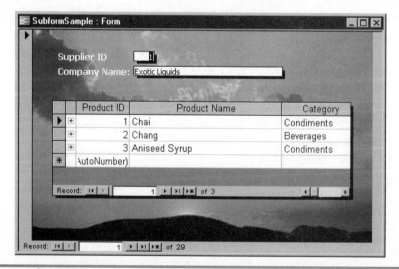

Figure 12-16 A form that contains a subform, as seen in Form view

Now let's take a look at the same form in Design view (shown in Figure 12-17). As you can see, the design grid contains three controls: two Text Box controls and one Subform/Subreport control. (There are actually five controls if you count the two Label controls that are linked to the Text Box controls.) The Subform/Subreport control is added in the same way that you add any other bound control.

To add a Subform/Subreport control to a form, click the Select Objects button in the Toolbox, click the Subform/Subreport button, and then click somewhere within the design grid. Once the control has been added, you can resize it and format it as necessary so that it is displayed properly in the form. Next you must identify the table that the control will be bound to. To do this, you must know how tables are related in your database. If you are not sure, open the Relationships window and view the relationships between the tables. (For information about relationships, see Module 5.)

Once you've identified the related tables, open the properties for the Subform/Subreport control and select the Data tab. From the drop-down list associated with the Source Object property, select the related table. (Make certain that the table name is preceded by the word Table so that you're not picking a different type of object with the same name.) When you select the table, a value is added to the Link Child Fields property and to the Link Master Fields property. The new values are the names of the fields that are related in the two tables. Once all the properties have been configured, close the properties dialog box.

After you've added the Subform/Subreport control, view the form in Form view to make certain that it is correctly displaying the data. View several records and watch how the data in the related table changes. As you can see, only data related to the records displayed by the form is displayed in the subform.

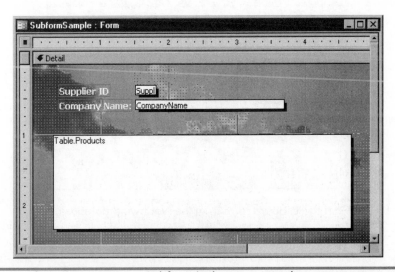

Figure 12-17 A form that contains a Subform/Subreport control, as seen in Design view

Creating Switchboards

When developing a data-driven application in Access, you might find it useful to create forms that allow you to structure your application so that users will have easy access to objects within your database. To facilitate this functionality, Access supports the use of a type of form, known as a *switchboard,* that contains unbounded controls that perform specific actions, such as opening another form or a report. For example, the Northwind database includes the Main Switchboard form (shown in Figure 12-18) that appears when you first open the database file.

The Main Switchboard form does not contain any bound controls, only unbound controls, including one Image control, one Label control, and seven Command Button controls. Each of the Command Button controls performs an action when the user initiates an event. For example, when the user clicks the Categories button, the Categories form appears. The event initiates a call to a function in an expression that is defined in a module. The function performs the action. You can also use a macro to define the action that is to be performed. (Macros and modules are discussed in Module 15.)

You create a switchboard as you would any other type of form. Figure 12-19 shows the Main Switchboard form as it appears in Design view. As you can see, the switchboard is made up of controls that are placed on the design grid. You place these controls in the same way that you place other types of controls. For controls that must perform an action, you must configure the event properties with the necessary expressions, macros, or modules. You can also format the controls and the switchboard form to provide the look and feel that you want to give your application.

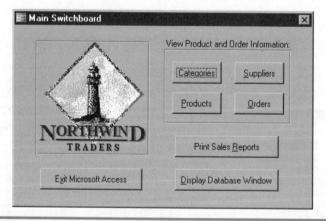

Figure 12-18 The Main Switchboard form from the Northwind database, as seen in Form view

Figure 12-19 The Main Switchboard form from the Northwind database, as seen in Design view

NOTE

You can also use the Switchboard Manager utility to create a switchboard. However, I find that using the utility is a bit cumbersome and somewhat limited in what you can do, compared to creating a switchboard in Design view. In addition, a switchboard that you create from scratch tends to be easier to manage and format. To access Switchboard Manager, click the Tool menu, point to Database Utilities, and then click Switchboard Manager. For information on how to use this tool, see Access online Help.

Configure a Switchboard to Open at Startup

Once you have created a switchboard, you can configure the database to have the switchboard open when the database file is opened. To do this, click the Tools menu and then click Startup. In the Startup dialog box, select the switchboard form from the Display Form/Page drop-down list and then click OK.

By default, when you open a database file the database window appears. If a switchboard is configured to open, it appears over the database window. However, you can also choose to display only the switchboard form when you start the application. In the Startup dialog box, clear the Display Database Window check box. The next time the database file is opened, only the form will be displayed.

Project 12-1 Creating a Form in the Consumer Advocacy Database

In this module, you learned about forms and the various types of controls you can add to a form. You also learned how you can enhance a form to make it more user-friendly. Now you will create your own form in the consumer advocacy database. The form will be based on the Staff table and will include six bound controls—one a Combo Box control and the rest Text Box controls. The form will also include a calculated control and an unbound control that is used to provide a title for the form. After you've added the controls to the form, you will change the background color of the form and the controls, save the form, and view it in Form view. From there, you can view information about the organization's staff.

Step by Step

1. If they're not already open, open Access and then open the ConsumerAdvocacy.mdb database file.

2. If necessary, select the Forms object type in the database window, and then click New. The New Form dialog box appears.

3. Ensure that Design View is selected in the list, select Staff from the drop-down list, and click OK. The new form opens in Design view.

4. Click the Select Objects button in the Toolbox, then click the Text Box button, and finally click in the upper-left area of the design grid. The new control is added to the grid.

5. Click the Properties button on the Form Design toolbar. The properties dialog box appears.

6. Select the Data tab, and in the Control Source property, type the following expression:

   =[NameFirst] & " " & [NameLast]

   Close the properties dialog box. The expression is added to the control.

7. Resize the Text Box control to allow enough room for the full name of each staff member.

8. In the Label control linked to the Text Box control, type **Full Name:** and then resize the control as necessary.

9. In the Field List, select the Address1, Address2, City, State, and PostalCode fields, and then drag them to the design grid directly beneath the Full Name control.

10. Align and size all controls as necessary. You will be using the field names for the Label controls. The field names are assigned to the controls automatically, so you don't have to change those names.

11. Click the Select Objects button in the Toolbox, then click the Combo Box button, and finally click the design grid, to the right of the other controls. Resize and reposition the new control as necessary.

12. Open the properties for the Combo Box control and select the Data tab.

13. From the drop-down list for the Control Source property, select PositionID. Ensure that the Table/Query option is selected for the Row Source Type property.

14. In the Row Source property, click the Build button. The Query Builder window and the Show Table dialog box appear, with the dialog box active.

15. Double-click the Positions table and then close the Show Table dialog box. The Query Builder window becomes active.

16. In the Positions table object, double-click the PositionID field and then double-click the PositionType field. The fields are added to the design grid.

17. In the Sort row of the PositionType column in the design grid, select the Ascending option.

18. Close the Query Builder window. A message appears, asking you to confirm the changes that you're about to make.

19. Click Yes. You're returned to the properties dialog box.

20. On the Format tab, type **2** in the Column Count property and type **0";1"** in the Column Widths property.

21. Close the control's properties.

22. In the Label control linked to the Combo Box control, type **Position:** and then resize the control as necessary.

23. Click anywhere in the design grid so that no controls are selected. Select a color from the Fill/Back Color option on the Formatting (Form/Report) toolbar. The color of the design grid changes to the new color.

24. Select all the controls on the design grid, and then click the Bold button on the Formatting (Form/Report) toolbar.

25. Select the Text Box and Combo Box controls without selecting the linked Label controls. Select a color from the Fill/Back Color option on the Formatting (Form/Report) toolbar. The color is added to the controls. Apply any other necessary formatting to the controls.

(continued)

12

Creating and Configuring Forms

Project
12-1

Creating a Form in the Consumer Advocacy Database

26. Click the Select Objects button in the Toolbox, then click the Label button, and finally click the top center of the design grid. The control is added to the grid. If a warning icon appears, click the Ignore Error option. The warning tells you that the control is not bound to any fields. In the Label control, type **Consumer Advocacy Database**. Center the control and apply any desired formatting. The Form window should now look similar to the one in the following illustration:

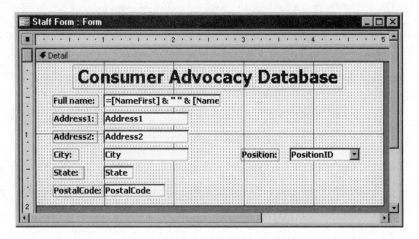

27. Click the Save button on the Form Design toolbar. The Save As dialog box appears.

28. Type **Staff Form** in the Form Name text box and then click OK.

29. Click View on the Form Design toolbar to switch to Form view. Your form should now look similar to the one in the following illustration:

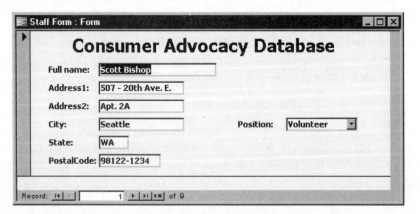

Project Summary

In this project, you created five bound controls by selecting them from the Field List. By using this method, you did not need to identify the data source for the controls. However, for the Combo Box control, you had to identify not only the control source but also the source of the values that are displayed in the form. You achieved this by creating a query that returned the necessary information. In addition to the Combo Box control, you added a Text Box control that calculated the values that would be displayed in the form. In this case, you used an expression to concatenate the first name and last name of each staff member. Now that you have a feel for how to create forms, you should experiment with adding different types of controls and applying different formatting. In Module 15, you will learn more about creating macros and modules, which will give you even greater flexibility in the types of controls that you can add to your forms.

Module 12 Mastery Check

1. What is a form?

2. How should you open a new form if you want to link a table to the form?

3. What three windows appear in Design view when you open a new form that is associated with a table?

4. What is a control?

5. Which button must you select in the Toolbox before selecting one of the control buttons?

6. What steps should you take to add a control to a form (without using a wizard)?

7. You're creating a form that is associated with a table in your database. You plan to add several bound Text Box controls. From which object in Design view should you add the controls?

   A. The design grid

   B. The Field List

   C. The Form window

   D. The Toolkit

8. Which type of control should you add to a form if you want to concatenate two fields into one control?

   A. Bound

   B. Switchboard

   C. Calculated

   D. Unbound

9. What controls are added to the design grid when you use the Toolbox to add a Text Box control?

10. How do you use the Field List to add more than one Text Box control at a time?

11. Which property in a bound control specifies the field that the control is bound to?

    A. Row Source Type

    B. Row Source

    C. Bound Column

    D. Control Source

12. Which control should you use if you want to group together Yes/No controls?

13. Which types of controls allow you to apply conditional formatting?

    A. Text Box

    B. Combo Box

    C. List Box

    D. Check Box

14. What tabs are included in the properties dialog box for a control?

15. What two tools can you use to format a control?

Module 13

Creating and Configuring Reports

CRITICAL SKILLS

13.1 Create Reports in Design View

13.2 Configure Headers and Footers

13.3 Sort and Group Data

13.4 Use Parameter Queries in a Report

In Module 12, you learned how to create and configure forms that you could add to your database. In this module, you will learn how to add reports to your database. Reports are similar to forms in many ways. Like forms, reports are data objects that enhance your application by providing an interface between the users and the data in the database. In addition, you create and configure reports in much the same way you do forms. However, forms and reports serve different purposes. As you've already seen, forms are interactive. They allow users to view and manipulate data as well as trigger events that cause actions to occur. Reports, on the other hand, are used primarily to provide information in a concise format. They do not contain such controls as command buttons or option groups. They are meant only to present information. Reports also provide greater flexibility for grouping and summarizing data than forms do. In this module, you will learn how to create reports, configure headers and footers, sort and group data, and use parameter queries in a report.

CRITICAL SKILL
13.1 # Create Reports in Design View

Reports allow you to present information in a way that can be easily printed and disseminated throughout your organization. The report interfaces with the database so that data can be deployed in a way that is meaningful to the target audience. For example, you can create a report that serves as a customer catalog that describes your company's products and services. Or you can create a report that provides financial information to bookkeepers and accountants. There is almost no limit to the types of reports that you can create and the ways that you can present information.

Reports can be as simple or as complex as you want to make them. For example, the report shown in Figure 13-1 is as simple a report as you can create. It displays product information from the Northwind database. As you can see, the report contains no column headings, no titles, and no special formatting. As you work through this module, you'll learn how a report like this can be enhanced so that it presents the information in a more readable and useful manner.

Opening a New Report

As with forms, there are a number of methods that you can use to create a report. You can use a wizard or one of the AutoReport tools, or you can create the report in Design view, which is the method that we will focus on in this module. The first step in creating a report in Design view is to select the Reports object type in the database window and then use one of the following methods to open the report in Design view:

- Double-click Create Report In Design View.
- Click the New button in the database window.

● Click the Insert menu and then click Report. (For this method, you do not have to select the Reports object type first.)

For a report to be effective, it must be linked to data in the database. To create a report that is linked to data, you must associate the new report to a table or query, so you should use the second or third option to open the new report. When you select one of these two options, the New Report dialog box appears. In this dialog box, you can select the method that you want to use to create the report and, optionally, you can select the table or query on which the report will be based.

To create a report in Design view, select the Design View option from the list box in the New Report dialog box. Next, select the table or query from the drop-down list at the bottom of the dialog box, and then click OK. Once the new report opens in Design view, you can start adding controls to the design grid.

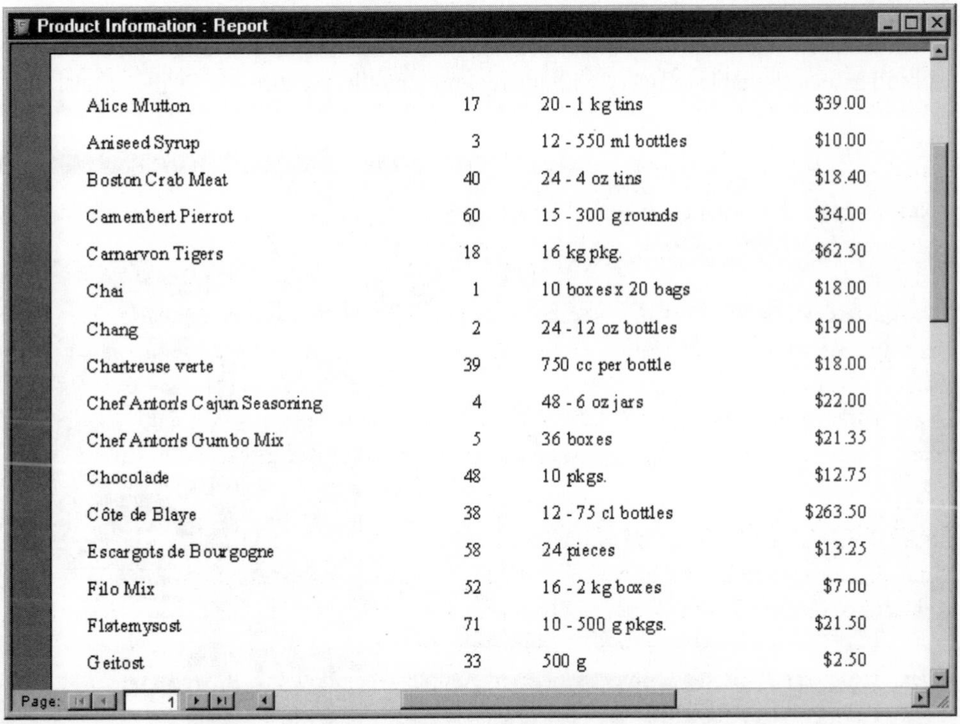

Product Information : Report			
Alice Mutton	17	20 - 1 kg tins	$39.00
Aniseed Syrup	3	12 - 550 ml bottles	$10.00
Boston Crab Meat	40	24 - 4 oz tins	$18.40
Camembert Pierrot	60	15 - 300 g rounds	$34.00
Carnarvon Tigers	18	16 kg pkg.	$62.50
Chai	1	10 boxes x 20 bags	$18.00
Chang	2	24 - 12 oz bottles	$19.00
Chartreuse verte	39	750 cc per bottle	$18.00
Chef Anton's Cajun Seasoning	4	48 - 6 oz jars	$22.00
Chef Anton's Gumbo Mix	5	36 boxes	$21.35
Chocolade	48	10 pkgs.	$12.75
Côte de Blaye	38	12 - 75 cl bottles	$263.50
Escargots de Bourgogne	58	24 pieces	$13.25
Filo Mix	52	16 - 2 kg boxes	$7.00
Fløtemysost	71	10 - 500 g pkgs.	$21.50
Geitost	33	500 g	$2.50

Page: 1

Figure 13-1 The Product Information report in the Print Preview window

Navigating the Design View Interface

When you open a new report in Design view, three windows appear: the Report window, the Toolbox, and the Field List, as shown in Figure 13-2. As you can see, the Design view interface that is used for creating reports is similar to the interface used for creating forms. One of the main differences is in the design grid, which includes three sections: Page Header, Detail, and Page Footer. The Detail section is the same as what you saw in the Form window. However, the Page Header and Page Footer sections are new. As the names imply, these sections are used for adding header and footer information to your report. I'll be discussing headers and footers later in this module, in the section "Configure Headers and Footers."

NOTE

The Field List appears only if you select a table or query from the New Report dialog box when you first open the new form.

If you open a new report by double-clicking the Create Report In Design View option, you can still associate a table or query with the report by modifying the report's properties. You

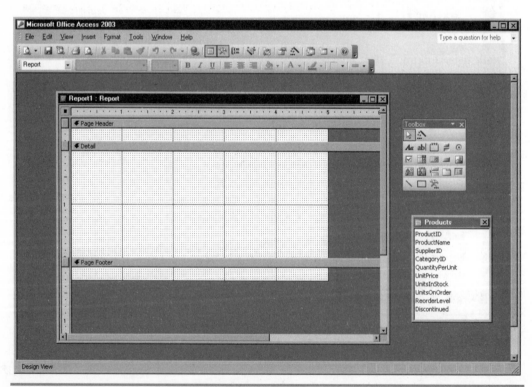

Figure 13-2 Opening a new report in Design view

can access the report's properties in the same way that you accessed a form's properties: Select the report and then click the Properties button on the Report Design toolbar. You can also double-click the box near the top-left corner of the Report window, to the left of the top ruler and directly above the left ruler. When the Report dialog box appears, select the Data tab. From the drop-down list for the Record Source property, select the table or query that you want to associate with the report.

TIP

You can configure the properties for each section of the design grid. If you refer back to Figure 13-2, you'll see that each section is preceded by a heading that identifies the section. For example, the Detail heading precedes the Detail section. To the left of that heading is a box. The Report window displays a box for each section. To open the properties for a section, double-click the box. You can then configure properties specific to the selected section.

You can add or remove the Toolbox and Field List in Design view by clicking the appropriate options (Toolbox or Field List, respectively) on the Report Design toolbar. The Field List can be displayed only if the report is associated with an underlying table or query. Also, you can move all three windows and resize them as necessary.

Adding Controls to a Report

Adding a control to a report is similar adding a control to a form. First, ensure that the Control Wizards button in the Toolbox is not selected. If necessary, click the Select Objects button in the Toolbox, then click the button for the control type that you want to add, and finally click in the design grid where you want to locate the control. When you add a control to the design grid, it is displayed in the same way it is displayed for a form. Figure 13-3 shows the Report window for the Product Information report that you viewed in Figure 13-1. As you can see, the design grid contains four controls. Each one is a Text Box control that is bound to a field in the Products table. Notice that header and footer sections are not used for this report. Because they're not

Figure 13-3 The Product Information report in Design view

used, they're not displayed in Design view. Later in this module, in the section "Configure Headers and Footers," you will learn how to display and remove the header and footer sections and how to use these sections in your reports.

NOTE

You may have noticed that the Text Box controls shown in Figure 13-3 do not include the linked Label controls that are added to the design grid when you add Text Box controls. For reports, you'll often find that you want to remove a Label control because of the way that you plan to lay out the report. To remove the control, simply select the control and press DELETE. The Label control will be removed without affecting the Text Box control. Later in the module, in the section "Configure Headers and Footers," you will learn how to add a separate Label control as a column heading above the Text Box control to identify the values being returned by the report.

The big difference between report controls and form controls is that report controls are not interactive. For example, you can add a Text Box control that is tied to a field in the underlying table, but users will not be able to enter or modify data when viewing the report. You can also add a Combo Box control, but you cannot interact with the data in any way, and the control does not display data in the same way that it would in a form.

Another difference between report controls and form controls is that report controls do not trigger events. If you were to view the Event tab in the control's properties, you would see that no event properties are listed. As a result, you cannot trigger an event when working with the data displayed by a control.

NOTE

Although you cannot configure event properties for report controls, you can configure event properties for the report itself or for the individual sections within the report, such as the Detail section. For information on configuring event properties, see Module 12.

Ask the Expert

Q: You state that you can add Image and Object Frame controls to a report. When should you add a picture through an Image control rather than through an Object Frame control?

A: An Image control is used simply to add a picture to the report. On the other hand, an Object Frame control adds a container that displays an OLE object. You can either embed the object by using an Unbound Object Frame control or link the object by using a Bound Object Frame control. An Image control loads faster that an Object Frame control. Once the Image control is added to the report, users cannot take any further actions with the picture; they can only view it as it appears in the report. In most cases this will be adequate. On the other hand, if users must be able to view the picture in its native application or be able to edit the picture, you should use an Object Frame control. If you decide to use an Object Frame control, the decision to embed the image or link it depends on how the image will be accessed and stored in the future. If the picture will be used only in the context of the report, you should use an Unbound Object Frame control. If, on the other hand, you want to maintain the picture in a central location where it can be modified by different users at various times, use the Bound Object Frame control so that the picture displayed in the report is always the most current image available.

For the most part, the controls that you will be adding to a report are bound Text Box controls, Image and Object Frame controls, and enhancement controls such as Label and Line controls.

Using Multiple Columns in a Report

For some reports, you might find that you want to display information in multiple columns. This is particularly useful for reports that contain just a few types of information spread out over multiple pages, leaving much of each page unused. For example, the report shown in Figure 13-4 displays only two types of information and uses only half of each page.

You can display information like this in multiple columns. This allows you to streamline the look of the report so that fewer pages are used and so that the report is more readable to those viewing it. To display the report information in columns, you must configure the settings on the Columns tab of the Page Setup dialog box, which is shown in Figure 13-5. The Columns tab allows you to set the number of columns, the spacing between rows and columns, the size of the columns, and the way in which data is displayed in the columns.

If you were to configure the Product Sales report with the settings shown in Figure 13-5, the information would be displayed in two columns and there would be .5 inches between the two columns. In addition, the information would be displayed down the first column before starting at the top of the second column, rather than across and then down. Figure 13-6 shows you what the report would look like if you applied these settings.

You can access the Page Setup dialog box by clicking the File menu and then clicking Page Setup. You do not have to be in Design view to configure the column-related options. You can also configure them from the Print Preview window or by selecting the report in the database window and then accessing the Page Setup dialog box. Once you have configured the options, click OK. The column settings are immediately applied to the report.

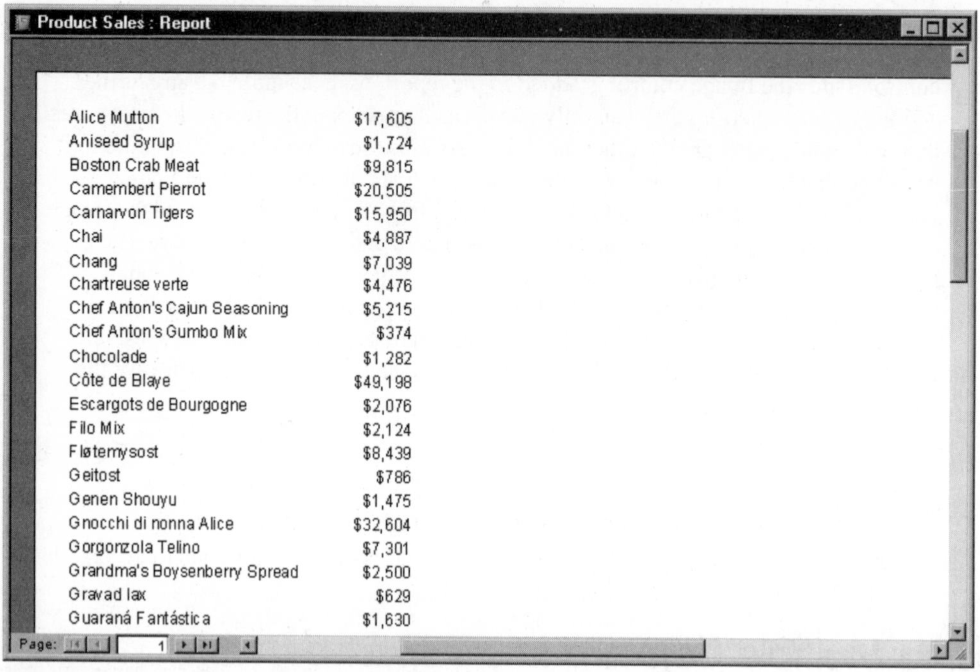

Figure 13-4 The Product Sales report displayed in a single column

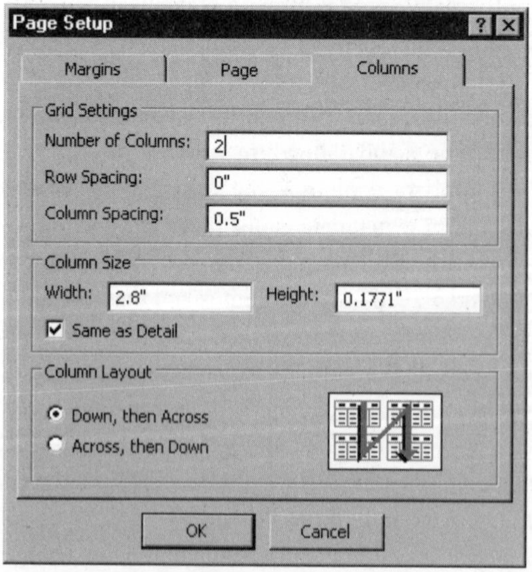

Figure 13-5 The Columns tab of the Page Setup dialog box

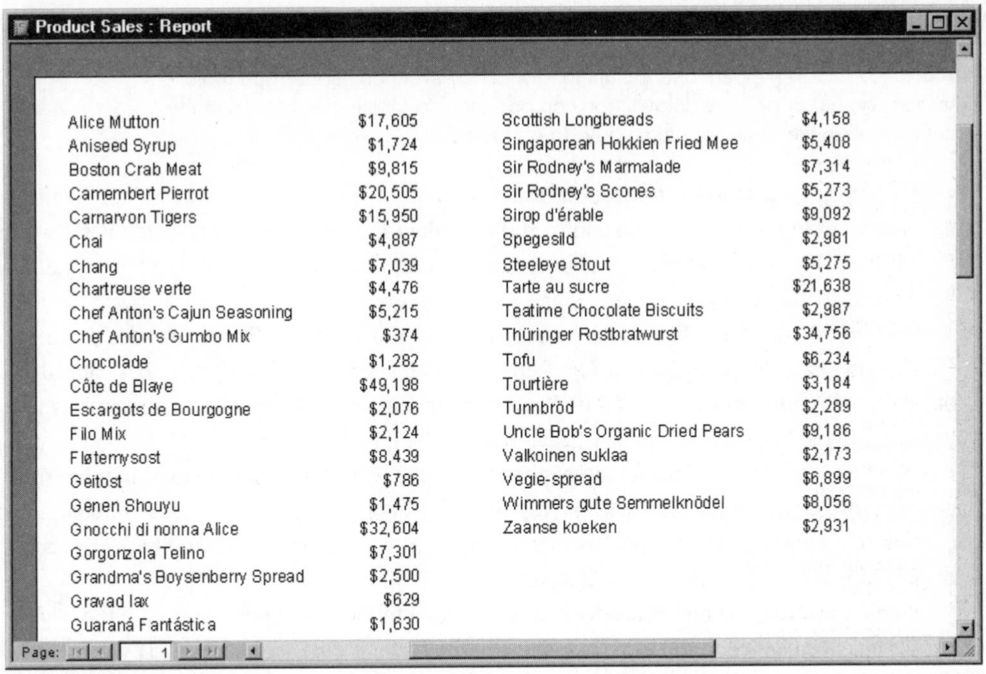

Product Sales : Report

Alice Mutton	$17,605	Scottish Longbreads	$4,158
Aniseed Syrup	$1,724	Singaporean Hokkien Fried Mee	$5,408
Boston Crab Meat	$9,815	Sir Rodney's Marmalade	$7,314
Camembert Pierrot	$20,505	Sir Rodney's Scones	$5,273
Carnarvon Tigers	$15,950	Sirop d'érable	$9,092
Chai	$4,887	Spegesild	$2,981
Chang	$7,039	Steeleye Stout	$5,275
Chartreuse verte	$4,476	Tarte au sucre	$21,638
Chef Anton's Cajun Seasoning	$5,215	Teatime Chocolate Biscuits	$2,987
Chef Anton's Gumbo Mix	$374	Thüringer Rostbratwurst	$34,756
Chocolade	$1,282	Tofu	$6,234
Côte de Blaye	$49,198	Tourtière	$3,184
Escargots de Bourgogne	$2,076	Tunnbröd	$2,289
Filo Mix	$2,124	Uncle Bob's Organic Dried Pears	$9,186
Fløtemysost	$8,439	Valkoinen suklaa	$2,173
Geitost	$786	Vegie-spread	$6,899
Genen Shouyu	$1,475	Wimmers gute Semmelknödel	$8,056
Gnocchi di nonna Alice	$32,604	Zaanse koeken	$2,931
Gorgonzola Telino	$7,301		
Grandma's Boysenberry Spread	$2,500		
Gravad lax	$629		
Guaraná Fantástica	$1,630		

Page: 1

Figure 13-6 The Product Sales report displayed in two columns

---

CRITICAL SKILL
13.2 Configure Headers and Footers

As you saw earlier in this module, you can configure headers and footers for a report. In fact, you can configure a report header and footer and a page header and footer. A report header is inserted at the beginning of a report, and a report footer is inserted at the end of a report. A page header, on the other hand, is inserted at the top of each page of the report, and a page footer is inserted at the bottom of each page.

When you first open a new report in Design view, the Report window displays the Page Header and Page Footer sections in the grid. However, you can also display the Report Header and Report Footer sections by clicking the View menu and then clicking Report Header/Footer. If you click this option again, the sections are removed from the Design grid. You can also add or remove the Page Header and Page Footer sections by clicking the View menu and then clicking Page Header/Footer.

NOTE

You can also add headers and footers to forms. However, the header and footer sections do not appear by default. You can add them to or remove them from the design grid in the same way that you add and remove them from reports.

Once you've displayed the sections that you want to configure, you can add any controls that you want to them. Let's take a look at the Product Information report, which is shown in Figure 13-7. We looked at the report in Figure 13-1 and Figure 13-3. Now the report includes header and footer sections.

As you can see in the figure, the report includes controls in the Report Header, Page Header, and Page Footer sections. The Report Header section contains one Label control that reads "Product Information." The Page Header section contains four Label controls that provide column headings at the top of each page in the report. The Page Footer section contains one Text Box control that inserts the page number, the word "of," and the total number of pages at the bottom of each page in the report. The Report Footer section does not contain any controls. To view the report, click the View button on the Report Design toolbar. The report is displayed in the Print Preview window, as shown in Figure 13-8.

As you can see, the report header has been added to the top of the report, and the page header has been added to the top of the page in the form of column headings. If you were to view the next page, you would see only the column headings, not the report heading. In addition, if you were to scroll down to the bottom of the first page of the report, you would see the page number written as "1 of 3."

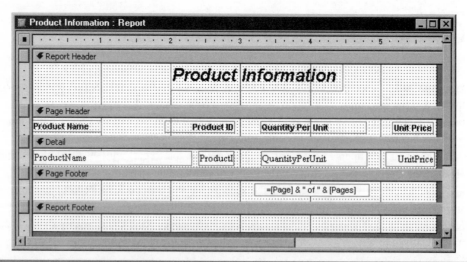

Figure 13-7 Configuring the Product Information report with a report header, a page header, and a page footer

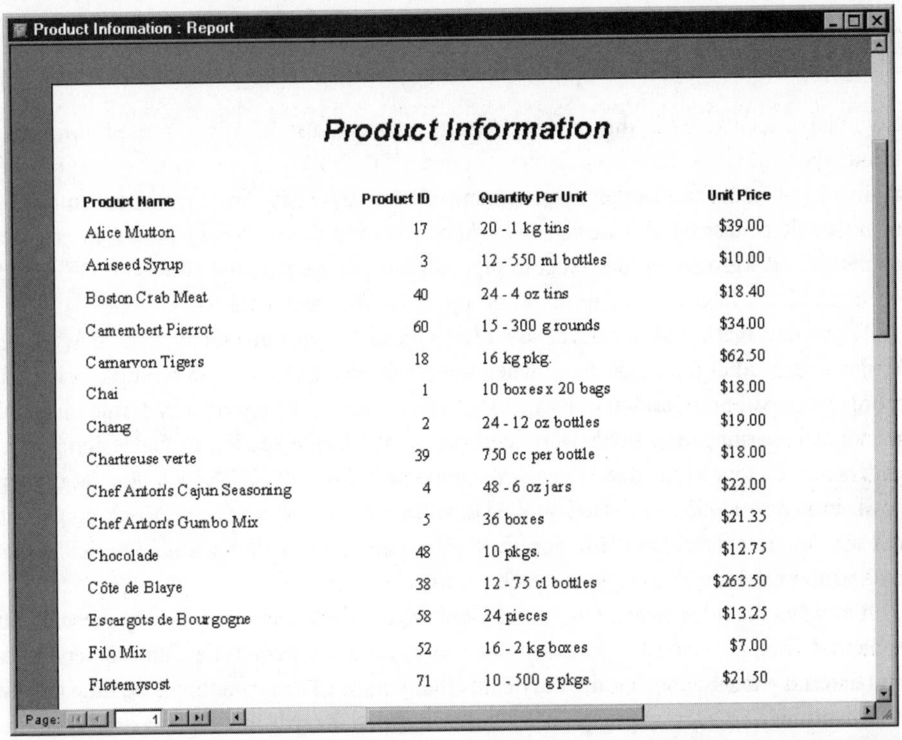

Product Information : Report

Product Information

Product Name	Product ID	Quantity Per Unit	Unit Price
Alice Mutton	17	20 - 1 kg tins	$39.00
Aniseed Syrup	3	12 - 550 ml bottles	$10.00
Boston Crab Meat	40	24 - 4 oz tins	$18.40
Camembert Pierrot	60	15 - 300 g rounds	$34.00
Carnarvon Tigers	18	16 kg pkg.	$62.50
Chai	1	10 boxes x 20 bags	$18.00
Chang	2	24 - 12 oz bottles	$19.00
Chartreuse verte	39	750 cc per bottle	$18.00
Chef Anton's Cajun Seasoning	4	48 - 6 oz jars	$22.00
Chef Anton's Gumbo Mix	5	36 boxes	$21.35
Chocolade	48	10 pkgs.	$12.75
Côte de Blaye	38	12 - 75 cl bottles	$263.50
Escargots de Bourgogne	58	24 pieces	$13.25
Filo Mix	52	16 - 2 kg boxes	$7.00
Fløtemysost	71	10 - 500 g pkgs.	$21.50

Page: 1

Figure 13-8 Viewing the report header and the page header in the Product Information report

Progress Check

1. What sections are included in the design grid when you open a new report in Design view?

2. How do you add the Toolbox to Design view?

3. How do you add a control to the design grid?

4. In which section of a report would you add a Label control that displays text at the beginning of a report only?

---

1. Page Header, Detail, and Page Footer

2. Click the Toolbox button on the Report Design toolbar.

3. First ensure that the Control Wizards button in the Toolbox is not selected. If necessary, click the Select Objects button in the Toolbox, then click the button for the object type that you want to add, and finally click in the design grid where you want to locate the control.

4. The Report Header section

13.3 Sort and Group Data

As you have seen so far in this module, reports provide a useful way to present information to various types of users. Reports offer a great deal of flexibility in how you organize and format the displayed data. For example, you can specify exactly what data should be displayed and how it should be displayed. You can also add headers and footers, change fonts, insert pictures, and modify background colors. Access supports another feature that allows you to enhance your report even further—the ability to group and sort related data.

The reports that we've looked at so far have presented data in a linear fashion, with records listed one right after the other. Even when we configured a report with multiple columns, the records were still presented in the same way. In each case, the report was defined in a similar manner. The participating fields were identified in the Detail section of the design grid, and headers and footers were added to enhance the report. For example, if you look at the report shown in Figure 13-9, you'll see that the Detail section includes four Text Box controls that are each bound to a field in the underlying table. This report will generate a basic list that contains the values in each field for each record.

If a report includes only a few records, displaying the records in this way presents little problem. However, when a report includes many records, viewing the data can become a cumbersome process, and finding the details that you need can sometimes be time consuming and frustrating. To address this problem you can group records in a report based on the values in a specific field.

To group records in a report, you must use the Sorting And Grouping dialog box, as shown in Figure 13-10. This dialog box allows you to specify the participating fields and set options related to each field.

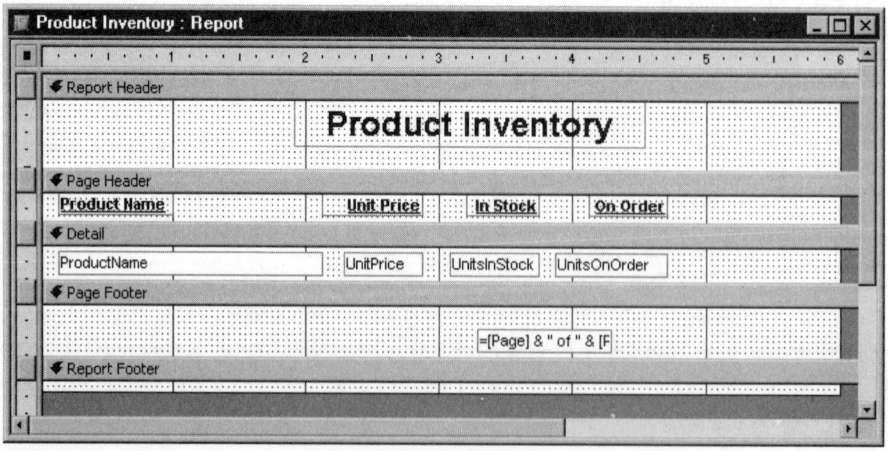

Figure 13-9 The Product Inventory report in Design view

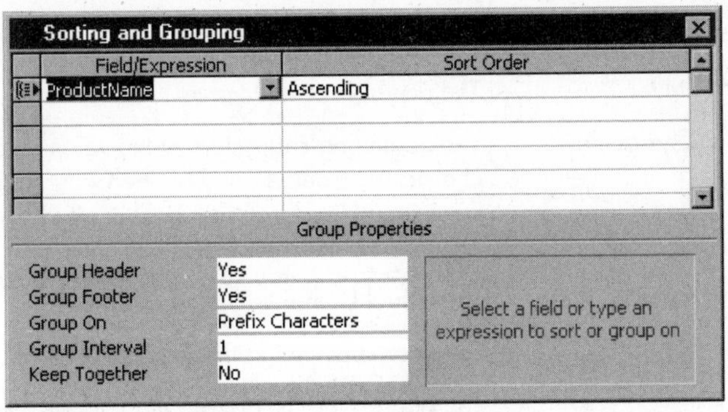

Figure 13-10 The Sorting And Grouping dialog box

To access the Sorting And Grouping dialog box, click the Sorting And Grouping button on the Report Design toolbar. When the dialog box appears, select a field name from the drop-down list in the first row of the Field/Expression column. The records will be grouped based on the values in the selected field. After you've identified a field, select a sort order in the Sort Order column. Next you must configure the group properties, as necessary. Five properties are supported for each field:

- **Group Header**   This property adds a header section to the design grid. The section is specific to the field whose values you're grouping together.

- **Group Footer**   This adds a footer section to the design grid. The section is specific to the field whose values you're grouping together.

- **Group On**   This property specifies how values will be grouped together.

- **Group Interval**   This specifies the number of characters or the interval on which to base the group. For example, you can specify that a Number field be based on an interval value of 100. As a result, records will be grouped together in intervals of 100. For instance, 128, 132, and 153 will be in one group, and 209, 226, and 288 will be in another group.

- **Keep Together**   This specifies whether groups smaller than one page in length are kept together across page breaks. This property does not affect groups larger than one page. If you configure this property to keep groups together, you must also ensure that the Keep Together property for the group header and footer sections of the design grid is set to Yes.

The options available in the Group On property vary according to the data type of the grouped field. Table 13-1 describes the options available for each data type for fields that can be grouped together.

Data Type	Group On Option	Groups Records Based On
Text	Each Value	The actual Text field value.
	Prefix Characters	The beginning characters of the value. The number of characters is determined by the Group Interval property. For example, if Group Interval is set to 1, the records are grouped by the first character only.
Date	Each Value	The actual Date field value.
	Year	The year specified in the Date field value.
	Qtr	The quarter that is inferred in the Date field value.
	Month	The month specified in the Date field value.
	Week	The week that is inferred in the Date field value.
	Day	The day specified in the Date field value.
	Hour	The hour specified in the Date field value.
	Minute	The minute specified in the Date field value.
Number, Currency, or AutoNumber	Each Value	The actual Number, Currency, or AutoNumber field value.
	Interval	The value specified in the Group Interval property. For example, if the Group Interval property specifies 1000, records will be grouped together based on the specified numerical field value and according to increments of a thousand.

Table 13-1 Options Available in the Group On Property

In order for a field to be grouped, you must select Yes for the Group Header property, the Group Footer property, or both. Otherwise, the field values will only be sorted, rather than grouped. The data is sorted based on how sorting is configured for each field. However, the sort order applies only to data as it is displayed in the report. It does not affect data in the underlying table.

Once you set up grouping in the Sorting And Grouping dialog box, close the dialog box and add the necessary controls to the header and footer sections in the design grid.

Configuring Group Headers and Footers

For each field that is grouped, a Group Header section, a Group Footer section, or both are added to the design grid if the fields' Group Header or Group Footer properties are set to Yes.

You can add controls to the grid sections in the same way you add controls to other sections. Controls added to the group header section are displayed at the beginning of each group. Likewise, controls added to the Group Footer section are displayed at the end of each group.

When a group header or footer is added to the design grid, it is assigned a name that is based on the field that is being grouped. For example, the Sorting And Grouping dialog box shown in Figure 13-10 is configured to group the ProductName field on the value's prefix character (just the first character because the Group Interval property is set to 1). In addition, both the Group Header property and the Group Footer property are set to Yes. If you take a look at Figure 13-11, you'll see how the group header and footer sections are added to the grid and named ProductName Header and ProductName Footer.

As you can see, the Label controls used to provide column headings are added to the ProductName Header section. If you refer back to Figure 13-9, you'll see that these controls were part of the Page Header section. However, now that the controls have been moved, the column heads will appear at the beginning of each group, rather than the beginning of each page. Figure 13-12 shows how the report will now look when it is displayed in the Print Preview window.

Notice that the report displays data in groups based on the first letter of the ProductName value. This is because the Prefix Characters option was set for the Group On property. In addition, because the ProductName file is sorted in ascending order, the groups are displayed alphabetically, starting with *A*. In addition, each group begins with column headings and ends with a line. The Line control was added to the ProductName Footer section and therefore appears after each group.

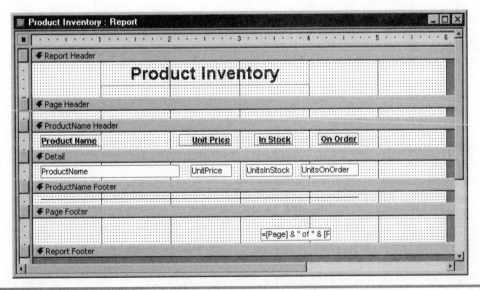

Figure 13-11 Adding a group header and footer to the Product Inventory report

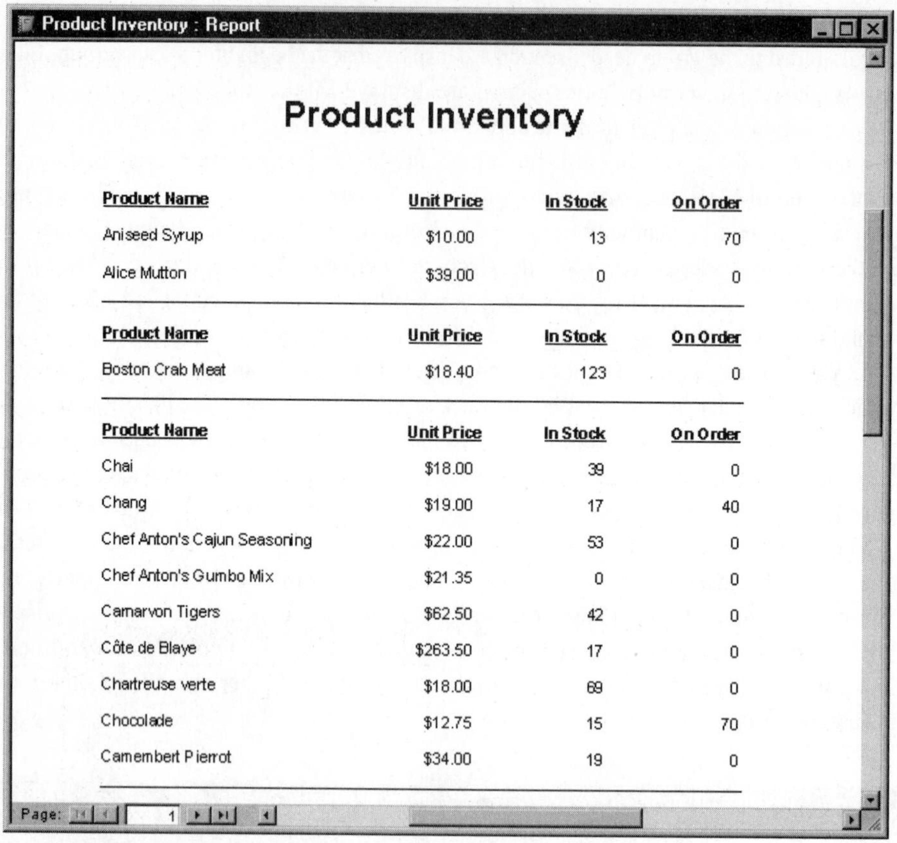

Figure 13-12 Viewing the group header in the Product Inventory report

As you can see in Figure 13-12, by grouping records together and using group headers and footers, you can create a report that is far more readable and that presents data that is easier to access and understand.

Summarizing Grouped Data

Once you group data in a report, you might find it useful to summarize part of the data. In Module 11, you learned how to summarize data in queries by using aggregate functions to calculate values in a field. As you'll recall, an aggregate function is a type of function that applies summary calculations to groups of data. For example, you can use the Avg aggregate function to find the average of a group of values.

You can also use aggregate functions in a calculated Text Box control that is added to a group footer. For example, you can add a calculated Text Box control to the Product Inventory report that you saw in Figure 13-11 and Figure 13-12. The control can be configured with a Sum aggregate function, as shown in Figure 13-13.

The Sum aggregate function is part of the expression defined in the Control Source property on the Data tab of the control's properties. The expression calculates the total of UnitsInStock values and inserts that total at the end of each group. As you can see in Figure 13-14, nothing else has changed in the report and no data has been affected, other than what is returned by the aggregate function. The Text Box control simply provides the group total for the participating field.

You can use other aggregate functions, such as Avg or Count, and you can configure aggregated calculated controls on other fields. In addition, you can summarize data from the entire report by adding the control to the report footer. For example, by adding the same control you saw in the group footer in Figure 13-13 to the report footer, you can have the report include the UnitsInStock total for the entire report. In fact, if you were providing totals for each group, most users would no doubt expect to see a grand total at the end of the report.

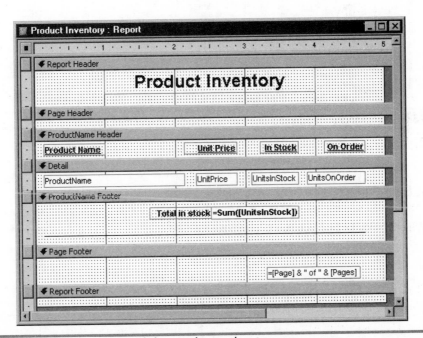

Figure 13-13 Adding summarized data to the Product Inventory report

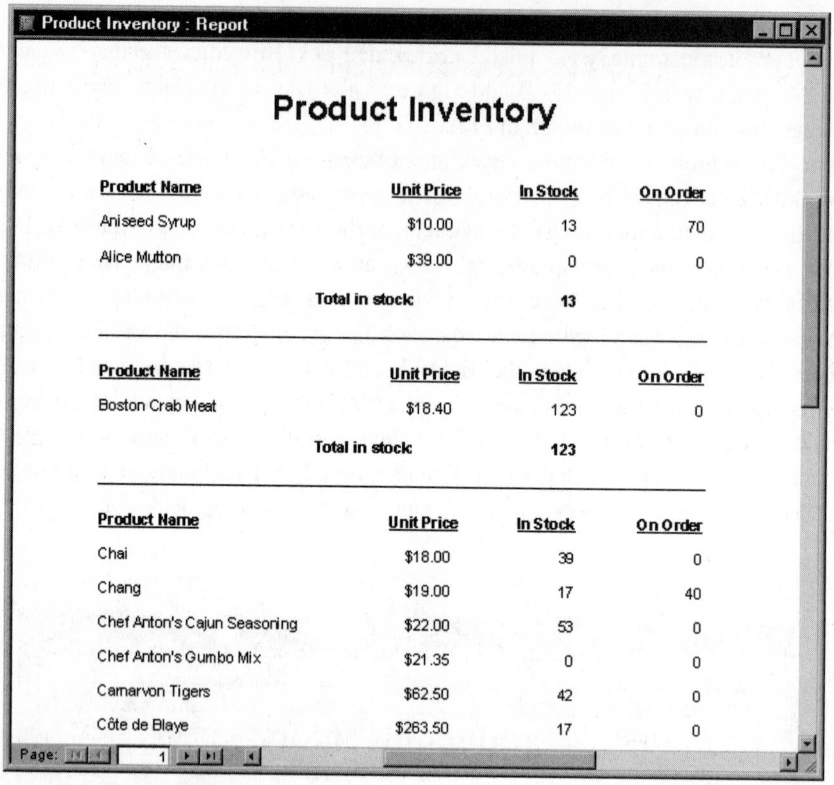

Figure 13-14 Viewing summarized data in the Product Inventory report

Progress Check

1. Which dialog box do you use to group records?

2. What properties can you configure for a grouped field?

3. What name is assigned to a group header?

4. What type of functions do you use to summarize grouped data?

---

1. The Sorting And Grouping dialog box
2. Group Header, Group Footer, Group On, Group Interval, and Keep Together
3. A group header is assigned a name that is based on the field that is being grouped
4. Aggregate functions

CRITICAL SKILL
13.4 Use Parameter Queries in a Report

Access allows you to create a type of query that defines a parameter within the query definition. This type of query is called a parameter query. The parameter acts as a placeholder that allows you to specify a value whenever you run that query. Before the query can return data, a value must be provided for the parameter. The value is then used to complete the query, and the data is returned. For example, Figure 13-15 shows a query definition that defines a parameter on the Country field.

The actual parameter ([Enter name of country:]) is specified in the Criteria section of the design grid. By enclosing the value in brackets, you're telling Access to treat this value as a parameter. The rest of the query is defined as you would normally expect. The query returns values from the CompanyName field and the ContactName field. The values returned depend on the value specified for the parameter, and the parameter is based on the Country field. As a result, the records returned will be only those with a Country value that matches the name provided for the parameter.

When you run a query that includes a parameter, Access prompts you for a value for that query. For the previous example, you'll be prompted for the name of a country, as shown in Figure 13-16. Notice that the name of the parameter—Enter name of country:—is printed

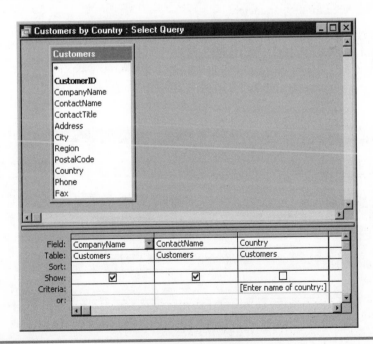

Figure 13-15 The Customers by Country parameter query

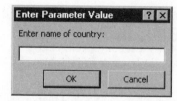

Figure 13-16 The Enter Parameter Value dialog box

above the text box where you enter the parameter value. After you enter the value, click OK, and the query will be executed.

Once you have created a parameter query, you can base your report on that query. As you can see Figure 13-17, you simply define the report as you would any other type of report. In this case, Text Box controls are added to the Detail section, and Label controls are added to the Page Header section. The label controls will act as column headings for the values returned by the Text Box controls.

When you view a report that is based on a parameter query, you are prompted for a parameter value when you open the report. You're prompted for the value in the same way that you would be prompted if you were running the query directly. When the Enter Parameter Value dialog box appears, type in a value and click OK. The report will then be generated based on the value you entered for the parameter.

Adding Parameter Values to a Report

You can use the parameter value in your report if you want that value displayed. You simply create a Text Box control and define an expression that includes the static text plus the name

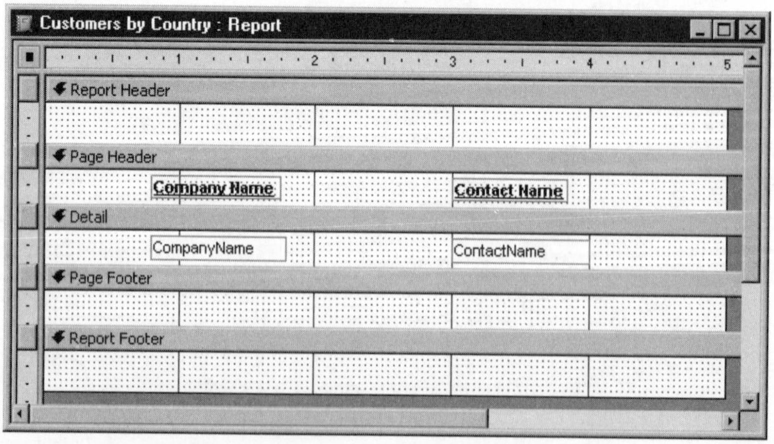

Figure 13-17 The Customer by Country report in Design view

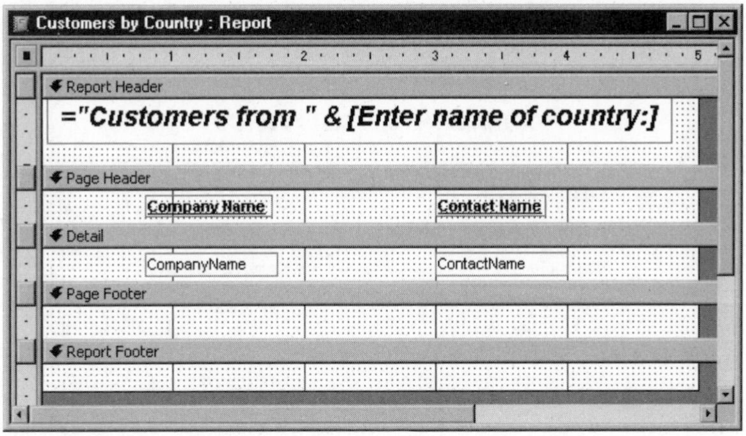

Figure 13-18 Adding the parameter value to the Customers by Country report

of the parameter, enclosed in brackets. For example, Figure 13-18 shows how the parameter can be used as part of a heading for the entire report. By adding a Text Box control to the Report Header section, you can display the static text and the parameter value at the top of the report.

Notice that the Text Box control includes an expression that begins with an equal (=) comparison operator, then specifies the text "Customers from " (including a space after "from"), then adds the concatenation (&) operator, and finally ends with the name of the parameter. The parameter returns the value that is specified when you run the report. Figure 13-19 shows how the report will look if you enter "France" as the parameter value. The report returns only those companies that are located in France. At the top of the report is a title based on the Text Box control in the Report Header section.

Project 13-1 Creating a Report in the Consumer Advocacy Database

Project
13-1

As you've seen in this module, reports provide a great deal of flexibility in presenting different types of information to users. You will now create a report in your consumer advocacy database. The report will provide the names of staff members in your organization, and the names will be grouped according to the cities in which the staff members are located. The report will also show the number of staff members in each city and the total number of staff members in the entire organization. Once you've created the report, you will save it to your database and then view it in the Print Preview window.

(continued)

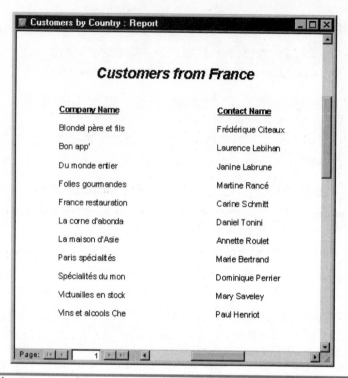

Figure 13-19 The Customers by Country report in the Print Preview window

Step by Step

1. If they're not already open, open Access and then open the ConsumerAdvocacy.mdb database file.

2. If necessary, select the Reports object type in the database window and then click the New button. The New Report dialog box appears.

3. Ensure that Design View is selected, select the Staff table from the drop-down list, and click OK. The new report opens in Design view. The Report window includes three sections in the design grid: Page Header, Detail, and Page Footer.

4. Click the View menu, and then click Report Header/Footer. The Report Header section and the Report Footer section are added to the design grid.

5. Click the View menu, and then click Page Header/Footer. The Page Header section and the Page Footer section are removed from the design grid. You will not be adding controls to these sections in this project.

6. Drag the NameFirst field from the Field List to the Detail section of the design grid.

7. Select the Label control linked to the Text Box control that you just added, and then press DELETE. The Label control will be removed from the design grid.

8. Position the Text Box control toward the left of the Detail section and directly at the top of the grid.

9. Repeat steps 6 through 8 to add the NameLast field to the design grid. Position the Text Box control to the right of the first control.

10. Reduce the size of the Detail section so that it is large enough to display only the two controls.

11. Click the Sorting And Grouping button on the Report Design toolbar. The Sorting And Grouping dialog box appears.

12. In the Field/Expression column of the first row, select the City field from the drop-down list. Set the Group Header and Group Footer properties to Yes, and close the dialog box. The City Header and City Footer sections are added to the design grid.

13. Add two Label controls to the City Header section of the design grid. Position the controls directly over the two Text Box controls in the design grid. The Label controls will act as column headings for the values returned by the Text Box controls.

14. Type **First Name** in the first Label control, and type **Last Name** in the second Label control. Add bold and underline formatting to the text.

15. Use the Field List to add a Text Box control to the City Header section. The control should be based on the City field. Position the Text Box and Label controls at the top of the section, all the way to the left of the grid.

16. In the Label control linked to the Text Box control that you just added, type **Location:** as the displayed value. Add bold formatting to the Label control and the linked Text box control. Change the color of the lettering of both controls. If necessary, resize the City Header section so that only the four controls are displayed.

17. In the City Footer section, add a Text Box control at the top left of the grid. In the Label control that is linked to the Text Box control, type **Total number of staff members in this city:** as the displayed value. In the Text Box control, type **=Count([NameLast])**. Add bold formatting to the Label control and the linked Text Box control. Change the color of the lettering of both controls.

18. In the City Footer section, add a Line control beneath the Label and Text Box controls. If necessary, resize the City Footer section so that only the three controls are displayed.

(continued)

19. In the Report Footer section, add a Text Box control at the top left of the grid. In the Label control that is linked to the Text Box control, type **Total number of staff members for all cities:** as the displayed value. In the Text Box control, type **=Count([NameLast])**. Add bold formatting to the Label control and the linked Text Box control. Change the color of the lettering of both controls. If necessary, resize the Report Footer section so that only the two controls are displayed.

20. Add a Label control to the Report Header section. In the control, type **Staff Location by City**. Change the font to a different font type and change font size to 18 points. Center and resize the Label control. Resize the Report Header section if necessary, but leave a little extra space beneath the Label control. The Form window should now look similar to the following illustration:

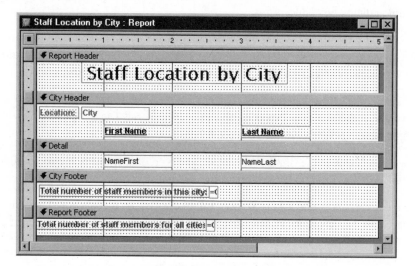

21. Click the Save button on the Report Design toolbar. The Save As dialog box appears.

22. Type **Staff Location by City** in the first text box, and then click OK.

23. Click View on the Report Design toolbar to switch to the Print Preview window. Your report should now look similar to the following illustration:

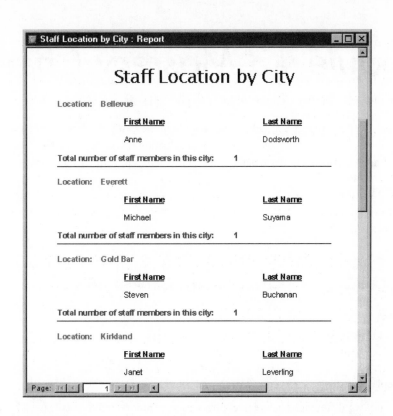

Project Summary

The report that you created was made up of five sections. You added a combination of Label controls and Text Box controls to provide data about your staff members. You also added a Line control to separate the groups. The report was based on the Staff table, and the information was grouped according to the values in the City field. You could have created other types of groups or formatted the report in different ways. You should also spend time looking at the sample reports in the Northwind database. Review the reports in Design view, and be sure to look at the Sorting And Grouping dialog box for grouped reports to see how those groups were configured. As you'll see, there is almost no limit to the types of reports that you can create in Access.

✔

Module 13 Mastery Check

1. What methods can you use to open a new report in Design view?

2. You're creating a report that is linked to a table in the database. You open a new report in Design view by clicking the New button and selecting the table in the New Report dialog box. Which windows appear when you open the new report in Design view?

   A. Report

   B. Report Design

   C. Toolbox

   D. Field List

3. Which sections appear in the design grid when you open a new report in Design view?

   A. Detail

   B. Group Header

   C. Page Header

   D. Report Header

4. What are two differences between controls used in reports and controls used in forms?

5. How do you display report information in columns?

6. How do you display the Report Header section in the design grid?

7. You're creating a report and you want to add column headings that appear at the top of each page. In which section of the design grid should you add the Label controls?

   A. Detail

   B. Page Header

   C. Report Header

   D. Group Header

8. You're creating a report that will include grouped data. The group will be based on the LastName field of the underlying table. You want the data to be grouped alphabetically based on the first letter of the LastName value. How should you configure the group properties?

9. Which Group On options are available for a Currency field?

   A. Each Value

   B. Prefix Character

   C. Qtr

   D. Interval

10. How must Group On properties be configured for a field to be grouped, rather than sorted?

11. You're creating a report that includes grouped data. The data is grouped based on the HomeState field of the underlying table. What name is automatically assigned to the group header section?

   A. HomeState

   B. HomeState Header

   C. HomeState Group Header

   D. HomeState Header (Group)

12. You're creating a report that includes grouped data. The data is grouped based on the InStock field of the underlying table. You want the report to include the total of InStock values for each group. How should you set up the group?

13. A(n) _____ is a type of function that applies summary calculations to groups of data.

14. What is a parameter query?

15. You're creating a report based on a parameter query. The name of the parameter used in the query is [Enter your last name:]. You want the report to include "Report for" and the parameter value in a title at the top of the report. You add a Text Box control to the Report Header section. What expression should you specify in the Text Box control?

Module 14

Creating and Configuring Data Access Pages

CRITICAL SKILLS

14.1 Learn about Data Access Pages

14.2 Create a Data Access Page

14.3 Group Data in a Data Access Page

14.4 Add Special Controls to a Data Access Page

As the number of Internet- and intranet-based solutions has steadily increased, so too has the number of mechanisms for delivering content to these environments. Many desktop applications allow you to save a file as a Hypertext Markup Language (HTML) page that can be posted to the Web. Access also supports functionality that allows you to deliver content to Internet and intranet environments. For example, you can export data to an HTML file or to an Extensible Markup Language (XML) file. In addition, you can create data access pages, which are HTML files that allow users to view and modify data in an Access database. In this module, you will learn how to create a data access page; group data on that page; and add a spreadsheet, chart, or PivotTable to a page. Once the data access pages have been created, you can publish them to a web server on your Internet or intranet site so that users can access data through their Internet Explorer browsers.

CRITICAL SKILL
14.1 Learn about Data Access Pages

In many ways, a data access page is similar to a form or a report. Like a form, a data access page allows users to view and modify data in the Access database. Like a report, a data access page allows users to view grouped and summarized information that is based on data in the database. In addition, the process of creating a data access page is similar to that for creating forms and reports—you add controls that determine what data is displayed and how it is displayed.

Despite the similarities between data access pages and forms or reports, there are also many differences, which you'll discover as you work through this module. One of the most significant differences is that a data access page is intended to ultimately be viewed through the Internet Explorer browser, rather than through the Access interface window, which forms and reports are viewed through. For example, the Northwind database includes the Review Orders data access page, which is shown in Figure 14-1. As you can see, the page can be viewed in Internet Explorer.

The Review Orders data access page displays information about customer orders. The orders are first grouped together by year and then by order ID. In addition to individual order information, the data access page includes year totals and order totals. You can view information related to a particular order by clicking the plus (+) sign next to the order ID. As you can see, data access pages support many of the features available in forms and reports and, like forms and reports, data access pages offer you quite a bit of flexibility in design. However, as you'll see, data access pages are a very different type of data object.

Working with Data Access Pages

If you open the Northwind.mdb database file and select the Pages object type in the database window, you'll see a list of data access pages that are included with the sample database. For example, you'll see the Review Orders data access page, which is shown in Figure 14-1. However, unlike forms and reports, the pages listed in the database window are not the actual

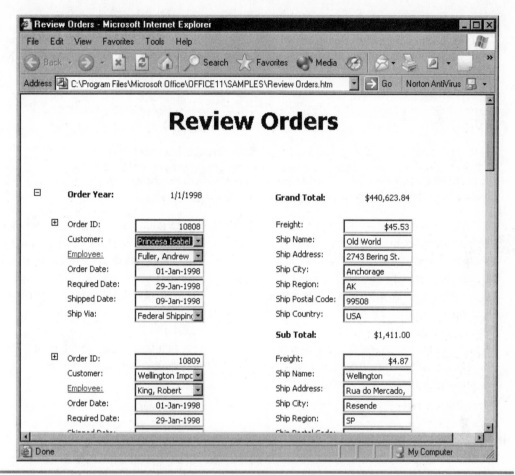

Figure 14-1 The Review Orders data access page, as shown in Internet Explorer

data objects but are links to HTML files that are stored in a folder on your computer. When you access a data access page by using one of the links in the database window, you're accessing the HTML file from where it is stored, rather than within the database file. Only the data access page link is stored within the Access database file; the actual data access page is stored separately as an HTML file.

You can open a data access page through the Access interface (by using a link) or through the Internet Explorer browser. Internet Explorer allows you to interact with the page as you would with any HTML file on an Internet or intranet site. The data access page is connected to the Access database and displays data from that database. If you modify the data that is being displayed in the data access page, the data within the database will be modified. However, if you simply change *how* the data is displayed—by sorting or filtering data, for example—the underlying data is unaffected. To view or modify data in a data access page on a web server, you must be using Internet Explorer 5.01 with Service Pack 2 or later. In addition, the extent to which you can view and modify data depends on the permissions that you've been granted to the database objects.

CAUTION

Because a data access page is stored as an HTML file separate from the Access database file, Access security has no control over the data access page HTML file. To protect the data access page, be sure to apply the appropriate security to the folder, share, or web server where the data access page is stored.

Although data access pages can be opened directly from a folder on a computer or on the network, they are most effective when they are published to a web server. If they are published, users will be able to view and access data stored in an Access database directly through an Internet or intranet web site. The process of publishing your data access pages and allowing data access through the pages varies from environment to environment and product to product, and a discussion of this process is beyond the scope of this book. Still, you should be aware that ultimately the purpose of a data access page is to support a web application on your Internet or intranet system. You would normally not view a data access page through the Access interface or by opening it directly from a folder or network share unless you needed to implement the page or verify its contents.

NOTE

A data access page displays content directly from the Access database. This means that the database must be available to the page when it is published to a web site. In other words, the page must correctly reference the data source location, the database must be available, and users must be granted the proper access permissions to the site and the database. For information on Access security, see Module 6. For information on web site access and publishing to a site, work with your network administrator or Internet service provider (ISP).

Viewing Data Access Pages

When first creating and configuring a data access page, you will often want to view how the finished page will look as you're working on it. The easiest way to view the page is through the Page View window. From the Pages tab in the database window, double-click the data access page link. The page opens in Page view. If you're working in Design view, click the View button on the Page Design toolbar to switch to Page view. The Page window allows you to see the page as it will look in Internet Explorer. Figure 14-2 shows how the Review Orders data access page looks in the Page view window.

Review Orders

Order Year:	1/1/1998

Grand Total: $440,623.85

Order ID:	10808	Freight:	$45.53
Customer:	Princesa Isabel	Ship Name:	Old World
Employee:	Fuller, Andrew	Ship Address:	2743 Bering St.
Order Date:	01-Jan-1998	Ship City:	Anchorage
Required Date:	29-Jan-1998	Ship Region:	AK
Shipped Date:	09-Jan-1998	Ship Postal Code:	99508
Ship Via:	Federal Shipping	Ship Country:	USA

Sub Total: $1,411.00

Order ID:	10809	Freight:	$4.87
Customer:	Wellington Impc	Ship Name:	Wellington
Employee:	King, Robert	Ship Address:	Rua do Mercado,
Order Date:	01-Jan-1998	Ship City:	Resende
Required Date:	29-Jan-1998	Ship Region:	SP
Shipped Date:	07-Jan-1998	Ship Postal Code:	08737-363

Figure 14-2 The Review Orders data access page, as shown in Page view

You can also view the page directly in Internet Explorer. When in Design view or Page view, click the down arrow on the View button on the Page Design or Page View toolbar, and then click Web Page Preview. When you click the button, an instance of Internet Explorer is launched and the page is displayed. You can also view a data access page in Internet Explorer directly from a folder or network share. One way to do this is to locate the HTML file in the folder or share where it is stored and then double-click the file. The file will open in Internet Explorer. For example, if you installed Access into its default location, you can open the Review Orders data access page by going to the C:\Program Files\Microsoft Office\Office11\Samples folder and double-clicking the Review Orders.htm file.

TIP

To make it possible for an HTML file to be opened automatically in Internet Explorer, you must have Internet Explorer installed on your system, and your system's folder properties must be configured to open HTML files in Internet Explorer. If Internet Explorer is the only browser on your computer, the folder properties should already be configured this way.

If you want to be able to view the data access page through a web site, you must publish the page to the appropriate Internet or intranet web server. You will need to open Internet Explorer and enter in the Uniform Resource Locator (URL) that indicates where the page is located. However, publishing a data access page should be the last step in the implementation process. You should first view the page in the Page view window as you're creating it and again once it has been fully configured. Only after the page has been completed and fully tested should it be published to a web site.

CRITICAL SKILL
14.2 Create a Data Access Page

Access provides a number of methods for creating a data access page. You can use the Page wizard, the AutoPage feature, or Design view. You can also create a data access page from an existing HTML file. As with other data objects, our focus will be on using Design view to create a data access page.

NOTE

If you create a data access page in Access 2003, you cannot view the page in Design view in Access 2000 or Access 2002. In addition, you cannot view the page in Page view in Access 2000 or Access 2002 unless you install the Microsoft Office 2003 Web Components, which are the Component Object Model (COM) controls that are installed with Office 2003. For information about the Office web components, go to the Microsoft web site at http://www.microsoft.com.

Opening a New Data Access Page in Design View

The first step in creating a new data access page is to open the page in Design view. The process of opening a new data access page in Design view is similar to that for opening a new report or form in Design view. Select the Pages object type in the database window, and then take one of the following steps:

- Double-click Create Data Access Page In Design View.

- Click the New button at the top of the database window.

- Click the Insert menu and then click Page. (You do not have to select the Pages object type to use this method.)

When you use either of the last two methods to open a new data access page in Design view, the New Data Access Page dialog box appears. Select Design View from the list and then click OK. The New Data Access Page dialog box also allows you to specify a table or query as the source of the data. However, specifying a table at this time is not as useful as it was with forms and reports. The data access page Design view interface allows you to easily select fields from the necessary tables and queries.

Once you open a data access page in Design view, one of your first steps should be to save the file. To do so, click Save on the Page Design toolbar. When the Save As Data Access Page dialog box appears, navigate to the appropriate folder, provide a name for the HTML (.htm) file, and click Save. You might receive a message saying that the ConnectionString property for the page specifies an absolute path. If necessary, modify the property to specify a Universal Naming Convention (UNC) path, in the format *Servername\sharename\folder*. This way, the page will be able to connect to the Access database from any location on the network. If you're publishing the page to a web site, you'll need to work with the web administrator to determine what location to specify in the ConnectionString property.

TIP

To access the page properties for a data access page, select the page and then click the Properties button on the Page Design toolbar. Be sure that no objects or sections in the design grid are selected when you click the Properties button. You can also right-click the title bar of the Data Access Page window and select Page Properties. The ConnectionString property is located on the Data tab.

Ask the Expert

Q: You state that one method that you can use to create a data access page is to create one from an existing HTML file. How do you create a data access page from an existing HTML file?

A: Access makes the process of creating a data access page from an existing HTML file relatively straightforward. You open the file in Design view and modify it as necessary. To start the creation process, double-click the Edit Web Page That Already Exists option in the database window. You can also click the New button and then select Existing Web Page from the list. After you use either of these methods, the Locate Web Page dialog box will appear. Navigate to the folder where the HTML file is located, select the file, and then click Open. The HTML page will open in Design view, with the existing content preserved. You can modify the content, add new content, and add controls, as you would with a new data access page in Design view.

Navigating the Design View Interface

When you open a new data access page in Design view, the Data Access Page window appears and, optionally, the Field List and the Toolbox, as shown in Figure 14-3. If the Field list or the Toolbox is not displayed, click the Field List or Toolbox button on the Page Design toolbar. You can also use these buttons to hide the Field List and Toolbox.

Using the Data Access Page Window

The Data Access Page window is very different from the Form window and the Report window in Design view. Although the Data Access Page window contains a design grid where you can add controls, it also contains a space outside the grid where you can enter HTML text. The space where you can enter HTML text is any part within the Data Access Page window that does not contain a section of the design grid. If you refer again to Figure 14-3, you'll see that the Data Access Page window includes space above and below the design grid. You can add text to any HTML paragraph in that space. (You'll learn how to add text later in this module, in the section "Adding HTML Paragraphs to a Data Access Page.")

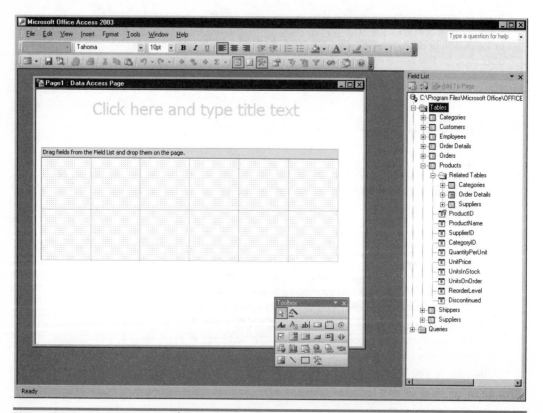

Figure 14-3 Opening a new data access page in Design view

Using the Toolbox

When working with forms and reports in Design view, you were able to use the Toolbox to add controls the design grid. You can also use the Toolbox to add controls to a data access page and to take actions related to adding controls. However, because data access pages are implemented as HTML files, some of the controls that you can add are different from those for forms and reports. Table 14-1 describes the buttons that are included in the Toolbox by default. The table describes the buttons as they appear, left-to-right, in the Toolbox. The table also indicates whether a wizard is available for a particular control type.

Button	Description	Wizard?
Select Objects	Indicates that a control button can be selected so that you can add that control to the design grid. When the Select Objects button is selected, you can then click one of the control buttons to add that control to the data access page. If the Control Wizards button is also selected, a wizard will be launched when you try to add a control to the data access page, if a wizard is available for that particular control.	N/A
Control Wizards	Indicates that a wizard should be launched when you click a control button to add a control to the design grid. This applies only to those buttons that have wizards associated with them. Once you select the Control Wizards button, it remains selected until you deselect it. It does not matter whether the Select Objects button is selected. You must manual deselect the Control Wizards button if it is selected to prevent a wizard from being launched.	N/A
Label	Adds descriptive text, such as a title.	No
Bound Span	Adds a control that displays data from the database. The control binds HTML text to a Text or Memo field. A Bound Span control makes pages load faster in Internet Explorer, but the data displayed by the control cannot be edited	No
Text Box	Adds a control that displays data from the database.	No

Table 14-1 Control-Related Buttons Available in the Toolbox

Button	Description	Wizard?
Scrolling Text	Adds a marquee that displays scrolling text within the control.	No
Option Group	Groups together a set of option buttons, toggle buttons, or check boxes so that only one of the options can be selected.	No
Option Button	Adds a button that supports a selected or deselected setting. The button represents a Yes/No value in the database.	No
Check Box	Adds a check box that supports a selected or deselected setting. The button represents a Yes/No value in the database.	No
Dropdown List	Adds a control that combines a text box with a drop-down list. This control is similar to the Combo Box controls used for forms and reports.	Yes
List Box	Adds a box that displays a list of values.	Yes
Command Button	Adds a button that initiates an action.	Yes
Expand	Adds a plus (+) sign that allows users to expand and collapse grouped records.	No
Record Navigation	Adds a navigation bar that allows users to move through records. This is similar to the navigation bar that is automatically added to the bottom of a form.	No
Office PivotTable	Adds a PivotTable to the data access page.	No
Office Chart	Adds a chart to the data access page.	No
Office Spreadsheet	Adds a spreadsheet to the data access page.	No
Hyperlink	Adds a hyperlink to a data access page.	No
Image Hyperlink	Adds a picture that acts as a hyperlink to a file or web page.	No
Movie	Adds a movie file to a data access page.	No
Image	Adds a picture to the data access page.	No
Line	Adds a straight line to the data access page.	No
Rectangle	Adds a rectangle to the data access page.	No
More Controls	Allows you to access additional controls that are installed on your computer.	N/A

Table 14-1 Control-Related Buttons Available in the Toolbox *(continued)*

Using the Field List

As you can see in Figure 14-3, the Field List is very different from the Field List window that you saw for reports and forms. Rather than displaying only the fields from one table or query, the Field List provides a hierarchical view of all of the tables and queries in your database. Each table or query node includes a list of the fields in that table or query. To access the fields, click the plus (+) sign to the left of the node. You can also view a list of any other tables that are related to a table. When you expand the table node, you'll see a folder named Related Tables. To view the related tables, expand the Related Tables folder.

Adding Controls to a Data Access Page

The easiest way to get started adding controls to a data access page is to use the Field List to add bound Text Box controls. You simply drag and drop the field from the Field List to the design grid. For example, Figure 14-4 shows three Text Box controls that have been added to the design grid. The controls are based on fields in the Customers table.

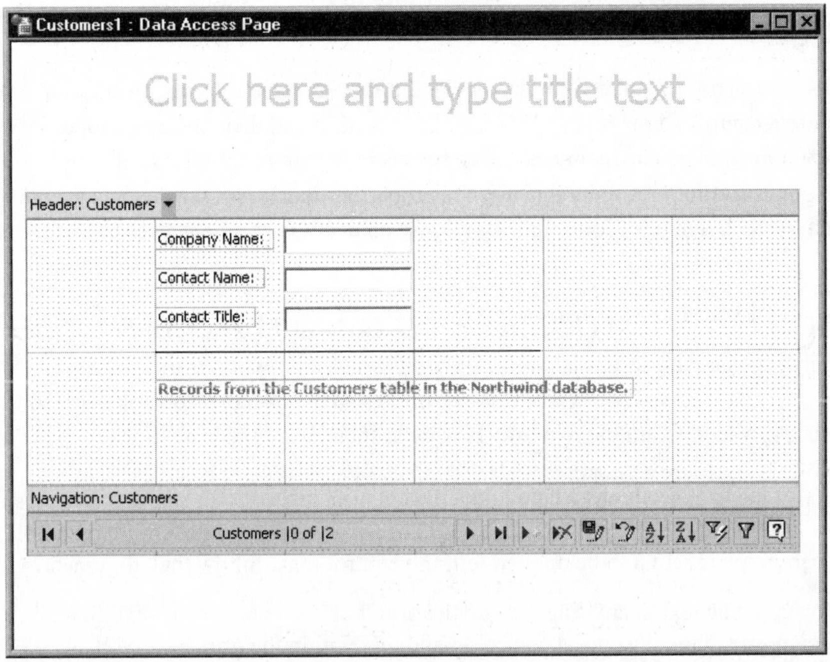

Figure 14-4 The design grid and the Record Navigation control in the Data Access Page window

When you add a bound Text Box control by using the Field List, Access creates two sections in the design grid. The first section is a header section that is assigned a name based on the underlying table. For example, the header section shown in Figure 14-4 is called Header: Customers. The second section that is added is a navigation section, which is automatically populated with a Record Navigation control. In Figure 14-4, this section is named Navigation: Customers.

You can also add a caption section to the design grid. A caption section is added above the header section. The caption section provides yet one more area in which to add controls or set up a different format. To add the caption section to the design grid, click the down arrow next to the name of the header section and then click Caption. In some cases, you can also add a footer section. Click the down arrow next to the name of the header section and then click Footer.

In addition to using the Field List to add bound Text Box controls to the design grid, you can use the Toolbox to add other controls. To add a control to a form without using a wizard, first verify that the Control Wizards button is not selected. If it is selected, deselect it. Next, click the Select Objects button if it is not already selected, then click the applicable control button, and finally click within the design grid where you want to locate the control. If a wizard is available for a control and you want to use that wizard, click the Control Wizards button, then click the control button, and finally click within the design grid to launch the wizard.

You can also format the controls, as you did for reports and forms. In addition, you can configure a control's properties by selecting the control and then clicking Properties on the Page Design toolbar. The main difference between the control properties dialog boxes for data access pages and form or reports is that the properties dialog box for the data access page does not include an Event tab. You cannot configure an event for a data access page control.

Adding HTML Paragraphs to a Data Access Page

Another way that data access pages differ from forms and reports is that the usable workspace within the Data Access Page window is not limited to the design grid. You can add text or controls anywhere within the window. However, there are some limitations:

- You can add controls anywhere in the design grid, but you can add controls outside the grid only according to the way the HTML paragraphs are set up. For example, if a paragraph is set up to be aligned left, the control must follow that alignment.

- You can type text in any line outside the grid, but you cannot type text directly in the design grid. You must use a control to add text within the grid.

- You cannot move controls from within the grid to outside the grid, or vice versa.

Generally, you should use the design grid to add controls. The design grid allows you to place and size the controls with precision. On the other hand, you will usually want to type general text that is not related to a specific control outside the design grid as an HTML paragraph.

To add HTML text to a data access page, simply click within an existing paragraph outside the design grid and start typing. By default, a paragraph is added above the design grid and below. In addition, a special title paragraph is also included and is indicated by the *Click here and type title text* placeholder. To add a title, simply click anywhere within the placeholder and type in a title. Figure 14-5 shows the Data Access Page window with text added to the paragraphs above and below the design grid. Notice also that a title has been added.

Once you have added HTML text, you can format it by selecting the text and then using the options on the Formatting (Page) toolbar. You can also format the text through the properties dialog box. Simply select the text and then click the Properties button on the Page Design toolbar. After you've formatted the text, you can view the data access page in Page view by clicking the View button on the Page Design toolbar. Figure 14-6 shows how the page being designed in Figure 14-5 looks in Page view.

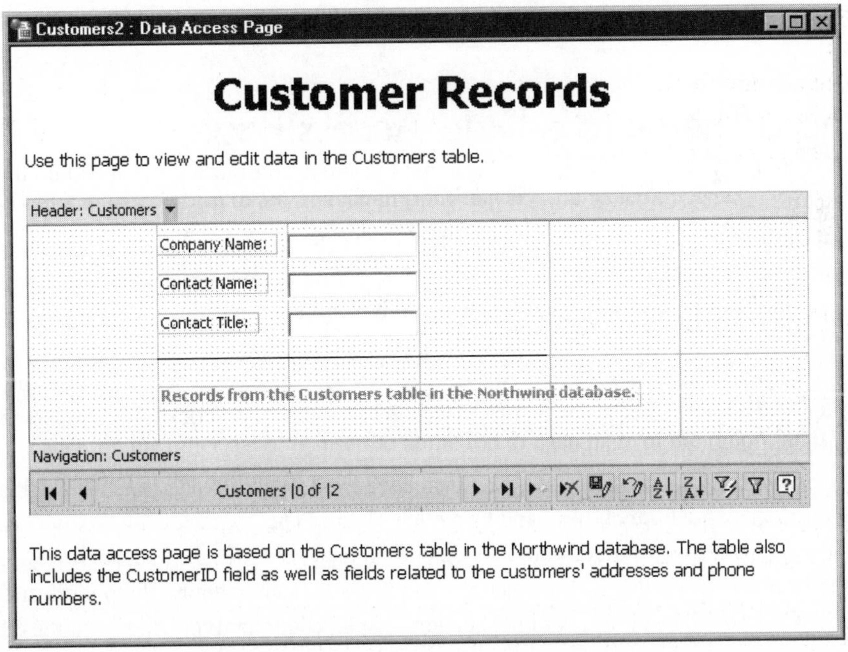

Figure 14-5   Adding HTML text to the Data Access Page window

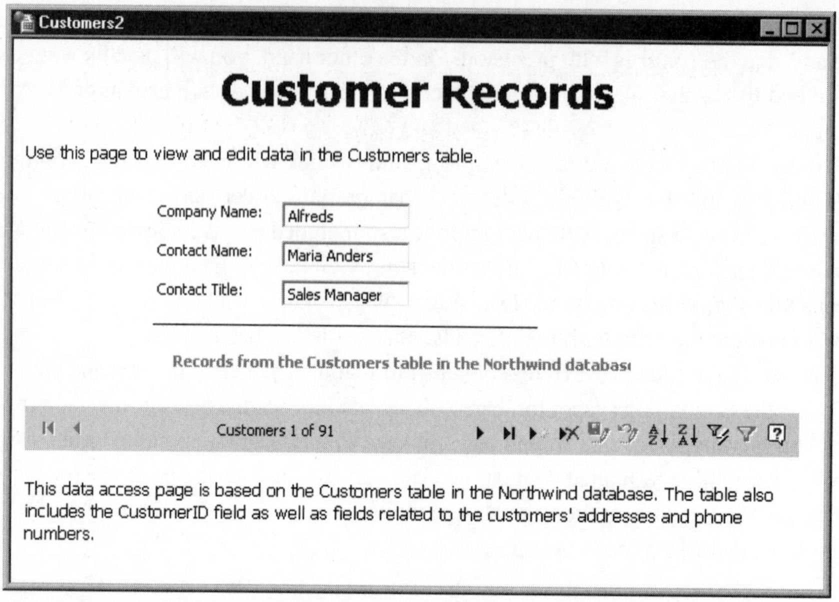

![Customers2 data access page showing Customer Records form with Company Name: Alfreds, Contact Name: Maria Anders, Contact Title: Sales Manager, and a navigation bar showing Customers 1 of 91]

Figure 14-6 Viewing the Customers2 data access page in Page view

Adding a Theme to a Data Access Page

If you go to nearly any web site, you'll see that the site is configured with a certain look and feel that provides a consistency to all the pages in the site. Such things as font styles and background colors all lend to the overall effect of the site. Access allows you to configure your data access pages with their own appearance by applying themes to the various pages. A *theme* is a set of preconfigured format settings that can be applied to multiple data access pages to give those pages a consistent look and feel.

Access makes applying a theme to a data access page an easy process. You simply open the Theme dialog box, shown in Figure 14-7, select a theme, and click OK. The theme is immediately applied to the current page.

To access the Theme dialog box, you must have the data access page open in Design view. From there, click the Format menu and then click Theme. The Theme dialog box includes a list of available themes that can be applied to the current data access page. You can review each theme to determine whether it contains the styles that you want to apply. Simply select the theme from the Choose A Theme list. A sample page is displayed in the right window of the dialog box.

NOTE

The first time you try to add a theme to a data access page you might receive a message saying that the themes are not installed in your system. Follow the steps on the screen to install the themes. You will need the Office installation CD.

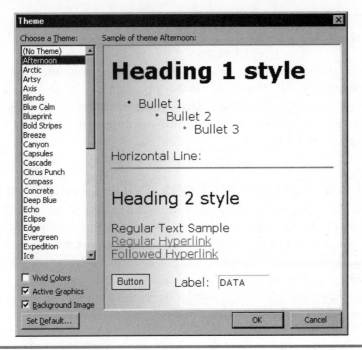

Figure 14-7 The Theme dialog box

Progress Check

1. What type of file is created when you create a data access page?

2. What version of Internet Explorer must you use to view or modify data in a data access page on a web server?

3. Which control should you add to the design grid if you want to display a picture on your data access page?

4. What type of control can you add to a data access page by using the Field List?

---

1. An HTML file
2. Internet Explorer 5.01 with Service Pack 2 or later
3. An Image control
4. A bound Text Box control

CRITICAL SKILL

14.3 Group Data in a Data Access Page

In Module 13, you learned how to group and summarize data in reports so that you could present the data in a useful format. You can also group and summarize data in a data access page; however, the process for grouping data is very different for data access pages from what you saw for reports. In this section, you will learn how to group data in a data access page and how to summarize that data.

Working with Group Sections in the Design Grid

The process of grouping data in Design view involves a number of steps. The best way to show you how this process works is to walk you through the steps necessary to create an example data access page. In this example, we will create a data access page based on customer and order data in the Northwind database. The goal is to create a data access page that provides a list of orders placed by each customer.

To begin the process of creating a data access page that groups data, open a new page in Design view, verify that the Field List is displayed, and follow these steps:

1. Create a bound Text Box control based on the CustomerID field in the Customers table. The CustomerID field will form the basis for the group. All orders will be grouped according to the CustomerID value.

2. Verify that the Text Box control is selected, and then click the Promote button on the Page design toolbar. This creates the top-level group. The header section is assigned the name Header: Customers-CustomerID. In addition, a new section named Header: Customers has been added to the design grid. The new section is indented and will be used for the second-level group.

3. Beneath the Customers node in the Field List, expand the Related Tables node, and then expand the Orders node. The Orders table is related to the Customers table, so you can use fields from the Orders table in your group.

4. Create a bound Text Box control in the Header: Customers section of the design grid. The control should be based on the OrderID field beneath the Order node in Related Tables. By adding this control, you're identifying the records that will be grouped under each CustomerID value. When you add the control, the section name changes to Header: Orders.

5. In the Header: Orders section, add another Text Box control based on the ShippedDate field in the Orders table in Related Tables.

6. Resize the design grid for each section, add an HTML title, and format the controls as necessary. Be sure to save the page and provide a name consistent with whatever naming conventions you're using for HTML files.

Your new data access page, as it appears in the Data Access Page window, should look similar to the one in Figure 14-8. Notice that the second-level header and navigation sections are indented to set them apart. Also notice that an Expand control was automatically added to the top level header section.

Once you have added all the necessary text and controls and formatted the data access page, you can view the page in Page view, as shown in Figure 14-9. In the figure, the third customer (with the customer ID of ANTON) is expanded to show five of the orders for that customer. Only five records in each group are displayed because the DataPageSize property for both groups is configured to display only five records.

TIP

You can configure group properties by clicking the down arrow at the top of the header section and then clicking Group Level Properties.

Now that you've seen how to create a data access page that includes two group levels, let's add another group to see what effect that has on the page. In this example, we will add a third

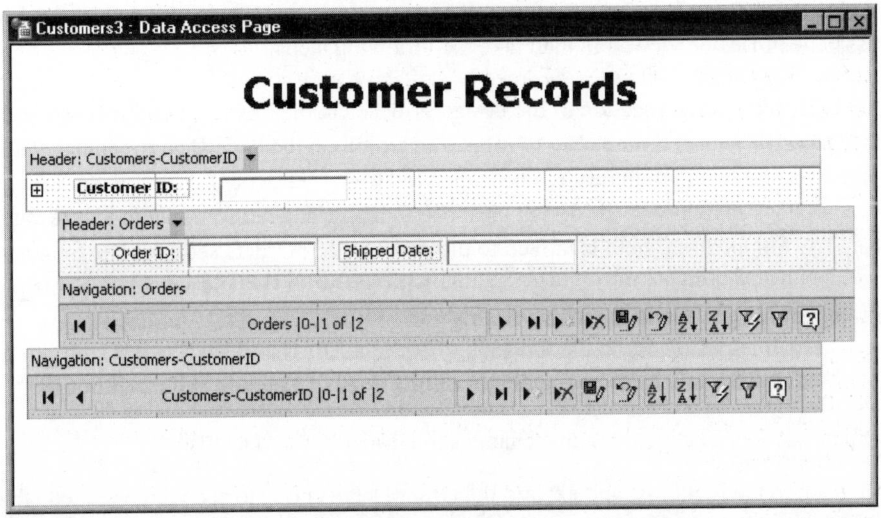

```
Customers3 : Data Access Page                                    _□×

                    Customer Records

Header: Customers-CustomerID ▼
⊞    Customer ID:       [                      ]

    Header: Orders ▼
         Order ID: [          ]    Shipped Date: [          ]
    Navigation: Orders
     ◄◄  ◄          Orders |0-|1 of |2       ► ►◄ ► ►× ▓ ⁊ ↕↑ ↕↓ ▽ ▽ ?
Navigation: Customers-CustomerID
 ◄◄  ◄         Customers-CustomerID |0-|1 of |2   ► ►◄ ► ►× ▓ ⁊ ↕↑ ↕↓ ▽ ▽ ?
```

Figure 14-8 Grouping data on a data access page

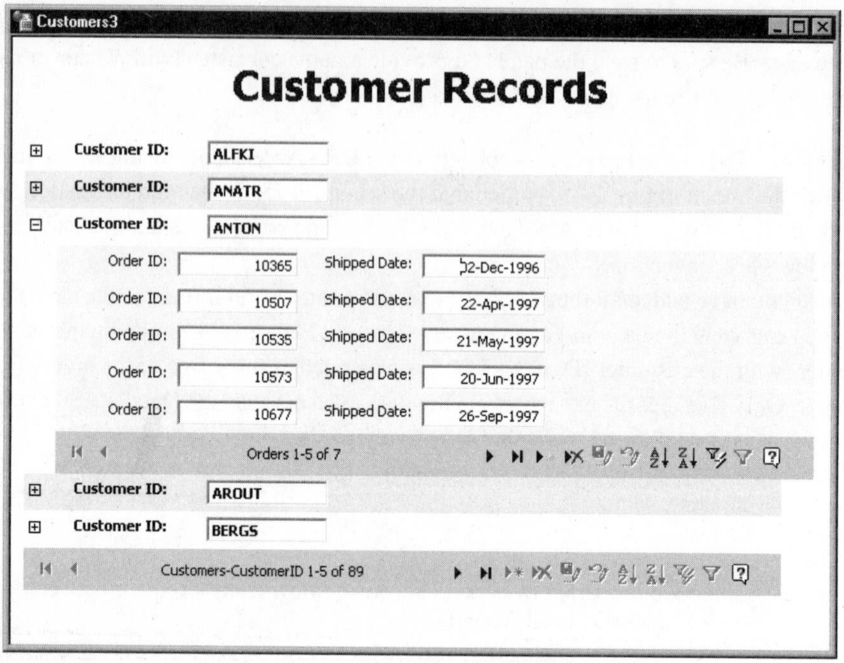

Figure 14-9 Viewing grouped data in the Page view window

group level that provides product information about each order. Once more, open the data access page in Design view, and then take the following steps:

1. In the Header: Orders section of the design grid, select the Text Box control associated with the OrderID field, and then click the Promote button on the Page Design toolbar. The name of the second-level group header is changed to Header: Orders-OrderID. In addition, two new sections are added to the design grid: one for the group header and one for the navigation bar. The ShippedDate field is moved to the new Header: Orders section. The field is moved because its values cannot be grouped along with the OrderID field values. (For the purposes of this exercise, we will delete this field.)

2. Expand the Related Tables node beneath the Orders table, and then expand the Order Details node. Add the UnitPrice, Discount, and Quantity fields to the new Header: Orders section. The section name changes to Header: Order Details.

3. Go back to the Field List and expand the Order Details node to access the related tables. Beneath the Related Tables node, expand the Products table and add the ProductID and the ProductName fields to the Header: Order Details section.

4. Apply any necessary formatting, including background colors and lines.

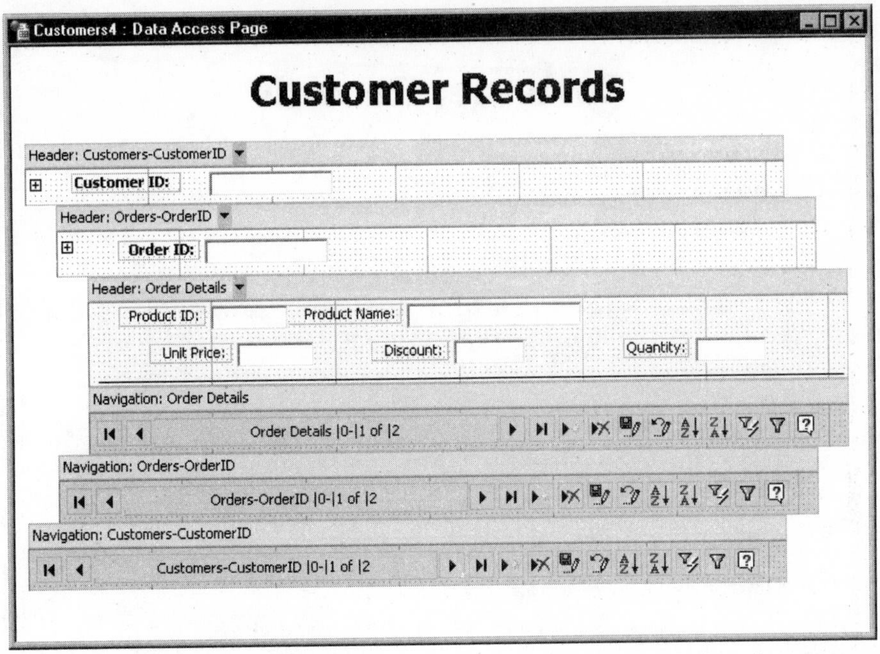

Figure 14-10 Creating multiple groups in a data access page

After you've added the third group to your data access page and modified the formatting, your page design should look similar to that shown in Figure 14-10.

As you can see, the third group is indented from the second group, which is indented from the top-level group. Your data will now be organized first by customer ID, then by order ID, and then by product information. You can now view the page in Page view, as shown in Figure 14-11. In this figure, the data access page is expanded for the second customer, and is again expanded for the first order placed by that customer. As a result, you are able to view product information for that order.

Summarizing Data

As you saw when creating reports, it is often useful to summarize grouped data in order to provide yet more information to the users. You can also summarize data in a data access page, although the process is very different from the one you use to present this information in reports.

When you summarize data, you must identify the control whose field you want to summarize and then identify the aggregate function that will be used for the summary. A new summarized

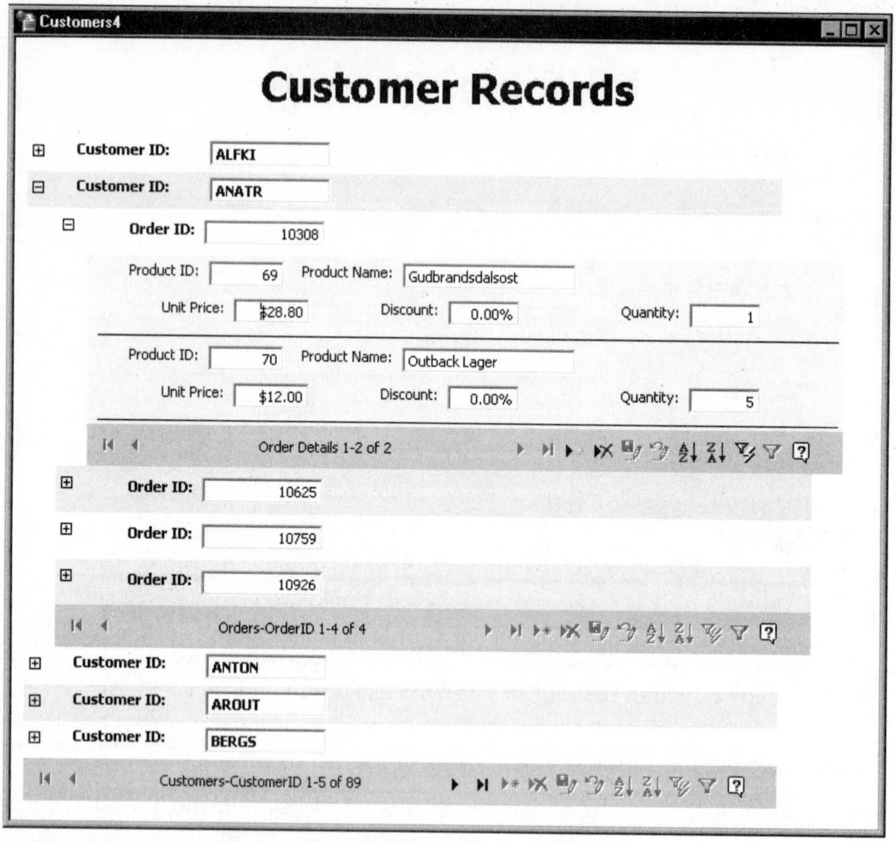

Figure 14-11 Viewing multiple groups in the Page view window

control is then automatically added to the group header or footer one level above the group where the original control is located. Let's take a look Figure 14-12 to help clarify this. The data access page is based on the last example that we looked at, only now it contains a footer section and four additional controls that contain summary data.

NOTE

You can add a footer section by clicking the down arrow at the top of the header section and then selecting Footer. The footer section is not available for the lowest-level group in a data access page with grouped data.

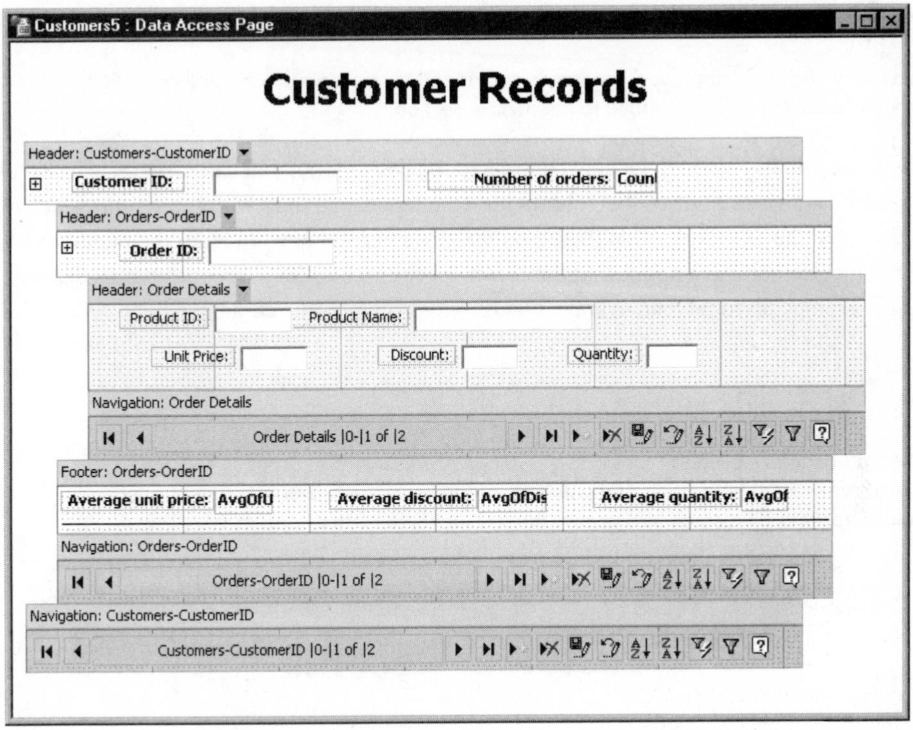

Figure 14-12 Summarizing data in a data access page

The first new control is located in the Header: Customers-CustomerID section of the design grid. The control is based on the OrderID field in the Orders table and it uses the Count aggregate function to arrive at the number of orders for a particular customer. To add this control, select the Text Box control in the Header: Orders-OrderID section, click the down arrow on the AutoSum button on the Page Design toolbar, and then click Count. A new Text Box control is automatically added to the Header: Customers-CustomerID section, and the ControlSource property for that control is configured with the value CountOfGroupOfOrderID: GroupOfOrderID. You can then resize and reformat the control as you would any other Text Box control.

The other three controls that contain summary data have been added to the Footer: Orders-OrderID section and are based on controls in the Header: Order Details section. In each case, the original Text Box control was selected, and then the Avg aggregate function was used to create a summarized control in the group footer one level above the group where the original control was created. For example, to find the average unit price for all the products in an order, you select the Unit Price Text Box control, click the down arrow in the AutoSum button on the Page Design toolbar, and then click Average. A new control is automatically added to the footer.

NOTE

If a footer section is displayed, the new summarized controls are added to that section, otherwise the controls are added to the header section.

Once you have added the new controls to the design grid, you can view the data access page in Page view. Figure 14-13 shows how the report will look with the summarized controls. Notice that the top-level group (based on the customer ID) now includes the number of orders for that customer. Also notice that the footer for the second-level group contains the average price, average discount, and average quantity for each product contained in an order.

NOTE

The DataPageSize property for each group has been set to 3 in order to give you a better overview of how this report will look in Page view. However, the summarized values apply to all records in a group, not just the three records displayed.

Customers5	▲

Customer Records

⊟ **Customer ID:** ALFKI **Number of orders:** 7

⊟ **Order ID:** 10643

Product ID: 28 **Product Name:** Rössle Sauerkraut
Unit Price: $45.60 **Discount:** 25.00 **Quantity:** 15

Product ID: 39 **Product Name:** Chartreuse verte
Unit Price: $18.00 **Discount:** 25.00 **Quantity:** 21

Product ID: 46 **Product Name:** Spegesild
Unit Price: $12.00 **Discount:** 25.00 **Quantity:** 2

|◀ ◀ Order Details 1-3 of 3 ▶ ▶| ▶* ▶✕ ⁎⁎ ⁎⁎ A↓ Z↓ ⁎⁎ ⁎⁎ ?

Average unit price: $25.20 **Average discount: 25.00%** **Average quantity: 12.67**

⊞ **Order ID:** 10692

Average unit price: $43.90 **Average discount: 0.00%** **Average quantity: 20.00**

⊞ **Order ID:** 10702

Average unit price: $14.00 **Average discount: 0.00%** **Average quantity: 10.50**

|◀ ◀ Orders-OrderID 1-3 of 7 ▶ ▶| ▶* ▶✕ ⁎⁎ ⁎⁎ A↓ Z↓ ⁎⁎ ⁎⁎ ?

Figure 14-13 Viewing summarized data in the Page view window

Ask the Expert

Q: When viewing HTML pages, I have been able to view the HTML code by opening the page in a text editor such as Notepad. Can I view the code used in a data access page?

A: Access provides a convenient tool for viewing the HTML code and other scripts that are used to create the page. When your data access page is open in Design view, click the Microsoft Script Editor button on the Page Design toolbar. This launches the Script Editor in a separate window, where you can view and modify the data access page. Unlike a text editor, the Script Editor uses colored fonts to designate different elements within the page. For example, HTML tags are shown in one color, the content enclosed in those tags is another color, and any script contained on the page is yet another color. This makes it far easier to find the specific elements that you're looking for and edit the HTML and script text as necessary. You can also add other elements to the page, such as HTML tags or Jscript and VBScript objects. In addition, the Script Editor includes a set of debugging tools that allow you to test and troubleshoot your pages. Keep in mind, however, that you should be very careful when working with the Script Editor. Do not make any changes unless you're confident that the steps you're taking are correct. Otherwise, you could cause your data access page to stop working properly.

CRITICAL SKILL

14.4 Add Special Controls to a Data Access Page

Access allows you to add several different types of special controls to your data access pages, including spreadsheets, charts, and PivotTables. Each of these types of controls extends the functionality of a data access page and allows users to view data in ways not available with the other types of controls or with basic HTML text. This section shows you to how to add spreadsheets, charts, and PivotTables to your data access pages. Each one of these controls supports a rich set of features and can be used extensively to display data in different ways that make the presentation and analysis of data easier for the user. I recommend that you also refer to Access online Help and spend time experimenting with the controls so that you can gain a better understanding of how they work and what you can do with them.

Adding a Spreadsheet to a Data Access Page

The Office Spreadsheet controls that you can add to data access pages are similar to the types of spreadsheets that you find in Microsoft Office Excel. When a spreadsheet is displayed on a data access page, users can cut, copy, and paste data; find the totals for rows and columns of data; sort and filter data; and export the data to an Excel spreadsheet. Users can also access a Help file that is specific to the spreadsheet control.

You add an Office Spreadsheet control in the same way you add any other control from the Toolbox. Once you have placed the control on the design grid, resize it so that it can display the expected amount of data. To resize the control or set the control's properties, select the control once and configure it in the same way you would other controls. To add data to the spreadsheet or work with the individual cells, select the control again. This surrounds the spreadsheet with hash marks to indicate that you can now work within the spreadsheet. Figure 14-14 shows a data access page with an Office Spreadsheet control added to the design grid. Notice that the spreadsheet is surrounded with hash marks.

You can add data to the spreadsheet by typing it into each cell or by cutting and pasting it from another source. You can also import data from a web page, text file, or XML file by using the Commands And Options dialog box. (To access the dialog box, click the Commands And Options button on the navigation bar at the top of the spreadsheet.) Once the data has been

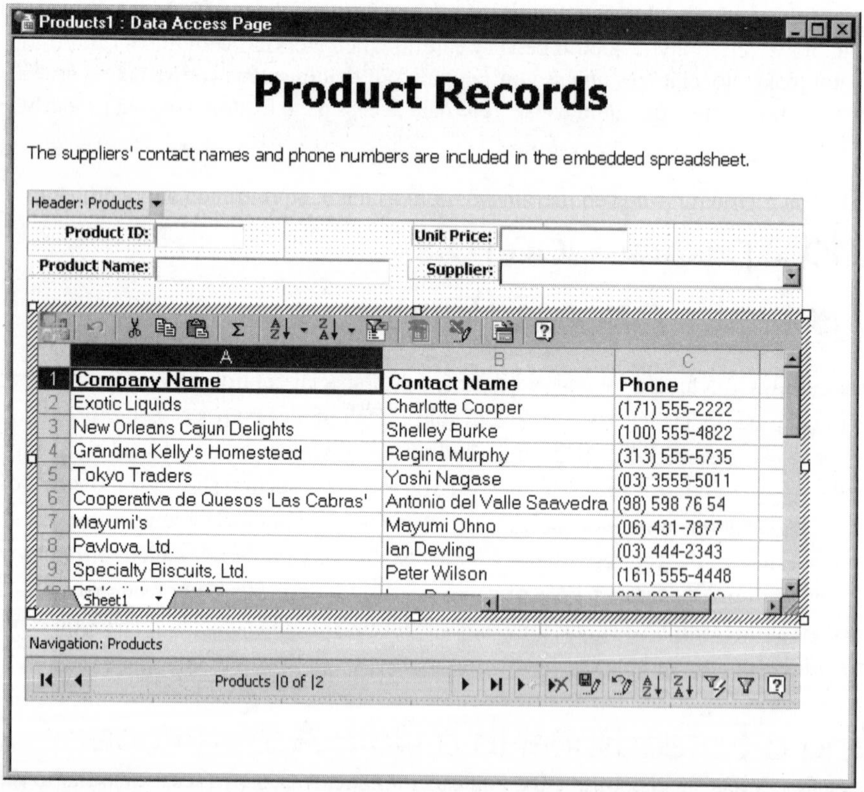

Figure 14-14 Adding an Office Spreadsheet control to a data access page

added, you can use the navigation bar to manipulate the data. This is the same navigation bar that the users will see and use when they work with the spreadsheet in Internet Explorer.

For example, to add the data that is shown in Figure 14-14, you can first export the data in the Customers table to an Excel spreadsheet. Next, open the spreadsheet, move the Phone column so that it is next to the ContactName column, and then select the values from the CompanyName, ContactName, and Phone columns. Next, copy the data to the clipboard, and return to the data access page (in Design view). Select the first cell (1A) in the spreadsheet control, and then paste the data from the clipboard into the spreadsheet.

Another method that you could have used is to create a query that returns the information that you want and then export the data to a text file. Next, you would use the Commands And Options dialog box to import the data into the spreadsheet. Figure 14-15 shows how the data access page appears in Page view. As you can see, the spreadsheet looks similar to how it appears in Design view, and much of the functionality is the same.

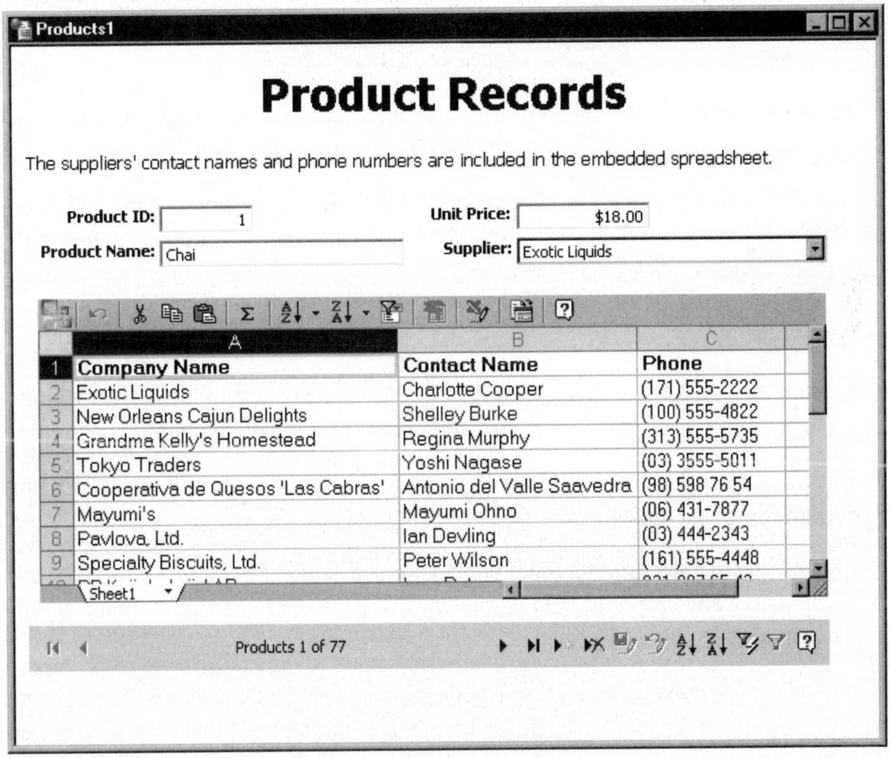

Figure 14-15 Viewing a spreadsheet in a data access page

Adding a Chart to a Data Access Page

Adding an Office Chart control to a data access page is different in many ways from adding a spreadsheet to the page. After you have added the control, you can select it once to resize it and set the control's properties. To work within the chart, select the control again so that hash marks are displayed around the control. From there, you must configure the chart to determine which data should be used.

Let's take a look at an example that demonstrates how to add a chart to a data access page. This example is based on a query named Sales By Category, which I created in the Northwind database. To add a chart based on this query, take the following steps:

1. You would begin by adding an Office Chart control to the design grid and positioning and resizing it as necessary. Initially, only a box is added to the grid. The box says Microsoft Office Web Components.

2. While the control box is still selected, you would select the box again. This adds hash marks around the box and opens the Commands And Options dialog box, which displays the Data Source tab.

3. Next, you would select the Data From A Database Table Or Query option, select the Data Details tab, and then click Edit. The Select Data Source dialog box appears.

4. Now you would navigate to the Northwind.mdb file, select the file, and then click Open. If the Data Link Properties dialog box or the Enter MS JET OLE DB Initialization Information dialog box appears, click OK. When the Select Table dialog box appears, select the Sales By Category query and then click OK. You should be returned to the Commands And Options dialog box.

5. You would now select the Type tab, select the Pie Chart type, and then select the last pie chart option in the right window. Next, you would close the dialog box.

6. Next, you would right-click the control box and select Field List from the shortcut menu. The Chart Field List dialog box appears.

7. You would expand the Product Sales node, and then select the Product Sales subnode. Next you would drag and drop that field to the Drop Data Fields Here section in the control. A pie chart is added to the control.

8. You would expand the CategoryName node, and then select the CategoryName subnode. Next, you would drag and drop that field to the Drop Category Field section in the control. The pie chart now includes several sections. Close the Chart Field List dialog box.

9. Now you would click the Show/Hide Legend button in the navigation bar at the top of the chart. A legend is added to the control.

10. You would right-click within the control box and select Commands And Options from the shortcut menu. In the Commands And Options dialog box, you would select the Show/Hide tab and clear the Field Buttons/Drop Zones check box. Now you would close the dialog box.

Your chart in Design view would look similar to the one in the Data Access Page window shown in Figure 14-16. The pie chart is divided into sections. Each section represents a product category. The size of each section is based on the amount of sales for that product.

When you display the data access page in Page view, you can see the same pie chart and legend, as shown in Figure 14-17. Notice that the navigation bar above the legend includes several options that are grayed out. If users select the actual chart, they can then select which options to display by using the Show Top/Bottom Items button on the navigation bar. If they select the legend, they can sort the product categories by using the two sort buttons. Other options on the navigation bar are available depending on the type of chart displayed and how the control is configured.

Figure 14-16 Adding an Office Chart control to a data access page

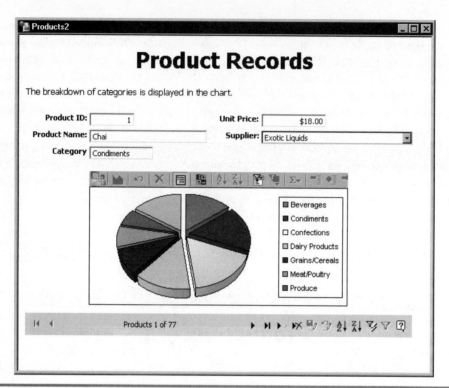

Figure 14-17 Viewing a chart in a data access page

Adding a PivotTable to a Data Access Page

A PivotTable is an Office object that is similar to an Excel spreadsheet. However, a PivotTable supports more dynamic types of analysis than a spreadsheet can provide. For example, a PivotTable can include calculations in individual cells, totals for the rows that contains those cells, and totals for the columns, all of which can be recalculated immediately. The PivotTable can also calculate subtotals and grand totals. It can also use a field's value as a row or column heading and then perform calculations on that heading. For more information on using PivotTables, see Access online Help and Office Help.

To add a PivotTable to a data access page, you must first add the Office PivotTable control to the design grid. As with spreadsheets and charts, you can resize and reposition the control by selecting it once. To add or configure data within the PivotTable, you must select the control a second time, which surrounds the control with hash marks. You then drag fields from the Field List to the appropriate section in the control box.

For example, Figure 14-18 shows a PivotTable that includes information from the Categories table in the Northwind database. You can add this information simply by dragging and dropping the CategoryName field and the Description field from the Field List to the Drop Totals Or Detail Fields Here section of the control. You can then use the Commands And Options dialog box to configure how you want the data displayed and the control configured.

When you view the data access page in Page view, you'll see that the navigation bar above the PivotTable provides a greater number of options than that for a spreadsheet, as shown in Figure 14-19. However, the data access page shown in the figure provides only a simple example of a PivotTable. PivotTables are very powerful tools, and a thorough discussion of them is beyond the scope of the book. However, you might find it useful to spend additional time learning about PivotTables and the various functions that they support.

Figure 14-18 Adding an Office PivotTable control to a data access page

Figure 14-19 Viewing a PivotTable in a data access page

Project 14-1 Creating a Data Access Page in the Consumer Advocacy Database

In Project 13-1 of Module 13, you created a report in the consumer advocacy database that was based on the Staff table. In the report, you listed the names of the staff members according to the cities in which they lived. You will now create a data access page that is similar to the report. The data access page will be based on fields in the Staff table, and you will group staff member names according to city. You will also add a summarized field that provides the total number of staff members per city. Once you create the data access page, you will save it to the database and view it in Page view and in Internet Explorer.

Step by Step

1. If they're not already open, open Access and then open the ConsumerAdvocacy.mdb database file.

2. If necessary, select the Pages object type in the database window and then double-click Create Data Access Page In Design View.

3. If a message appears that provides information about Access versions, read the message and click OK. The new data access page opens in Design view.

4. If the Field List is not displayed, click the Field List button on the Page Design toolbar.

5. In the Field List, expand the Staff node. Drag the City field to the design grid and drop it near the top-left corner. The section name changes to Header: Staff, and a navigation section is added to the design grid.

6. With the new Text Box control selected, click the Promote button on the Page Design toolbar. An Expand control is added to the left of the Text Box and Label controls. In addition, two new sections are added to the design grid.

7. In the Label control associated with the Text Box control, type **City**. Resize and reposition the Text Box and Label controls as necessary and apply bold formatting to both controls.

8. Drag the NameFirst and NameLast fields from the Field List to the Header: Staff section and position them side by side.

9. Delete the two Label controls associated with the new Text Box controls.

10. Click the down arrow at the top of the Header: Staff section and then click Caption. A section named Caption: Staff is added to the group.

11. If the Toolbox is not displayed, click the Toolbox button on the Page Design toolbar.

12. Add two Label controls to the Caption: Staff section . Type **First Name** in the first label control and **Last Name** in the second Label control. Position the two controls above the Text Box controls in the Header: Staff section.

13. Resize the Caption: Staff section and the Header: Staff section to make them smaller so that only the controls are displayed.

14. Drag the StaffID field from the Field List and drop it in the Header: Staff-City section, to the right of the City Text Box control. The control is added and automatically configured with the Count aggregate function.

(continued)

15. In the Label control associated with the new Text Box control, type **Total number of staff members:** (including the colon).

16. At the top of the Data Access Page window—in the *Click here and type title text* placeholder—type **Staff Members by City**.

17. In the HTML paragraph beneath the title, type **Click the plus (+) sign next to the city name to view a list of staff members in that city**. The Data Access Page window should now look like the following illustration:

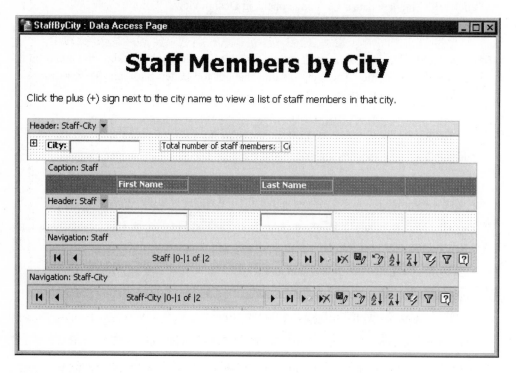

18. Click the Save button on the Page Design toolbar. The Save As Data Access Page dialog box appears.

19. Name the file StaffByCity.htm and then click Save. A message box appears warning about the absolute path defined in your data access page.

20. Click OK.

21. Click View on the Page Design toolbar. The page is displayed in the Page view window, as shown in the following illustration:

22. Expand the various cities to view the names of the staff members in those cities.

23. Click the down arrow on the Page View toolbar and then click Web Page Preview. Internet Explorer is launched, and the data access page is displayed.

24. Expand the various cities to view the names of the staff members in those cities.

25. Close Internet Explorer and then close the Page view window.

Project Summary

In this project, you created a data access page that displayed a list of staff members according to the cities in which they live. You could have displayed other information or grouped the staff members based on different criteria. You could have also applied more extensive formatting or added a theme to your design. I recommend that you experiment with data access pages so that you become comfortable with the various ways that you can put together a page and display different types of data.

Module 14 Mastery Check

1. What is one of the most significant differences between a data access page and a form or report?

2. What are the shortcuts listed on the Pages tab of the database window linked to?

3. What two conditions must be met for you to be able to access a database through a data access page that you're viewing through a web server?

4. What methods can you use to open a new data access page in Design view?

5. How do you display the Toolbox when you're in Design view?

6. Which control should you use if you want to add only descriptive text to the design grid?

   A. Text Box

   B. List Box

   C. Line

   D. Label

7. What is displayed in the Field List for a data access page in Design view?

8. What is the easiest way to add a bound Text Box control to the design grid?

9. In what parts of the Data Access Page window can you type in text?

10. How do you type HTML text directly in the Data Access Page window?

11. You are creating a data access page that will contain grouped data. You add a bound Text Box control to the design grid. The field that the control is based on will form the basis for the group. What should your next step be?

12. Which group property should you set to determine the number of records displayed per group?

   A. DefaultSort

   B. DataPageSize

   C. GroupOn

   D. GroupInterval

13. You are creating a group that is based on the CustomerID field in the Customers table. You add a bound Text Box control to the design grid and promote the control. What name will be assigned to the header section that contains the CustomerID Text Box control?

   A. Header: Customers-CustomerID

   B. Header: Customers

   C. Header: CustomerID-Customers

   D. Header: CustomerID

14. What actions can a user take in an Office Spreadsheet control?

15. What is a PivotTable?

Module 15

Creating Macros
and Modules

CRITICAL SKILLS

15.1 Create Macros for Events

15.2 Assign Macros to Events

15.3 Create Modules for Events

363

n Module 12, you learned how to create forms and configure the properties associated with them. As you'll recall, many of these properties were related to events, and each event property could be associated with an expression, a macro, or a module. In fact, you can configure event properties for most types of controls that can be added to a form, for sections within a form, and for the form as a whole. You can also configure event properties for sections within a report and for an entire report. In this module, you will learn how to create the macros that perform the actions triggered by the events. You will also learn how to associate an existing macro to an event property. In addition, you will be introduced to Visual Basic for Applications (VBA), the language used within modules, and you will learn how to create a basic module that can respond to an event. (For information about creating expressions, see Module 11.)

Create Macros for Events

Macros have been a mainstay of many desktop applications since the inception of those applications. However, the macros that you create in an Access database are different from those you'll find in such applications as Microsoft Office Word or Excel. In those types of applications, a macro merely records a set of keystrokes that can be repeated at any time when the user calls the macro. However, a macro in Access is quite different. An Access macro is a data object—stored within the database file—that identifies one or more predefined actions that are performed when an event occurs.

You can associate a macro with an event property so that the macro runs when the event occurs. When the macro runs, the actions within the macro are performed. For example, you can create a macro that opens a form when a user clicks a command button. In this case, the action is the opening of the form, and the event is the user's click on the button. Access supports a variety of predefined actions for each event, and each event can be defined with more than one action. As a result, you can define macros that are as simple or as complex as you need.

Using the Macro Window

To create a macro, you must use the Macro window. In the Macro window, you can select actions, add comments that describe each action, and configure arguments that define the specifics of the action. To open the Macro window for a new macro, take one of the following steps:

- Select the Macros object type in the database window and then click the New button at the top of the window.

- Click the Insert menu and then click Macro.

When the Macro window appears, you can begin creating your macro. At any point during the process, you can save the macro by clicking the Save button on the Macro Design toolbar. When the Save As dialog box appears, enter the name of the macro in the Macro Name text box and then click OK.

The Macro window is divided into two main sections, as shown in Figure 15-1. The top section is a design grid that contains two columns (Action and Comment) and multiple rows. The number of rows displayed depends on how you've sized the window. Each row in the design grid can contain one action, one comment, or one action and one comment, or the row can be left blank. Each action is selected from a list of predefined actions. Comments are used only to document the action of the macro and do not affect the actions taken by the macro. They are useful for explaining how the macro is used and to which event it's attached.

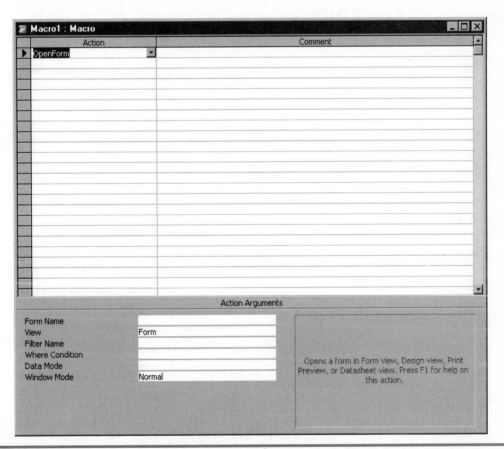

Figure 15-1 Creating a macro in the Macro window

The bottom section of the Macro window is divided into two panes. The left pane contains the arguments that can be configured for a specific action. An *argument* is a qualifier for the specified action. It provides a detail about how the action should be carried out. For example, one of the arguments associated with the OpenTable action is Table Name. The arguments displayed apply only to the action identified in the active row of the design grid. If no action is specified for that row, no arguments will be displayed. In addition, some actions have no arguments associated with them.

The right pane in the bottom section provides information about the specific action or argument that is selected. You don't interact with this section, although it is useful when you are configuring a macro.

Creating a Basic Macro

The first step you take when you create a macro is to choose an action. To choose an action, select it from the drop-down list in the first row of the Action column. The drop-down list includes all of the predefined actions available to the macro. For the most part, the action names are self-explanatory. For example, the Close action closes the specified window, and the Save action saves the specified object.

Once you have selected an action, you can add a comment in the Comment column in the same row where you added the action. Although comments are not mandatory, you should add comments when appropriate to help explain the purpose of the macro and to provide information to anyone else who might need to view the macro definition.

NOTE

You can also add a comment to a row that does not contain an action. This can be useful to introduce a set of actions or to describe the purpose of the macro as a whole.

After you've identified the action and, optionally, added a comment, you should configure the action's arguments. For many actions, some arguments are required and some are optional. In addition, some argument settings must be selected from a drop-down list, while others need to be typed into a text box. You'll have to look at each argument individually to determine how to configure it. When you select an argument, be sure to view the bottom-right pane of the Macro window for information about that argument.

If you want to include additional actions in your macro, add them as you did the first action: Select an action from a blank row, add a comment if desired, and configure the arguments. Repeat the process for each action, and be sure to save the macro to the database.

Now that you have an overview of the steps necessary for creating a macro, let's take a look at an example. Figure 15-2 shows the definition for the OpensCustomersForm macro, as it appears in the Macro window. Two actions have been identified for this macro: Beep and OpenForm.

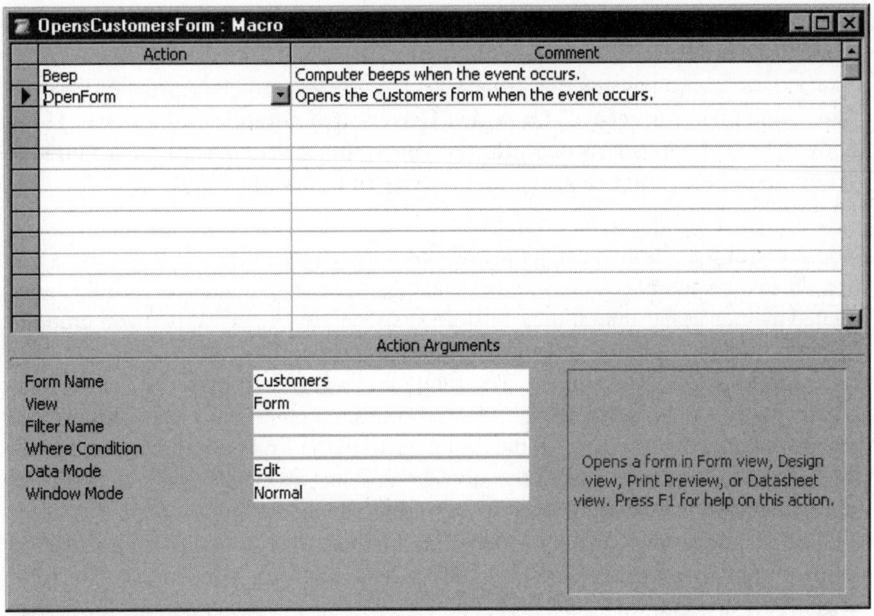

Figure 15-2 Creating the OpensCustomersForm macro

The Beep action causes your computer to beep when the event occurs. The Beep action has no arguments associated with it; however, you can still add a comment to the row that contains this action, as has been done in this example.

The second action, OpenForm, is a bit more complicated than Beep. The OpenForm action has six arguments associated with it. As you can guess, the Form Name argument requires the name of the form, which you must select from the drop-down list associated with the argument. The list contains the names of all the forms in the database.

The next argument is View. Like Form Name, the View argument requires a value, which by default is Form. The View argument indicates what view will be used when the form is opened. For example, you can open the form in Design view or Form view. In this case, the default value of Form is used. The Filter Name and Where Condition arguments do not require a value, nor are any assigned in this example. The Filter Name argument can be a query or a filter saved as a query, and the Where Condition argument can be an expression that limits the records returned.

The Data Mode argument is another optional argument that refers to how users will be able to interact with the form when it opens. For example, you might want users to be able to view data but not modify it. In this example, Edit mode is selected, so users can view and modify data. However, if this argument were left blank, the users' editing options would depend on how the form itself was configured.

Ask the Expert

Q: I have one form (or record) for which I've created a number of macros. If I need to modify the form (or record), those macros might also need to be updated. Can I group macros together to make them easier to find and edit?

A: You can group multiple macros together into one macro object. This has the advantage of reducing the number of macro objects in the database, and it makes finding and editing related macros easier than if they're stored as separate objects. When you group macros together, you are essentially creating one macro and assigning different names to different sets of actions within that macro. To group macros together, open the Macro window as you normally would, and click the Macro Names button on the Macro Design toolbar to add the Macro Name column to the design grid. In the first row of the grid, type a name for the first macro in the Macro Name column, select an action, add a comment if you wish, and configure the arguments. If you want to include multiple actions in one macro, add actions to the rows directly beneath the first row, but do not assign a macro name to these rows. When you're ready to create a second macro, add a name in a blank row after all the rows for the first macro, and then add the necessary actions for the second one. Any action that you define is assigned to the group whose name immediately precedes that action. When Access processes a macro, it begins with the row that contains the macro name and stops when it find another macro name or discovers no more macros.

The last argument—Window Mode—determines how the form window will be displayed when the form opens. For example, you can choose to display it normally or minimize it as an icon. In the OpensCustomersForm macro, Normal mode is selected.

Once you've configured the arguments, the macro is complete. However, after a macro has been created, it won't do anything until it is associated with an event. You'll learn how to associate a macro with an event later in this module, in the section "Assign Macros to Events."

Adding Conditions to a Macro

There might be times when you want an action triggered only under certain circumstances. For example, suppose that you have a form that displays information about your company's inventory. One of the controls in the form provides the number of items in stock, and you want to remind users to place an order if the number drops below 20. You can create a macro that displays a message only when the number is changed to a value less than 20. If the amount is 20 or more, no message is displayed. When a condition is defined on an action, the condition must evaluate to true for the action to be taken. If the condition evaluates to false, Access skips to the next action.

To add a condition to an action, you must first add the Condition column to the design grid of the Macro window. You add the column by clicking the Conditions button on the Macro Design toolbar. The column is added to the left of the Action column. In the Condition column, type an expression next to the action that should be executed if the condition evaluates to true. You can use Expression Builder to create your condition. To access Expression Builder, click the Build button on the Macro Design toolbar.

By default, a condition applies only to the action contained in the row in which the condition is defined. If you want a condition to apply to more than one action, you must specify the condition in those rows as well. However, if the actions are sequential, you can use an ellipsis (…) to continue the condition to the next action. To do this, simply specify the condition in the first row and then add an ellipsis to the Condition column in the next row. You can continue to use an ellipsis in each additional row, as long as the actions are sequential.

Now let's take a look at an example of a macro that is defined with conditions on the actions. Figure 15-3 shows the OpensCustomersTable macro. The macro contains three actions. Conditions are defined on the first and third actions, and an ellipsis is used for the condition in the second action. The macro will be associated with an event on the ContactTitle control in the Customers form of the Northwind database. The control displays data from the ContactTitle field in the Customers table.

The first condition in the macro is defined on the OpenTable action. The condition specifies that the value in the ContactTitle field must equal Owner. If the condition evaluates to true, the Customers table will be opened. The second action uses an ellipsis in the Condition column.

Condition	Action	Comment
[ContactTitle]="Owner"	OpenTable	Opens the Customers table if the ContactTitle value is Owner.
...	Beep	Beeps if the ContactTitle value is Owner.
[ContactTitle]<>"Owner"	MsgBox	Displays a message unless the ContactTitle value is Owner.

Action Arguments

Message	The Customers table opens only if th
Beep	Yes
Type	None
Title	Contact Not Owner

Enter a conditional expression in this column.

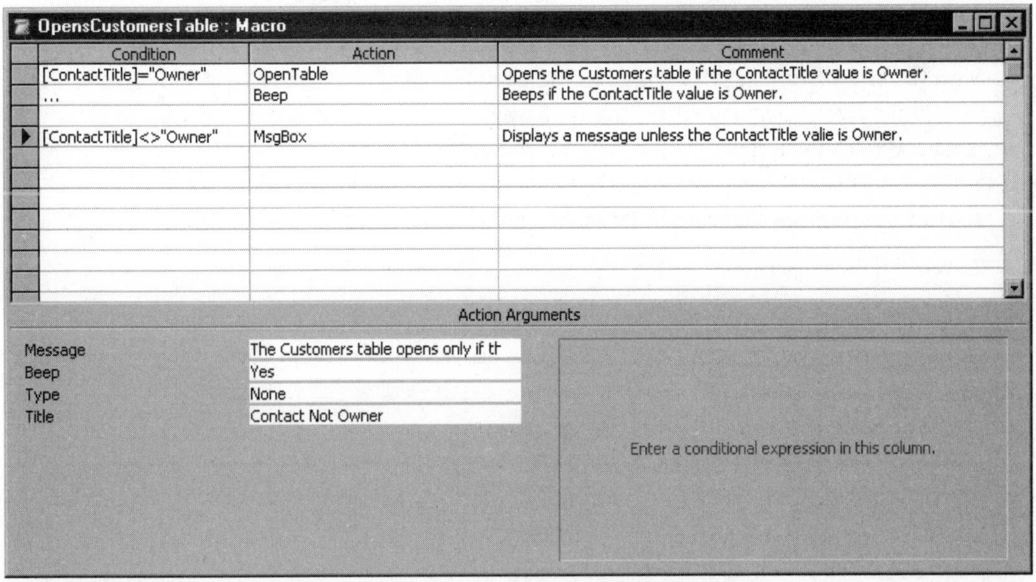

Figure 15-3 Adding conditions to the OpensCustomersTable macro

Figure 15-4 Displaying a message box when an event occurs

As a result, the condition defined for the first action must also be met for the second action. In other words, the value in the ContactTitle field must equal Owner if the computer beep action is to be carried out.

The third action in the OpensCustomersTable macro is MsgBox, which opens a message box (shown in Figure 15-4) when the event occurs. The condition defined for this action specifies that the ContactTitle value must *not* equal Owner. If the condition evaluates to true, the message box will be displayed.

NOTE

If you compare Figure 15-4 to Figure 15-3, you'll see that the message box title and text are defined in the arguments for the MsgBox action.

When combined, the conditions in the OpensCustomersTable macro define an either/or situation. In programming language, this is often referred to as an "If...Then...Else" condition— *if* the ContactTitle value equals Owner, *then* open the Customers table and make the computer beep, or *else* display a message box.

Progress Check

1. How does a macro in Word differ from a macro in Access?

2. When does a macro run?

3. At a minimum, what are the two primary steps that you take when creating a macro?

4. What symbol do you use to repeat a condition?

---

1. A Word macro records a set of keystrokes that can be repeated at any time when a user calls the macro. However, an Access macro is a data object—stored within the database file—that identifies one or more actions that are performed when an event occurs.
2. A macro runs when the event to which it is assigned occurs.
3. You must select an action and, if appropriate, configure the action's arguments.
4. The ellipsis (...)

CRITICAL SKILL
15.2 Assign Macros to Events

Once you've created a macro, you can assign that macro to one or more events. Macros can be assigned to events associated with any of the following objects:

- Forms

- Sections within forms

- Controls within forms

- Reports

- Sections within reports

Until a macro is assigned to an event, none of the actions defined within the macro will be taken. To assign a macro to an event, you must open the properties for the specific object, select the Event tab, and then select the event. When you select the event, a down arrow is displayed. Click the down arrow to open a drop-down list of all the macros in the database. From the list, select the macro that you want to run when the event occurs.

Let's take a look at an example to demonstrate how this works. Suppose you want to associate the OpensCustomersTable macro (which we used in the previous example) with an event in the Customers form. Specifically, you want the macro to run when users click the ContactTitle control. To do so, you must open the form in Design view and then open the properties dialog box for the control. In the case of the ContactTitle control, the properties open in the Text Box: ContactTitle dialog box, as shown in Figure 15-5. The figure shows the Event tab with the list of macros opened for the On Click event. From the list of macros, you would select the OpensCustomersTable option, close the dialog box, and then save the form. You can then switch to Form view to test the macro.

The first record that would appear when you opened the Customers form in Form view would probably display a ContactTitle value of Sales Representative. (If you had applied any filters to the form or changed any of the data, you might see a different value.) If you were to click the Text Box control, the Contact Not Owner message box would appear and the computer would beep. Clicking OK closes the message box. You could then go to the second record, which would display a ContactTitle value of Owner. Clicking the Text Box control would open the Customers table and cause the computer to beep. As you can see, the macro would not run until the user clicks the Text Box control, and the action taken depends on the value displayed in the Text Box control.

When you're associating a macro with an event (on the Event tab of the object's properties), you can select any macro from the list. If you're selecting a macro from a macro group, you must select one of the options that has a two-part name. The first part of the name is the name of the macro object, and the second is the macro name used within the object. For example, the

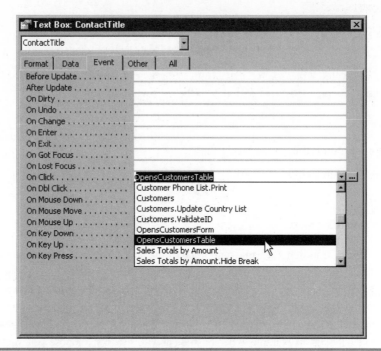

Figure 15-5 Selecting an existing macro for an Event property

Customers macro in the Northwind database is a group macro that contains two macros: the Update Country List macro and the ValidateID macro. If you want to attach the ValidateID macro to an event, you must select Customers.ValidateID.

Adding a New Macro

Access provides a second option for associating a macro with an event: You can create the macro when you are configuring the event property. To do this, first open the form or report in Design view, and then open the properties for the object whose event you want to configure. On the Event tab, select the event property and then click the Build button that appears to the right of the event when you select it. When the Choose Builder dialog box appears, select Macro Builder and then click OK. (You can also double-click Macro Builder.)

When you click OK, the Macro window and the Save As dialog box appear, with the Save As dialog box active. In the Macro Name text box, type in a name for the new macro and then click OK. The dialog box closes and the Macro window becomes active. You can then define the macro as you have other macros. Once you've completed the definition, save the macro and close the Macro window. You're then returned to the properties dialog box, and the name of the new macro is added to the event. You can also use that macro for other events; it is added to the list of macros available to each event.

Project 15-1 Create a Macro for an Event

So far in this module, you have learned how to create a macro and associate a macro with an event. In this project, you will create a macro named StaffAfter1996 in the consumer advocacy database. The macro will open the EmployeesHiredAfter1996 query or will display a message box. The message box will be displayed only if the PositionID value in the Staff table equals VOL. Before you create the macro, you will first add a Command Button control to the Staff Form form that you created in Module 12. From there, you will create a macro directly from the On Click event property for the new control. After you have created the macro, you will save the form and then test the new Command Button control.

Step by Step

1. If they're not already open, open Access and then open the ConsumerAdvocacy.mdb database file.

2. Select the Forms object type, click Staff Form, and then click the Design button at the top of the database window. The form opens in Design view.

3. If necessary, open the Toolbox, and ensure that the Select Objects button is selected and that the Control Wizards button is deselected.

4. In the Toolbox, click the Command Button control type and then click within the design grid to add the control to the form.

5. In the Command Button control, type **Staff After 1996**, and then resize and position the command button as necessary.

6. Open the properties for the command button and select the Event tab.

7. Select the On Click event property and then click the Build button next to the property. The Choose Builder dialog box appears.

8. Double-click Macro Builder. The Macro window and the Save As dialog box appear, with the dialog box active.

9. In the Macro Name text box, type **StaffAfter1996**, and then click OK. The Save As dialog box closes and the Macro window become active.

10. Click the Conditions button on the Macro Design toolbar. The Condition column is added to the design grid.

11. In the first row of the Condition column, type **[PositionID]<>"VOL"** (including the quotation marks), and in the first row of the Action column select OpenQuery from the drop-down list. Several arguments are added to the lower-left pane.

(continued)

12. In the first row of the Comment column, type **Displays the EmployeesHiredAfter1996 query.**

13. In the Query Name argument, select EmployeesHiredAfter1996.

14. In the second row of the Condition column, type **[PositionID]="VOL"** (including the quotation marks), and in the second row of the Action column select MsgBox from the drop-down list. Several arguments are added to the lower-left pane.

15. In the second row of the Comment column, type **Displays message box if PositionID equals VOL.**

16. In the Message argument, type **The EmployeesHiredAfter1996 query will not open for the Volunteer position.**

17. In the Type argument, select Information.

18. In the Title argument, type **Incorrect Position**.

19. Click the Save button on the Macro Design toolbar, and then close the Macro window. You're returned to the properties dialog box. The StaffAfter1996 macro has been added to the On Click event property.

20. Close the properties dialog box, click the Save button on the Form Design toolbar, and then click the View button on the toolbar. The form is displayed in Form view, displaying the first record in the Staff table. The record includes a Position value of Volunteer.

21. Click the Staff After 1996 button. The Incorrect Position message box appears.

22. Click OK.

23. Navigate to the second record, which contains a Position value of Employee.

24. Click the Staff After 1996 button. The EmployeesHiredAfter1996 query is displayed in Datasheet view.

25. Close the query and then close the form.

Project Summary

In this project, you created a macro that set up an If…Then…Else condition. If the PositionID value equals VOL, then a message box is displayed, or else the EmployeesHiredAfter1996 query is displayed. The If…Then…Else condition is set up by defining two actions. The first action contains a condition in which the PositionID value equals anything except VOL. The second action contains a condition in which the PositionID value equals VOL. You can create macros for any form or report event. Experiment with the Macro window and with associating macros with events. However, if you're creating a macro that modifies data, you might want to practice on a backup copy of the database so that you do not inadvertently delete or change data.

CRITICAL SKILL
15.3 Create Modules for Events

For the beginning Access developer, macros are a very effective method for defining actions that can be taken on specified events. However, as you become more experienced in developing Access applications, you'll find that modules are far more flexible and powerful tools for defining actions that can be taken in response to events. A module, as you'll recall, is an object that contains blocks of code written in VBA (Visual Basic for Applications). Modules can perform most actions that macros can perform but are generally more versatile. At the same time, they are usually more difficult to create and maintain.

Access supports two type of modules: module objects and Access class objects. Module objects are the modules that you see when you select the Modules tab of the database window. They are distinct data objects stored within the database window, but separate from any other objects. Module objects contain *procedures*—blocks of related VBA code—that can be referenced from anywhere in the database. Access class objects, on the other hand, are stored with either forms or reports, and are not separate data objects. Like module objects, class objects contain procedures, but the code within these procedures is related only to the associated form or report. As a result, class objects, rather than module objects, are the modules used to define the actions related to an event. You would use module objects when you want to create frequently used procedures that can be run from anywhere within the database and that are not tied to events within a specific object.

Both types of modules can support a wide variety of actions. However, the focus of this section is modules that are used to define actions that respond to events. As a result, our discussion will be limited to creating class objects that are made up primarily of *event procedures,* procedures that carry out actions in response to specified events. Before I go into the details of creating modules and event procedures, I want to first introduce you to VBA. The VBA language is an object-oriented programming language that is both extensive and complex. All modules are written in VBA. However, a detailed discussion of VBA is far beyond the scope of this book, although you still need a rudimentary understanding of VBA to create a module. Therefore, this discussion can serve only as an introduction to VBA and, consequently, only as an introduction to the basics of module design. As you continue to build Access applications, I encourage you to refer to more comprehensive resources on VBA so that you can build robust modules, not only to respond to events, but to carry out other actions within your Access database.

Understanding VBA

A module written in VBA is made up of two sections of code: declarations and procedures. Declarations normally represent only a small portion of the module, while procedures represent the bulk of the code.

Declarations

A module always begins with a declaration section. There are two primary declaration statements that are used at the beginning of a class module. The first of these is the Option Compare statement, which determines the default comparison method that should be used to compare and sort character string data. The Option Compare declaration statement can take one of three arguments:

- **Binary** This argument specifies that comparisons of string values are based on the underlying binary representation of those characters.

- **Text** This argument specifies that comparisons of string values are based on a case-insensitive text sort order. The text sort order is determined by your system's locale, as specified by the Office locale ID. Your system's *locale* refers to the language (specific to location) configured for your installation of the Microsoft Office System, and the *locale ID* identifies that language.

- **Database** This argument is used only within the context of Access. When it is specified, string comparisons are determined by the locale ID of the database in which the comparisons are made.

The Option Compare Database declaration statement is always used to begin an Access class object.

The second declaration statement that is often included in a class object is the Object Explicit declaration. This statement specifies that all variables and constants used within the class object must be explicitly declared. (I discuss variables and constants later in this section.) The Object Explicit statement takes no arguments.

Procedures

Procedures are made up of blocks of VBA code that perform an operation or calculate a value. Procedures are sometimes referred to as *subprograms* that can be called by other operations. VBA supports two types of procedures:

- **Sub procedures** This type of procedure performs an operation but does not return a value. For example, you can use a sub procedure to open a form or display an error message. The most common type of sub procedure in an Access module is the event procedure.

- **Functions** This type of procedure performs a calculation or comparison and then returns a value based on that operation. You already saw examples of built-in functions when you learned about expressions. For example, the Date function returns the current date. You can also create your own functions in VBA and then use those functions in expressions wherever function use is permitted.

Because our focus is on creating event procedures, our discussion will be limited to creating class objects that are defined with sub procedures. A sub procedure is made up of three types of statements:

- **Declaration**   This type of statement declares a variable or constant. A *variable* is a uniquely named item that contains data that can change during the execution of a procedure. You can think of a variable as a named storage location that contains data that can be modified throughout the course of the procedure. A *constant* is also a uniquely named item that holds a value; however, that value doesn't change.

- **Assignment**   This type of statement assigns a value to a variable or a constant. An assignment statement can appear only after the applicable declaration statement.

- **Executable**   This type of statement initiates an action that can execute functions and methods as well as loop and branch through blocks of code. A *method* is either an action that an object can perform or a function or statement that operates on a specific object. For the purposes of creating event procedures, a method generally refers to an action such as opening a table, going to a record, or closing a form.

If you declare a constant or variable in your procedure, you must do it at the beginning of the procedure, before you assign values or define actions. You can also declare variables and constants in the declaration section at the beginning of the class object. Variables and constants declared at the beginning of the class object can be used in any of the sub procedures defined within that object. Variables and constants declared within a sub procedure can be used only within that procedure.

Once you declare a variable or constant, you then use an assignment statement to assign a value to it. You can also use the variable or constant in an executable statement. However, you do not need to use variables and constants in your procedures in order to create an executable statement. Many sub procedures contains only executable statements, with no declaration or assignment statements.

Now let's take a look at a code sample to give you a better idea of what the VBA code for a class object module might look like. This code is written for a Command Button object on the Customers form of the Northwind database. When the user clicks the button, the related module takes one of two actions: It opens the CompanyOwners query if the ContactTitle value equals Owner, or it opens the CompanyNonowners query if the ContactTitle value does not equal Owner. The following code example includes a declaration section and a sub procedure:

```
1    Option Compare Database
2    Option Explicit
3    Private Sub Command46_Click()
4    'This event procedure opens the CompanyOwners query _
5        if the ContactTitle value equals Owner _
6        and opens the CompanyNonowners query _
```

```
7              if the ContactTitle value does not equal Owners
8    Dim strTitle As String
9    strTitle = Me!ContactTitle
10    If strTitle = "Owner" Then
11        DoCmd.OpenQuery "CompanyOwners", acViewNormal, acReadOnly
12   Else
13        DoCmd.OpenQuery "CompanyNonowners", acViewNormal, acReadOnly
14   End If
15   End Sub
```

NOTE

The line numbering is added in this example only to help explain the VBA code. It is not part of the code. In addition, the tabs have no effect on the code and are added only to make the code more readable.

The first two lines of code represent the declaration section. The first statement—Option Compare—determines the default comparison method. Because the Database argument is used, string comparisons are determined by the locale ID of the database in which the comparisons are made. The second statement—Option Explicit—indicates that constants and variables must be declared if they are used in the module.

Line 3 is the first line of the sub procedure. The Private keyword indicates that the procedure is available only within the module and is not available to other modules. The Sub keyword indicates that the block of text is a sub procedure, rather than a function. Command46_Click is the name of the sub procedure. When you access the module through an event property, Access automatically assigns a name based on the type of control and event. The sub procedure ends with Line 15. All sub procedures must be terminated with the End Sub statement.

Lines 4 through 8 contain a comment that explains the purpose of the procedure. The comment has no effect on the VBA code. Notice that the comment begins with an apostrophe. Also notice that, because the comment continues past one line, an underscore is added at the end of the line to indicate that the statement continues on the next line.

Line 8 declares a variable named strTitle. The Dim keyword is used to indicate that a variable is being declared. The As String keywords mean that the String data type is being assigned to the variable. Line 9 assigns an initial value to the strTitle variable. In this case, the variable is assigned the value in the ContactTitle field returned by the Customers form. Because the sub procedure applies to the Customers form, you don't have to provide a fully qualified name but instead can use the Me keyword (to indicate the current object) and the exclamation point (!) to separate the items.

Lines 10 through 14 create an If…Then…Else construction. If the strTitle variable is equal to Owner, then the statement in Line 11 is executed. Otherwise, the statement in Line 13 is executed. Lines 11 and 13 each contain an execution statement. The statements both begin with DoCmd.OpenQuery. DoCmd is an object in the Access class library. The DoCmd object contains numerous methods that you can use to perform actions in response to an event. The

DoCmd methods have many counterparts in macro actions. For the event procedures that you will be creating for class object modules, you will primarily be using DoCmd and its methods.

When you specify the DoCmd object, you must always specify a method, which is separated from the object name by a period. In the case of the code example here, the method used is OpenQuery. Following the method are values that are assigned to the arguments supported by the selected method. In the case of the previous example, the arguments specify the name of the query, the view in which the query should be displayed, and the type of access that the users will be allowed. For example, Line 11 opens the CompanyOwners query in normal view, and users will have read-only access.

Using the Microsoft Visual Basic Window

Now that you have a better understanding of the VBA code that makes up a class object module, let's take a look at how that code appears in the Microsoft Visual Basic window. The Microsoft Visual Basic window allows you to create and modify the VBA code that makes up a module. The method that you use to access the window depends on whether you're creating a new module or editing an existing one and on the type of module you're creating or editing. Depending on what you want to do, you can use any of the following options to access the Microsoft Visual Basic window:

- To create a class object module for a specific event in a form or report, open the form or report in Design view and then open the properties for the form, report, section, or control whose event you want to configure with an event procedure. On the Event tab, select the event property, click the Build button, and then double-click Code Builder.

- To edit a class object module for a form or report, open the form or report in Design view and then click the Code button on the Form Design or Report Design toolbar.

- You can also edit a class object module for a form or report through the database window. Select the Forms or Reports object type and then select the form or report. Click the Tools menu, point to Macro, and then click Visual Basic Editor.

- To create a module object, select the Modules object type in the database window and then click the New button at the top of the window. You can also click the Insert menu and then click Module.

- To edit an existing module object, select the Modules object type in the database window and then click the Design button at the top of the database window.

If you're editing an existing module, you can use any method to open the Microsoft Visual Basic window and then select the appropriate module from within the window. Figure 15-6 shows how the Microsoft Visual Basic window displays the different modules and the VBA code. The left pane displays the modules hierarchically. At the top of the hierarchy is the name of the database. At the next level are the two types of modules: the Microsoft Office Access Class Objects node and the Modules node.

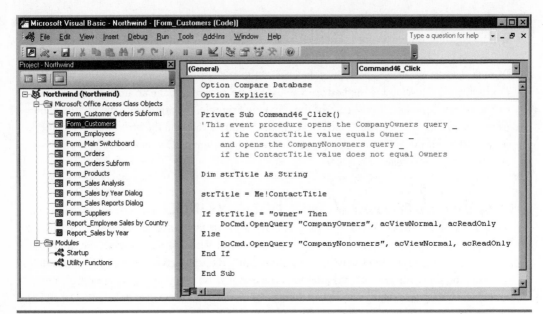

Figure 15-6 The Microsoft Visual Basic window displaying the Form_Customers class object module

The Microsoft Office Access Class Objects node contains the existing class objects that are associated with the forms and reports in the Northwind database. Only one class object can exist for each form or report. If a form or report requires multiple sub procedures, the sub procedures are listed in the same module. Access automatically assigns names to the class objects. For example, the class object for the Employees form is Form_Employees. Class objects are not added to the database until a module is created. The Modules node at the bottom of the left pane contains the object modules that are included in the Northwind database.

The right pane in the Microsoft Visual Basic window displays the VBA code that is contained in the selected module. In this pane you can edit the code as necessary and add procedures. Each event procedure is associated with a specific object and a specific event for that object. For example, the sub procedure shown in Figure 15-6 is named Command46_Click. Command46 is the name of a Command Button control in the Customers form. (This is a control that I added to test the code in the module.) The Click part of the procedure name is based on the fact that this procedure was created for the On Click event for the Command46 control.

The code within the Microsoft Visual Basic window is displayed in different colors, depending on the type of code element. For example, comment text appears in green and keyword text appears in blue, but you can change the color and the font. Click the Tools menu, and then click Options. When the Options dialog box appears, select the Editor Format tab and make the desired changes.

Creating a Class Object Module

When you write VBA code to respond to an event in a form or report, you are basically writing an event procedure for the specific control and event. As a result, you do not have to worry about whether a class object module already exists. If one does not exist, Access automatically adds a new class object and provides the start of a procedure by adding the Sub statement and the End Sub statement. If a class object already exists, Access adds the Sub/End Sub statements and you can work within that block.

To create a sub procedure for an event, open the form or report in Design view, open the object properties, select the event, and click the Build button. In the Choose Builder dialog box, double-click Code Builder. The Microsoft Visual Basic window appears with the sub procedure already started and the cursor inserted between the Sub and End Sub statements. Type in the VBA code, save your changes, and close the Microsoft Visual Basic window. You're returned to the Event tab of the control's properties dialog box. Notice that [Event Procedure] is added to the event property. The event property must be set with this property if the event procedure is to be executed.

TIP

The class object is part of the form or report. Whenever you save the form or report, whether in the Design view window or in the Microsoft Visual Basic window, you are saving both the form or report design as well as the class object. As a result, you should be careful when making changes in one window and then switching to another window. You might inadvertently save a change that you do not want to make.

Project 15-2 Create a Module for an Event

In Project 15-1, you created a macro (for the Staff Form form) that opens a query or displays a message box, depending on the PositionID value displayed in the form. You will now create a module that performs the same actions as the macro. In this module, you will write an event procedure that uses an If…Then…Else construction to determine which action to take. If the PositionID value is VOL, then a message box will be displayed saying that the query cannot be opened for this position. If the PositionID value is anything other than VOL, the EmployeesHiredAfter1996 query will be displayed. Once you have created the event procedure, you will test it by opening the form in Form view and clicking the command button for a Volunteer position and for an Employee position.

(continued)

Step by Step

1. If they're not already open, open Access and then open the ConsumerAdvocacy.mdb database file.

2. Click the Forms tab, select the form named Staff Form, and then click the Design button at the top of the database window. The form opens in Design view.

3. Open the properties for the Staff After 1996 Command Button control and select the Event tab.

4. Delete the macro name from the On Click event property and then click the Build button. The Choose Builder dialog box appears.

5. Double-click Code Builder. The Microsoft Visual Basic window appears. The Form_Staff Form class object has been added to the list of modules, and the first and last statements of a sub procedure have been added to the right pane. In addition, an Option Compare statement has been added to the macro.

6. On the line beneath the Sub statement, type **If Me!PositionID = "VOL" Then** and then press ENTER.

7. On the next line, press TAB. Type **MsgBox** and then add a space. A pop-up message box appears and displays the syntax used for this function. The syntax includes the arguments that are associated with the function. The current argument is in bold.

8. Type **"The query will not open for this position.",** (including the quotation marks, period, and comma). A drop-down list appears, displaying the options available for the *Buttons* placeholder.

9. Double-click vbDefaultButton1, and then add a comma.

10. Type **"Incorrect Position"** (including the quotation marks), and then press ENTER.

11. In the MsgBox line you just created, insert an underscore (_) directly in front of vbDefaultButton1, and then press ENTER. The MsgBox statement is now split into two lines.

12. Move down to the line after the MsgBox statement. Type **Else** and then press ENTER.

13. On the next line, type **DoCmd.** (including the period). A drop-down list appears, displaying all the methods available to the DoCmd object.

14. Double-click the OpenQuery method. The method is added to the statement.

15. Type a space. A pop-up message box appears and displays the syntax used for this method.

16. Type **"EmployeesHiredAfter1996",** (including the quotation marks and comma). A drop-down list appears displaying the options for the *View* placeholder.

15

Creating Macros and Modules

Project
15-2

Create a Module for an Event

17. Double-click the acViewNormal option, and then type a comma. A drop-down list appears displaying the options for the *DataMode* placeholder.

18. Double-click the acReadOnly option and then press ENTER.

19. On the next line, type **End If** and save the file. Your VBA code should now look similar to the following:

```
Option Compare Database
Private Sub Command13_Click()
If Me!PositionID = "VOL" Then
    MsgBox "The query will not open for this position.", _
    vbDefaultButton1, "Incorrect Position"
Else
    DoCmd.OpenQuery "EmployeesHiredAfter1996", acViewNormal, acReadOnly
End If
End Sub
```

Note that some lines were indented in the above code to make the code more readable.

20. Close the Microsoft Visual Basic window. You're returned to the properties for the Command Button control. Notice that [Event Procedure] has been added to the On Click property.

21. Close the properties dialog box and then click View on the Form Design toolbar. The form is displayed in Form view, and the first record in the Staff table is displayed. The Position value should be Volunteer.

22. Click the Staff After 1996 button. The Incorrect Position message box appears.

23. Click OK and then move to the second record in the table. The Position value should be Employee.

24. Click the Staff After 1996 button. The EmployeesHiredAfter1996 query opens in Datasheet view.

25. Close the query and then close the form.

Project Summary

The VBA code for this module includes a declaration section and a sub procedure. The declaration section is made up only of an Option Compare statement. The sub procedure is an event procedure that performs one of two actions, depending on the PositionID value. The first action is based on the MsgBox function, which creates a message box that includes message text, an OK button, and a title. The second action is based on the OpenQuery method in the DoCmd object. This method opens the EmployeesHiredAfter1996 query in normal view and gives users read-only access. You can, of course, create far more complex procedures, and you

(continued)

can include multiple procedures within a module. As I stated earlier, the information presented here is meant only as an introduction to VBA. As you continue to develop larger and more complex Access applications, you will want to spend the time necessary to learn more about VBA and the various types of procedures that you can create.

Module 15 Mastery Check

1. A(n) _____ is a data object—stored within the database file—that identifies one or more predefined actions that are performed when an event occurs.

2. With what type of form or report property do you associate a macro?

3. How do you open the Macro window?

4. What is the purpose of a comment in a macro?

5. You are creating a macro on the On Click event property. You add the OpenForm action and type in a comment. What other step must you take?

6. What is the purpose of the lower-right pane in the Macro window?

7. How do you choose an action in a macro?

8. You are creating a macro. You open the Macro window by selecting the Macros object type in the database window and then clicking the New button at the top of the window. You create the macro, and then save it to the database. What other step must you take?

9. How do you add a condition to an action in a macro?

10. A(n) _____ is an object that contains blocks of code written in VBA. The code can include declarations and procedures that perform operations or calculate values.

11. Which types of procedures does VBA support?

    A. Declarations

    B. Sub procedures

    C. Assignments

    D. Functions

12. What is the difference between a declaration statement and an assignment statement?

13. Which statements can be used in the declaration section of a module?

  A. Option Explicit

  B. Option Compare Database

  C. Private Sub Command46_Click()

  D. DoCmd.OpenQuery "CompanyOwners", acViewNormal, acReadOnly

14. Which object in VBA provides most of the methods that you need to create execution statements in an event procedure?

  A. OpenForm

  B. Option Explicit

  C. DoCmd

  D. Dim

15. What symbol do you use to precede a comment in VBA code?

Part IV

Appendixes

Appendix A

Answers to Mastery Checks

Module 1: Working with Access Databases

1. **Which toolbar is displayed by default at the top of the main Access window?**

   A. Database

   B. Web

   C. Task Pane

   D. Query Design

   A is the correct answer.

2. **From which task panes can you open a file?**

   A. Search Results

   B. File Search

   C. New File

   D. Getting Started

   B and **D** are the correct answers.

3. **Which database engine does a typical Access data file use?**

   Jet

4. **What object types are listed in the database window?**

   Tables, queries, forms, reports, pages, macros, and modules

5. **What do you use the Design button for in the toolbar on the database window?**

   To open a selected object in Design view, which allows you to view object definitions and layouts

6. **Which group is included in a database file by default?**

   Favorites

7. **Which type of object contains predefined requests for data?**

   A. Forms

   B. Reports

   C. Queries

   D. Pages

   C is the correct answer.

8. **Which type of object contains procedures written in Visual Basic?**

A. Modules

B. Reports

C. Macros

D. Pages

A is the correct answer.

9. **How do you add an object shortcut to a group?**

Right-click the object name in the database window, point to Add to Group, and click the group name.

10. **Which toolbar button on the database window should you use to execute a macro?**

A. New

B. Run

C. Preview

D. Open

B is the correct answer.

11. **What are the three types of new database files supported by Access?**

Files that contain blank databases, database files based on existing files, and database files based on templates

12. **What methods can you use to open the New File task pane?**

Clicking the Create A New File link on the Getting Started task pane, selecting New file from the drop-down list at the top of the task pane window, or clicking the New button on the database toolbar

13. **What steps do you take to create a blank database?**

To create a blank database, take the following steps:

1. In the New File task pane, click the Blank Database link.

2. In the File name text box of the File New Database dialog box, type the name of the new database file.

3. Click Create.

14. **From which sources can you choose a template to create a database file?**

From a set of templates installed on your computer or from templates available online

15. **How do you access the properties of a database object?**

By selecting Database Properties from the File menu

Module 2: Creating a Data Model

1. **Which structure within the relational model is made up of similar data that form columns within a table-like structure?**

   A. Tuple

   B. Attribute

   C. Relation

   D. Domain

   B is the correct answer.

2. **The _____ is based on the mathematical principles of set theory and predicate logic, which define a database structure that maintains data consistency and accuracy.**

   Relational model

3. **What is a relation in the relational model?**

   A relation is a set of related data collected into columns and rows to form a table-like structure.

4. **What is a domain in the relational model?**

   A domain specifies the type of data that can be stored in an attribute.

5. **What is the common name used in an RDBMS to refer to a relation?**

   A. Column

   B. Attribute

   C. Field

   D. Table

   D is the correct answer.

6. **How does a data type differ from a domain?**

   A data type defines the format of the data that can be entered into a field. A domain can provide a far more comprehensive set of restrictions, such as defining the format and restricting the values that can be entered.

7. **Which normal form states that each record in a table must be different?**

   A. First

   B. Second

   C. Third

   D. Fourth

   A is the correct answer.

8. Which normal form is violated if non-primary-key fields are dependent on each other?

A. First

B. Second

C. Third

D. Fourth

    C is the correct answer.

9. You have two tables in your database, one that lists the names of actors and one that lists the names of movies. An actor can appear in one or more movies. A movie can star one or more actors. What type of relationship exists between the two tables?

A. One-to-one

B. One-to-many

C. Many-to-one

D. Many-to-many

    D is the correct answer.

10. You're developing a data model for your Access database. A many-to-many relationship exists between two tables. What should you do?

Create a third table that establishes two one-to-many relationships.

11. What is SQL?

SQL is a computer language used to implement the relational model into an RDBMS. SQL was developed to support the creation of relational databases, the management of objects within those databases, and the manipulation of data stored in those objects.

12. You're working with an Access database and you want to modify the data in one of the tables. Which type of SQL statement will be used to modify the data?

A. Data Definition Language

B. Data Control Language

C. Data Manipulation Language

    C is the correct answer.

13. What is a data model?

A data model is a visual representation of the tables and their fields as they will be implemented in your Access database. The model also defines the relationships between the tables, allowing the developer to see how data is related within the database.

14. **What is the first step that you should take when creating a data model?**

    A. Group together related information.

    B. Define the possible relationships that might exist between data.

    C. Identify the initial entities.

    D. Normalize the data structure

    C is the correct answer.

15. **You're creating a data model and you've normalized the data structure. What is the next step that you should take?**

    A. Define the relationships between tables.

    B. Group together related information.

    C. Denormalize the appropriate structures.

    D. Identify possible entities.

    A is the correct answer.

Module 3: Managing Access Tables

1. **You want to view the table definition for the Employees table. Which view should you use?**

   Design view

2. **Which toolbar is displayed when you are viewing the data contained in a table?**

    A. Database

    B. Table Design

    C. Table Datasheet

    D. Formatting (Datasheet)

    C is the correct answer.

3. **How do you display the subdatasheet associated with a record that you're viewing in Datasheet view?**

    A. Click the plus sign associated with the record.

    B. Click the minus sign associated with the record.

    C. Click the Database Window button on the Table Datasheet toolbar.

    D. Click the row selector arrow for that record.

    A is the correct answer.

4. **How is a table's primary key indicated in Design view?**

    A key icon appears at the left of the row or rows that contain the primary key fields.

5. **What five methods does Access provide for creating tables?**

Creating tables in Design view, creating tables in Datasheet view, creating tables by using the Table wizard, creating tables by importing data, and creating tables by linking to data in another table

6. **What types of characters can you use in a field name?**

Letters, numbers, and spaces

7. **You're creating a field that will uniquely identify each record in your table. The field values will be a mix of letters and numbers. Which data type should you use?**

A. AutoNumber

B. Text

C. Memo

D. Number

    B is the correct answer.

8. **How does the Text data type differ from the Number data type?**

The Text data type can contain letters and numbers, but the numbers cannot be calculated. The Number data type can contain numerical values only, but they can be calculated.

9. **You're creating a new table in the database. You want to create only the basic table at this time, but will refine the table settings at a later time. What settings must you configure when creating the table?**

A. Field names

B. Data types

C. Descriptions

D. Primary key

    A and **B** are the correct answers.

10. **How do you create a table by simply entering data?**

You enter the data in Datasheet view. Access assigns the data types based on that data and configures the properties with default settings.

11. **Which table creation method should you use if you want to select fields from sample tables?**

A. Creating a table in Design view

B. Creating a table in Datasheet view

C. Creating a table by using the Table wizard

D. Creating a table by linking data

    C is the correct answer.

12. **What feature does Access include that updates field references in a data object if that field name changes?**

Name AutoCorrect

13. **What can happen to data in a table if you change a data type?**

Data can be lost if you change a data type because the new data type might not permit certain values.

14. **What happens to data in a field when you delete that field?**

The data is also deleted.

15. **You want to add a new field to a table after the existing fields. How do you add a field to the end of the listed fields?**

Open the table in Design view, select the Field Name column in the first empty row, enter the field information, and save the table.

Module 4: Managing Table Properties

1. **Which properties are available for every field type except OLE Object?**

A. Default Value

B. Format

C. Indexed

D. Validation Rule

    B and **C** are the correct answers.

2. **What is the default value assigned to the Field Size property of a Text field?**

A. 25

B. 50

C. 75

D. 100

    B is the correct answer.

3. **You're configuring the Field Size property of a Number field. You want to store whole numbers ranging from 10 through 100. Which Field Size option should you use?**

A. Byte

B. Integer

C. Single

D. Double

    A is the correct answer.

4. **You're configuring a Text field for your table. You want all the values to be displayed in lowercase and printed in red. What setting should you use for the Format property?**

   <[Red]

5. **You're configuring the Format property for a Number field. You want the numbers to be displayed with a thousands separator and you want the display to be based on the regional settings as they're configured in the operating system. Which Format option should you use?**

   A. General Number

   B. Currency

   C. Fixed

   D. Standard

   D is the correct answer.

6. **A(n) _____ is a type of filter that determines how data is entered into a field. It provides users with a fill-in-the-blank type format that limits the way data can be entered.**

   Input mask

7. **For which fields can you define a default value?**

   A. Hyperlink

   B. Currency

   C. AutoNumber

   D. OLE Object

   A and **B** are the correct answers.

8. **How should you configure a Text field's properties if you want to allow zero-length stings in that field?**

   Set the Allow Zero Length property to Yes.

9. **Which language's characters will be compressed if you set the Unicode Compression property to Yes?**

   A. Chinese

   B. English

   C. Japanese

   D. German

   B and **D** are the correct answers.

10. **You're configuring a Number field, and you set the Field Size property to Decimal. Which property should you configure to set the total number of digits in the field?**

A. Format

B. Precision

C. Required

D. Scale

    B is the correct answer.

11. **A(n) _____ is an expression that is made up of operators, literal values, and other elements that together create a formula that defines the acceptable value range.**

Validation rule

12. **You're creating an expression that limits numerical values to the range of 100 through 200, inclusive. Which expression should you use?**

A. 100 Between 200

B. 100 <> 200

C. >= 100; <= 200

D. >= 100 And <= 200

    D is the correct answer.

13. **On what fields should you create an index?**

You should create an index on any field that you intend to query frequently or that is used to create a relationship with another table.

14. **How do you create a lookup field?**

Select the Lookup Wizard option in the Data Type column of the field, and then follow the steps in the wizard.

15. **Which lookup field property indicates whether the source of the data is a table or a list?**

A. Row Source

B. Row Source Type

C. List Rows

D. Limit To List

    B is the correct answer.

16. **What is the difference between table object properties and table design properties?**

Table object properties are those properties that apply to the general characteristics of the table as an object within the database. Table design properties are those properties that you access through Design view and that are related to the table data.

Module 5: Managing Table Relationships

1. Which type of relationship requires the creation of a junction table to form two relationships of another type?

A. One-to-one

B. One-to-many

C. Many-to-one

D. Many-to-many

   D is the correct answer.

2. _____ refers to the state of the database in which data in one or more fields in one table is kept consistent with data in one or more fields in another table.

Referential integrity

3. You're configuring a one-to-many relationship between two tables. What is the name of the field in the child table that references a field in the parent table?

A. Primary key

B. Unique index

C. Foreign key

D. Junction

   C is the correct answer.

4. Which actions are prevented when referential integrity is enforced?

A. Adding records to the child table if a foreign key field contains a value that does not exist in the related parent field

B. Deleting a record in the child table if a related record exists in the parent table

C. Changing a value in the primary key or unique index field of the parent table if a record in the child table will be left without an associated record in the parent table

D. Changing a value in the foreign key field of a child table if that change results in the record not being associated with a record in the parent table

   A, **C**, and **D** are the correct answers.

5. How are primary key fields represented in the Relationships window?

Primary key fields are shown in bold type.

6. How do you add tables to the Relationships window?

Click the Show Table button on the Relationship toolbar to open the Show Table dialog box. You can then add tables to the table relationship layout diagram in the Relationships window.

7. **You're creating a relationship between the Publishers table and the Books table. You want to create a one-to-many relationship, with the Publishers table as the parent table and the Books table as the child table. Both tables contain a PublisherID field, which is the primary key in the Publishers table. What should you do first?**

   A. Select the foreign key in the Publishers table, drag it to the Books table, and drop it on the primary key in the Books table.

   B. Select the primary key in the Publishers table, drag it to the Books table, and drop it on the PublisherID field in the Books table.

   C. Select the primary key in the Books table, drag it to the Publishers table, and drop it on the PublisherID field in the Publishers table.

   D. Select the foreign key in the Books table, drag it to the Publishers table, and drop it on the primary key in the Publishers table.

   B is the correct answer.

8. **How do you enforce referential integrity in a relationship?**

   Select the Enforce Referential Integrity check box in the Edit Relationships dialog box.

9. **You're creating a new relationship between two tables in your database. You want any changes made to the primary key of the parent table to be cascaded down to the foreign key of the child table. Which option or options should you select?**

   A. Cascade Delete Related Records

   B. Related Table/Query

   C. Cascade Update Related Fields

   D. Enforce Referential Integrity

   C and **D** are the correct answers.

10. **You're creating a relationship between two tables. The parent table includes a primary key that is made up of one AutoNumber field. How should the foreign key field be configured?**

    The foreign key must be configured as a Number field with the field size set to Long Integer.

11. **A(n) _____ is a type of query that matches the values in the related fields of two tables in order to return results that combine data from the tables.**

    Join

12. **How are the join properties configured by default?**

    The query results will include only those records with matching values in the joined fields (the primary key from the parent table and the foreign key from the child table).

13. **What methods can you use to save the table relationship layout in the Relationships window?**

    Click the Save button on the Relationship toolbar, select Save from the File menu, press CTRL-S, or right-click anywhere in the Relationships window (except on a table) and then select Save Layout from the shortcut menu.

14. **What actions can you take in the Edit Relationships dialog box?**

You can change fields, add fields, and set the referential integrity options. You can also create new relationships or modify the join type.

15. **How do you delete a relationship?**

To delete a relationship, right-click the relationship line and then select Delete from the shortcut menu. You can also delete a relationship by selecting the relationship and then selecting Delete from the Edit menu.

Module 6: Managing Database Security

1. **What security concerns should you be aware of when password-protecting a database file?**

The password is stored in an unencrypted form, so the security of the database can be compromised. In addition, protecting your database with a password applies to the file as a whole. Once the database is opened, users can access any of the objects within the database, unless user-level security has been configured.

2. **Which component in the Access security model is a type of access right that is granted to a specific user?**

A. User account

B. Workgroup

C. Permission

D. Object

C is the correct answer.

3. _____ mode is the state in which you can open a database file that prevents any other users from opening the file while you're using it.

Exclusive

4. **What is the difference between a workgroup and a group account?**

A workgroup is a set of users who access the databases in the same instance of Access. A group account is a type of security account in an Access workgroup that contains a set of user accounts.

5. **How many workgroups can Access be associated with at any one time?**

A. Exactly one

B. One for each WIF that has been created

C. One for each database object

D. As many as necessary

A is the correct answer.

6. **What is the name of the default WIF that is created when you install Access?**

System.mdw

7. **Which types of security accounts does Access support?**

A. Workgroups

B. Users

C. Groups

D. Objects

B and **C** are the correct answers.

8. **What is the name of the default user account that is created automatically by Access?**

Admin

9. **Which group are all users added to by default?**

A. Admin

B. Admins

C. Security

D. Users

D is the correct answer.

10. **What type of access does the Admin account have?**

Full access to all objects in all databases

11. **How do you add a user account to a workgroup?**

In the User and Group Accounts dialog box, click the New button. When the New User/Group dialog box appears, enter a name for the user and a personal ID, and then click OK.

12. **How must you configure the Admin account in order to implement user-level security?**

You must assign a password to the Admin account in order to implement user-level security.

13. **You created a user account in a workgroup, and you want to allow the user to view the data in the database but not make any changes. Which permission should you assign?**

A. Open Exclusive

B. Administer

C. Read Data

D. Read Design

C is the correct answer.

14. **Which object type supports the Open Exclusive permission?**

A. Database

B. Table

C. Form

D. Macro

   A is the correct answer.

15. **What does encoding a file accomplish?**

Encoding a file compacts the file and prevents word processing and utility programs from being able to read the file.

Module 7: Modifying Data in an Access Database

1. **What information is displayed in the Datasheet view window?**

The Datasheet view window displays the data in a table in a column/row structure. Each field is represented by a column, and each record is represented by a row.

2. **What methods can you use to move from one field to the next?**

You can click on the field that you want to move to, press TAB or ENTER to move to the next field, or use the appropriate arrow key to move to the field above, below, to the right, or to the left of the current field.

3. **What types of fields does character data apply to?**

A. Number

B. Text

C. Memo

D. Currency

   B and **C** are the correct answers.

4. **How are fractions handled in a numerical field if the Field Size property is configured as an integer?**

Fractions are rounded to the nearest whole number.

5. **What type of value can you enter into an AutoNumber field?**

You cannot enter a value in an AutoNumber field or change an existing value.

6. Your field is configured with the Date/Time data type, and the Format property is configured with the Long Date option. Which values will the field accept?

A. 815

B. 8/15

C. 0815

D. 8-15

B and **C** are the correct answers.

7. How do you insert a new object into an OLE Object field?

Right-click the field and then click Insert Object in the shortcut menu. In the Microsoft Office Access dialog box, select the type of object from the Object Type list, and then click OK. This will launch the appropriate application in which you can create the embedded document.

8. What are the four elements that can be included in a value in a Hyperlink field?

Display name, URL or UNC, subaddress, and screen tip

9. How do you enter data in a field that is configured with a lookup list?

You must select the value from a drop-down list that is available for the specific field.

10. How do you select consecutive records in a table?

Select the first record in the group of records that you want to select, press and hold down SHIFT, and then click the last record in that group. You can also select the first record, hold down the left mouse button, and highlight the consecutive records to select all of them.

11. Which type of field contains a check box that you can select or clear?

A. Hyperlink

B. AutoNumber

C. Memo

D. Yes/No

D is the correct answer.

12. Which key can you use to switch between Navigation mode and Edit mode in the Datasheet view window?

A. F2

B. INSERT

C. ENTER

D. F10

A is the correct answer.

A

13. How do you edit a value in a Hyperlink field?

Right-click the field, point to Hyperlink, and then click Edit Hyperlink. When the Edit Hyperlink dialog box appears, make the necessary corrections.

14. You're working in Datasheet view and you're entering values into various fields. You want to change the behavior of the keyboard when you press ENTER so that the insertion point moves to the next record. What should you do?

Click the Tools menu, and then click Options. When the Options dialog box appears, select the Keyboard tab. In the Move After Enter section, select the Don't Move option, and then click OK.

15. How do you delete an entire value in a field?

Use TAB or the arrow keys to move the cursor to that field in order to highlight the entire field, and then press BACKSPACE or DELETE. If you're in Edit mode, press F2 to switch to Navigation mode, which will highlight the entire field, and then press BACKSPACE or DELETE.

Module 8: Finding, Sorting, and Filtering Data

1. What option should you select in the Find and Replace dialog box if you want to search the entire table, rather than one field?

Select the name of the table in the Look In drop-down list.

2. What options are available in the Match drop-down list in the Find and Replace dialog box?

Any Part Of Field, Whole Field, and Start Of Field

3. In what circumstances should you select the Search Fields As Formatted check box in the Find And Replace dialog box?

You should select this option if you want to search records with values based on how they're displayed, rather than how they're actually stored in the database.

4. What should you type in the Find What text box of the Find And Replace dialog box if you want to find a zero-length string value?

A. **Null**

B. **Is Null**

C. Single-quotes ('')

D. Double-quotes ("")

   D is the correct answer.

5. You're using the Find And Replace dialog box to search for a customer name. You know the first three letters of the last name (Bur) but do not know the full last name or how many letters are in the name. What should you type in the Find What dialog box?

A. **Bur?**

B. **Bur#**

C. **Bur***

D. **Bur!**

> **C** is the correct answer.

6. What is the purpose of the Replace With text box on the Replace tab of the Find And Replace dialog box?

The Replace With text box allows you to specify a new value for your records.

7. How is a table sorted by default if the primary key is not an AutoNumber field?

If a type of field other than AutoNumber is used as the primary key, the values are sorted in ascending order (A through Z if alphabetical, 1 and up if numerical).

8. Which types of fields does Access allow you to sort?

A. Text

B. Number

C. AutoNumber

D. OLE Object

> **A**, **B**, and **C** are the correct answers.

9. You're creating a filter on the Employees table in the Northwind database. You want to filter out all records except those records with a Last Name value of Fuller. Which filter method is the easiest to use in this situation?

A. Filter by excluded selection

B. Filter by selection

C. Filter by using advanced options

D. Filter by form

> **B** is the correct answer.

10. How do you remove a filter from a table?

Click the Remove Filter button on the Table Datasheet toolbar, right-click any value and then click Remove Filter/Sort in the shortcut menu, or click the Records menu and then click Remove Filter/Sort.

11. How does filtering by selection differ from filtering by excluding a selection?

When filtering by selection, you're identifying the records that should be included in the view. When filtering by excluding a selection, you're identifying the records that should be excluded from the view.

12. **You're using the Filter By Form window to create a filter on a table. How do you define the filter criteria for that table?**

Select a value for each field that you want to include in the filter criteria.

13. **In addition to field values, what other elements can you include in your criteria in the Filter By Form window?**

Expressions and wildcards

14. **What information is included in the Filter window that is used for advanced filters?**

The Filter window includes a graphical representation of the applicable table and a grid that is used to define the criteria for the participating fields.

15. **What information can you define for each field in the Filter window?**

The sort order and one or more conditions for the filter criteria

Module 9: Importing, Exporting, and Linking Data

1. **You're importing data from another Access database into your Access database. Which data objects can you import into your database?**

   A. Macros

   B. Forms

   C. Reports

   D. Tables

   A, B, C, and **D** are the correct answers.

2. **What database file can you import into an Access table, but not link to?**

   A. dBase

   B. Lotus

   C. Paradox

   D. SQL Server

   B is the correct answer.

3. **Which data sources allow you to insert imported data directly into a table?**

   A. Access tables

   B. dBase files

   C. Excel spreadsheets

   D. Text files

   C and **D** are the correct answers.

4. What would prevent you from inserting Excel data into an existing table?

You cannot import data into an existing table if the data in any way conflicts with the primary key or any other constraints that exist on the table.

5. What is the difference between a delimited text file and a fixed width text file?

The values in a delimited text file are separated by a character (such as a tab), and the values in a fixed width text file are evenly aligned.

6. What is XML?

XML is a language standard that is used to describe and deliver data in various environments.

7. What is the difference between importing data and linking data?

When you import data, the data is copied into a table in your database. When you link data, the data remains in the external data source, but you can view and manipulate an image of that data from within your database.

8. What is the main difference between importing an object from an Access database and linking to an object in an Access database?

You can import any data object from an Access database into your database, but you can link only to tables in the external database.

9. What name is provided by default to a table that is linked to a dBase file?

The linked table is assigned the same name as the dBase file.

10. To which file type can you export a module?

A. XML file

B. Access database file

C. Text file

D. dBase file

   B and **C** are the correct answers.

11. Which object types in an Access database can you export to another Access database?

All object types

12. You're exporting data to a dBase file. How long can the filename be?

A dBase filename is limited to 11 characters: 8 characters for the actual name and 3 characters for the .dbf file extension.

13. You're exporting data into a text file. During the export process, you determine that the file will be formatted as a delimited file. What other decision must you make if the file is delimited?

You must decide what character will be used to separate values.

14. **Which XML-related file stores the data presentation?**

A. .xml

B. .xsd

C. .xsl

D. .xls

    C is the correct answer.

15. **What is the difference between importing and exporting data?**

When you import data, you're copying data from another data source into your database. When you export data, you're copying data out of your database to another data source.

Module 10: Querying an Access Database

1. **Which type of query retrieves and displays a subset of data from one or more tables?**

A. Make-table

B. Append

C. Select

D. Crosstab

    C is the correct answer.

2. **In what window are the results of a select query displayed?**

Datasheet view

3. **Which rows are included by default in the design grid of the Design view window for a select query?**

A. Sort

B. Total

C. Append To

D. Show

    A and **D** are the correct answers.

4. **How do you view the results of a query when in Design view without actually running the query?**

Click the View button in the Query Design toolbar to open the query in Datasheet view.

5. **What is the main difference between a single-table query definition and a multiple-table query definition?**

In a multiple-table query definition, you can include fields from different tables in the same design grid.

6. A(n) _____ query is a type of query that groups together related data and summarizes values associated with that data.

Crosstab

7. You're creating a crosstab query in the Design view window. For one of the fields, you want the values grouped together to form a row for each unique value. Which option should you use in the Crosstab cell?

A. Row Heading

B. Column Heading

C. Value

D. (not shown)

   A is the correct answer.

8. You're creating a crosstab query in the Design view window. One of the fields is configured with the Column Heading option. Which option should you use in the Total row of the design grid?

A. Where

B. Sum

C. Group By

D. Count

   C is the correct answer.

9. What are the four types of action queries?

Make-table, update, append, and delete

10. What is the difference between an update query and an append query?

An update query modifies existing data in a table. An append query takes the records returned by the query and inserts them into an existing table.

11. A(n) _____ query is a type of query that creates a table based on the results generated from that query.

Make-table

12. Which types of action queries directly affect data or tables that already exist in a database?

A. Make-table

B. Update

C. Append

D. Delete

   B, **C**, and **D** are the correct answers.

13. **What information do you identify in an update query definition?**

In an update query definition, you identify which records in a table should be modified and what the new values should be.

14. **What is the main difference between an append query and a make-table query?**

A make-table query creates a new table when the query is generated and then inserts data into that table, but an append query inserts data into a table that already exists.

15. **You're creating a delete query in the Design view window. You drag the asterisk from the table object to the Field cell of the column in the design grid. Which option is added the Delete cell of that column?**

A. Value

B. From

C. Group By

D. Where

    B is the correct answer.

Module 11: Adding Expressions to Your Queries

1. **Which component of an expression is used to compare or calculate data?**

A. Operator

B. Function

C. Identifier

D. Literal

    A is the correct answer.

2. **How is an identifier different from a literal?**

An identifier is the name of an Access database object, such as a table or field. A literal is a value that is used exactly as you type it into an expression.

3. **What components must be included in a statement for that statement to be considered an expression?**

For a statement to qualify as an expression, it must include at least one operator and one of the other three elements (literal, identifier, or function).

4. **Which type of operator should you use if you want to compare two conditions in an expression?**

A. Comparison

B. Arithmetic

C. Logical

D. Concatenation

    C is the correct answer.

5. **Which expression should you use if you want to return a Date/Time value that is the same as or later than January 1, 1999?**

   >=#1/1/99#

6. **Which expression should you use if you want to add a value of 25 to the OnOrder field?**

   [OnOrder]+25

7. **Which operator should you use to connect two conditions in which at least one of those conditions must evaluate to true?**

   A. In

   B. Or

   C. Like

   D. And

   B is the correct answer.

8. **Which expression should you use if you want to join the FirstName field and the LastName field into one field in your query results?**

   [FirstName]&" "&[LastName]

9. **You are defining a select query, and you want to return only those records whose OrderDate value is after the current date. Which expression should you use?**

   A. Between [OrderDate] and Date( )

   B. <Date( )

   C. Date( )+[OrderDate]

   D. >Date( )

   D is the correct answer.

10. **What symbol should you use in an expression to separate a parent object from a child object?**

    Exclamation point (!)

11. **Which type of literals must be enclosed in quotation marks?**

    A. Text

    B. Object

    C. Numerical

    D. Date/Time

    A is the correct answer.

12. **Which type of query expression allows you to include a calculated field in your query results?**

A. Criteria

B. Field

C. Aggregate

D. Multiple row

> **B** is the correct answer.

13. **What is an aggregate function?**

A type of function that allows you to apply summary calculations to groups of data

14. **You want to extract the year out of the DateDelivered field, which is configured as a Date/Time field. Which function should you use?**

Year

15. **Which row in the design grid of the Design view window includes options that are aggregate functions?**

The Total row

Module 12: Creating and Configuring Forms

1. **What is a form?**

A form is an interface between a user and the data within the database. By using a form, a user can view and modify data without having to access the database directly or know how the database is structured.

2. **How should you open a new form if you want to link a table to the form?**

Click the New button at the top of the database window, or click the Insert menu, and then click Form.

3. **What three windows appear in Design view when you open a new form that is associated with a table?**

The Form window, the Toolbox, and the Field List

4. **What is a control?**

A control is an object that displays data, performs an action, or enhances the appearance of a form.

5. **Which button must you select in the Toolbox before selecting one of the control buttons?**

The Select Objects button

6. **What steps should you take to add a control to a form (without using a wizard)?**

To add a control to a form without using a wizard, first verify that the Control Wizards button is not selected. If it is selected, deselect it. Next, click the Select Objects button if it is not already selected, then click the control button, and finally click within the design grid where you want to locate the control.

7. You're creating a form that is associated with a table in your database. You plan to add several bound Text Box controls. From which object in Design view should you add the controls?

A. The design grid

B. The Field List

C. The Form window

D. The Toolkit

   B is the correct answer.

8. Which type of control should you add to a form if you want to concatenate two fields into one control?

A. Bound

B. Switchboard

C. Calculated

D. Unbound

   C is the correct answer.

9. What controls are added to the design grid when you use the Toolbox to add a Text Box control?

The Text Box control and a linked Label control

10. How do you use the Field List to add more than one Text Box control at a time?

Select all the fields in the Field List that you want to add as bound controls and drag them at one time to the design grid.

11. Which property in a bound control specifies the field that the control is bound to?

A. Row Source Type

B. Row Source

C. Bound Column

D. Control Source

   D is the correct answer.

12. Which control should you use if you want to group together Yes/No controls?

The Option Group control

13. Which types of controls allow you to apply conditional formatting?

A. Text Box

B. Combo Box

C. List Box

D. Check Box

   A and **B** are the correct answers.

14. What tabs are included in the properties dialog box for a control?

Format, Data, Event, Other, and All

15. What two tools can you use to format a control?

The Formatting (Form/Report) toolbar and the Format tab of the properties dialog box

Module 13: Creating and Configuring Reports

1. What methods can you use to open a new report in Design view?

Double-click Create Report In Design View, click the New button in the database window, or click the Insert menu and then click Report. For the first two methods, you must first select the Reports object type in the database window.

2. You're creating a report that is linked to a table in the database. You open a new report in Design view by clicking the New button and selecting the table in the New Report dialog box. Which windows appear when you open the new report in Design view?

A. Report

B. Report Design

C. Toolbox

D. Field List

A, **C**, and **D** are the correct answers.

3. Which sections appear in the design grid when you open a new report in Design view?

A. Detail

B. Group Header

C. Page Header

D. Report Header

A and **C** are the correct answers.

4. What are two differences between controls used in reports and controls used in forms?

Form controls can be interactive, but report controls cannot. In addition, form controls can trigger events, but report controls cannot.

5. How do you display report information in columns?

Configure the settings on the Columns tab of the Page Setup dialog box.

6. How do you display the Report Header section in the design grid?

Click the View menu and then click Report Header/Footer.

7. You're creating a report and you want to add column headings that appear at the top of each page. In which section of the design grid should you add the Label controls?

A. Detail

B. Page Header

C. Report Header

D. Group Header

> **B** is the correct answer.

8. You're creating a report that will include grouped data. The group will be based on the LastName field of the underlying table. You want the data to be grouped alphabetically based on the first letter of the LastName value. How should you configure the group properties?

Set the Group On option to Prefix Characters, and set the Group Interval property to 1.

9. Which Group On options are available for a Currency field?

A. Each Value

B. Prefix Character

C. Qtr

D. Interval

> **A** and **D** are the correct answers.

10. How must Group On properties be configured for a field to be grouped, rather than sorted?

You must select Yes for the Group Header property, the Group Footer property, or both.

11. You're creating a report that includes grouped data. The data is grouped based on the HomeState field of the underlying table. What name is automatically assigned to the group header section?

A. HomeState

B. HomeState Header

C. HomeState Group Header

D. HomeState Header (Group)

> **B** is the correct answer.

12. You're creating a report that includes grouped data. The data is grouped based on the InStock field of the underlying table. You want the report to include the total of InStock values for each group. How should you set up the group?

Add a Text Box control to the InStock Footer section. Create an expression in the Text Box control that uses the Sum aggregate function to total the values in the InStock field.

A

Answers to Mastery Checks

13. A(n) _____ is a type of function that applies summary calculations to groups of data.

Aggregate function

14. **What is a parameter query?**

A parameter query is a type of query that defines a parameter within the query definition. The parameter acts as a placeholder that allows you to specify a value whenever you run that query. Before the query can return data, a value must be provided for the parameter. The value is then used to complete the query, and the data is returned.

15. **You're creating a report based on a parameter query. The name of the parameter used in the query is [Enter your last name:]. You want the report to include "Report for" and the parameter value in a title at the top of the report. You add a Text Box control to the Report Header section. What expression should you specify in the Text Box control?**

="Report for "&[Enter your last name:]

Module 14: Creating and Configuring Data Access Pages

1. **What is one of the most significant differences between a data access page and a form or report?**

A data access page is intended to ultimately be viewed through the Internet Explorer browser, rather than through an Access interface window, as forms and reports are viewed.

2. **What are the shortcuts listed on the Pages tab of the database window linked to?**

HTML files stored separately from the database file

3. **What two conditions must be met for you to be able to access a database through a data access page that you're viewing through a web server?**

You must be using Internet Explorer 5.01 with Service Pack 2 or later as your browser, and you must have been granted the proper permissions to the database objects.

4. **What methods can you use to open a new data access page in Design view?**

Double-click Create Data Access Page In Design View; click the New button at the top of the database window; or click the Insert menu and then click Page. For the first two methods, you must first select the Pages object type in the database window.

5. **How do you display the Toolbox when you're in Design view?**

Click the Toolbox button on the Page Design toolbar.

6. **Which control should you use if you want to add only descriptive text to the design grid?**

   A. Text Box

   B. List Box

   C. Line

   D. Label

   D is the correct answer.

7. **What is displayed in the Field List for a data access page in Design view?**

   The Field List provides a hierarchical view of all the tables and queries in your database. Each table and query node includes a list of the fields in that table or query.

8. **What is the easiest way to add a bound Text Box control to the design grid?**

   Drag and drop the field from Field List to the design grid.

9. **In what parts of the Data Access Page window can you type in text?**

   You can type in text on any line outside the design grid, but you cannot type text directly in the design grid. You must use a control to add text within the grid.

10. **How do you type HTML text directly in the Data Access Page window?**

    Click within an existing paragraph outside the design grid and type in the text.

11. **You are creating a data access page that will contain grouped data. You add a bound Text Box control to the design grid. The field that the control is based on will form the basis for the group. What should your next step be?**

    Verify the that Text Box control is selected, and then click the Promote button on the Page Design toolbar.

12. **Which group property should you set to determine the number of records displayed per group?**

    A. DefaultSort

    B. DataPageSize

    C. GroupOn

    D. GroupInterval

    B is the correct answer.

13. **You are creating a group that is based on the CustomerID field in the Customers table. You add a bound Text Box control to the design grid and promote the control. What name will be assigned to the header section that contains the CustomerID Text Box control?**

    A. Header: Customers-CustomerID

    B. Header: Customers

    C. Header: CustomerID-Customers

    D. Header: CustomerID

    A is the correct answer.

14. **What actions can a user take in an Office Spreadsheet control?**

Users can cut, copy, and paste data; find the totals for rows and columns of data; sort and filter data; and export the data to an Excel spreadsheet. Users can also access a Help file that is specific to the spreadsheet control.

15. **What is a PivotTable?**

A PivotTable is an Office object that is similar to an Excel spreadsheet. However, a PivotTable supports more dynamic types of analysis than a spreadsheet can provide. For example, a PivotTable can include calculations in individual cells, totals for the rows that contains those cells, and totals for the columns. The PivotTable can also calculate subtotals and grand totals, and it can use a field's value as a row and column heading and then perform calculations on that heading.

Module 15: Creating Macros and Modules

1. **A(n) _____ is a data object—stored within the database file—that identifies one or more predefined actions that are performed when an event occurs.**

Macro

2. **With what type of form or report property do you associate a macro?**

An event property

3. **How do you open the Macro window?**

Select the Macros object type in the database window and then click the New button at the top of the window. You can also click the Insert menu and then click Macro.

4. **What is the purpose of a comment in a macro?**

A comment is used only to document the action of the macro; it does not affect the actions taken by the macro.

5. **You are creating a macro on the On Click event property. You add the OpenForm action and type in a comment. What other step must you take?**

You must configure the action's arguments.

6. **What is the purpose of the lower-right pane in the Macro window?**

The lower-right pane provides information about the specific action or argument that is selected.

7. **How do you choose an action in a macro?**

To choose an action, select it from the drop-down list in the applicable row of the Action column.

8. **You are creating a macro. You open the Macro window by selecting the Macros object type in the database window and then clicking the New button at the top of the window. You create the macro, and then save it to the database. What other step must you take?**

After you create and save the macro, you must associate it with an event.

9. How do you add a condition to an action in a macro?

To add a condition to an action, you must first add the Condition column to the design grid of the Macro window. Click the Conditions button on the Macro Design toolbar. The column is added to the left of the Action column. In the Condition column, type an expression next to the action that should be executed if the condition evaluates to true.

10. A(n) _____ is an object that contains blocks of code written in VBA. The code can include declarations and procedures that perform operations or calculate values.

Module

11. Which types of procedures does VBA support?

A. Declarations

B. Sub procedures

C. Assignments

D. Functions

   B and **D** are the correct answers.

12. What is the difference between a declaration statement and an assignment statement?

A declaration statement declares a variable or a constant. An assignment statement assigns a value to the variable or constraint.

13. Which statements can be used in the declaration section of a module?

A. Option Explicit

B. Option Compare Database

C. Private Sub Command46_Click()

D. DoCmd.OpenQuery "CompanyOwners", acViewNormal, acReadOnly

   A and **B** are the correct answers.

14. Which object in VBA provides most of the methods that you need to create execution statements in an event procedure?

A. OpenForm

B. Option Explicit

C. DoCmd

D. Dim

   C is the correct answer.

15. What symbol do you use to precede a comment in VBA code?

An apostrophe (')

Appendix B

Keyboard Shortcuts

A large part of this book's focus has been on teaching you how to create and configure the objects necessary to store data in an Access database. However, once a data-driven application has been created, the database's users will spend most of their time viewing and modifying data. Quite often, users will be accessing data through Datasheet view or Form view. Because of this, Access provides a variety of keyboard shortcuts that help users navigate through and manipulate data. This appendix describes the shortcuts that users most often need. However, these shortcuts represent only a portion of those that Access supports. I encourage you to also refer to Access online Help for a complete listing of the keyboard shortcuts.

Editing Data in Datasheet View and Form View

When working in Datasheet view or Form view, you will often want to edit and manipulate the data within the fields. Access provides a number of shortcuts that you can use when working in Edit mode in either of these views to navigate through the data in a field and select that data. Table B-1 lists the most commonly used Edit mode shortcuts and describes the purpose of each one.

Shortcut	Purpose
F2	Switches between Edit mode and Navigation mode. In Navigation mode, the cursor's insertion point isn't visible and an entire field is selected at the cursor's location. In Edit mode, the insertion point is visible and the field is no longer selected, which allows you to move from character to character within a field.
RIGHT ARROW	Moves the insertion point one character to the right.
CTRL-RIGHT ARROW	Moves the insertion point one word to the right.
LEFT ARROW	Moves the insertion point one character to the left.
CTRL-LEFT ARROW	Moves the insertion point one word to the left.
END	Moves the insertion point to the end of the field.
HOME	Moves the insertion point to the beginning of the field.
SHIFT-RIGHT ARROW	Selects data or extends the selected data one character to the right of the insertion point.
CTRL-SHIFT-RIGHT ARROW	Selects data or extends the selected data one word to the right of the insertion point.
SHIFT-LEFT ARROW	Selects data or extends the selected data one character to the left of the insertion point.
CTRL-SHIFT-LEFT ARROW	Selects data or extends the selected data one word to the left of the insertion point.

Table B-1 Shortcuts for Navigating Data in Edit Mode

Shortcut	Purpose
CTRL-C	Copies the selected characters to the clipboard.
CTRL-X	Deletes the selected characters and copies them to the clipboard.
CTRL-V	Pastes the contents of the clipboard at the insertion point or where the characters are selected.
DELETE	Deletes the selected characters or deletes the character to the right of the insertion point.
BACKSPACE	Deletes the selected characters or deletes the character to the left of the insertion point.
CTRL-DELETE	Deletes all characters to the right of the insertion point (in Edit mode) or deletes the value in the selected field (in Navigation mode).
CTRL-Z	Undoes the most recent modification.
ALT-BACKSPACE	Undoes the most recent modification.
ESC	Undoes changes in the current field or current record. If the current field and other fields have been changed, you must press ESC twice: first to undo the changes in the field, and then to undo the other changes.

Table B-2 Shortcuts for Modifying Data

Whether you're working in Edit mode or Navigation mode, you will often find that you want to copy, move, or delete entire values or characters within those values. Access supports a number of shortcuts that assist in the editing of data. Table B-2 lists the most commonly used shortcuts available for modifying data and describes the purpose of each one.

Navigating Fields and Records in Datasheet View

You will often find it necessary to view and edit data within a table or query. In many cases, you will be viewing that data in Datasheet view. Access supports numerous shortcut keys that can be used in this view to move from field to field and record to record. Table B-3 lists the most commonly used shortcuts available for navigating through records and fields in Datasheet view and describes the purpose of each one.

Shortcut	Purpose
TAB	Moves to the next field.
RIGHT ARROW	Moves to the next field.
SHIFT-TAB	Moves to the previous field.
LEFT ARROW	Moves to the previous field.
HOME	Moves to the first field in the current record (in Navigation mode).
END	Moves to the last field in the current record (in Navigation mode).
UP ARROW	Moves to the current field in the previous record.
DOWN ARROW	Moves to the current field in the next record.
CTRL-UP ARROW	Moves to the current field in the first record (in Navigation mode).
CTRL-DOWN ARROW	Moves to the current field in the last record (in Navigation mode).
CTRL-HOME	Moves to the first field in the first record (in Navigation mode).
CTRL-END	Moves to the last field in the last record (in Navigation mode).
CTRL-A	Selects all records.
CTRL-SHIFT-SPACEBAR	Selects all records.
SHIFT-UP ARROW	Extends the selected field or record to the previous field or record.
SHIFT-DOWN ARROW	Extends the selected field or record to the next record.
PAGE UP	Moves the view up one screen.
PAGE DOWN	Moves the view down one screen.
CTRL-PAGE UP	Moves the view to the left one screen.
CTRL-PAGE DOWN	Moves the view to the right one screen.
F5	Moves to the record number box on the navigation bar. From there, you can enter a record number and then press ENTER to go to that record.

Table B-3 Shortcuts for Navigating Fields and Records in Datasheet View

Navigating Fields and Records in Form View

Form view, like Datasheet view, displays data stored in the tables in the database. As a result, users will often use forms to access and modify that data. Access provides a number of shortcuts that allow users to move from field to field and from record to record. Table B-4 lists the most commonly used shortcuts available to navigate through records and fields in Form view and describes the purpose of each one.

Shortcut	Purpose
TAB	Moves to the next field.
SHIFT-TAB	Moves to the previous field.
HOME	Moves to the first field in the current record (in Navigation mode).
END	Moves to the last field in the current record (in Navigation mode).
CTRL-HOME	Moves to the first field in the first record (in Navigation mode).
CTRL-END	Moves to the last field in the last record (in Navigation mode).
PAGE UP	Moves the view up the form if only part of the form is displayed and then, at the top of the form, moves to the previous record. If the entire form is displayed, PAGE UP moves to the previous record.
PAGE DOWN	Moves the view down the form if only part of the form is displayed and then, at the bottom of the form, moves to the next record. If the entire form is displayed, PAGE DOWN moves to the next record.
CTRL-PAGE UP	Moves to the current field in the previous record.
CTRL-PAGE DOWN	Moves to the current field in the next record.
F5	Moves to the record number box on the navigation bar. From there, you can enter a record number and then press ENTER to go to that record.

Table B-4 Shortcuts for Navigating Fields and Records in Form View

Index

Symbols

+ (addition operator), 243
* (asterisk)
    as multiplication
      operator, 243
    as wildcard character,
      86, 165
& (concatenation operator), 244
/ (division operator), 243
= (equal-to operator), 241, 242
! (exclamation point)
    in expressions, 246
    as wildcard, 165
^ (exponentiation operator), 244
> (greater-than operator), 241, 242
>= (greater-than-or-equal-to
    operator), 242
- (hyphen)
    in datasheet windows, 50
    as subtraction operator, 243
    as wildcard, 165
< (less-than operator), 242
<= (less-than-or-equal-to
    operator), 242
<> (not-equal-to operator), 242, 248
(number sign)
    in expressions, 247
    as wildcard, 165
+ (plus sign)
    as addition operator, 243
    in datasheet windows, 50
? (question mark), as wildcard,
    86, 165
" (quotation marks), in
    expressions, 247
[] (square brackets), as
    wildcard, 165
- (subtraction operator), 243

A

Access class objects
    creating in Microsoft Visual
      Basic window, 379,
      381–384
    defined, 375
    editing in Microsoft Visual
      Basic window, 379
    in forms and reports, 375,
      380, 381
    in Microsoft Visual Basic
      window, 379, 380, 381
    module code example,
      377–378
    vs. module objects, 375
    Northwind VBA code
      example, 377–378
    overview, 375, 380
    procedures in, 375, 376–379
    as type of module, 375
    when to use, 375
accounts, security. See also group
    accounts; user accounts
    assigning permissions,
      128–132
    changing logon passwords,
      126–127
    configuring step by step,
      134–137
    group type, 120, 123,
      125, 126
    managing, 123–128
    user type, 119, 123,
      125–126
action queries
    consumer advocacy
      database example,
      234–236
    creating append queries,
      231–233
    creating delete queries,
      233–234
    creating make-table queries,
      227–228
    creating update queries,
      229–231
    defined, 212
    expressions in, 258
    overview, 226
active record, defined, 50

addition operator (+), 243
Admin user account, 128, 130
Administer permission, 128
Admins group, 125–126
Admins group account, 130
adp files, defined, 9
aggregate functions
    creating queries, 255–257
    defined, 246
    overview, 246
    summarizing grouped data
      in reports, 314–316
Allow Zero Length property, 73,
    81, 82, 148
ampersand (&), 244
And operator, 243, 249
angle brackets (<>), 242
Append dialog box, 231–232
append queries, 231–233
arithmetic operators, 242–243
assignment statements, 377
asterisk (*)
    as multiplication
      operator, 243
    as wildcard, 86, 165
attributes
    columns as, 25
    defined, 24–25
    fields as, 25
    illustrated, 25
AutoForm tools vs. Design view,
    268–269
AutoNumber field
    data type, defined, 57
    editing values, 152
    entering data, 144
    Field Size property, 75
    Format property, 76–77
    Group On property options
      for reports, 312
    list of properties supported,
      72–73
    New Values property, 85
    and primary key, 59

B

Between operator, 242
blank databases, creating, 17, 21
blank fields, allowing, 81, 82
bound controls, 276, 277–279
Bound Object Frame control,
    273, 305
Bound Span control, 335
brackets ([]), as wildcard, 165
Build button
    and Default Value
        property, 81
    and events, 286, 287
    and Input Mask property, 74
    and Row Source
        property, 277

C

calculated controls, 276, 279
calculated field expressions,
    253–255
Caption property, 72, 78, 80
captions, creating, 78, 80
CCur function, 245, 246
character fields. *See* Memo field;
    Text field
charts, adding to data access pages,
    352–354
Check Box control
    for data access pages, 336
    for forms, 272, 279–280
class objects
    creating in Microsoft Visual
        Basic window, 379,
        381–384
    defined, 375
    editing in Microsoft Visual
        Basic window, 379–380
    in forms and reports, 375,
        380, 381
    in Microsoft Visual Basic
        window, 379, 380, 381
    module code example,
        377–378
    vs. module objects, 375
    Northwind VBA code
        example, 377–378

overview, 375, 380
procedures in, 375, 376–379
as type of module, 375
when to use, 375
Clipboard task pane
    copying records, 149, 150
    defined, 8
    illustrated, 150
Codd, E.F., 24
columns
    as attributes, 25
    as fields, 25
    in reports, 305–307
Combo Box control
    conditional formatting,
        281–282
    for forms, 272, 277–279
Command Button control
    for data access pages, 336
    for forms, 272, 286
comparison operators, 241–242
concatenation operator (&), 244
conditional formatting, 281–282
conditions, adding to macros,
    368–370
Confirm Workgroup Information
    dialog box, 122, 123
ConnectionString property, 333
Control Wizards control
    for data access pages, 335
    for forms, 272
controls
    adding to data access pages,
        337–338
    adding to forms, 275–279
    adding to forms using Field
        List, 274–275
    adding to forms without
        using wizards, 273
    adding to reports, 303–305
    binding to Yes/No fields,
        279–280
    bound, 276, 277–279
    calculated, 276
    configuring properties,
        283–288
    defined, 75, 271
    formatting on forms,
        280–281

forms *vs.* reports, 303, 304
grouping on forms, 280
list for data access pages,
    335–336
list for forms, 272–273
modifying property
    defaults, 287
properties dialog box, 277,
    279, 283–288
role of Toolbox, 271–273
unbound, 276, 279
copying database records, 149–151
criteria expressions, 248–253
crosstab queries
    creating in Design view,
        221–225
    defined, 212
    Northwind examples,
        221–225
    overview, 221
Currency field
    data type, defined, 57
    Decimal Places property, 84
    entering data, 144
    Format property, 76–77
    Group On property options
        for reports, 312
    list of properties supported,
        72–73
cursor, Datasheet view, 153

D

Data Access Page window, 334.
    See also data access pages
data access pages
    adding charts to, 352–354
    adding controls to, 337–338
    adding HTML paragraphs
        to, 338–340
    adding PivotTables to,
        354–356
    adding spreadsheets to,
        349–351
    adding themes to, 340–341
    consumer advocacy
        example, 356–359
    creating from existing
        HTML files, 333

creating in Design view,
332–349
Customer Records example,
339–348
vs. forms and reports,
328, 338
grouping data in, 342–349
as HTML files, 328, 329, 330
listing in database
window, 328
Northwind examples,
328–330
overview, 328–330
role of Data Access Page
window, 334
role of Field List, 337–338
role of Toolbox, 335–336
summarizing data, 345–348
viewing, 330–332
viewing in Internet
Explorer, 329–330, 331
viewing in Page view,
330–331
Data Control Language (DCL), 33
Data Definition Language
(DDL), 33
Data Manipulation Language
(DML), 33
data models
bookstore example, 34–38
consumer advocacy
example, 38–43
creating, 38–43
identifying tables and fields,
34–35
logical *vs.* physical, 34
normalizing data, 35–36
overview, 33–34
data objects
database objects as, 19
list of types, 12
properties, 19
shortcuts to, 13
Data tab, control properties dialog
boxes, 277, 279, 284–286
data types. *See also* fields
changing in table Design
view, 66
defined, 25–26

vs. domains, 25–26
list, 57
selecting for table fields,
56–57
database engines, 9
database files. *See* databases; .mdb
files; Northwind database
database objects, 19–20. *See also*
data objects
Database Properties dialog box
Contents tab, 20
Custom tab, 20
General tab, 20
illustrated, 19
overview, 19
Statistics tab, 20
Summary tab, 19, 20
Database toolbar
OfficeLinks button, 204
overview, 6–7
showing/hiding, 7
database window
creating tables from, 54–55
illustrated, 11
Modules tab, 375
Northwind example, 11
overview, 11–14
Pages tab, 330
selecting Tables object type,
48, 51
toolbar buttons, 13–14
Database wizard, 18
databases
adding data to tables,
142–151
adding tables, 53–65
blank, creating, 17, 21
creating, 15–21
creating from existing
databases, 17, 18, 20–21
decoding, 133–134
encoding, 132–133
exporting data from,
202–207
importing data into,
184–195
linking to, 195–199
naming, 18
new, 15–21

opening, 9–15
opening in exclusive
mode, 118
password-protecting,
118–119
renaming, 18
DataPageSize property, 348
Datasheet view
adding records to tables,
142, 143
creating tables, 59–60
cursor in, 153
entering data in, 59–60
illustrated, 49, 60
Navigation mode *vs.* Edit
mode, 153
Northwind Employees table,
142, 143, 148
Northwind query results,
212, 213, 218, 219
opening tables, 48
viewing filtered data, 171
viewing tables, 48–51
window overview, 49–50
Date function, 245
Date/Time field
data type, defined, 57
entering data, 144–145
Format property, 77, 78
Group On property options
for reports, 312
Input Mask property, 78
list of properties supported,
72–73
DateAdd function, 245
dBase
exporting Access data to,
203–204
importing databases
from, 187
linking to databases,
197–198
DCL. *See* Data Control Language
(DCL)
DDL. *See* Data Definition
Language (DDL)
decimal numbers, configuring
appearance, 84
Decimal Places property, 73, 84

declarations
  in modules, 375, 376
  in sub procedures, 377
  VBA code in, 376
Decode Database As dialog box,
  133–134
default properties, modifying for
  controls, 287
Default Value property
  applicable fields, 72
  Build button, 81
  when to use, 80–81
Default View property, 94
Delete button, 14
Delete Data permission, 128
delete queries, 233–234, 258
denormalization, 29
Description property, 94
Design button, 14
Design view
  adding tables in, 55–58,
    64–65
  vs. AutoForm tools, 268–269
  changing table settings,
    65–68
  creating calculated field
    expressions, 253–255
  creating criteria expressions,
    248–253
  creating crosstab queries,
    221–225
  creating data access pages,
    332–349
  creating expressions,
    248–257, 260–262
  creating forms, 268–275
  creating queries step by
    step, 260–262
  creating queries with
    aggregate functions,
    255–257
  creating reports, 300–307
  creating select queries,
    212–218
  creating tables, 55–58
  Data Access Page
    window, 334
  Form window, 269, 270, 271
  vs. Forms wizard, 268–269
  illustrated, 52

Lookup tab, 90, 91
  opening tables, 51
  overview, 51–53
  Report window, 302
  switching to Form view, 277
  viewing tables in, 51–53
Display buttons, 14
division operator (/), 243
DML. *See* Data Manipulation
  Language (DML)
DoCmd object, 378–379
domains
  vs. data types, 25–26
  defined, 25
  illustrated, 25
Dropdown List control, 336

E

Edit Hyperlink dialog box,
  153–154
Edit menu, defined, 7
Edit mode, 153
Edit Relationships dialog box, 107,
  109, 111, 112
embedding objects, 145–146, 153,
  305. *See also* OLE Object field
Encode Database As dialog box,
  132–133
encoding databases, 132–133
engines, database, 9
Enter Parameter Value dialog box,
  216, 317–318
equal operator (=), 241, 242
event procedures, 375, 381–384
Event tab, control properties dialog
  boxes, 286, 287, 371, 372
events
  adding to forms, 286
  assigning macros to,
    371–374
  configuring properties, 286,
    287, 371, 372
  consumer advocacy database
    example, 373–374
  creating macros for,
    364–370, 373
  creating modules for,
    381–384
  defined, 286

Excel
  adding spreadsheets to
    Access data access
    pages, 349–351
  exporting Access data to
    spreadsheets, 204
  importing spreadsheet data
    into Access, 187–192
  linking from Access
    databases to
    spreadsheets, 198
  and OfficeLinks button, 204
exclamation point (!)
  in expressions, 246
  as wildcard, 165
exclusive mode, 118
executable statements, 377
Expand control, 336
Export dialog box, 202, 203
Export Table To dialog box,
  202–203
Export Text wizard, 205–206
Export XML dialog box, 207
exporting data
  from Access databases,
    202–207
  consumer advocacy
    database example,
    207–209
  to dBase databases, 203–204
  to Excel spreadsheets, 204
  to other Access databases,
    202–203
  to text files, 205–206
Expression Builder, 81, 258–260
Expression Is option, 281, 282
expressions
  in action queries, 258
  adding to queries, 248–258
  calculated field type, 253–255
  creating in Design view,
    248–257, 260–262
  creating in Expression
    Builder, 258–260
  criteria type, 248–253
  functions in, 244–246,
    250–252
  identifiers in, 246–247,
    250–252
  literals in, 247, 248–250

multiple, 252–253
operators in, 240, 241–244,
248–250
overview, 240–241
for validation rules, 86
external data sources
importing, 184–195
linking to, 195–199

F

Favorites group, 13
Field Has Focus option, 281, 282
Field List
for data access pages,
337–338
for forms, 273–275
for reports, 302, 303
Field Size property, 72, 75
Field Value Is option, 281, 282
fields
adding to tables, 55–58, 67,
68–69
allowing blanks, 81–82
as attributes, 25
bookstore example, 34–35
calculated, in expressions,
253–255
changing listed order, 68
changing names and
descriptions in table
Design view, 66
character type, 144
columns as, 25
configuring properties, 72–85
creating and viewing
indexes, 88–89
creating captions, 78, 80
date/time type, 144–145
deleting from tables, 67–68
editing data, 152–154
entering data, 143–147
entering default values, 80–81
finding data in, 162–167
list of data types, 57
list of properties supported,
72–73
lookup, 89–92
moving between, 143

naming, 56
numerical type, 144
as primary key, 58, 59
requiring values, 81–82, 148
selecting data type, 56–57
sorting on, 168–170
summarized, 257
updating data, 152–155
viewing description, 50
writing description, 57
File menu, defined, 7
File Search task pane, 8, 10
files, recently used, changing
number displayed, 10. *See also*
databases
Filter By Form window, 174–175
Filter property, 94
Filter window, 175–178
filtering table records
creating advanced filters,
175–178
by excluded selection,
172, 173
by form, 174–175
Northwind examples,
171–12, 173, 175–177
overview, 170–171
by selection, 171–172, 173
filters *vs.* queries, 178
Find and Replace dialog box
Find tab, 162–165
Replace tab, 162, 165–167
finding data. *See also* File Search
task pane
Northwind example,
178–179
values in tables, 162–165
first normal form, 26–27
footers, report
configuring, 307–309
for grouped fields, 312–314
foreign keys, 37, 105
Form view, switching to, 277
Form window, 269, 270, 271.
See also forms
Format property
applicable fields, 72
Date/Time field, 77, 78
Memo field, 76

numeric value fields, 76–77
overview, 75
Text field, 76
Yes/No field, 77
Format tab, control properties
dialog boxes, 279, 284, 285
formatting
conditional, 281–282
controls on forms, 280–281
field data in tables, 75–77
forms
adding bound controls,
277–279
adding calculated
controls, 279
adding controls to, 275–279
adding unbound controls, 279
class objects in, 375, 381
configuring properties, 283
consumer advocacy database
example, 294–297
creating in Design view,
268–275
creating multiple tabs,
288–289
creating subforms, 289–291
creating switchboards,
292–293
vs. data access pages,
328, 338
defined, 9
Design view *vs.* Forms
wizard *vs.* AutoForm
tools, 268–269
importing from other
Access databases,
184–186
Northwind Customers form,
268, 269
vs. reports, 300
role of Field List, 273–275
role of Form window, 271
role of Toolbox tools,
271–273
as type of interface, 268
viewing elements in Design
view, 268–275
ways to create, 268–269
Forms object type, defined, 12

Forms wizard *vs.* Design view, 268–269
function procedures, 376
functions
    aggregate, 246, 255–257, 314–316
    in expressions, 240, 244–246, 250–252
    in validation rules, 86

G

Getting Started task pane
    defined, 8
    opening database files, 10, 15
    overview, 5, 6, 7–8
greater-than operator (>), 241, 242
greater-than-or-equal-to-operator (>=), 242
group accounts
    adding groups to workgroups, 126
    configuring, 126
    defined, 120
    User and Group Accounts dialog box, 123, 125
grouping
    controls on forms, 280
    data access page data, 342–349
    data objects, 13
    report data, 310–316

H

headers, report
    configuring, 307–309
    for grouped fields, 312–314
Help menu, defined, 7
Help task pane, defined, 8
HTML files, data access pages as, 328, 329, 330
Hyperlink control, 336
Hyperlink field
    data type, defined, 57
    editing values, 153–154
    entering data, 146–147
    list of properties supported, 72–73

hyperlinks, adding to databases, 146–147
hyphen (-)
    as arithmetic operator, 243
    as wildcard, 165

I

identifiers
    in expressions, 241, 246–247, 250–252
    in validation rules, 86
Image control
    for data access pages, 336
    for forms, 273
    for reports, 304–305
Image Hyperlink control, 336
IME Mode property, 73, 83
IME Sentence Mode property, 73, 83
Import dialog box, 185–186
Import Objects dialog box, 186
Import Spreadsheet wizard, 188–190, 191, 192
Import Text wizard, 193–194
Import XML dialog box, 194–195
importing data
    consumer advocacy database example, 199, 200–201
    from dBase databases, 187
    from Excel spreadsheets, 187–192
    vs. linking to data, 196
    from other Access databases, 184–186
    overview, 184
    from text files, 192–194
    from XML files, 194–195
In operator, 242
Index property, 88–89
Indexed property, 73
indexes
    creating on multiple fields, 90
    creating on single field, 88
    overview, 88
    viewing, 88
Indexes dialog box, 89

Input Mask property
    applicable fields, 72
    Date/Time field, 78
    mask examples, 78, 79
    overview, 147
    predefined masks, 78
    Text field, 78
Input Mask wizard, 78, 79, 80
input masks, defined, 77
Input Method Editor (IME), 83
Insert Data permission, 128
Insert menu, defined, 7
Is operator, 242

J

Jet database engine, 9
join properties, 109–110
joining workgroups, 123

K

keyboard, setting options, 154–155

L

Label control
    for data access pages, 335
    formatting, 280–281
    for forms, 272, 280–281
languages, and Unicode compression, 82–83
launching Microsoft Access, 4–6
less-than operator (<), 242
less-than-or-equal-to operator (<=), 242
Like operator, 241, 242, 249
Line control
    for data access pages, 336
    for forms, 273
Link Child Fields property, 94
Link dialog box, 196–197
Link Master Fields property, 94
Link Tables dialog box, 197–198
linking
    consumer advocacy database example, 199, 201
    to Excel spreadsheets, 198

to external data sources, 195–199
vs. importing data, 196
inserting hyperlinks, 145–146
to other Access databases, 196–197
to text files, 199
List Box control
    for data access pages, 336
    for forms, 272, 277–278
literals
    expression examples, 248–250
    in expressions, 241, 247
    in validation rules, 86
logical operators, 243–244
logon passwords, changing, 126–127
lookup fields
    changing property settings, 90–92
    defined, 89
    list of properties, 92
    overview, 89–90, 148
Lookup Wizard data type, 57, 72–73, 89–92
Lotus 1-2-3, importing databases from, 187, 188

M

Macro window, 364–366
macros
    adding conditions to, 368–370
    assigning to events, 371–374
    consumer advocacy database example, 373–374
    creating for events, 364–370, 373
    vs. modules, 375
    OpensCustomersForm example, 366–370
Macros object type, defined, 12
make-table queries, 227–228
many-to-many table relationships, 29, 30, 31, 37, 42, 102
.mdb files
    creating, 15–21
    defined, 9

opening, 9–15
Memo field
    data type, defined, 57
    entering data, 144
    Format property, 76
    list of properties supported, 72–73
menu bar
    defined, 6
    illustrated, 6
    list of menus, 7
menus, 6, 7
Microsoft Office. *See* Excel; Word, and Office Links button
Microsoft Office Access dialog box, 145, 146
Microsoft Visual Basic window
    creating class objects, 379, 381–384
    creating module objects, 379
    editing class objects, 379
    editing module objects, 379
    illustrated, 380
    Microsoft Office Access Class Objects node, 379, 380
    Modules node, 379, 380
    overview, 379
Microsoft Word. *See* Word, and Office Links button
minus sign (-)
    as arithmetic operator, 243
    in datasheet windows, 50
Modify Design permission, 128
module objects
    vs. class objects, 375
    creating, 379
    defined, 375
    editing, 379
    overview, 375
    as type of module, 375
    when to use, 375
modules. *See also* class objects; module objects
    declarations, 375, 376
    defined, 375
    vs. macros, 375
    overview, 375
    procedure code, 375, 376–379

VBA code example, 377–378
Modules object type, defined, 12. *See also* module objects
More Controls Toolbox button
    for data access pages, 336
    for forms, 273
Movie control, 336
moving database records, 149, 151
multiple-table select queries, 217–219
multiplication operator (*), 243

N

naming
    database files, 18
    fields, 56
    groups, 13
Navigation mode, 153
New button, 14
New File task pane
    creating blank databases, 17, 21
    creating database files from templates, 18–19
    creating databases from existing files, 17, 18, 20–21
    creating new database files, 15–21
    defined, 8
    illustrated, 16
    opening, 16
New Form dialog box, 269, 270
new records, adding to tables, 142–143
New Table dialog box, 54, 55
New Values property, 73, 85
normal forms, 26–28
normalization
    bookstore example, 35–36
    consumer advocacy database example, 39–41
    defined, 26
    first normal form, 26–27
    second normal form, 27–28
    third normal form, 28
    violating rules, 29

Northwind database
  class object module VBA
    code, 377–378
  creating new database file
    from, 20–21
  crosstab query example,
    221–225
  Customers form, 268, 269
  Customers table in Design
    view, 52–53
  data access page examples,
    328–331, 350–351, 353,
    354, 355–356
  database window, 11
  defined, 10
  defining table relationships,
    104–107
  Employees Properties dialog
    box, 92, 93
  Employees table in
    Datasheet view, 142,
    143, 148
  filtering Products table
    records, 171–172, 173,
    175–177
  Main Switchboard form,
    292–293
  opening, 10, 11–14, 15
  Properties dialog box, 19
  report examples, 300–319
  select query example,
    212–219
  sorting Products table
    records, 168, 169–170
not-equal-to operator (<>),
  242, 248
Not operator, 243, 244
null values, finding, 164
Number field
  data type, defined, 57
  Decimal Places property, 84
  entering data, 144
  Field Size property, 75
  Format property, 76–77
  Group On property options
    for reports, 312
  list of properties supported,
    72–73
  Precision property, 84–85

Scale property, 84, 85
number sign (#)
  in expressions, 247
  as wildcard, 165
numeric values. *See also*
  AutoNumber field; Currency
  field; Number field
  configuring decimal number
    appearance, 84
  entering data into fields, 144

O

Object Frame control, 304–305
objects
  changing ownership, 131
  changing permissions,
    129–130
  defined, 120
  embedding, 145–146,
    153, 305
  importing from other
    Access databases,
    184–186
  linking to *vs.* importing, 196
Office Chart control, 336
Office PivotTable control, 336
Office Spreadsheet control, 336
OfficeLinks button, 204
OLE Object field
  data type, defined, 57
  editing objects, 152–153
  entering data, 145–146
  list of properties supported,
    72–73
one-to-many table relationships,
  29, 30–31, 37, 38, 42, 102,
  103–105
one-to-one table relationships, 29,
  30, 31, 102
Open button, 14
Open Exclusive permission, 128
Open/Run permission, 128
opening
  database files, 9–15
  databases in exclusive
    mode, 118
  Microsoft Access, 4–6
  New File task pane, 16

Northwind.mdb file, 10,
  11–14, 15
  tables in Datasheet view, 48
  tables in Design view, 51
OpensCustomersForm macro,
  366–372
operators
  arithmetic, 242–243
  comparison, 241–242
  concatenation, 244
  in expressions, 240,
    241–244, 248–250
  logical, 243–244
  in validation rules, 86
Option Button control
  for data access pages, 336
  for forms, 272, 279
Option Group control
  for data access pages, 336
  for forms, 272, 280
Or operator, 243, 244
Oracle, importing data from, 188
Order By property, 94
Orientation property, 94
Other tab, control properties dialog
  boxes, 286–288

P

Page Break control, 273
Page view, 330–332
Pages object type, defined, 12.
  See also data access pages
Paradox, importing databases
  from, 187, 188
parameter queries, 216, 317–319
passwords
  changing user logons,
    126–127
  protecting database files,
    118–119
permissions
  assigning to security
    accounts, 128–132
  changing ownership, 131
  configuring, 129–130
  defined, 120
personal IDs, 125, 126

PivotTables, adding to data access pages, 354–356
plus sign (+)
    as addition operator, 243
    in datasheet windows, 50
pound sign (#), in expressions, 247
Precision property, 73, 84–85
Preview button, 14
primary key
    assigning to fields, 58, 59
    changing in table Design view, 66–67, 69
    configuring, 58, 59
    defined, 27, 37
    including multiple fields, 59
    and indexes, 88, 89
    in Relationships window, 105
    as sorting default, 167
procedures. *See also* event procedures
    in class objects, 375, 376–379
    in module objects, 375
    VBA code in, 376–379
projects, defined, 9

Q

queries
    action type, 212, 226–237, 258
    adding expressions to, 248–258
    aggregate functions in, 255–257
    append type, 231–233
    crosstab type, 212, 221–225
    delete type, 233–234, 258
    vs. filters, 178
    importing from other Access databases, 184–186
    make-table type, 227–228
    operator examples, 242, 243–244
    parameter type, 216, 317–319
    role of field indexes, 88
    select type, 212–221
    summarized fields in, 257

types, defined, 212
    update type, 229–231, 258
Queries object type, defined, 12
Query Builder, 277–278
question mark (?), as wildcard, 86, 165
quotation marks ("), in expressions, 247

R

RDBMS (relational database management systems), 4, 24–31. *See also* relational model
Read Data permission, 128
Read Design permission, 128
recently used files, changing number displayed, 10
Record Navigation control, 336
records
    active, 50
    adding to tables, 142–143
    copying, 149–151
    entering data into fields, 143–147
    filtering, 170–178
    finding data in, 162–167
    moving, 149, 151
    new, creating, 142–143
    rows as, 25
    sorting, 167–170
    updating, 152–155
Rectangle control
    for data access pages, 336
    for forms, 273
referential integrity, 103, 107, 109
relational database management systems (RDBMS), 4, 24–31
relational model
    bookstore example, 34–38
    data structures, 24–26
    normalization, 26–28
    overview, 24
    table relationships, 28–31
    terminology, 24–26
relations, 24, 25
relationships, table
    adding data to tables, 156–158

bookstore example, 36–37, 103–104
configuring join properties, 109–110
consumer advocacy data model example, 41–43
consumer advocacy step-by-step creation example, 112–114
creating in Relationships window, 106–114
creating in Table Wizard, 61–62
defining in Relationships window, 106–107
deleting in Relationships window, 112
many-to-many, 29, 30, 31, 37, 42, 102
modifying in Relationships window, 111–112
Northwind example, 104–107
one-to-many, 29, 30–31, 37, 38, 42, 102, 103–105
one-to-one, 29, 30, 31, 102
overview, 102–104
saving layouts, 110–111
Relationships window
    adding tables to, 106
    consumer advocacy example, 112–114
    creating table relationships, 106–114
    defining relationships, 106–107
    deleting relationships, 112
    modifying existing relationships, 111–112
    modifying table definitions, 108
    navigating, 104–106
    opening, 105
    overview, 104
    saving layouts, 110–111
replacing values in tables, 165–167
Report window, 302, 303. *See also* reports
reports
    adding controls to, 303–305
    class objects in, 375, 381

configuring group headers and footers, 312–314
consumer advocacy database example, 319–323
creating in Design view, 300–307
vs. data access pages, 328, 338
vs. forms, 300
grouping data, 310–316
headers and footers in, 307–309
importing from other Access databases, 184–186
multiple columns in, 305–307
navigating Design view interface, 302–303
overview, 300–301
parameter queries in, 317–319, 320
role of Field List, 302, 303
role of Report window, 302, 303
role of Toolbox, 302, 303
sorting data, 310–316
summarizing grouped data, 314–316
ways to create, 300–301
Reports object type, defined, 12
Required property, 72, 81, 82, 148
Review Orders data access page
listed in database window, 328
viewing in Internet Explorer, 329–330, 331
viewing in Page view, 330–331
right-clicking in menu area, 7
rows, as records, 25
Run button, 14

S

saving table relationship layouts, 110–111
Scale property, 73, 84–85
ScreenTips, 7
Scrolling Text control, 336

Search Results task pane, defined, 8
second normal form, 27–28
security. *See* passwords; user-level security
Security wizard, 120
Select Objects control
for data access pages, 335
for forms, 272
select queries
consumer advocacy database example, 219–220
defined, 212
multiple-table, creating, 217–219
Northwind examples, 212–219
overview, 212
single-table, creating, 212–217
Set Database Password dialog box, 119
Show Table dialog box, 105, 214
single-table select queries, 212–217
slash (/), as division operator, 243
Smart Tags property, 73, 83–84
Sorting and Grouping dialog box, 310, 311–313
sorting database records
on multiple fields, 169–170
Northwind example, 178–180
on primary key, 167
in reports, 310–316
on single field, 168–169
spreadsheets
adding to data access pages, 349–351
exporting Access data to, 204
importing Excel data from, 187–192
linking Access databases to, 198
SQL Server, importing data from, 188
SQL Server database engine, 9
SQL (Structured Query Language)
importing data, 188
overview, 31–33

types of statements, 33
viewing statements, 228
SQL view, 228
square brackets ([]), as wildcard, 165
Start menu, Windows XP, 4–5
starting Microsoft Access, 4–6
sub procedures
creating, 381
defined, 376
overview, 377
types of statements, 377
Subdatasheet Expanded property, 94
Subdatasheet Height property, 94
Subdatasheet Name property, 94
subdatasheet window, 50–51
Subform/Subreport control, 273, 289–291
subforms, creating, 289–291
subprograms. *See* procedures, in module objects
subtraction operator (-), 243
summarized fields, 257
summarizing grouped report data, 314–316
Switchboard Manager, 293
switchboards
configuring to open at startup, 293
creating, 292–293
illustrated, 292, 293
Northwind example, 292, 293
System.mdw file, 120

T

Tab control, 273, 289, 290
Table Properties dialog box, 93–94
Table wizard, 60–62
tables
adding data to, 142–151
adding fields to, 55–58, 67, 68–69
adding records to, 142–143
adding to databases, 53–62
adding to Relationships window, 106

bookstore example, 34–38
changing field settings,
    65–69, 95
configuring field properties,
    72–85, 95
configuring table design
    properties, 92–97
configuring table object
    properties, 92–93
consumer advocacy
    example, 39–43, 63–65,
    156–158
copying and moving
    records, 149–151
creating in Datasheet view,
    59–60
creating in Design view,
    55–58
creating in Table Wizard,
    60–62
deleting data from, 156
deleting fields from, 67–68
filtering records, 170–178
finding data, 162–167
importing from other Access
    databases, 184–186
list of design properties, 94
list of field data types, 57
list of field properties, 72–73
many-to-many relationship
    between, 29, 30, 31, 37,
    42, 102
Northwind Customers table
    in Design view, 52–53
Northwind Employees table
    in Datasheet view, 142,
    143, 148
one-to-many relationship
    between, 29, 30–31, 37,
    38, 42, 102, 103–105
one-to-one relationship
    between, 29, 30, 31, 102
opening in Datasheet
    view, 48
opening in Design view, 51
referential integrity
    between, 103, 107, 109
relationships between, 28–31
relationships overview,
    102–104

replacing data, 165–167
sorting records, 167–170
updating field data, 152–155
viewing in Datasheet view,
    48–51
viewing in Design view,
    51–53
ways to create, 53–54
Tables object type, 12, 48, 51
tabs, creating for forms, 288–289
task panes. *See also* New File task
pane
    changing, 7–8
    Clipboard task pane, 8,
        149, 150
    complete list, 8
    displaying window, 8
    Getting Started task pane, 5,
        6, 7–8
    opening, 8
    returning to previous pane, 8
    viewing drop-down list, 8
Template Help task pane,
    defined, 8
templates, creating database files
    from, 18–19
Text Box control
    conditional formatting,
        281–282
    for data access pages, 335
    formatting, 280–281
    for forms, 272, 277
Text field
    data type, defined, 57
    default field values, 73, 74
    entering data, 144
    Field Size property, 75
    Format property, 76
    Group On property options
        for reports, 312
    Input Mask property, 78
    list of properties supported,
        72–73
text files
    exporting Access data to,
        205–206
    importing data from,
        192–194
    linking to, 199

themes, adding to data access
    pages, 340–341
third normal form, 28
Toggle Button control, 272, 279
toolbars
    Database toolbar, 6–7
    in database window, 13–14
    Web toolbar, 7
Toolbox
    for data access pages,
        335–336
    vs. Field List, 274–275
    for forms, 271–273
    for reports, 302, 303
Tools menu, defined, 7
Try It box, 80
tuples
    defined, 25
    illustrated, 25
    rows as, 25

U

unbound controls, 276, 279
Unbound Object Frame control,
    273., 305
UNC (Universal Naming
    Convention), 333
Unicode, defined, 82
Unicode Compression property,
    73, 82–83
Uniform Resource Locators
    (URLs), 332
Universal Naming Convention
    (UNC), 333
Update Data permission, 128
update queries, 229–231, 258
updating table data, 152–155
URLs (Uniform Resource
    Locators), 332
user accounts
    adding users to workgroups,
        125–126
    configuring, 125–126
    defined, 119
    User and Group Accounts
        dialog box, 123, 125
User and Group Accounts
    dialog box

Change Logon Password tab, 127
Groups tab, 126, 127
overview, 123, 125
Users tab, 123, 125–126
User and Group Permissions dialog box
Change Owner tab, 131
Permissions tab, 129–130
user-level security
assigning permissions to accounts, 128–132
changing logon passwords, 126–127
configuring step by step, 134–137
creating workgroups, 121–123
encoding and decoding files, 132–134
vs. file password protection, 119
joining workgroups, 123
managing accounts, 123–128
overview, 119–120
Users group account, 130

V

Validation Rule property
applicable fields, 72
defining rules, 85–88
expression elements, 86
overview, 85–86, 86–88
rule examples, 86, 87
Validation Text property, 87–88, 94
Valudation Rule property, 94
View menu, defined, 7
viewing
data access pages, 330–332
field indexes, 89
form elements, 268–275
tables in Datasheet view, 48–51
tables in Design view, 51–53
views, switching, 277

Visual Basic for Applications (VBA)
class object module example, 377–378
code example, 377–378
defined, 375
overview, 375–379
window, 379–380
Visual FoxPro, importing data from, 188

W

Web toolbar, 7
WIFs (workgroup information files)
associating databases with, 124
defined, 119
managing, 120–123
wildcards
in expressions, 86
in Filter By Form window, 175
in searches, 164–165
searching for as values, 166
Window menu, defined, 7
Windows Explorer
opening database files in, 10
starting Microsoft Access from, 4
Windows XP
opening database files, 10
starting Microsoft Access, 4–6
wizards
Database, 18
Export Text wizard, 205–206
Import Spreadsheet, 188–190, 191, 192
Import Text wizard, 193–194
Input Mask, 78, 79, 80
Security, 120
Table, 60–62
Word, and OfficeLinks button, 204

Workgroup Administrator dialog box, 121
Workgroup Information File dialog box, 121, 122
workgroup information files. *See* WIFs (workgroup information files)
Workgroup Owner Information dialog box, 121, 122
workgroups
adding groups, 126
adding users, 125–126
creating, 121–123
defined, 119
joining, 123
managing, 120–123
worksheets. *See* spreadsheets

X

XML (Extensible Markup Language) files
exporting Access data to, 207
importing data from, 194–195
.xml files, 207
.xsd files, 207
.xsl files, 207

Y

Yes/No field
binding controls to, 279–280
data type, defined, 57
entering data, 145
Format property, 77
list of properties supported, 72–73

Z

zero-length string values, finding, 164
Zoom dialog box, 251

INTERNATIONAL CONTACT INFORMATION

AUSTRALIA
McGraw-Hill Book Company
Australia Pty. Ltd.
TEL +61-2-9900-1800
FAX +61-2-9878-8881
http://www.mcgraw-hill.com.au
books-it_sydney@mcgraw-hill.com

CANADA
McGraw-Hill Ryerson Ltd.
TEL +905-430-5000
FAX +905-430-5020
http://www.mcgraw-hill.ca

GREECE, MIDDLE EAST, & AFRICA (Excluding South Africa)
McGraw-Hill Hellas
TEL +30-210-6560-990
TEL +30-210-6560-993
TEL +30-210-6560-994
FAX +30-210-6545-525

MEXICO (Also serving Latin America)
McGraw-Hill Interamericana Editores
S.A. de C.V.
TEL +525-1500-5108
FAX +525-117-1589
http://www.mcgraw-hill.com.mx
carlos_ruiz@mcgraw-hill.com

SINGAPORE (Serving Asia)
McGraw-Hill Book Company
TEL +65-6863-1580
FAX +65-6862-3354
http://www.mcgraw-hill.com.sg
mghasia@mcgraw-hill.com

SOUTH AFRICA
McGraw-Hill South Africa
TEL +27-11-622-7512
FAX +27-11-622-9045
robyn_swanepoel@mcgraw-hill.com

SPAIN
McGraw-Hill/
Interamericana de España, S.A.U.
TEL +34-91-180-3000
FAX +34-91-372-8513
http://www.mcgraw-hill.es
professional@mcgraw-hill.es

UNITED KINGDOM, NORTHERN, EASTERN, & CENTRAL EUROPE
McGraw-Hill Education Europe
TEL +44-1-628-502500
FAX +44-1-628-770224
http://www.mcgraw-hill.co.uk
emea_queries@mcgraw-hill.com

ALL OTHER INQUIRIES Contact:
McGraw-Hill/Osborne
TEL +1-510-420-7700
FAX +1-510-420-7703
http://www.osborne.com
omg_international@mcgraw-hill.com

Sound Off!

Visit us at **www.osborne.com/bookregistration** and let us know what you thought of this book. While you're online you'll have the opportunity to register for newsletters and special offers from McGraw-Hill/Osborne.

We want to hear from you!

Sneak Peek

Visit us today at **www.betabooks.com** and see what's coming from McGraw-Hill/Osborne tomorrow!

Based on the successful software paradigm, Bet@Books™ allows computing professionals to view partial and sometimes complete text versions of selected titles online. Bet@Books™ viewing is free, invites comments and feedback, and allows you to "test drive" books in progress on the subjects that interest you the most.

Mc